Rioting for Representation

Ethnic riots are a costly and common occurrence during political transitions in multi-ethnic settings. Why do ethnic riots occur in certain parts of a country and not others? How does violence eventually decline? Drawing on rich case studies and subnational analysis from Indonesia between 1990 and 2012, this book argues that patterns of ethnic rioting are not inevitably driven by intergroup animosity, weakness of state capacity, or local demographic composition. Rather, local ethnic elites strategically use violence to leverage their demands for political inclusion during political transition and that violence eventually declines as these demands are accommodated. Toha breaks new ground in showing that particular political reforms–increased political competition, direct local elections, and local administrative units partitioning–in ethnically diverse contexts can ameliorate political exclusion and reduce overall levels of violence between groups.

RISA J. TOHA is Assistant Professor of Political Science at Yale-NUS College in Singapore. Her work has focused on questions related to political violence, identity, and political economy, appearing in journals such as the *British Journal of Political Science, Terrorism and Political Violence,* and *Contemporary Southeast Asia.*

Problems of International Politics

Series Editors

Keith Darden, *American University*

Ian Shapiro, *Yale University*

The series seeks manuscripts central to the understanding of international politics that will be empirically rich and conceptually innovative. It is interested in works that illuminate the evolving character of nation-states within the international system. It sets out three broad areas for investigation: (1) identity, security, and conflict; (2) democracy; and (3) justice and distribution.

Titles in the Series

Rioting for Representation

Local Ethnic Mobilization in Democratizing Countries

Risa J. Toha

Yale-NUS

CAMBRIDGE
UNIVERSITY PRESS

University Printing House, Cambridge CB2 8BS, United Kingdom

One Liberty Plaza, 20th Floor, New York, NY 10006, USA

477 Williamstown Road, Port Melbourne, VIC 3207, Australia

314–321, 3rd Floor, Plot 3, Splendor Forum, Jasola District Centre, New Delhi – 110025, India

103 Penang Road, #05–06/07, Visioncrest Commercial, Singapore 238467

Cambridge University Press is part of the University of Cambridge.

It furthers the University's mission by disseminating knowledge in the pursuit of education, learning, and research at the highest international levels of excellence.

www.cambridge.org
Information on this title: www.cambridge.org/9781316518977
DOI: 10.1017/9781009004190

First published 2022

A catalogue record for this publication is available from the British Library.

ISBN 978-1-316-51897-7 Hardback

For David

Contents

Figures

Tables

Acknowledgments

Growing up as a woman with a mixed ethnic heritage in the 1980s–1990s in Jakarta, Indonesia, I knew firsthand the generosity, warmth, and openness that many Indonesians regularly bestow on people outside their community. Thus, the waves of violence against churches and against ethnic Chinese minorities in the late 1990s came as a deep shock. I wanted to understand why and how people from different communities, who had previously lived a seemingly harmoniously, could so suddenly commit such horrific violence against each other. It took me many years to formulate my answer this question, and even then, only partially. I never would have gotten to this point without the long list of friends, allies, and mentors who have helped me along the way. My thanks in the following pages pale in comparison to the gift of time, insights, resources, and encouragement many people have shared with me.

My PhD dissertation committee members at the University of California Los Angeles (UCLA) – Michael Ross, Barbara Geddes, Daniel Posner, Daniel Treisman, and Andreas Wimmer – were the best advisers a student could have. They believed in me and my project from the very start, and each of them prodded me to think more carefully about a particular dimension of the bigger question that I was grappling with and made the dissertation much better. I also benefited from conversations with Art Stein, Kathy Bawn, and Miriam Golden earlier in the dissertation process. My friends at UCLA saw the beginnings of this book and celebrated every victory. I thank in particular Devorah Manekin, Natasha Behl, Anoop Sarbahi, Jae-Hyeok Shin, Brian Min, Jessica Preece, Julia Kim, and Linda Hasunuma for their conversations and encouragement.

During my graduate training, I received financial support from various organizations that enabled me to conduct field research, present at conferences, and acquire a new language (Tagalog) for future comparative work. I thank the Pacific Rim Research Program, UCLA Graduate Summer Research Mentorship, UCLA Institute for Social

Research, the Lemelson Fellowship, the Harvey Fellowship from the Mustard Seed Foundation, and the Foreign Language for Area Studies fellowship for funding my graduate research. I am grateful to Barbara Gaerlan, Michael Ross, Geoffrey Robinson, and Robert Lemelson and the UCLA Center for Southeast Asian Studies for their commitment to supporting young scholars studying Southeast Asia and creating a home for us at UCLA.

My very first fieldwork experience was during my work as a consultant at the World Bank office in Jakarta's Social Development Unit. I am grateful to Scott Guggenheim and Sri Kuntari for recruiting me to join their team, and to my colleagues Sandra Usmany and Mbak Atis for patiently showing me the ropes on how to "do" fieldwork in post-conflict areas. I am also grateful for the institutional home I found at the Centre for Strategic and International Studies (CSIS) in Jakarta during later rounds of field research.

As an Indonesia Postdoctoral Fellow at the Ash Center for Democratic Governance and Innovation at the Kennedy School, I benefited from research support and conversations with Jay Rosengard, Malcolm McPherson, and David Dapice. Elizabeth Osborn and Trisiawati Bantacut deftly ensured that we didn't lack anything. My co-fellows in the Indonesia program – Maggie Triyana, Djayadi Hanan, Nelden Djakababa, Agung Pambudhi, Nugroho Hanan, and Pak Muhadjir – understood very well the joys and challenges of researching Indonesia as Indonesians. I count this solidarity in the journey a big blessing.

At Wheaton College, I thank my colleagues Leah Seppanen Anderson, Larycia Hawkins, Michael McKoy, Amy Black, Bryan McGraw, Tess Duncan, Amy Reynolds, Christine Folch, and Winnie Fung, who shared their wealth of experience on how to be an effective scholar and a good human being at the same time.

At Stanford University's Shorenstein APARC, I am grateful to Don Emmerson and Lisa Blaydes for their time and feedback on the manuscript. APARC gave me ample space and support to develop a significant portion of this manuscript in 2014.

Finally, Yale-NUS, my home for the last six years, has nurtured me as a scholar. As an assistant professor at this new college, I found camaraderie and friendship in Anju Paul, Claudine Ang, Shaoling Ma, Rochisha Narayan, Julien Labonne, Guillem Riambau, Steven Oliver, Xing Xia, Chin-Hao Huang, Rohan Mukherjee, and Parashar Kulkarni. This good group of scholars have encouraged my musings and inspired me with their good humor, commitment, and creative endeavors.

Advice and mentoring conversations from my senior colleagues at the college – Terry Nardin, Joanne Roberts, Jane Jacobs, and Jeanette Ickovics – have also been very important in helping me navigate the book's publication process and tenure-track journey.

Parts of the book were presented at various seminars and conferences over many years. I thank panel/seminar/workshop participants at APSA, MPSA, AAS, Wheaton College, University of California San Diego IRPS, Harvard Kennedy School of Government, Singapore Management University, Northern Illinois University Center of Southeast Asian Studies series, and Southeast Asia Research Group (SEAREG). Steven Wilkinson, Tom Pepinsky, Yuhki Tajima, Daniel Slater, and Alex Debs read earlier versions of the manuscript and were incredibly generous with their time and insights. I also thank Eddy Malesky, Allen Hicken, Donald Horowitz, Meredith Weiss, Amy Liu, Sarah Shair-Rosenfield, Kai Ostwald, Sana Jaffrey, S. P. Harish, Nico Ravanilla, Jamie Davidson, Terence Lee, Ted Hopf, Soo Yeon Kim, Eve Warburton, Colm Fox, Thomas Power, Ed Aspinall, Marcus Mietzner, Michele Ford, Walid Jumblatt Abdullah, Sana Jaffrey, Jake Ricks, Eunsok Jung, Johana Birnir, Ed Aspinall, Daniel Ziblatt, Frances Rosenbluth, and Kikue Hamayotsu for their feedback on this project, and on my more recent works on election violence that have emerged out of this book.

I am indebted to the people I met in Jakarta, Poso, Palu, Ambon, Ternate, Banggai, and Kei, who welcomed me and shared their stories with me. I hope I have captured their stories well enough that they will recognize themselves in the book.

Anjali Hazra, Rachel Quek, Sintus Runesi, Merry Alianti, Carissa Lim, Natasha Kristina, Wisha Jamal, Anmei Zeng, and Kenisha Alicia have provided research assistance throughout the years.

Thanks to two anonymous reviewers for their excellent comments that have strengthened this book, and to John Haslam at Cambridge University Press for signing this book and Ian Shapiro for including this book in the Problems of International Politics series. My sincere thanks also to Tobias Ginsberg, Roisin Munelly, Aparna Nair, and Franklin Mathews Jebaraj for seeing this book through the production process.

At Princeton, I found many lifelong friends: Jen Kwong, Jamie Chan, Jeff Lee, Jung Ju, Sally Kim, Diana Lee, David Kim, Jane Kim, Danielle Shin, Sonia Lee, Juewon Khwarg, and Gregory Lee. Sonia Lee did not get to see this book, but I hope she knows how her insights about writing many years ago have kept me going amid frustrating moments. Gregory Lee and Jeanette Park Lee are such dear friends; I cherish the time our two families were a 15-minute drive away.

My parents, Frans Toha and Riris K. Toha-Sarumpaet, modeled for me what co-parenting, mutual respect, and a strong work ethic look like. My sisters, Astrid and Thalia Toha, were my first friends in life and I am grateful for their friendship.

Finally, my husband, David Fernandez, and our three children, Ezra, Naomi, and Judah. Ezra sat through a number of classes and presentations quietly with a book in his hands. Naomi regularly wrote many stories next to me, and presented me with handmade cards celebrating every milestone of the book. Judah has no concept of what this book is about, or what I do for a living, but he cannot love me any more, or less, even if he had had that piece of information. David has not read a single word of this manuscript, but his stubborn faith in my abilities and steadfast commitment and sacrifices for our family made this book possible. This book is dedicated to him.

1 Introduction

The end of a regime is often accompanied by a severe outbreak of violence. The hopefulness that surrounded the 2011 Arab Spring uprisings, for example, was shattered by civil conflicts. Coptic Christians in Egypt, who had marched hand in hand with Muslims on Tahrir Square in January 2011, saw their churches and properties destroyed, and their co-religionists and clergy members kidnapped and slain, within months of the revolution. Clashes between ethnic groups erupted as dictators fell following pro-democracy protests in Tunisia, Yemen, and Libya. Violence also followed the collapse of apartheid in South Africa, the breakup of Yugoslavia, the 2010 revolution in Uzbekistan, and political transitions in Iraq, Burundi, Sudan, and Nigeria. In fact, nearly half of all democratic transitions between 1973 and 2000 involved some kind of conflict (Karatnycky and Ackerman 2005). Of the 408 communal conflicts around the world that occurred between 1989 and 2013, 74.51% occurred in countries that are neither fully democratic nor authoritarian, 17.15% in democracies, and 6.12% in autocracies.[1]

Indonesia's experience at the end of 32 years of authoritarian rule was no exception. Following the Asian financial crisis and a series of protests demanding political and economic reforms, President Soeharto announced his resignation on May 21, 1998. Within months of Soeharto's ouster, an argument between a Muslim and a Christian youth in Ambon in Maluku province, escalated into widespread clashes. Though previously touted as a model of interethnic and interreligious harmony, Ambon became the site of one of the most violent severe, complicated, and protracted violence between Christians and Muslims in recent history.

Yet even as Ambon was embroiled in sectarian violence during Indonesia's democratic transition in the late 1990s and early 2000s, its neighboring district, Maluku Tenggara, remained relatively peaceful in comparison. Whereas in Ambon hundreds of people died and the

---

[1] These calculations are based on the Uppsala Conflict Data Program (UCDP) non-state conflict database and the Polity IV data. See Toha (2017) and Figure B.1. in Appendix B.

clashes continued for years, in Maluku Tenggara the fighting lasted three months with far fewer deaths. Within months of the initial clash, refugees who had fled Maluku Tenggara were welcomed back with traditional ceremonies and both Christian and Muslim residents spoke of the conflict as a *musibah* (disaster) (Thorburn 2002).

This variation in the extent of local ethnic violence during a political transition raises important questions. What accounts for the onset of ethnic riots at a time of transition? Why do some parts of a transitioning country erupt in violence while others remain quiet? What factors account for the subsequent dissipation of violence? Why does conflict subside more quickly in some areas than in others?

The question of why groups fight each other during political transitions is one of the most debated issues in political science. Existing answers tend to fall into a few broad categories.[2] The first group of explanations, now outdated, focused on the inherent incompatibilities between ethnic groups. This view assumed that ethnic identities are fixed and that ethnic groups are inherently at odds with each other because individuals favor members of their own group over outsiders. Yet plenty of evidence from diverse settings suggests that violence between groups is not automatic. On the contrary, intergroup peace seems to be the norm, not an anomaly (Fearon and Laitin 1996). Furthermore, the same pairs of ethnic groups are sometimes allies in one context and enemies in another (Varshney 2009). In sub-Saharan Africa, for example, ethnic Chewas and Tumbukas are allies in Zambia and adversaries in Malawi (Posner 2005). Intrinsic differences across ethnic groups thus cannot account for the onset of violence during political transitions.

A second, more popular, type of explanation focuses on the strategic uses of violence between groups. It highlights elites' material interests and expected gains from mobilizing ethnic loyalties, particularly around elections. Scholars have argued that elites manipulate and politicize identities when they believe that they can win an election by persuading in-group members to vote along ethnic lines. This logic has been applied to incidents of ethnic rioting in South Asia (Wilkinson 2004) and election violence in countries of sub-Saharan Africa.

Based on this line of argument, violence should be more prevalent in the run-up to elections and should be more common amidst competitive elections. During Indonesia's democratic transition, however, although in some localities riots did erupt before elections, clashes escalated and

---

[2] In Chapter 2, I provide a more thorough discussion of these explanations.

continued well after the elections in many administrative units where violence happened. In Ambon, clashes spread and worsened after the 1999 election, whereas in Maluku Tenggara violence ended exactly three months before election. Electoral strategy alone cannot account for the pattern of violence in Indonesia's democratic transition.

A third category of explanations emphasizes structural factors, claiming that groups fight because of economic inequalities and grievances over their living conditions (Mancini 2008). But Ambon and Maluku Tenggara were relatively similar in terms of their levels of economic development and inequality between groups. Furthermore, both are ethnically and religiously diverse. In most cases, economic inequality between groups and the demographic composition within a country do not change drastically over time, which means these factors alone cannot explain why some riots started and ended relatively quickly during political transitions.

A good explanation of ethnic riots during political transitions must account for why they erupt in certain parts of a country and not others, why they subsequently decline, and how the incentives and decisions of actors involved in violence mobilization both shape and are influenced by institutional reforms. I attempt to answer these questions based on data from Indonesia.

The Argument in Brief

Given the prevalence of demands for change and the weakness of institutions in transitioning countries, a better approach to explaining why ethnic riots occur and subsequently decline during political transitions should take into account the unique characteristics of countries in transition. In many transitions, those who had access to power in the previous regime will want to protect their positions, and those excluded under the prior regime will push for changes in the political arrangement to favor them in the new government. In mature democracies with strong institutions, this negotiation of political influence and control of state resources typically occurs through formal political channels, such as elections. But in weakly institutionalized settings, these formal institutions may not function well, may be subject to drastic changes, or may disproportionately benefit a subset of the population at the expense of others who have been excluded. Consequently, citizens in weakly institutionalized settings must find alternative ways to voice their demands and get their government to listen to them.

To characterize the actions that groups may take during a political transition, I borrow from Albert Hirschman's (1970) seminal framework of organizational decay in *Exit, Voice, and Loyalty*. I argue that strategic local political actors in transitioning countries will *voice* their demands for seats in the new government, *exit* their local administrative units, or remain *loyal* and continue to endure unfavorable arrangements. These strategies are not mutually exclusive.

The voice and exit strategies require further explanation. Local actors in weakly institutionalized settings can voice their demands by two alternative forms of political engagement: voting or violence (Dunning 2011; Machado, Scartascini, and Tommasi 2011). I conceptualize violence as one form of voice, particularly during a political transition when institutions are weak. Local ethnic elites will interpret initial election results as a signal of the likely new configuration of power in the new government. To the extent that initial elections are competitive, previously excluded groups can assume that contestation, turnover, and ultimately political inclusion are plausible near-term outcomes. If elections are not competitive, excluded groups will perceive that the status quo is likely to continue despite overall democratic transition. When elections in transitioning countries fail to usher in the political access desired by excluded local actors, disgruntled people may express their voice by mobilizing violence.

On the other hand, incumbent ethnic elites who enjoyed insider status up to the moment of transition will also want to secure their position in the new regime. Whereas previously excluded local actors would interpret increased competition as a hopeful sign of possible entry, old guards of the prior regime view it as a threat to their place in the new government. They, too, will have an incentive to use violence to demonstrate their disruptive capacity in the new regime, should their interests be ignored. For both previously excluded and incumbent elites, violence serves as an effective signal of the group's mobilizational capacity and the threats they pose if their demands are unheeded. The more damaging the violence and the larger the number of people participating, the greater the signal of capacity and threat. To the extent that these demands for political inclusion are met in the new regime, local elites will have a vested interest in making the new arrangement work and will stop relying on violence to agitate for change. Violence will dissipate as institutions become stronger and more effective in channeling demands.

Conceptualized in this manner, my account does not attribute ethnic riots during a democratic transition in multiethnic societies to cultural incompatibilities, economic inequality, or electoral campaigns. Rather, ethnic riots serve a formative purpose in the country's long-term political development, helping to cement a group's status in the country's landscape of political actors and signal to others that the group cannot be ignored in the new political configuration. When these demands are accommodated, the group's position is legitimated in the new government.

Beyond voicing their demands, local ethnic groups can push for more access to local politics through the exit option. Exit can entail several actions at the individual level, including migration (Okamoto and Wilkes 2008) and, capital flight (Pepinsky 2009), or leaving organizations (Hirschman 1978). At the level of local administrative units, however, one previously understudied manifestation of exit is the carving out of new administrative units (i.e., a new district or municipality) from existing ones. This splitting of administrative units is akin to secession or partitioning, but at the subnational rather than the national level. When an existing district is split into multiple separate units, the number of seats and government positions increases, while the size of the population within each new unit declines. This gives groups concerned about exclusion from the new local government a greater chance of winning elections in the new units. Whether ethnic groups in transitioning countries choose the strategy of voice or exit, violence during political transition will decline once their demands for political inclusion are accommodated.

This argument implies several observable implications. Broadly, one would expect that the patterns of rioting should rise and fall depending on local actors' demand for political access and their ability to reach an agreeable power-sharing solution in the new government. Therefore, political transitions in ethnically diverse countries will not be universally violent but will be vulnerable to ethnic clashes if ethnic groups have been politically excluded in the previous government and ethnic groups can be readily mobilized. In comparisons across different countries, the empirical data should indicate that greater levels of political exclusion are positively associated with violent political transitions, all things being equal. At the subnational level, the same implication should apply as well; that is, more politically exclusive areas should experience higher rates of violence than those with less exclusion. Another implication of the argument is that violence should decline once these demands are accommodated through increased political competition, leadership turnover, and better representation of ethnic groups in local government positions.

In this book, relying on statistical and case-study analysis of local-level experiences during Indonesia's democratic transition from 1990 through 2012, I argue that local actors tend to mobilize violence to signal their demands for greater inclusion, and that violence declines when these demands are met.

Why Indonesia

Indonesia is a vast, archipelagic country with more than 17,500 islands located between Asia and Australia. It is a middle-income country, more than 85% Muslim, with more than one thousand ethnic groups and six official religions recognized by the government. Indonesia's first tier of administrative units consists of 34 provinces, which are further subdivided into second-tier units, districts (*kabupaten*) and municipalities (*kota*).[3] Despite the overall Muslim majority composition at the national level, religious and ethnic composition varies considerably across districts and municipalities. The abundance of administrative units and the variation between units along important dimensions allow for a systematic examination of local environmental precursors of violence.

Beyond the number of observations available for analysis, Indonesia provides a good laboratory to study the local dynamics of ethnic riots because such outbreaks are episodic, not routine (Varshney, Tadjoeddin, and Panggabean 2008; Tadjoeddin and Murshed 2007). They are rare occurrences, but they were particularly prevalent during the years immediately after Soeharto's ouster in 1998. The timing of riots during Indonesia's democratization mirrors the pattern of clashes in other transitioning countries, including Romania (Huntington 1991), Nigeria (Suberu 2001), Uzbekistan, and Georgia (Garthoff 2000). Aggregate statistics on ethnocommunal riots in Indonesia over time show that they spiked drastically shortly after Soeharto's ouster, reached its peak within the following year, and quickly declined thereafter.[4]

Geographically, ethnic rioting during Indonesia's democratic transition was concentrated in a few hot spots while most of the country remained peaceful. Specifically, 85.5% of all casualties in ethnic riots in the late 1990s and early 2000s in Indonesia occurred in 15 districts and

---

[3] Indonesia has four tiers of administrative units below the central government. The first tier is the provinces (*propinsi*, or Daerah Tingkat I in New Order parlance); the second consists of districts/regencies (*kabupaten*) and municipalities (*kota*) and was referred to as Daerah Tingkat II during the New Order; the last two are sub-districts (*kecamatan*) and villages (*desa* and *kelurahan*). Municipalities and districts are at the same layer of government, but municipalities are urban whereas districts are generally more rural. By districts, I refer to an administrative unit, not an electoral district, unless otherwise indicated.

[4] See Figures 5.2 and 5.3 for the temporal and spatial distribution of ethnic riots during Indonesia's political transition.

municipalities where just 6.5% of the country's total population resided (Varshney, Tadjoeddin, and Panggabean 2008). This variation in levels of violence across administrative units provides the opportunity for a careful inquiry into why violence erupted in some places and not others.

Third, the nationwide consistency in the reform process following the autocrat's ouster facilitates analysis. After President Soeharto resigned in 1998 following decades of authoritarian rule, Indonesia went through a six-year period of transition, implementing a series of important reforms and consolidating democracy.[5] In 2001, Indonesia began a "big-bang decentralization" that entailed the granting of political and fiscal autonomy to local governments, the proliferation of administrative units, and the direct election of local executives. The timing and process of these reforms were centrally determined, enabling an examination of causal relationships that otherwise would be more difficult to discern.

Contributions of the Book

This book contributes to our understanding of the challenges of democratic development. First, its most notable contribution to the literature is its emphasis on local politics. I have shown that it is not sufficient to focus simply on exclusion, competition, and incentives that shaped the behavior of political actors at the highest levels of government. My analysis of broad patterns across districts and municipalities in Indonesia demonstrates that local political exclusion in districts and municipalities at the onset of democratic transition matters as well. Amid broader political reforms at the national level, ethnic elites in districts and municipalities evaluated their prospects in the new regime in terms of their representation in local government. As much as local elites may have rejoiced over changes in Jakarta, these changes rang hollow if not followed by their group's inclusion in important positions at home.

With this framing, the book interacts with different bodies of literature that seldom engage each other. It borrows insights that others have articulated in explaining the onset of civil wars and armed rebellions, applying them to explain the emergence of ethnic riots, which are usually considered to have little in common with more protracted, highly violent, and coordinated types of violence. Most prior studies that have demonstrated the relationship between political exclusion of ethnic groups and violence have focused on civil wars (Cederman, Hug,

---

[5] The years 1998–2001 are considered the years of Indonesia's transition to democracy, as reflected in the Polity IV index score for Indonesia, which jumped from −7 in 1998 to 6 in 2001.

and Krebs 2010; Cederman, Wimmer, and Min 2010) and nationalist mobilizations (Beissinger 2002; Wimmer 2002). Horowitz (1985) has observed that ethnic groups disappointed with election results may resort to military coups to seize power from the ruling government, as demonstrated by a series of coups in the Congo-Brazzaville, Sierra Leone, Nigeria, and Togo in 1966–1967. While ethnic riots may occur alongside civil wars and military coups, the literature so far has not examined their onset as a unique category of violence that is associated with political exclusion at the local level. In this book, I argue that local actors are also preoccupied with concerns about entry and representation, even when they do not mobilize a secession or an armed rebellion against the state.

Second, I leverage the creation of new administrative units in Indonesia as a lens to examine whether and how accommodating demands for political inclusion ameliorates violence. Many studies have focused on power-sharing arrangements, electoral systems, and quotas and reservations as institutional solutions to violent conflict. Another body of literature has focused on secession and partitioning as a helpful (or unhelpful) solution to ethnic wars (Chapman and Roeder 2007; Kaufman 1996; Sambanis 2000). Yet another body of literature has examined administrative unit proliferation in the context of decentralization (Malesky 2009; Pierskalla and Sacks 2017; Grossman and Lewis 2014). But we know relatively little about the role of subnational territorial partitioning and boundary revisions in cultivating peace after violence. In this book, I treat administrative unit proliferations as local actors' exit and a solution to prior violence and demands for greater representation and control over state resources. District creation can function as a political tool for mitigating exclusion by carving out separate units for previously warring groups and granting each group greater control over state resources. To my knowledge, this monograph is the first to bring together ethnic rioting, political transition, and the creation of new administrative units in a cohesive framework that is then analyzed over a large number of observations with a range of methods.

Third, this book contributes to the literature on riots. Extant literature on riots has been mostly based on cases in South Asia and, to some extent, in Western Europe and the United States, where the political salience of identity-based loyalties has developed in the context of mature political institutions. Indonesia, perhaps along with other countries in Southeast Asia more generally, showcases an opposite situation: ethnic groups have historically had strong institutions and networks, whereas the state was largely absent or weak (Tajima 2014; Scott 2010).

The turn toward ethnic networks, narratives, and communities during a political transition was possible because these infrastructures were readily available and more effective than the state-affiliated political apparatus. Given the stickiness of ascriptive identities and the failures of formal political institutions in many transitioning countries, a careful study of Indonesia should also inform our understanding of other weakly institutionalized and diverse countries.

Fourth, for scholars of Indonesia, this book offers a new explanation of ethnic riots during a political transition that moves beyond national-level politics and provides systematic evidence at the subnational level, using a mixed-methods approach combining both comparative case studies and time-series analysis of administrative units from 1990 through 2012. Although pioneering works on violence during Indonesia's political transition have articulated the importance of elites' machinations in shaping violence, consistent with the argument offered in this book, the evidence presented here establishes a broad pattern across time and space in Indonesia, articulating how *local* elites' mobilization and coordination shapes both the rise and decline of violence. This book should also be of interest to policymakers, both in Indonesia and in other multiethnic new democracies, who seek to manage ethnic loyalties and avoid future outbursts of violence.

Organization of the Book

This book has two main parts. The first part develops my theoretical framework and arguments, and I present my research design and a set of implications of my theory. In the second part, these implications are examined through a large-*n* statistical analysis of districts and municipalities in Indonesia, and then in an empirically rich case study of four districts where rioting occurred at varying levels of intensity during the country's democratic transition. Finally, in the conclusion of the book, I discuss the relevance of the book's theoretical framework and findings beyond Indonesia.

In Chapter 2, I develop a theory of how local political exclusion drives ethnic riots in multiethnic countries during a political transition. I start by outlining a set of assumptions and unique characteristics of countries in transition, and by demarcating the boundaries of the argument. I outline existing explanations of the onset of ethnic riots and discuss their limitations in explaining why ethnic riots rise and subsequently decline during political transitions in multiethnic countries. Applying Hirschman's framework of strategies in organizational decay, I argue that excluded ethnic groups in countries undergoing political transitions can choose to voice their grievances and demands, threaten to exit the district, or continue to endure the existing political arrangement. I argue that ethnic riots in democratizing countries are driven by local elites' resentment over continued political exclusion and are by-products of their attempts to push for entry into politics. Following a disappointing election, excluded local elites turn to their networks – which in ethnically diverse areas will usually be ethnic networks – to mobilize violence as a means of amplifying their demands for inclusion. Once their demands for inclusion have been met and the violence has served its purpose, rioting will decline. This chapter elaborates and extends Hirschman's logic to account for why, where, and when ethnic fighting erupts and subsequently stops in transitioning countries.

Chapter 3 traces the development of ethnic cleavages in Indonesia across three significant time periods. Although the inhabitants of the archipelago now known as Indonesia have always encompassed various cultural, ethnic, linguistic, and religious groups, the political salience of their identities has fluctuated based on the policies of the authorities at the time. At times, ethnic groups engaged in violence to challenge their treatment by existing authorities. These precedents for using violence to contest existing political configurations and to renegotiate the boundaries of who is "in" or "out" set the stage for my examination of the more recent mobilizations of violence during Indonesia's democratic transition.

Chapter 4 provides a macro-historical context of Indonesia's 32 years of authoritarian rule under President Soeharto and the country's subsequent transition to democracy in 1998. Soeharto's combined strategy of rapid development, depoliticization of the masses, and preferential treatment of specific groups carried important implications for the local political representation of ethnic groups. During Soeharto's New Order regime, Golongan Karya (better known as Golkar), the political organization associated with Soeharto, developed a deep and dominant presence in villages throughout the country, effectively crushing alternative forces of political mobilization and engagement. Furthermore, in ethnically diverse areas, Golkar coopted and colluded with local members of certain ethnic communities while snubbing others. As such, even though Golkar was not an ethnic party in the traditional sense, in ethnically diverse districts, Golkar officials who rose through the bureaucratic ranks appeared to come from one group at the expense of others, thereby exacerbating the politicization of ethnic identities over time.

Chapter 5 investigates the relationship between political exclusion and ethnic riots. Earlier studies of the relationship between political exclusion and armed conflict have mostly relied on cross-national analyses that examined exclusion at the national level. However, given my task of explaining subnational variations in ethnic riots during a time of political transition, it is important to study political exclusion at the local level. This chapter examines how the onset of ethnic riots correlates with two indicators of political exclusion: competitiveness of district elections and dominance by Golkar. Assuming that electorally uncompetitive districts present greater barriers to entry for opposition candidates, I show that districts with lower electoral competition at the onset of democratization were more likely to experience higher levels of violence than those with fiercer competition.

Chapter 6 discusses the specific relationships between Golkar's entrenchment, the exclusion of local ethnic elites, and the mobilization of riots in two high-conflict Indonesian provinces, Central Sulawesi and Maluku. By comparing two pairs of districts – Ambon and Maluku Tenggara in Maluku province, and Banggai and Poso in Central Sulawesi province – I demonstrate the importance of local elites' framing, mobilization, and organization of violence. Although the four districts are relatively similar in their religious and ethnic composition, level of economic development, and dependence on the state, Ambon and Poso experienced some of the most protracted and intense ethnocommunal violence in Indonesia's recent history, while their two neighboring districts, Maluku Tenggara and Banggai, respectively, were relatively peaceful by comparison. Relying on interviews with bureaucrats, community leaders, and former combatants, I show that these diverging outcomes can be attributed to local elites' initial political configuration at the onset of the democratic transition, and to their actions and responses to trigger events.

Chapter 7 explains the dissipation of violence. Consistent with my theory, once political exclusion was ameliorated in conflict-ridden districts, the level of violence dropped. The creation of new districts and the implementation of direct elections of local executives accommodated these demands for inclusion. Whereas previously excluded political hopefuls faced impenetrable barriers to election, the creation of new districts multiplied the number of elected positions and increased the likelihood of opposition electoral victories, particularly in post-conflict areas where the electorate was already receptive to ethnic appeals and likely to vote for members of their ethnic group.

In Chapter 8, I summarize my findings and discuss their implications and contributions to existing literatures and policymaking. I identify remaining unanswered questions and outline possible trajectories of future research on political exclusion, institutional accommodation of excluded actors, and demobilization of participants in violence in countries in political transition.

2   Exclusion and Violence during Democratic Transitions

Why do clashes between groups occur in some places during political transitions in multiethnic settings and not in others? What explains the return to peace in some contexts and extended violence in others? Existing accounts have focused on the importance of political actors' strategic interests during power shifts, state capacity, and structural factors such as inequality and grievances between groups. These accounts, however, have highlighted political actors' scramble and strategic maneuvers at the national level. As such, they cannot address why some areas within a country remained peaceful when some others erupted in violence during a political transition.

This chapter develops a theory of how local political exclusion drives ethnic riots in multiethnic countries during political transition. I start by defining key terms and describing the unique characteristics of countries in transition. I discuss existing accounts of the onset of ethnic riots and their limitations in explaining why ethnic rioting rises and subsequently declines during political transitions in multiethnic countries. I argue that ethnic riots in democratizing countries are driven by local elites' demands for inclusion in local politics. This deployment of ethnic riots as a form of political engagement is particularly prevalent in weakly institutionalized multiethnic settings, where institutions are less reliable and where available local networks tend to be ethnic based. Once a group's demands for inclusion have been met and violence has served its purpose, rioting will decline. I derive a set of observable implications and hypotheses to be examined in the subsequent empirical chapters.

Key Terms

Ethnic Riots

In this book, I do not attempt to explain all kinds of identity-related violence, let alone all political violence, but only ethnic riots during a country's democratic transition. In line with other constructivists who view ethnic identity as fluid and malleable (Barth 1969; Hobsbawm 1996), I define ethnic identity as a subjective sense of belonging to a group based on a perception of commonly shared, descent-based attributes.[1] Like Chandra (2006); Posner (2005), I use the terms *ethnic* and *ethnicity* as broad umbrella terms that include various dimensions of ascriptive identities such as religion, ethnicity, tribe, and language.[2]

Horowitz (2001) defined ethnic riots as "intense, sudden, though not necessarily wholly unplanned lethal attack by civilian members of one ethnic group on civilian members of another ethnic group, the victims chosen because of their group membership."[3] Clashes between Hindus and Muslims in India, Christians and Muslims in northern Nigeria, or Hutus and Tutsis in Rwanda and Burundi, along with the anti-Chinese violence of 1969 in Malaysia and the Tulsa race riots in 1921 in the United States, are examples of ethnic riots.

Based on this definition, many incidents of violence do not qualify as ethnic riots. Although local ethnic grievances contributed to some instances of violence in 1965–1966 in Indonesia, the anti-communist killings in Indonesia in these years were not ethnic riots because the victims were generally targeted due to their supposed ideological leanings, not their ethnic affiliations.[4] I also exclude mob violence

---

[1] For a thorough review of what ethnic identity is and is not, see Chandra (2012b).

[2] This practice of using the terms *ethnic* and *ethnicity* as a big umbrella category for all kinds of ascriptive identities is common in the ethnic politics. For example, Chandra (2004) wrote, "I take the term 'ethnic group' to refer to the nominal members of an ascriptive category such as race, language, caste, tribe, or religion" (Chandra 2004, 2). Similarly, Donald Horowitz stated that "ethnicity easily embraces groups differentiated by color, language, and religion; it covers tribes, races, nationalities, and castes" (Horowitz 1985, 53). Rothchild (1997); Birnir (2007); Kasfir (1979); and Posner (2005) adopted a similarly broad approach. The aggregation of ethnicity and religion under the umbrella term *ethnic* is not empirically useful in some cases. McCauley (2017) and Sidel (2006), for example, have analyzed religious violence as a completely separate category from other kinds of identity-related violence.

[3] Although much has been written on ethnic riots, there is surprisingly little disagreement over what constitutes an ethnic riot. Other definitions are largely consistent with Horowitz (2001), although their particular emphases may vary slightly. Brass (1997) defines an ethnic riot as "an event involving a large number of massed persons from opposing ethnic groups engaged in assaults on persons, lives, and property." Though he does not specify cutoffs for what counts as a large number of persons, other social scientists also define riots as necessarily involving large crowds (Olzak and Shanahan 1996; Wilkinson 2009; Rude 1981). Because there is no specified upper bound for the size of groups engaged in rioting, this definition can encompass genocidal violence, as long as the victims are targeted on the basis of their ethnic identification. Wilkinson (2004) emphasizes the non-state identity of the individuals engaged in violence and excludes riots against the police or any other state apparatus.

[4] In some instances, however, individuals were targeted over various community-level grievances, apart from their membership in communist organizations (Robinson 1995).

against one individual (e.g., street justice or lynchings) unless the incident was triggered by an ethnicity-related offense or led to a bigger clash between ethnic groups. Violence by an individual against a large group, such as terrorism or sniper shootings, is also not part of an ethnic riot unless it occurred within the context of prior ethnocommunal violence.[5] Similarly, incidents that directly involve state security personnel as a party engaged in violence are excluded, since these clashes do not occur between two groups of civilians divided along ethnic lines. For this reason, civil wars; secessionist violence; police violence; mass mobilizations and demonstrations criticizing government policies; and nationalist mobilizations against a ruling government are excluded. However, incidents of violence carried out by civilian individuals at the behest of state-affiliated actors who deliberately incite ethnic hatred, mobilize crowds, and allow initial trigger events to escalate would fall into this category. In these cases, the individuals directly involved and engaged in the act of violence are civilians, even though they may have been responding to prompting, sponsorship, and coordination from within the government.

In the broader literature, scholars have used the terms *communal, racial, religious, ethnonationalist,* and *ethnocommunal* clashes to refer to ethnic riots. Some distinguish between ethnocommunal and communal events, using the latter term for clashes that are not ethnically motivated (Tajima 2014). I follow the same practice. Since ethnocommunal violence is the category of interest in my study, I use the terms *riots, violence,* and *ethnocommunal violence* interchangeably.

Political Exclusion

Broadly, political exclusion refers to the institutional barriers to participation, representation, and access to political and economic resources faced by a specific group within a state. The specific manifestations of political exclusion can vary, however.

The crudest form of political exclusion is the denial of citizenship and access to the rights and protection that citizens generally enjoy, such as the right to vote or to a fair trial (Chatty, Mansour, and Yassin 2013). The ethnic Rohingyas in Myanmar, for example, lack the right to vote and have repeatedly been driven from their homes, forced into ghettos without any provision of basic services, or killed.

---

[5] Targeted sniper shootings in Poso, Central Sulawesi, where ongoing clashes between Christians and Muslims occurred from 1998 through 2007, would fall under the category of violence analyzed in this book because they sharpened divisions and arguably prolonged the violence (Sidel 2006).

The Romas in Macedonia have similarly been denied citizenship unless they were legally residing in Macedonia when Yugoslavia collapsed and had applied for naturalization within one year of the state's dissolution. Many of the 54,000 officially registered Romas in Macedonia still carry identification cards designating them as foreigners, lack birth certificates, and cannot access many state services as a result (UNHCR 2017).

Beyond the basic issue of citizenship, political exclusion can also refer to the lack of representation of a subset of a country's population in the political system (Wimmer 2002; Cederman, Wimmer, and Min 2010; Gurr 2000; Asal et al. 2016). Political representation is an important manifestation of inclusion because diverse groups have distinct positions, experiences, and perspectives (Young 2000), and because having their voices at the table in policymaking processes should help to prevent the further perpetuation of structural inequalities (Williams 1998; Mansbridge 1999; Kymlicka 1995). Scholars have distinguished between symbolic and substantive representation. Symbolic representation refers to simply placing people affiliated with marginalized groups in government positions, whereas substantive representation implies enabling representatives of marginalized groups to advocate for policies and decisions that would benefit those whom they claim to represent (Pitkin 1967; Htun 2016). For instance, the introduction of quotas for female politicians in many Latin American countries has increased the number of women in politics, but many elected female officials do not necessarily advocate for policies on behalf of women (Htun 2016). In this framework, women could be symbolically represented yet still substantively excluded. Among the various categories of a country's population, empirical studies have focused mostly on the political representation of groups organized along ethnic (Reilly 2001; Cederman, Wimmer, and Min 2010), gender (Shair-Rosenfield 2012; Arriola and Johnson 2014), and class (Carnes 2016) lines.

A third form of political exclusion concerns government policies that influence a group's ability to attain economic, political, and social resources. A group may possess citizenship and voting rights but still be victimized by exclusionary policies that influence its members' well-being. Mylonas (2012, 22), for example, defines exclusionary policies as "policies that aim at the physical removal of a non-core group from the host state (or specific areas of it)." Exclusionary policies can be as severe as population exchange, segregation, internal displacement, or genocide. But actions of lesser severity can still deny a group access to economic, political, and social resources. The ethnic Chinese in Indonesia, for example, are by law considered citizens, though up until

2006 they were categorized as citizens of foreign descent (*WNI keturunan asing*), distinct from indigenous Indonesians (*WNI asli*). Up until 2000, Chinese languages, religion, and schools were banned. It took another six years before a new citizenship law was passed, removing the prior requirements for Chinese Indonesians to go through additional legal steps to affirm their Indonesian citizenship (Chandra 2012a). Similarly, African Americans in some northern US states held voting rights as early as the 1840s, but they risked endangering their lives if they actually tried to exercise this right (Tocqueville 1988).

In such situations, political exclusion usually accompanies social exclusion, by which a particular group is granted a lower social status. In the case of many women, descendants of Africans, and indigenous people in Latin America, political exclusion reinforces and reflects the groups' already inferior social status (Htun 2016). Notably, however, it does not necessarily imply subordination in every sphere; in some cases, in fact, ethnic groups may be excluded politically because they are perceived as superior in other spheres. Examples of market-dominant and yet politically excluded ethnic minorities in Southeast Asia fit this category (Chua 2003; Glaeser 2005).

In this book, I use the term *political exclusion* to refer to situations where an ethnic group lacks meaningful representation in local politics and has little or no hope of placing group members in important positions in local government.

Demands

Violent mobilizations during political transitions in countries around the world have articulated all kinds of demands, ranging from a complete overhaul of the political system to demands for greater redistribution. The People Power movement in the Philippines that upended Ferdinand Marcos' autocratic rule, for example, was a broad-based movement seeking the establishment of an electoral democracy. South Korea's democratic transition in June 1987 followed weeks of riots against the party nomination of Roh Tae-woo for the presidency, the deaths of university students, and demands for direct presidential elections (Lee 2018). Protesters in South Africa's New Defiance Campaign and general strike in 1989 pushed to abolish apartheid (Teorell 2010). Indonesia's own transition to democracy in 1998 was preceded by months of student protests against rising fuel prices and demands to remove Soeharto. All these demands sought major changes in the institutionalized political arrangements.

Another frequently expressed demand during political transitions is for redistribution of resources, typically for the benefit of those who are economically disadvantaged or their representatives. This category and demands for political reforms are, of course, not always mutually exclusive. In fact, seminal theories of regime change have modeled democratization as the outcome of distributive conflicts between different socioeconomic groups. Boix (2003), for example, has suggested that democratization occurs when inequality is low and when elites have less incentive to repress the poor's demands for greater redistribution. Similarly, Acemoglu and Robinson (2006) have argued that countries are more likely to transition to democracy when they are at intermediate levels of inequality, where the poor would be sufficiently aggrieved to mobilize demands for redistribution but the elites would not be so threatened by potential losses in the new regime as to repress these demands. Even skeptics of this theory, such as Haggard and Kaufman (2012), have found that distributive conflict was present in more than 50% of all democratic transitions from 1980 to 2000. As one illustration, Mali's democratic transition in 1992 began with economic grievances and urban protests against structural adjustment measures (Haggard, Kaufman, and Teo 2016). Mass mobilizations protesting against pervasive corruption also preceded electoral reforms in Kenya in 1997 (Ndegwa 1998). Albania's economic collapse in 1990 prompted hundreds of thousands of protesters to demand elections and wage increases (Biberaj 1999).

Although many books on violent mobilizations during political transitions have focused on national-level demands for a massive overhaul of the country's political system and significant redistribution of resources, this book considers a different category of demands, revolving around access to local politics. It examines the incentives and concerns of local bureaucrats, civil servants, party activists, religious leaders, and community figures in districts and municipalities. While democratic transition was happening at the national level and politicians were wheeling and dealing to protect their interests under the new government, local actors in districts and municipalities were concerned about protecting their interests and ensuring access to the spoils of the state. In practice, these demands may be manifested in a push for a co-ethnic executive leader, a new political party, or a legal recognition of economic and political control of traditional communities among others.

Transition to Democracy

This book examines the onset of ethnic riots in multiethnic countries undergoing a transition to democracy. The study of democratization has spawned numerous books and captured scholars' attention, particularly during democracy's "third wave" in the 1990s as many post-communist countries transitioned to democracies. Although some have argued that the transition paradigm is now outdated (Carothers 2002), it is still useful to distinguish countries in political transition from their more mature and stable counterparts. In this book, a transition to democracy, or democratization, is defined as a process that starts with the ouster of an authoritarian regime and ends with the consolidation of democracy.

The point at which democracy is considered consolidated has been a subject of many years of scholarly debate. Some have advocated a multidimensional approach to measuring consolidation (Linz and Stepan 1996; Abulai and Crawford 2010; Schedler 2001), while others have proposed a simple longevity threshold to separate unconsolidated from consolidated democracies (Huntington 1991). Broadly, democracy is considered consolidated when it is "the only game in town" and its legitimacy is widely accepted by the country's political actors (Linz and Stepan 1996, 5). Linz and Stepan (1996, 5–6) clarified further that democracy is consolidated when "no significant political groups seriously attempt to overthrow the democratic regime or secede from the state," when "the overwhelming majority of the people believe that any further political change must emerge from within the parameters of democratic formulas," and when political actors "become subjected to, and habituated to, the resolution of conflict within the specific laws, procedures and institutions sanctioned by the new democratic process." Carothers (2002, 7) similarly described consolidation as "a slow but purposeful process in which democratic forms are transformed into democratic substance through the reform of state institutions, the regularization of elections, the strengthening of civil society, and the overall habituation of the society into the new democratic 'rules of the game.'" In practice, this broader and more holistic understanding of democratic consolidation has been operationalized by various indices that capture the multiple dimensions in their empirical analyses (Schneider and Schmitter 2004).

Another alternative approach uses a test or threshold to determine when a democracy is consolidated. For example, Huntington (1991) focused on the legitimacy of elections among political actors and offered the now-famous *two-turnover* test, according to which a democracy is consolidated only "if the party or group that takes power in the initial election at the time of transition loses a subsequent election and turns over power to those election winners, and if those election winners then peacefully turn over power to winners of a later election" (Huntington 1991, 267). Another alternative is the longevity threshold, which defines democracy as consolidated when twenty years with regular competitive elections have passed (Beetham 1994). Gasiorowski and Power (1998) set a twelve-year threshold after transition as a marker for democratic consolidation. But this test-based approach is also insensitive to contexts (Schedler 2001) and captures only a very narrow aspect of consolidation (Abulai and Crawford 2010). It does not provide any information about the quality of elections; outbursts of protests and violence; the presence of electoral malpractice; or non-electoral dimensions of consolidation, such as constitutional arrangements or the legitimacy of democracy. Recognizing that no approach is perfect, I have adopted the *two-turnover* test to identify the point at which democracy is consolidated.

In limiting the scope of argument to countries transitioning to democracy, I do not address political transitions or authoritarian breakdowns generally. Democratizing countries are a small subset of these groups. A number of recent works on authoritarian collapses use the ouster of an authoritarian incumbent as the starting point of the political breakdown (Brownlee 2009). However, an autocrat's ouster may lead to a variety of outcomes. Some have argued that it must not be automatically conflated with democratization, since in many instances it represents mere moments of autocratic weakness that are quickly corrected and not any greater demand for democracy. Levitsky and Way (2015) have pointed out that historically, most authoritarian breakdowns have not led to democratization.[6] Some states, such as Great Britain, transitioned smoothly to consolidated democracies (Acemoglu and Robinson 2006). Egypt and Jordan, on the other hand, quickly relapsed into authoritarianism (Diamond 2008).[7] Moreover, some countries have remained stuck in a hybrid mix of democracy and autocracy, having democratic trappings but suffering from illiberal practices.[8] Even mature democracies may exhibit some features typically associated with authoritarianism.[9] For this reason, I refrain from using *authoritarian collapse* or *authoritarian breakdown* to label the group of cases to which my argument is applicable.

---

[6] Epstein et al. (2006); Przeworski et al. (2000); Tilly (2007) contested the notion that consolidation is automatic. Svolik (2014) provided an empirical examination of when and why certain transitional countries overcome the threat of authoritarian reversal and become consolidated.

[7] This description of recently transitioned democracies as "rolling back" into authoritarianism has been criticized by some who claim that these transitions were instead "moments of extraordinary incumbent weakness" and not meaningful movement toward democracy (Levitsky and Way 2015, 50).

[8] In the literature, these states have been referred to as semidemocratic, hybrid, competitive authoritarian, illiberal democracy, or partly free (Levitsky and Way 2002).

[9] For instance, Slater and Way (2017) have identified traits in the 2016 US presidential election that are common in elections in competitive authoritarian countries.

This approach also examines a relatively narrow temporal range. Although some scholars have started their analysis with the ouster of the incumbent, others have gone further back to the point of the country's liberalization. Tajima (2014), for example, began his analysis of Indonesia's authoritarian collapse at 1996, when the country began to liberalize. Ziblatt (2017) traced the adoption of democracy in Great Britain to the strong political party organization that the British Conservative Party had built over decades before the 1884 Reform Act, which many consider the turning point for British democratization. Though the incremental opening of a political system through various liberalizing policies shapes the opportunities and constraints available to political actors, it does not heighten uncertainties, distributive conflicts, and incentives for political mobilization as radically as the involuntary end of an autocrat's rule would, since political actors would expect the status quo to continue into the foreseeable future. As such, my analysis places the starting point of transition at the ouster of the incumbent. To avoid repetitiveness, I refer to transitioning or democratizing countries interchangeably, as well as to new or young democracies.

Existing Explanations of Ethnocommunal Violence

Existing explanations of ethnocommunal violence fall into several categories. The primordial view prioritizes the importance of ethnic diversity as the source of conflict between groups. According to this view, ethnicity matters simply because it is a "given" of society. Human beings are evolutionarily predisposed to view themselves as belonging to particular ethnic groups and are naturally inclined to favor fellow members of their group (van de Berghe 1981). Because of this ethnic nepotism, ethnically diverse societies are inevitably rife with tension, since individuals from different ethnic groups will take political, economic, and social actions based on a concern to favor their kin (Vanhanen 1999). This line of reasoning, however, has largely fallen out of favor. Empirically, the same pairs of ethnic groups may be peaceful in some times and places and at war elsewhere (Posner 2004). Furthermore, most interethnic relations are peaceful (Fearon and Laitin 1996), and many clashes have involved groups with a relatively short history of contact (Varshney 2009).

The second category of explanations of ethnic riots focuses on structural factors such as inequality between groups and competition for material resources. Gurr (1993), for example, argued that relative deprivation – the gap between what the material resources group has and what it thinks it deserves – drives discontentment and mobilizes people to rebel and protest against their governments. Olzak (1992) has argued that competition over jobs and public housing leads to clashes between groups. US race riots in the 1960s have been attributed to resentment and fears among whites that blacks were moving into white neighborhoods in large numbers and taking over their jobs (Spilerman 1976). In a study of countries in sub-Saharan Africa from 1990 through 2008, Fjelde and Ostby (2014) found that countries with higher levels of inequality (both vertical and horizontal) were more prone to violent communal conflicts. Similarly, a recent county-level study found that ethnic violence in the Xinjiang region of China was associated with horizontal inequality between the Han majority and the largest ethnic minority group (Cao et al. 2018). With regard to Indonesia, Tadjoeddin (2013) found that ethnic riots were concentrated in districts with a larger population of people with high levels of education but lower income levels, suggesting that these individuals may be disgruntled over their inability to achieve their aspirations.

Beyond inequality in access to material resources, numerous works have stressed the impact of political representation and inclusion on violence. Aristotle's *Politics* declared that "men ... cause revolutions when they are not allowed to share honors and if they are unjustly or insolently treated" (Aristotle 1944, 1316b). To maintain a peaceful polity, Aristotle (1944, 1308a) suggested treating those "outside the constitution well" and "bringing their leading men into the constitution." Niccolò Machiavelli echoed this idea and posited that when there are no laws in the republic to allow disgruntled people to articulate their grievances, "extra legal methods will be employed and without doubt these will have much worse consequences than legal ones" (Machiavelli 1531, 102). More recently, Lijphart (1977) argued that a "grand coalition" between important ethnic groups is necessary to maintain a peaceful plural polity. In his proposed consociational democracy, all ethnic groups are proportionately represented in the grand coalition, each group has mutual veto in decision-making, and each group enjoys a high degree of freedom to govern their affairs. In Lebanon from 1943 through 1975, he noted, the key groups were represented in a grand coalition of officeholders: "a Maronite president, a Sunni prime minister, a Shiite chairman of the legislature, and a Greek Orthodox deputy chairman and deputy prime minister" (Lijphart 1977, 148). Birnir (2007) has similarly demonstrated the importance of political inclusion for ethnic groups' peaceful electoral engagement. Legislative access, she argued, is what accounts for the peaceful political engagement of Turks in Bulgaria, Hungarians in Romania, and Catalans in Spain, and conversely for the violent mobilization of the Basques in Spain and the Tamils in Sri Lanka. When ethnic groups are unrepresented and excluded from formal politics, Birnir claimed, they will look for alternative means to voice their demands. Regime and party system stability in a plural setting, she stated, depends on the representation of ethnic political factions in politics. Cederman, Wimmer, and Min (2010) have made the same point from a different angle. Their cross-national analysis of all politically relevant ethnic groups from 1946 through 2005 showed that countries with politically excluded ethnic groups had a greater likelihood of civil war. Ethnic groups tend to fight when they are excluded from the highest political offices in the land.

The third group of explanations of ethnocommunal violence has focused on how local elites politicize identity-based loyalties for strategic and political purposes. Scholars in this camp treat ethnic groups as unitary, mobilizable coalitions organized to achieve common political, economic, and social goals (Bates 1983; Young 1976; Rabushka and Shepsle 1972). From this perspective, ethnic identity and diversity in and of themselves do not produce conflict; rather, conflict emerges when ethnic identity is politicized in such a way that whether one belongs to a particular group determines access to political and economic resources. In other words, in a multiethnic setting, some ethnic identities may be politically relevant, whereas others may not. The salience of ethnic identities is neither automatic nor fixed but is socially constructed and can be manipulated for instrumental reasons (Posner 2005).

One area that has received significant attention in the literature is how politicians strategically manipulate identity-based loyalties to their benefit through ethnic appeals and priming around elections. Examining incidents of Hindu–Muslim riots in India, Wilkinson (2004) argued that they were driven by local elites' electoral incentives. In anticipation of a competitive election, at the town level, politicians manipulated ethnic loyalties and fomented riots to prime members of their ethnic group to vote along ethnic lines, thereby helping their candidates to gain election. In this manner, ethnic riots function as a campaign tool that solidifies a coalition and mobilizes voters to support candidates from their ethnic group. Once riots have erupted, however, the relevant state governments can choose either to quell them decisively or to allow them to escalate. At the state level, Wilkinson (2004) further argued that the use of force to quell anti-minority violence depends on whether the incumbent government needs support from minority voters to win a competitive election.

Evidence from elsewhere supports this argument as well. Drawing on the Afrobarometer surveys of 35,000 respondents in 10 countries from 1999 through 2004, Eifert, Miguel, and Posner (2010) have found that proximity to election increases the likelihood that survey respondents will express views along ethnic lines. In the runup to the 1992 elections in Kenya, clashes between ethnic Kalenjins who backed the incumbent president, Daniel arap Moi, and non-Kalenjins were designed to intimidate voters into supporting Moi's party, Kenya African National Union (KANU) (Bekoe and Burchard 2017). In Nigeria, Collier and Vicente (2014) conducted an experimental study and found that voters were less likely to participate in elections when they thought they would be targeted with violence. Similarly, in a study based on newly declassified data from Afghanistan, Condra et al. (2018) demonstrated that insurgent attacks around elections reduced voter turnout, thereby highlighting another possible motivation for pre-election violence.

These explanations, however, are broadly about clashes between groups and the initiation of violence due to structural inequalities. They are not strictly about violence in countries in transition. With regard to violence during power shifts specifically, a fourth group of explanations focuses on the weakening of state security capacity. Posen (1993) argued that the temporary weakening of state security capacity during political transition in ethnically diverse settings heightens uncertainties and produces an ethnic security dilemma. Ethnic groups, now deprived of a strong state presence to guarantee their safety, arm themselves in anticipation of attacks from other groups. As each group arms itself, it alarms the other group, and tensions escalate until clashes erupt. In this view, peace is restored only when the state can enforce order again. Tajima (2014) expanded the focus to encompass non-state and informal security capacity, contending that communal riots are more common in villages with greater mismatches between informal and formal security institutions. When the state's security capacity is constrained during a political transition, communities whose informal security institutions have lower capacity struggled to respond to trigger events. In Tajima's view, violence will eventually decline and peace will return when the local communities have sufficiently improved their capacity to respond to trigger events.

Other than security capacity, the maneuvers of political entrepreneurs to secure control over political and economic resources have also been identified as a factor that drives violence during political transition. Snyder (2000) argued that in the context of democratic transitions, which allow for significant shifts in power configurations and the allocation of resources, politicians in ethnically diverse settings may find it useful to mobilize ethnonationalist sentiments to maintain their power. Gagnon (1994/1995) analyzed ethnic violence in Serbia, describing it as deliberately engineered by political actors who fomented violence for their personal gains.

Experts on Indonesia have also used this lens to explain violence during the country's democratic transition. Bertrand (2004, 3) claims that the country's democratic transition was a "critical juncture in Indonesia's post-independent history during which institutional transformation opened up channels to renegotiate the elements of the national model: the role of Islam in political institutions, the relative importance of the central and regional governments, the access and representation of ethnic groups in the state's institutions, as well as the definition and meaning of the Indonesian 'nation.'" In his view, at these crucial points of renegotiation of the national model, groups feel threatened and "seek to position themselves either to protect past gains, favorable definitions of national models, or institutions that provide them with protection and representation. Other groups fear that they will be subjected to discrimination or exclusion" (Bertrand 2004, 4–5). For Bertrand, ethnic and nationalist violence during Indonesia's democratic transition was a by-product of this renegotiation and shifts in political configuration at the national level.

In his analysis of riots, pogroms, and jihad from 1995 to 2005 in Indonesia, Sidel (2006, 210) argued that the "modalities of religious violence in Indonesia – its timing, location, forms, targets, protagonists, and processes of mobilization – have been decisively shaped by the broad constellation of religious authority in the country and by the possibility of articulating claims to represent (in both senses of the term) Islam in the world's most populous majority-Muslim nation-state." Whereas the late 1980s and the 1990s saw the ascendancy of those who claimed to represent Islam in Indonesia, the early 2000s brought "the eclipse and evisceration of the Islamic project in the country" in the form of the victory of Soeharto's opposition party, the Partai Demokrasi Indonesia-Perjuangan (PDIP) in the elections of June 1999 and its allocation of one-third of its seats in parliament to non-Muslim representatives (Sidel 2006, 210–211). In Sidel's view, religious violence during Indonesia's democratic transition was an expression of the anxieties of religious communities (and those who claimed to represent them) about a reversal of fortunes under the new government.

Whereas these scholars have focused on shifts and power struggles at the national level, others have carefully considered local factors and dynamics as determinants of violence. Their works have typically focused on either power struggles at the local level or the perceptions and experiences of participants in violence. van Klinken (2007) analyzed the interests and actions of elites in small towns in Indonesia's outer island provinces. Relying on extensive field research in West Kalimantan, Central Kalimantan, Central Sulawesi, Maluku, and North Maluku, van Klinken indicated that given the dependence of small-town local economies on the state, filling local government positions with fellow ethnic group members who would allocate state resources back to their ethnic community was an important priority. He claimed that the onset of political liberalization after Soeharto's ouster raised the stakes of elections. As local elites mobilized their ethnic communities to help them win elections, violence erupted. In explaining anti-Madurese violence in West Kalimantan, Davidson (2008) argued that the mobilization of violence against migrant Madurese in West Kalimantan solidified the ethnic Malay community in anticipation of competitive local elections in the province. Duncan (2013) and Al Qurtuby (2016), on the other hand, focused on the religious nature of violence in Maluku and North Maluku and showed that despite the rhetoric and framing of the violence as a political conflict by local and national elites, the rank-and-file fighters experienced the clashes as primarily a *religious* war between Christians and Muslims.

These various arguments have identified possible reasons why riots and instability may proliferate during political transition as the country's national model, constellation of power, and groups' access to resources are renegotiated. However, most of these studies have studied either national-level actors and events or a very small number of local cases.

The focus on national dynamics and actors alone is insufficient, since these should influence the entire country uniformly, but not all parts of a transitioning country experience violence. Why would events in Jakarta mobilize violence between Christians and Muslims in Poso, in the province of Central Sulawesi, but not in the neighboring district of Morowali? Presumably, the reversal of status that threatened Muslims' control over resources in Jakarta should also influence the political opportunities of Muslims everywhere in Indonesia (Davidson 2008).

Studies that examine a narrower number of cases offer very rich details on each case, but it remains to be seen whether the arguments made based on the limited cases can be generalized and applied to account for the geographical and temporal variation of ethnic riots within a country in transition. To attain a broader picture, one must take into consideration the conditions in not just the most violent areas of a transitioning country but also the regions that had relatively little or no violence during political transition.

Characteristics of Countries in Transition

Countries in transition exhibit a unique set of characteristics that distinguish them from established democracies and autocracies. First, they are weakly institutionalized. Scartascini and Tommasi (2012, 788) defined institutionalization as the degree to which formal political institutions "are indeed the places where societal actors focus their energies when trying to influence policy." In their framework, political actors in well-institutionalized countries view bargaining in the legislature, courts, and councils, as well as election campaigns, as opportunities to promote particular agendas. Political actors in less institutionalized countries, on the other hand, engage in informal political activities such as demonstrating and burning tires on the streets to articulate their preferences (Scartascini and Tommasi 2012). Acemoglu, Robinson, and Verdier (2004, 163) described *strongly institutionalized polities* (a term taken from Robert Powell) as countries where "formal political institutions, such as the constitution, the structure of the legislature, or electoral rules, place constraints on the behavior of politicians and political elites, and directly influence political outcomes." In contrast, in *weakly institutionalized polities*, "formal institutions neither place significant restrictions on politicians' actions nor make them accountable to citizens" (Acemoglu, Robinson, and Verdier 2004, 163). Other scholars have used the term *weakly institutionalized* to refer to countries that are emerging from conflict (Salehyan and Linebarger 2015), have high levels of civil conflict (Besley and Persson 2009), or are ethnically divided. This broad use of the term reflects a lack of clarity and consensus on the dynamics of political institutionalization, although there is some recognition in the literature that institutionalization is equivalent to having strong political institutions.

In countries moving from autocracy to democracy, opposition political parties may be so organizationally weak that they cannot effectively communicate information to voters (Tavits 2012), pay for expensive media and grassroots campaigns (Bartolini 2000; Grzymala-Busse 2002), or maintain a local presence (Geser 1999) that would help them succeed in the first democratic elections. The strength of political parties has important implications for whether a meaningful electoral competition and checks and balances on the chief executive can be accomplished (Kapstein and Converse 2008). In Tunisia in 2011 and the Philippines in 1986, for example, support for removing the autocratic regime was extremely broad, but the opposition movements in both countries lacked meaningful political organizations (Babatunde 2015). In addition, bureaucratic and police institutions are usually weak in times of transition (Migdal 1988). The weakened state security capacity allows illicit acts that otherwise would be severely penalized to go unchecked (Tajima 2014; Posen 1993). And since political institutions have less capacity, citizens are less likely to engage with and rely on them to communicate their demands or to push for specific policies.

The second characteristic that differentiates countries in transition from their stable counterparts is that political competition focuses on reform of the political system itself. After the collapse of communist regimes in Poland, Hungary, and the Czech Republic, for example, incoming new regimes sought to reform the state apparatus through privatization and decentralization (Suleiman 1999). After the 1986 People Power movement in the Philippines deposed President Ferdinand Marcos, his successor Corazon Aquino took immediate steps to ratify a new constitution that protected freedom of the press. Moreover, new democracies often introduce political and economic practices that change how decisions are made and who makes them. For example, many new democracies adopt a new constitution (Ordeshook 1997; Sunstein 2001), adopt a new electoral system (Shin 2015; Moser and Scheiner 2012), and implement decentralization (Treisman 2007). Although reforms and shifts in citizens' access to state resources also occur in mature democracies, the scale, intensity, and pace of reforms are usually much more tempered (Keefer 2007).

Third, many new democracies emerge from authoritarian rule plagued by poverty and gaping inequality. On average, countries that transitioned to democracy between 1960 and 2004 had approximately 20% of its population living on less than one dollar a day. The median per capita income for these countries was $850 in 2005 US dollars (Kapstein and Converse 2008). Thus, new governments must confront the additional burden of alleviating poverty quickly, with whatever resources they have.[10]

The fourth characteristic of countries in transition follows from the previous ones: distributive demands are usually very intense in this setting. Typically, a country undergoing transition has two types of groups, associated with either the *ancien regime* or its rising

---

[10] By comparison, mature democracies such as the United States, Canada, and Australia have had less than 5% of their population living in absolute poverty for at least the past two decades (Ravallion 2016). Mongolia, with a poverty rate of 30% and over 20 years of full democracy, is one of the few instances of both mature democracy and a high poverty rate.

rivals.[11] Both those who had power in the prior regime and those excluded from the old government will want to secure their interests in the new government (Haggard and Kaufman 1995; Albertus and Menaldo 2013; Ziblatt 2006). For the previously excluded, the period of transition presents an opportunity to renegotiate their position and to demand a better arrangement in the new government. Meanwhile, the beneficiaries of the old regime seek to protect their interests and ensure that they will not suffer severe losses in the new government.

Although distributive conflicts occur in non-transitioning countries as well, they are so intense and prevalent during political transitions that scholars have commonly described the adoption of democracy as an equilibrium outcome of the strategic considerations of conflicting groups (Boix 2003), or as a "pact" reached by conflicting groups (Stephan 1986).

Taken together, these initial conditions shape the constraints and opportunities available for individuals living in new democracies, and they produce strategic interactions that are unique to these settings (Haggard and Kaufman 1999). These characteristics differ considerably from those of mature democracies. In elaborating my core argument, I will show exactly how these distinctive characteristics matter in generating riots in new democracies.

My Argument

We have seen that countries undergoing political transition, relative to mature democracies, are often weak, are subject to drastic reforms, and disproportionately disadvantage those who are politically excluded. Given these starting conditions, individuals resort to non-institutional forms of political participation to impress their demands on the state.

To illustrate the strategies and considerations of disgruntled excluded groups in democratizing contexts, I extend Hirschman (1970)'s framework of exit, voice, and loyalty, which he used to explain individual responses to organizational decline. When a firm's performance deteriorates, Hirschman argued, individuals associated with the firm have three possible responses. They can *voice* their complaints and demand corrections to stop the decline, *exit* the organization by joining another

---

[11] In the literature, the *ancien regime* has been defined along various political and economic dimensions: landed elites (Bates and Lien 1985), those with mobile capital (Boix 2003), or the bourgeoisie (Moore 1966), for example. The previously excluded who demand greater redistribution may include the poor (Acemoglu and Robinson 2006), the middle class (Ansell and Samuels 2014), or the working class (Ansell and Samuels 2014), among others.

company or buying products from a different provider, or express *loyalty* to the organization by suffering the decline in silence.[12]

For Hirschman, voice, exit, and loyalty are not independent of each other, and which specific strategy individuals choose will depend on the elasticity of their demand and on the costliness and anticipated effectiveness of each strategy. Voice tends to be the action of choice when exit is too costly and difficult: "The voice option is the only way in which dissatisfied customers or members can react whenever the exit option is unavailable" (Hirschman 1970, 33). Conversely, "the presence of the exit alternative can therefore tend to atrophy the development of the art of voice" (Hirschman 1970, 43). For example, Hirschman elaborates, political asylum for dissidents, strategically and generously granted by a number of Latin American governments, could be seen as "conspiracy in restraint of voice" to reduce dissidents' likelihood to protest (Hirschman 1970, 61). For Hirschman, voice is a "residual of exit" – an option adopted when exit is difficult (Hirschman 1970, 30).

Loyalty mediates one's elasticity of demand and the calculation of costs and rewards associated with voice and exit (Hirschman 1970, 77). People's loyalty to their family, tribe, church, or state, for example, may reduce their willingness to exit these institutions despite institutional decay and unfavorable circumstances. In these contexts, exit may be unthinkable. Consequently, when exit options are blocked, the "principal way for the individual member to register his dissatisfaction with the way things are going in these organizations is normally to make his voice heard in some fashion" (Hirschman 1970, 76). The effectiveness of a loyalist's voice, however, depends on a credible threat of exit (Hirschman 1970, 83). In the context of party politics, voice would be effective to elicit party responsiveness when there are "very few parties, whose distance from each other is wide but not unbridgeable. In this situation, exit remains possible, but the decision to exit will not be taken lightheartedly" (Hirschman 1970, 84).

Although he recognized that exit and voice are not mutually exclusive, Hirschman believed that in a large number of organizations, one or the

---

[12] Hirschman defined exit as customers ceasing their patronage of the firm or members leaving the organization. Voice was described as "any attempt at all to change, rather than to escape from, an objectionable state of affairs, whether through individual or collective petition to the management directly in charge, through appeal to a higher authority with the intention of forcing a change in management, or through various types of actions and protests, including those that are meant to mobilize public opinion" (Hirschman 1970, 30). In practice, voice can be made manifest by a wide array of actions: writing letters to the editors, signing petitions, voting, filing a complaint, protesting, or waging armed rebellions. Loyalty is described as "a special attachment to an organization" (Hirschman 1970, 77).

other option dominates. In a market economy, for example, switching from one company to another is relatively low cost, and disappointed clients may not consider protesting to be worth the trouble. Exit is thus the standard response in a free market where many competing firms offer the same service. In a political community where institutionalized processes for articulating grievances exist, voice is the typical response.

In summarizing Hirschman's formulation, some have described exit and voice as ultimately in "a seesaw relationship: where one is predominant we expect a decline in the other" (Dowding and John 2012, 405).[13] This framework has been applied to a wide range of circumstances, from migration (Okamoto and Wilkes 2008; Adnanes 2004) to political parties and public policy (Dowding and John 2012). To this day, Hirschman's book remains one of the most impactful books in the academy.[14]

Hirschman's framework is helpful in explaining and predicting local ethnic groups' likely actions during a political transition in a weakly institutionalized setting. As discussed earlier, a period of political transition is rife with distributive demands, as both incumbent elites and rising challengers strive to secure their interests in the new government. In Hirschman's parlance, both incumbent elites and rising challengers face three possible courses of actions during political transition. First, they can remain passive and accept the status quo (loyalty in Hirschman's framework). Second, they can articulate their grievances and demands for political reforms, hoping that the new government will accommodate them (voice). Finally, they can exit their home districts and municipalities to the extent that they find their home environment intolerable, seeking alternative settings where they would enjoy a more favorable arrangement. Hirschman's original framework suggests that voice should increase when there is a reasonable expectation that it would be effective, when loyalty is strong, and when exit options are either unthinkable or extremely costly.

I contend that violence is a manifestation of voice during political transition to the extent that local actors can mobilize some networks to generate violence and perceive that their exclusion from office cannot be ameliorated otherwise. When local actors risk being excluded in the new government and when they can mobilize an existing network, they will use violence to signal their mobilizational capacity and to strengthen their demands for inclusion.

---

[13] Other extensions of Hirschman's work, however, have focused on the complementary relationship between exit and voice. See Pfaff and Kim (2003), for example.

[14] As a crude indicator, keying in the search term *exit, voice and loyalty* on Google Scholar on December 17, 2019, produced 159,000 results. Dowding and John (2012) did a similar search in 2011 and reported finding 13,600 entries.

In new democracies, results of the first few elections after a transition indicate the likely political configuration in the new government. In a well-institutionalized electoral democracy, citizens normally articulate their preferences and demands through voting. In countries that have very recently transitioned from authoritarianism, political institutions are usually weak and ineffective in articulating and aggregating the demands of those previously excluded from the regime. Opposition political parties, for example, may not have sufficient presence and capacity to mount a meaningful challenge in elections. The prior electoral rules may have been written to protect the interests of the former ruling regime and to preclude competition.

In this context, initial election results immediately after the autocrat's ouster communicate not only voters' preferences but also information about the likely configuration of the new government. To the extent that initial elections are competitive in a recently transitioned country, previously excluded groups may believe that electoral competition, turnover in leadership, and ultimately political inclusion are now realistic possibilities. On the other hand, if early elections remain uncompetitive and dominated by people associated with the former ruling regime, they signify continued regime entrenchment, indicating that excluded actors will likely remain barred from meaningful representation in local government despite pro-democratic reforms at the national level. Wright's (2008) cross-country analysis of the stability of 92 new democracies since 1946, for example, showed that new democracies that restrict political competition in initial elections are more prone to civil conflict, presumably because potential challengers do not foresee the possibility of gaining power through formal political means.

Given the costs of participating in violence, especially for regime outsiders who presumably have less access to state resources, one might wonder why excluded actors would use violence to leverage their demands during political transitions. In fact, models of war in the international relations literature suggest that rising challengers would typically maintain peace with a hegemon because war is so costly (Fearon 1995; Powell 1996). If war erupts, it will most likely be initiated by a hegemon seeking to arrest the challengers. Applying this logic to subnational actors, one would expect that excluded actors will not want to initiate violence.

Outside of the context of interstate wars, substantial empirical evidence similarly suggests that incumbent elites will be the ones turning to violence, to repress rising opposition (Gupta, Singh, and Sprague 1993; Moore 1998, 2000). Ruling elites' control over the state's security apparatus enables them to use violence to their benefit. By targeting dissidents with violence, authorities effectively increase the costs associated with participating in mass mobilizations against the state (Carey 2006). Empirical examples of incumbent elites' use of violence to stymie democratic movements abound, from Tiananmen Square to Bashar al-Assad's crackdown on democracy supporters in Egypt and Syria in 2011 (Brownlee, Masoud, and Reynolds 2015). Indeed, many studies have analyzed incumbents' use of repression in the face of challenges to their power (Tilly 1978; Lichbach 1987; Moore 1998; Carey 2006; Rudbeck, Mukherjee, and Nelson 2016; Wilson and Akhtar 2019).

Incumbent elites may also turn to violence during political transition as a response to perceived threats. The waves of violence against the Muslim Rohingyas during Myanmar's protracted political transition is one such example. In the run-up to the 2015 election, the country's first national election since 1990, anti-Rohingya sentiment and violence intensified as prominent Buddhist monks affiliated with the military and the military-affiliated Union Solidarity and Development Party (USDP) campaigned against the "Muslim threat" to Myanmar's demographic balance, culture, and politics. By portraying the opposition figure Aung San Suu Kyi's National League for Democracy (NLD) party, which had enjoyed Rohingya electoral support throughout the 1990s when Suu Kyi was under house arrest (Ellis-Petersen 2018), as "pro-Muslim" (ICG 2017, 14), many Buddhist nationalists actively encouraged voters to support candidates who would protect their interests in the 2015 election.

Shortly after the NLD's landslide victory in the 2015 national election and the inauguration of Suu Kyi's coalition government in 2016, the military launched operations in the Rakhine state in 2017 that effectively displaced over 750,000 people and killed thousands of Rohingyas (Simons and Beech 2019). When Suu Kyi appeared before the International Court of Justice in The Hague in December 2019, she denied accusations of genocide, refrained from criticizing the military generals who sit on her cabinet, and, instead, criticized the international community for failing to understand the matter (Simons and Beech 2019). Suu Kyi claimed that the military operations were a response to Rohingya insurgent violence, which began with the insurgent group's attacks on Border Police Guard bases (ICG 2017). The violence against the Rohingyas in Myanmar illustrates that the *ancien regime* can stir up violence not only to undermine challengers prior to an important election but also to further justify their control of key positions even after losing an election.

Despite the obvious costs of weaker challengers provoking violence against ruling elites, history is replete with examples of such

mobilizations. The Bougainville Revolutionary Army launched a secessionist campaign in late 1988, despite initially being severely outnumbered and outgunned by the Australia-backed Papua New Guinea
Defence Force (Rotheroe 1998). In the early days of the secessionist
struggle, the residents of the island were "a ragtag bunch of guerrillas
armed with catapults, bows and arrows" (Rotheroe 1998). Many ousters
of powerful autocrats around the globe were also initiated by opposition
groups, with little to no protection from the state military and security
personnel. The October Revolution of 2000 that removed Serbian
president Slobodan Milosevic began as a peaceful demonstration that
culminated a week later with hundreds of thousands of protesters
storming the parliament and burning the building (BBC 2010). The
Color Revolutions and the Arab Spring protests, despite subsequent
disappointments (Haring and Cecire 2013; Brownlee, Masoud, and
Reynolds 2013), began with small groups of individuals articulating
their grievances in spite of the authorities' repressive capacities. How
do we explain these cases wherein the weaker challengers mobilize
violence against ruling powers? Control over state resources and state
security capacity cannot account for them, as challengers usually have
no access to these and are under-resourced and outnumbered by
comparison.

My theory offers an explanation for this. I argue that such violence
can be expected during a political transition when formal political
channels fail to usher in the accommodation desired by excluded local
actors and when local networks can be readily mobilized to unleash
violence. In ethnically diverse, weakly institutionalized contexts, ethnic
groups provide a convenient vehicle for mobilization, for many
reasons. Shared social networks within an ethnic group help in-group
members to locate each other, coordinate, and sanction non-cooperative
behavior (Miguel and Gugerty 2005; Habyarimana et al. 2007). In-group
members may have a common political goal (Bates 1973). Individuals
belonging to the same groups may also share a set of technology (e.g.,
language, values, customs) that make coordination easier (Hardin 1995;
Spolaore and Wacziarg 2009). Ethnic groups often have traditional
leaders who enjoy their co-ethnics' respect and trust (Baldwin 2016;
Swidler 2013), along with traditional institutions with organizational
hierarchy and rules, committed members, and regular events and
gatherings that cultivate loyalty and norms within the group and
facilitate the recruitment of members who can be deployed for specific
goals.

Rather than accepting the status quo of exclusion in the new
government, local actors opt for mobilizing violence along ethnic lines

when they believe they can convincingly communicate to the central government both the urgency of their demands and their ability to pose a credible threat to the new government's stability if those demands are ignored. The authorities, fearing a further spread of violence that could weaken their position in the new government, may respond favorably by either encouraging political competition or allowing multiplication of positions to accommodate the increase in political players in the new regime. Once demands for greater political inclusion have been met and local actors enjoy a better representation in local politics, the violence has served its purpose and will decline. In signaling this mobilizational capacity and impressing upon the central government the urgency of accommodation, ethnic riots advance the push for political inclusion and establish the status of previously ignored groups in the new government.

In sum, the turn to ethnocommunal violence as a tool of political engagement during power shifts depends on the effectiveness of formal political institutions (such as elections) to accommodate a group's demands and the presence of readily mobilizable local networks of individuals who can conduct violence to leverage political actors' demands. When local networks can be mobilized and local political actors appear destined for exclusion in the new regime, violence becomes an effective weapon to signal groups' mobilizational capacity and to press for greater accommodation.

Figure 2.1 offers a visual presentation of the overall argument.

Aside from articulating their grievances, to the extent that exit options are available, excluded local ethnic groups can also push for the right

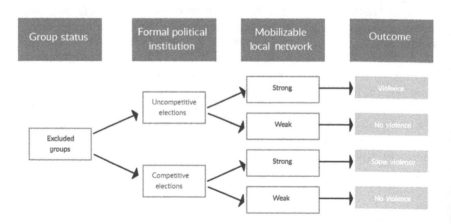

Figure 2.1 Diagram of the argument

to exit their politically exclusive home district or municipality. When an existing district is split into separate units, the number of seats and government positions is multiplied, while the size of the population within each new unit declines. In addition, a previously excluded group may represent a higher proportion or even a majority of the population in the new, smaller government unit. These changes give the group a greater chance of electoral success. Whether excluded ethnic groups in transitioning countries choose the strategy of voice or exit, violence during political transition will eventually decline once they attain important positions in their local government.

Although violence is often provoked by falling elites, rising challengers may also turn to violence during power shifts when certain conditions apply. I elaborate on these conditions in the following section.

Observable Implications

What does this theory of ethnic riots as a tool for articulating grievances in weakly institutionalized settings imply for the pattern of riot activity? My argument treats ethnic riots as a form of voice pushing for representation in the face of continued political exclusion from local governments. Where local political actors perceive that they will be excluded in the new government despite democratic transition at the national level, they will turn to local networks to mobilize violence as a means of pressing the authorities to accommodate them. In ethnically diverse settings, these networks are often ethnic in nature.

This argument has implications for both when and where violence occurs in multiethnic countries undergoing political transitions. Table 2.1 captures the basic expectations.

Political exclusion would aggrieve any local elites, but only in districts with an ethnically diverse population would this grievance then take on an ethnic turn. An ethnically homogeneous district, on the other hand, would offer little opportunity for enterprising local elites to politicize identities within a short time frame and incite violence. But ethnic heterogeneity alone does not predict violence. A second essential

Table 2.1. *Expectations of the argument*

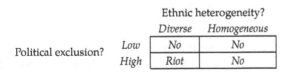

		Ethnic heterogeneity?	
		Diverse	*Homogeneous*
Political exclusion?	*Low*	No	No
	High	Riot	No

variable, political exclusion, is needed to motivate local ethnic leaders to turn to their ethnic networks for support as they demand inclusion in the new government.

The theory treats ethnic riots as strategic and political tools, not as automatic by-products of ethnic diversity. Ethnically diverse areas are not necessarily more prone to violence. Rather, ethnic identity must be politicized by exclusion along ethnic lines before it will produce outbursts of violence.

This claim of a non-relationship between ethnic diversity and violence, independent of political exclusion as a conditioning factor, produces the following testable hypotheses on the relationship between local ethnic diversity and violence.

Hypothesis 1: *Administrative units that are ethnically diverse but not politically exclusionary should be no more prone to violence than more ethnically homogeneous units.*

Hypothesis 2: *Historically, in the course of Indonesia's political development, the extent of intergroup clashes should rise and fall in tandem with policies that exclude ethnic groups.*

Given imperfect information and uncertainties surrounding groups' political status in the new government, initial election results provide cues on the likely ensuing political configuration in the new government. When initial election results after the collapse of an authoritarian regime suggest continued entrenchment of the former regime, we can expect the excluded ethnic groups to voice their discontent by mobilizing violence or to exit their administrative unit and seek to carve out a separate unit for themselves where they would be better represented. Therefore, administrative units that remain dominated by people affiliated with the former regime's ruling party should be more prone to violence and to district boundary revisions. This prediction generates two testable hypotheses on the association between political exclusion, district splits, and riots.

Hypothesis 3: *Electorally uncompetitive, ethnically diverse administrative units should have higher levels of ethnic rioting than other administrative units in transitioning countries.*

Hypothesis 4: *Administrative units where the former ruling party remains dominant in the initial elections are more prone to riots than those where challenger parties perform better in elections.*

Although my theory bears some resemblance to Wilkinson's (2004) logic regarding local elites in India who manipulated ethnic loyalties and generated violence for electoral gain, the implications are directly opposite. As in Wilkinson's argument, my framework also maintains that local elites set the agenda and mobilize ethnic sentiments, with the goal of placing members of their group in important elected positions. The similarity ends there, however. My argument differs in that political competitiveness is indicative of a country's openness and access to state power. Election results that indicate continued dominance by those affiliated with the incumbents in the prior regime suggest the half-hearted nature of supposed reforms and presage continued exclusion for some actors. This conceptualization of electoral competitiveness as a sign of more inclusion in the future has direct implications for the timing of riots. Because riots represent expressions of frustration with exclusion signaled in early election results, there should be more violence *after* elections than beforehand in the initial years after the ouster of an incumbent autocrat.

In Wilkinson's framework, on the other hand, riots are "brutal and effective forms of campaign expenditure, designed by politicians to solidify ethnic majorities and diminish the importance of other politically relevant identities – especially in marginal constituencies and among pivotal groups of undecided voters – *in the run up to elections*" (Wilkinson and Haid 2009, emphasis added). In this logic, ethnic riots would be more common before competitive elections, not afterward, because ethnic riots mobilize would-be supporters and harden their loyalty to co-ethnic candidates.

Of course, this prediction should be understood in terms of propensity, not in absolute terms. I am not arguing that incidents of violence between groups separated along ethnic lines will never happen before a competitive election in an ethnically diverse district in a transitioning country. Just as falling incumbents may provoke violence to deter the escalation of challenges to their rule, it is also possible that either ruling elites who view themselves as potential losers in the new regime or previously excluded political actors would provoke violence to signal their mobilizational capacity in advance of elections. In this framework, falling elites can be seen as expecting to be barred from the new government once the challengers gain power. They, too, can rely on violence to assert themselves and ensure that their concerns are heard.

Nonetheless, I argue that the use of violence as a form of voice to leverage demands would tend to happen after formal political institutions (i.e., elections) have been shown to be ineffective in aggregating political actors' demands favorably. In other words, although political actors may choose to launch their campaign of violence prior to elections to signal their demands during a political transition, my theory would suggest that they would tend to do so after disappointing elections. For scholars of conflict, this book's theory echoes the insights from recent works that have shown why, despite the costliness of conflict, weaker political actors may challenge more powerful ones in the interest of improving their access to resources (Monteiro and Debs 2019).

Because riots are essentially an expression of disappointment over election results that signal continued exclusion under the new government, we can expect the following.

Hypothesis 5: *There will be a higher level of violence after elections than beforehand.*

Electoral competitiveness in elections during authoritarian rule, however, should have no relationship with levels of ethnic rioting because, unlike in a democratic transition, competitiveness of elections under authoritarian rule would not signal information about the future political configuration after elections. This generates Hypothesis 6 as follows.

Hypothesis 6: *Electoral competitiveness is not associated with levels of ethnic rioting during authoritarian rule.*

Another implication is that local elites in politically exclusive districts can be expected to try to engineer violence by reframing trigger events in ethnic terms and by coordinating, funding, and mobilizing violence.

Hypothesis 7: *In ethnically diverse and politically exclusive administrative units, local ethnic elites will be more likely to play an active role in reframing, coordinating, and mobilizing ethnic riots.*

I also propose a new understanding of when violence should end. In my framework, violence ends when excluded actors have been accommodated; in Wilkinson's account, riots cease when incumbents win elections and retain power. If violence is a product of local elites' desire to attain positions in local government, then when these demands are met, we can expect the violence to decline. This accommodation of demands can be manifested in several ways. My argument would imply that riot-affected administrative units where elections have become more competitive over time and where turnover in leadership has happened should see a decline in violence.

Hypothesis 8a: *Administrative units with prior ethnic riots that have experienced electoral turnover should witness a decline in violence.*

Hypothesis 8b: *Administrative units with prior ethnic riots that have experienced an increase in electoral competitiveness should witness a decline in violence.*

Since another way to push for greater inclusion in local government is by exiting exclusive home administrative units and creating new ones, another set of implications derived from this theory concerns the patterns of administrative units' splits.

Hypothesis 9: *Administrative units with higher levels of political exclusion should be more likely to split than their counterparts.*

Since the theory expects politically exclusive administrative units to have higher levels of ethnic rioting during political transition, these units should also be more prone to splitting than those that were peaceful.

Hypothesis 10: *Administrative units with higher levels of ethnic rioting should be more likely to split than their counterparts*

To the extent that the splitting of administrative units is driven by local elites' desires to carve out a separate unit for themselves, this argument also carries implications for the characteristics of the newly partitioned, children units in conflict-affected areas. We can expect the newly created units to be more ethnically homogeneous than their parents, to have a majority population that is ethnically distinct from that of their parents, and to elect executive leaders of the same ethnic affiliation as the majority population.

Hypothesis 11a: *Newly partitioned units in conflict areas should be more ethnically homogeneous than their parent units*

Hypothesis 11b: *Newly partitioned units in conflict areas should have a majority population that is ethnically distinct from that of their parent units*

Hypothesis 11c: *Newly partitioned units in conflict areas should have more co-ethnic elected leaders after the split than before the split from the parent units*

In the following chapters, I test these hypotheses through both statistical and qualitative analyses.

Scope Conditions

This book tells a story about groups' strategic calculations during power shifts in plural settings. But I do not anticipate that my argument will hold in all such circumstances. For example, it should only apply to groups that have a reasonable chance of getting their demands accommodated. Participating and mobilizing violence in general is a costly endeavor, incurring the risks of deaths, injuries, and property loss among others. Participation in violence is even costlier for groups not part of the ruling coalition or the dominant group, since they do not control the state security forces and cannot anticipate any protection or immunity. Even beyond their hope of state security forces' protection, excluded groups may be particularly discouraged from using violence by the impact committing violent acts will have on their relationships with members of the dominant group once the riots have ended. Since violence is costly, groups will only turn to violence when they perceive a reasonable chance of success. In practice, this implies a few additional conditions about the groups, the authorities at which these demands are targeted, and the ordinary individuals whom local political actors would mobilize. I discuss each of these considerations in turn below.

At the group level, this story should apply only to excluded groups that are locally sufficiently large in number that they can become a minimum winning coalition (Posner 2017). If the group is quite small relative to others, and if its mobilization capacity is not great enough to challenge the incumbent electorally, it would be senseless to reveal the group's true extent of electoral support among the population by mobilizing violence. Hence, groups will not start down this path unless they can ultimately become effective political players, either on their own or within a coalition. This condition also implies that groups that participate in a large coalition at the national level but that are numerically very small in a particular local administrative unit will not mobilize locally.

A group's chance of success also depends on the characteristics of its counterpart in the political arena – the authorities. By definition, authorities in transitioning countries are exposed to uncertain situations and potential power shifts. Some authorities may be more receptive and open to demands for change than others. When precedents suggest that the authorities are willing to update their stances and policies in response to groups' political mobilization and demands, political actors will have a stronger basis for believing that their demands will be heeded. Conversely, inflexible authorities who never update their policy stances in response to popular demands will discourage excluded groups from mobilizing violently. In other words, the theory should apply to power shifts in multiethnic settings where the political atmosphere is such that popular demands have a decent chance of success.

Third, the lived experiences of the members of excluded groups must resonate with the narratives of exclusion that local group leaders are articulating to mobilize violence. Despite the strategic logic offered in this book, local elites need the participation of others in their community to launch a campaign of violence. The more their narrative of exclusion matches with the lived realities of ordinary individuals who would conduct the acts of violence, the more likely it is that local elites will attract supporters for their campaign. Empirically, this implies that mobilization during a political transition will work best if there are already grievances along group lines that can be readily politicized and framed by strategic political actors.

In sum, mobilization of violence by excluded actors is most likely when power shifts in multiethnic settings involve groups that are relatively large, an incumbent government that appears responsive to political mobilization, and individuals whose lived realities resonate with the narrative of exclusion and grievance that local political actors articulate.

Conclusion

In this chapter, I have introduced an explanation for why ethnic riots erupt in certain places within a country in transition. Recognizing that such countries are often weakly institutionalized and that some groups may still be disproportionately disadvantaged by existing political institutions, I argue that ethnic rioting is a manifestation of political engagement to press for entry in the new government. Applying Hirschman's framework of exit, voice, and loyalty, I contend that ethnic riots during a political transition function as a group's voice and that the violence will eventually decline when their demand is appeased or, alternatively, when an exit option becomes available through the creation of new administrative units.

I apply a mixed-methods approach, testing the theory's observable implications by using a combination of econometrics, archival work, and comparative case analyses. The book's focus and empirical strategies make several important and new contributions. First, the main dependent variable, ethnic riots, is usually considered separately from the types of political violence typically attributed to political exclusion. Ethnic riots are usually described in the literature as much less intense, shorter in duration, more episodic, and requiring less planning than armed rebellions, civil wars, or secessionist conflicts. In this book, I show that the patterns of ethnic rioting across subnational units in a transitioning country mirror the relationship between political exclusion and armed rebellions globally, in that more exclusive districts and municipalities are more prone to outbreaks of rioting.

Second, although some earlier case studies of specific episodes of ethnocommunal violence in Indonesia have acknowledged local elites' political motivation to generate violence during the country's democratic transition, this book is the first to provide broad statistical evidence on the relationship between district-level political exclusion and ethnic rioting.

Third, this book differs from earlier works that focused on the importance of electoral incentives in the mobilization of violence before elections. Previous studies of this relationship have been based on analyses of mature democracies with strong political institutions, which usually include strong ethnic political parties. My argument demonstrates that in the absence of strong political institutions or even of explicitly ethnic parties, local elites in ethnically diverse districts and municipalities can still turn to ethnic networks to mobilize violence in support of their demands.

Finally, the broad time range of my data, from 1990 through 2012, allows me to address some constraints that have affected previous empirical studies. Because the data cover 8 years before and 14 years after Soeharto's ouster in 1998, I can demonstrate how Golkar's dominance in Indonesian districts had no impact on rioting during Soeharto's autocratic rule, since there was no expectation of greater inclusion at that time. The post-Soeharto observations in my dataset facilitate the identification of district-specific characteristics associated with the decline of rioting and demonstrate that districts experienced much less violence after they became more politically inclusive.

3　The Emergence of Identity-Based Cleavages in Indonesia

Indonesia's ethnically diverse archipelago has been controlled by various types of polities since as early as the fourth century CE. The politicization of ethnic identity, forms of government, and levels of violence between groups have fluctuated over time and varied extensively across regions. Although it is impossible to summarize the early, colonial, and post-independence history, each of which has vast heterogeneity across regions, moments in time, and individuals' lived experiences, in this chapter I trace the country's broad historical trends, revealing drastic variations in the politicization of ethnicity over time. To capture the shifts in governance patterns and ethnic political arrangements in the archipelago, I distinguish three time periods: (1) the early modern period; (2) Dutch rule and Japanese occupation (1596–1945); and (3) Soekarno's regime (1945–1966). For each period, I describe the political landscape and policies that shaped intergroup relations.

Polities in the early modern period were greatly influenced by the islands' geography. The archipelago's strategic location meant that traveling between the islands or to other parts of the world was easy, but the dense forests and hilly terrains prevented authorities from easily projecting their power inland. Unhappy individuals could easily exit and avoid unpleasant rulers. To strike a compromise, many rulers used a system under which local enclaves were obliged to supply tributes at certain times of the year but were otherwise left alone to manage their affairs. The influx of travelers from outside the islands and between the islands exposed people living in the archipelago to many outside influences. Although ordinary people recognized the distinctions between groups, existing historical records suggest that early polities were not defined and organized along ethnic lines like more contemporary versions of ethnic-based nation-states.

When the Dutch arrived in Indonesia in the sixteenth century, they faced the same challenges of taming a vast archipelago with limited manpower, and they, too, relied on a form of indirect rule. Outside the main areas where they had established headquarters, they relied on local rulers who had signed treaties with them to manage internal affairs and left them alone as long as the transfer of goods continued as planned.

This arrangement had lasting ramifications for intergroup relations in Indonesia. First, the alliances with local rulers codified the authority of local rulers, as they were legally empowered to settle internal disputes and their territorial boundaries formed the basis of contemporary administrative units in Indonesia. Second, the Dutch governance of the peoples of the archipelago – whether intentionally or not – created distinct categories and hierarchies between indigenous *pribumi* and those of Chinese descent, between Muslims and non-Muslims, and between nominal and devout Muslims. Due to the governance, categorization, and separation of communities along ethnic lines, ethnic Chinese communities were perceived as a singular category of outsiders, distinct from other Indonesians. Non-Muslims, nominal Muslims, and ethnic Chinese were seen as close allies of the Dutch, since they were often favored by the colonial rulers in recruitment and alliances, and received special privileges that others did not. These categories and hierarchies across groups emerged during Dutch rule, and left an enduring legacy that shaped events during the Japanese occupation and the early years of independence.

As the nationalist movement gained momentum in the early twentieth century and then during the Japanese occupation, groups initially organized along ethnic lines and subsequently shifted to articulating demands for an independent, territorially unified, multiethnic state. When independence was finally declared, the state's founding documents, leaders' rhetoric, and initial appointments suggested the founders' aspiration for a united, centralized, multiethnic state. Yet, many dissenting groups, wanting greater autonomy and control over resources, became disgruntled, and mobilized armed uprisings along ethnic lines against the state.

Over several hundred years, the people of the archipelago now known as Indonesia experienced a broad gamut of political arrangements: a string of loosely connected and mostly independent small polities, a long and mostly indirect colonial rule by the Dutch, a brief but significant Japanese occupation, and a unified, centralized state burdened by groups' competing preferences. In this long arc of political development, ethnic identity became an important means of politically organizing groups in the archipelago only at certain junctures in time, and ethnic-based violent mobilization, while not entirely absent, was certainly not a constant.

Early Polities in Indonesia

Due to the islands' geography, the residents of Indonesia's archipelago prior to the arrival of Dutch merchants enjoyed significant autonomy and exposure to other cultures and people from outside the islands.

The Indonesian archipelago was not internationally recognized as a single, cohesive administrative polity until the twentieth century. English traveler George Samuel Windsor Earl coined the term *Indonesia* in 1850 to refer to the string of islands between Asia and Australia; up to that point, they were known as "the Eastern Seas," "the Eastern Islands," or "the Indian archipelago" (Elson 2008, 1). For centuries, the archipelago was home to numerous kingdoms, some bigger and more administratively complex than others. Although little is known about these early kingdoms prior to the seventeenth century,[1] historians generally agree that the archipelago's thick forests, mountainous terrains, and low population density played a significant role in shaping the polities' governance and ethnic composition.

Java has two long rivers that facilitated mobility and wet-rice cultivation,[2] but the other major islands are hilly and thickly forested, have shorter rivers that flow down from the highlands, and offer less agricultural land. Roads were difficult to maintain and often unreliable. Therefore, most settlements in these islands were concentrated along the coasts, where farming was easier. According to Reid's (1988, 14) estimates, Sumatra had about 5.7 people per square kilometer, Sulawesi had 6.3, Kalimantan had 0.9, and Maluku had 3.7 in 1600. Java was the most densely populated of the islands at the time, at about 30 people per square kilometer.[3]

Given the islands' physical fragmentation, low population density, and limited inland transportation (particularly during the rainy season), it was difficult to cultivate a centralized, politically unified territory with clearly defined boundaries. Instead, many early polities governed using the *mandala* system, wherein a principal governs from the inner circle at the center and radiates power with diminishing strength

---

[1] The era before European colonization has been traditionally divided between the "classical" (seventh to the early fifteenth century) and "precolonial" (fifteenth to early nineteenth century) periods. More recently, historians have adopted the term *early modern* to describe the period between the classical and colonial periods (i.e., the fourteenth or fifteenth to around the mid-nineteenth century) to avoid undue emphasis on the colonial period. See, for example, Andaya and Andaya (2015); Reid (1993); and Lieberman (2003).

[2] Java was Southeast Asia's primary producer of rice until the nineteenth century (Ricklefs 2008, 18).

[3] China, by comparison, had 110 million people in 1500 (Andaya and Andaya 2015).

to the outlying areas of the kingdom (Geertz 1973; Wolters 1982; Wheatley 1983). Under this system, the tributary areas were obliged to supply certain goods, at certain times of the year, to the center, following a set of court rituals but otherwise were largely left alone.[4] There were exceptions, of course. Lieberman (2003) noted that Java's denser population and markets facilitated more effective centralization. Mataram, a kingdom in Central Java (716–793), for example, built grand temples, water control systems, bridges, and roads using a system of bonded labor. The royals of Majapahit, a kingdom located in East Java in the fourteenth century, collected taxes, implemented a system of royal land certification, and went on tours of their core area (Lieberman 2003). Beyond these examples, scholars believe that Indonesia's inhabitants enjoyed significant local autonomy.

The islands' geography also influenced the archipelago's ethnic composition. Some scholars have argued that the islands' low population density, mountainous terrain, and the rivers flowing down from upland areas (particularly on the outer islands) facilitated the development of distinct ethnic groups. Whereas in Java the greater ease of movement along the rivers enabled a more cohesive culture, on the outer islands, where these geographical barriers are more pronounced, multiple ethno-linguistic groups can be found on relatively small islands. Andaya and Andaya (2015) have observed that Alor, an island in East Nusa Tenggara of just 2,800 square kilometers, has at least 20 different languages.[5]

The islands' maritime setting, abundance of natural resources, and annual monsoon cycle also made them prime stopping points for merchants, emissaries, explorers, and others. The population thus became accustomed to encounters with (and adaptations of) outside influences, particularly from India, China, and the Arab world. Indian influence was embraced on the archipelago at least as early as the fifth century, as demonstrated by discoveries of Buddha imagery from this time.[6] Likewise, gravestones uncovered from the eleventh century in East Java demonstrate Muslim influence in this area dating back to at

---

[4] One example of such a governing structure was Srivijaya. Described as "a loose assemblage of far-flung tributary ports" (Lieberman 2003, 782), Srivijaya was a maritime kingdom in southern Sumatra that claimed authority over much of Sumatra, parts of Java, Kalimantan, and the Malay peninsula (Wolters 1970).

[5] Papua, one of the archipelago's least populated major islands with eight to nine people per square kilometer, has at least 261 ethnic groups today (Ananta et al. 2015).

[6] In Kutai, East Kalimantan, inscriptions in Sanskrit were left by a king named Mulavarman, whose father was Asavarman and whose grandfather was named Kudunga. Mulawarman and Asavarman were both Sanskrit names, but Kudunga was not. These artifacts suggest that Indian influence had entered and been embraced by people in the archipelago before the fifth century (Coedes 1968, 18).

least this time (Ricklefs 2008).[7] Pires (1515, 142) described port towns in Java bustling with merchants from around the world and noted the presence of "Rumes, Turks, Arabs, Persians, Gujaratees, Kling, Malays, Javanese, and Siamese" at Pasai in Aceh. Both Marco Polo and Ibn Battuta noted that the northern coast of Sumatra was full of port-states, each with its own language (Reid 2010).

Despite this clear recognition of communal differences, existing historical records say very little about whether early states in the archipelago were defined along ethnic lines or whether ethnic categories served as a basis for inclusion or exclusion. The scant surviving records suggest a more fluid and accommodating picture. For example, Pires described the rulers of Java as "descended from Chinese, from Parsees and Kling, and from the nations we have already mentioned." He noted that "on account of the riches they have inherited from their antecessors, these men made themselves more important in Javanese nobility and state than those of the hinterland" (Pires 1515, 182). Pires also reported that a Chinese king sent one of his daughters to marry a king in Java. Family connections to China among ordinary Javanese and Malay merchants were described with pride in the 1500s (Reid 1996). To the best of my knowledge, none of the extant records explicitly describe ethnicity as a basis for political inclusion and governance. What we do know is that the archipelago in these early years was populated by many smaller kingdoms, most of them relatively decentralized. These polities were ethnically diverse, but ethnicity was most likely not a relevant category for political decisions or allocation of resources. This changed, however, with the arrival of the Dutch.

Dutch Rule

Like European explorers from other countries, the Dutch arrived in Bantam (now Banten, West Java) in 1596 in pursuit of spices. When their trading company, the United East Indies Company (Vereenigde Oost-Indische Compagnie or VOC), was established in 1602, the goal was to create a monopoly over trade and generate as much profit as possible.

This goal guided the VOC's, and later the Dutch colonial government's, engagement and approach to governing the inhabitants of the archipelago. Given the vastness of Indonesia (or the East Indies, as the Dutch called the territory) and the multitudes of kingdoms dotting

---

[7] Ricklefs wrote that Muslim emissaries from Arabia arrived in China as early as the third caliph's rule (644–656), implying that these travelers must have passed through Indonesian seas around that time as well.

the islands, the VOC's approach was to focus on resource extraction and to leave the work of governing the local population to local rulers as long as the company's trade interests were undisturbed.

Although colonial rule in the archipelago was by no means uniform throughout the 300 years of Dutch presence across thousands of islands, this section will show how the Dutch's indirect rule and classification of the islands' population along identity-based lines solidified boundaries between groups and left a durable impact on intergroup relations.

Ethnic Cleavage

Although established as a trading company, the VOC had "quasi-sovereign powers to enlist personnel on an oath of allegiance, wage war, build fortresses, and conclude treaties throughout Asia" (Ricklefs 2008, 30), powers that laid the groundwork for building a colonial empire. The VOC pushed the Portuguese out of Ambon in Maluku in 1605; it then seized Jayakerta on the northern coast of Java in 1619, renaming it Batavia (now Indonesia's capital, Jakarta).[8] To monopolize trade, it negotiated treaties, waged wars, and built outposts across the archipelago.[9] The VOC signed more than 1,000 treaties with local nobilities to secure its control over trade in the archipelago (Fox 2011). As a practice, wherever the company signed treaties, it also patrolled the seas, promised naval protection (in part to ensure that no ruler sold their goods to alternative buyers), and built fortresses or outposts. When treaties were violated, the VOC was quick to intervene, often with military might.[10]

Despite these powers, the company generally relied on local rulers to manage affairs for the most part. These local rulers – usually kings, sultans, chiefs, or customary leaders who shared the same ethnic background as the population – continued to host festivals and feasts, perform ceremonial rituals, build places of worship and architectural structures, and settle disputes (Ueda et al. 2016; Sutherland 2001).[11]

---

[8] At the time, Jayakerta was a vassal of Banten. Tome Pires (1515) had visited it a century earlier and described it as one of the finest ports on the island.

[9] By the end of the seventeenth century, the VOC had outposts in Banda, Ternate, Ambon, Malacca, Makassar, Padang, Banjarmasin, and Timor. Outside the archipelago, the company had branch offices in Sri Lanka, Formosa, Coromandel, Cape of Good Hope, Bengal, Surat, Persia, Malabar, and Japan. See Rei (2014, 30).

[10] On Banda island in 1621, the VOC deported, starved, and murdered the island's population to put an end to what it described as the "illegal smuggling" of spices (Ricklefs 2008, 32). At around the same time, the VOC launched a military campaign against Gowa rulers in Makassar that lasted until 1667 (Ricklefs 2008).

[11] In Maluku in particular, VOC also dealt with wealthy merchants (*orang kaya*) who wielded political and social authority in the community (Widjojo 2008).

In a letter dated September 12, 1618, VOC governor-general Jan Pieterszoon Coen asked officer Crijn van Raemborch to relay a message to the residents of Solor island, an island east of Flores in today's East Nusa Tenggara province of Indonesia:[12]

how noble, praiseworthy and good it is for a people that there is proper order, lawfulness and regulation in the community, indeed how orderly and well things go where there is sovereign authority, even in small measure, and to the contrary, how disorderly and troublesome is popular rule where each and everyone is master; how weak then is the community, overcome by troubles, and how difficult it is for us to have any dealings with so many headmen. For this reason, it would be better to choose a sovereign head and give that head full authority to be able to trade/deal with us and what is agreed with him all of you together should uphold and thus without any opposition, willingly accept (Colenbrander 1920).

This letter encapsulates the Dutch company's idea of indirect rule. To the extent that the VOC's trade interests were undisturbed, local rulers allied with the VOC continued to exercise authority over their community. In urban settings, the VOC appointed community "captains" (*kapitan*) or "lieutenants" (*letnan*) to maintain communal order, collect levies, and serve as the link between the company and the community. These captains were usually co-ethnics of the local population, residing in ethnic enclaves (*kampung*) within city boundaries. Makassar in the seventeenth century had various *kampungs*: Ternate, Banda, Butung, Melayu, and China, each with its ethnic head/captain (Sutherland 2001). In 1620 in Batavia, Coen appointed a Chinese merchant as the "Chinese captain" (*kapitan Cina*) to collect tax from fellow Chinese residents in the city and to settle "civil affairs among them" (Blussé 2003, 13). Malay captains performed similar functions for Malays in Batavia from 1644 through 1732 (Raben 1996).

This practice of nonintervention and reliance on ethnic chiefs continued when the company was liquidated and the Dutch colonial government took over control of the archipelago in 1799. When the cultivation system was initiated in 1830, the "native" regents, district, and village headmen were empowered to administer it (Furnivall 2010).[13] Annually, the government *Kolonial Almanak* volumes listed the names and titles of hundreds of sultans, rulers, and chiefs as the "Foremost Native Rulers" (Voornaamste Inlandse Vorsten) in the

---

[12] Quoted in Fox (2011, 133).
[13] In North Sulawesi, for example, *walak* chiefs were initially appointed to enforce the colonial coffee monopoly under the cultivation system (Henley 1996).

archipelago, codifying their influence and authority of hundreds of sultans, princes, princesses, and chiefs (Fox 2011, 136). As the Dutch intensified their administration and involvement in the nineteenth century, these local kings and sultans were recognized in subsequent *Kolonial Almanak* volumes as administrators of self-governing territories within the Dutch bureaucracy (Fox 2011, 141).

The boundaries between ethnic groups were hardened further by the colonial authorities' categorization and administration of people. The government divided the population into three broad categories: Europeans, the *pribumi* indigenous residents, and "foreign Orientals" (i.e., all individuals of Chinese, Arab, and South Asian descent, regardless of whether they were born in the archipelago).[14] Although ethnic Chinese communities in the archipelago were heterogeneous in terms of clan, language, place of origin, religion, and length of settlement (Pepinsky 2016, 1210), and many had migrated and settled in the archipelago long before the Dutch arrived, the colonial authorities viewed them as a single entity and as distinct from the rest of the indigenous population. In the 1930 colonial census, the ethnic Chinese were categorized as "foreign Orientals" and not included in the "indigenous population" group.

Beyond categorizations and descriptions of groups, the colonial government's system of "like [ruling] over like is welcome" solidified the boundaries between groups (Furnivall 1948, 225). The Government Regulation for the Netherlands Indies in 1854 specified that Dutch people and other Europeans were to be governed by laws and procedures akin to those that exist in the Netherlands, whereas the "natives" (which included the groups under the "foreign Orientals" category) were subjected to their own legal system (Fasseur 2007). The "like over like" principle implied creating separate public services, ministries, and departments for each category, including separate judiciaries. Furnivall (1948, 243–244) explained: "If civil disputes between natives come into court, they are decided according to native customary law, including thereunder any statutory laws that have been made applicable to natives. Religious matters between Muhammadans come before Moslem clerical tribunals."

---

[14] The term *pribumi*, or *bumiputra* (more popular in the 1900s in the East Indies), was coined to distinguish the indigenous population from Europeans and Asian migrants (Siddique and Suryadinata 1981–1982, 664). There were notable exceptions to this categorization. For example, Arabs in West Kalimantan in the 1800s were counted as indigenous rather than foreign Orientals (Somers Heidhues 2003, 28).

This distance between ethnic groups was also driven in part by the segregation of ethnic groups in the market. Long before the Dutch arrived, many Chinese migrants in the archipelago had established themselves as traders and middlemen between local producers and consumers. When the VOC regime began, this specialization was reinforced as the company contracted out the task of collecting tollgate taxes and farm revenues, along with other responsibilities, to members of the ethnic Chinese community (Lohanda 2002). During the cultivation system period, animosity between Chinese and indigenous farmers in Java grew because many of the sugar mills were operated and owned by ethnic Chinese, who charged farmers for the right to process their sugarcane in the mills and who were perceived to benefit from their relatively closer ties to the Dutch authorities.

Since the ethnic Chinese were barred from entering the civil service until 1913 (Lohanda 2002), by 1930, 57.7% of ethnic Chinese in Java were employed in the trade sector, whereas 65.3% of Javanese "natives" were employed in agriculture (Pepinsky 2016, 1212). This ethnic separation within the market strengthened group stereotypes, hardened the boundaries between groups, and occasionally spawned violent mobilizations. In October 1740, 10,000 ethnic Chinese in Batavia were killed by Dutch soldiers and local residents, following a revolt by Chinese sugar mill workers that killed 50 Dutch soldiers. As the Dutch forces drove out the Chinese from the city, fleeing Chinese groups encountered thousands of soldiers from the Sultans of Banten and Cirebon (Ricklefs 1983).

Beyond separate jurisdictions, rules, and ministries segregating the population along ethnic lines, restrictions on intergroup interactions further cemented the divide between groups. After the aforementioned October Massacre of 1740, the colonial authorities took measures to restrict intergroup interactions (Somers Heidhues 2009, 122).[15] Chinese migrants in Batavia were required to hold a resident's permit, and anyone found without it would be reported (Lohanda 1996). The Dutch also devised a zoning system (*Wijkenstelsel* and *Passenstelsel*) that regulated where individuals of Arab and Chinese descent could live

---

[15] Prior to the massacre, Batavia had a population of 1,275 Europeans and 4,199 Chinese, plus an unknown number of people in the surrounding countryside (Kuhn 2009). Blussé (1986) also indicated 4,199 Chinese in 1739. Somers Heidhues (2009, 144) noted that the consensus on the number of victims in this massacre may have been exaggerated. The clash was triggered by an influx of Chinese migrants into Batavia, underemployment, and rumors that Chinese migrants would be deported to Sri Lanka and thrown overboard along the way (Somers Heidhues 2009). The massacre triggered a series of anti-VOC uprisings, backed by Mataram forces.

and restricted them from traveling outside their quarters without an official permit. This permit requirement was particularly onerous, since a permit was needed each time a person wished to leave his or her city of residence, and could take up to twenty-four hours to process (Mobini-Kesheh 1999). The separation of groups applied to public services as well. When the colonial government began to build more government schools during the four decades of Ethical Policy (*Ethische Politiek*) period, they were segregated along racial lines. In addition to the "desa" schools that provided primary education to the rural indigenous population with Malay as the language of instruction, there were also separate Dutch-language schools for the natives (*Hollandsch-Indische School*, or HIS), Chinese (*Hollandsch-Chineesch School*, or HCS), and Europeans.

Consequently, over the years the Chinese in the archipelago came to see themselves as a separate and culturally distinct community. Granted, in some parts of Indonesia the *peranakan* Chinese were far more assimilated into the local community and were not as affected by these divisive colonial practices.[16] Nevertheless, when the nationalist movement began in the twentieth century, the dominant narrative of Indonesia did not include the ethnic Chinese (Elson 2008). When Indische Partij, the first archipelago-wide anti-imperialist group, was formed in 1912, it included elite Javanese and some Eurasians but very few ethnic Chinese (Elson 2008). Likewise, Sarekat Dagang Islam, the archipelago's first mass organization, drew its members from among Muslim indigenous traders, excluding Chinese merchants and manufacturers (Shiraishi 1997, 187–194).

The Dutch policies, whether intentionally or not, sharpened the boundaries between ethnic groups in the archipelago by providing historical precedents for administration along ethnic lines. The Dutch colonial rulers consistently described and managed groups along ethnic lines, lending legitimacy to ethnic boundaries and their use for political administration. We will see how subsequent political authorities in the islands referred to these ethnic boundaries and loyalties to legitimate their claims.

Religious Cleavage

Another dimension of identity that hardened and gained political salience during Dutch rule was religion. When the Dutch reached

---

[16] See Henley (1996, 69–72) for a discussion of the assimilation of ethnic Chinese into the Minahasa community in North Sulawesi.

Indonesia in the late sixteenth century, many coastal areas in the archipelago had embraced Islam.[17] In Maluku, the major kingdoms of Ternate, Tidore, and Bacan were ruled by Muslim kings when the VOC arrived (Heuken SJ 2008). Cornets de Groot, a Dutch resident of Gresik, East Java in 1822, reported that "the main points of the Islamic faith, which are carried out by many, are the *Shahada* [Confession of faith], the *sembayang* [daily prayer], the *puasa* [fast], the *zakat* [alms], *fitrah* [contribution at the end of the fast], and hajj [pilgrimage] ... The *puasa* is carried out by most Javanese of all classes" (quoted in Ricklefs 2012, 9).

Against this backdrop, the VOC generally adopted a noninterventionist approach to religion. The company frequently signed agreements with local kings that expressed respect for each other's religions. In 1657, the VOC promised "not to disturb [the people of Tidore] in their religion or faith, not to defy them, not to force them to accept the Christian religion, but to leave them as they think is necessary for their own salvation" (quoted in Steenbrink 2008, 116). To the extent that ministers and missionaries were hired and sent to the archipelago, they were tasked with providing sustenance for the faith of Dutch and local Christians.[18]

The VOC made a more concerted effort to convert inhabitants of the interior of the islands to Christianity, since many of them had not adopted a world religion (Wertheim 1959). They were offered a number of material benefits and incentives to convert. For example, after a major earthquake in Kaibobo in 1674, residents who fled to Haruku to escape were permitted to return home only after they had accepted Christianity. In 1677, the VOC sponsored a collective baptism of the population of

[17] The earliest evidence of an Islamic kingdom in the archipelago comes from 1211 CE, in the form of a gravestone of Sultan Sulaiman bin Abdullah bin al-Basir, found in the northern part of Sumatra. The first sultan of the Aceh Empire was buried in 1530 CE (Ricklefs 2008). In Java in 1639, Sultan Agung of Mataram sent an ambassador to Mecca who returned with authorization for him to take a new title, Sultan Abdullah Muhammad Matarani (Ricklefs 2008).

[18] A mandate to "maintain the public faith" appeared in the preamble of the VOC's charter in 1623, and subsequent private direction was given to the first two Governors-General that they must "promote the eastern trade in service of the propagation of the name of Christ" and "nominate ... without delay the ministers and teachers who join the fleet in order to stay in the Indies." Pursuant to this mandate, the VOC began sending teachers and missionaries, opening mission schools, training local Christians to become teachers, and commissioning Bible translations to facilitate religious education of Christians on the islands (Steenbrink 2008, 100). Over the course of two hundred years, the VOC sent 900 ministers to Dutch settlements in Asia and southern Africa (Taylor 1983, 22). In 1700, of the 18,117 European VOC personnel in the Indonesian archipelago, only 95 (or 0.5%) were employed in a religious capacity (Steenbrink 2008).

Kamarian, provided cows and rice for the celebration that followed, and gave clothes to the new converts (Steenbrink 2008). In 1635, the company introduced financial incentives for conversion (Steenbrink 2008). Under Coen, the VOC provided children attending a Christian school with a pound of rice, generating the term *rice Christians* (Wertheim 1959, 201). Additional incentives included eligibility for colonial civil service positions, freedom from slavery, and freedom from indigenous rulers (Ricklefs 2008).

This noninterventionist approach continued after the VOC was liquidated. Although policies concerning Islam in the archipelago were sparse, the colonial government regulation from 1854 stipulated that colonial administrators of the indigenous population were permitted to apply "religious laws, institutions, and customs of the natives, insofar as they are not in conflict with generally recognized principles of fairness and justice."[19] This regulation allowed Muslims to adhere to Islamic laws on inheritances and family relations. Islamic courts were established pursuant to this regulation in 1882 (Kaptein 2014). *Pesantrens* were subject to regular supervision, but these supervisory visits were intended only to ensure that the schools met Dutch hygiene standards; ordinary Muslims were generally left unencumbered to exercise their faith.

In the eyes of the local population, however, there was no doubt that the Dutch were European, and that the colonial staff, soldiers, and leaders were a religious "other." In 1614, Coen reported that many Muslim Malukans viewed the Dutch as pagans: "The Moors abhor us and therefore the Ternatans and Bandanese do not permit anyone from their families to marry any of us for any reason whatsoever. If sexual intercourse occurs, they terminate the pregnancy (they say) and untimely destroy the fruit and its creature that is born so that the mother will not produce pagan offspring" (quoted in Steenbrink 2008, 128). In the historic Malay poem *Sya'ir Perang Mengkasar* on the war against Gowa sultanate in Makassar in the 1660s, the Dutch were referred to as "godless infidels, and called all sorts of names like dogs, sinners, thieves, the cursed, and so forth" (Ng 2012, 374).[20]

Ordinary Indonesians called the Dutch *kapir londo* ("Dutch unbelievers"), suggesting both disdain and a perception that they were opposed

---

[19] *Regeeringsregelement* of 1854, article 75, cited in Kaptein (2014, 3).

[20] Although Ng (2012, 373) described the poem as "consciously Islamic," she noted that the poem recognizes that the Dutch had Muslim allies, the Buginese; that the Makassarese allied with the Protestant English; and that after Makassar's defeat, Muslim Buginese rose to prominence in South Sulawesi despite increasing Dutch involvement in the region (Ng 2012, 373–374).

to Islam (Noer 1973, 21). Conservative Muslim leaders framed their resistance to the Dutch as part of a greater holy war between Muslims and unbelievers.[21] In adjudicating conflicts between two Muslim local kings, the Dutch consistently sided with less conservative Muslim aristocrats (Wertheim 1959), further reinforcing the notion that they were anti-Islam.

Several measures further reinforced these perceptions. In recruiting local soldiers for the colonial army, the Koninklijk Nederlands Indisch Leger (KNIL), the Dutch exhibited a clear preference for Christians from Ambon, Timor, and Manado (Hack and Rettig 2006). Aside from the officers' ambivalence about the Javanese Muslim soldiers who comprised about 68% of the local troops, Ambonese soldiers also received better pay, enjoyed higher status, and received pensions. Despite their relatively small recruiting pool in Maluku, Ambonese soldiers represented nearly 21% of the Indonesian soldiers at one point (Hack and Rettig 2006, 52). They were deployed to counter anti-Dutch uprisings in Muslim-majority regions such as Aceh and Western Sumatra, and their sizable proportion among the troops provided another evidence that the Dutch favored their co-religionists.

Even in their dealings with Muslims in Indonesia, the colonial government appeared much more distrustful of radicalized Muslims. Anxious about the radicalization and mobilization of those who returned from hajj, the colonial government actively discouraged such pilgrimages. The influence coming from Saudi Arabia was viewed as bringing an "increasingly less tolerant spirit" and "a stricter, law-oriented" Islam.[22] Fearing that returning pilgrims were potential "instigators of fanaticism," the colonial government promulgated multiple regulations to restrict pilgrimages from the archipelago.[23] In 1825, pilgrims had to pay a large sum of money to obtain a travel permit for the journey to Mecca.[24] In 1830, another regulation stipulated that failure to pay this initial sum before departure would require a payment of twice the amount upon return (Noer 1973). At one point, Governor-General C. von Swoll prohibited Dutch ships from carrying pilgrims from Indonesia to

---

[21] For example, in Aceh, many anti-Dutch fighters "took an oath of resistance together after reading the forbidden *Hikayat Perang Sabil*," which referred to stories in the Quran and invoked the cause of the holy war (Reid 2013, 10–11).

[22] *Encyclopaedie van Nederlandsch Oost Indie*, quoted in Noer (1973, 28).

[23] Steenbrink (1993), quoted in Jung (2010, 291). K. F. Holle, who studied the social consequences of the hajj in Batavia, argued that returning pilgrims were dangerous because they could incite fanaticism and thus should not be trusted with positions in the colonial administration (Jung 2010).

[24] The permit cost was 110 florin; the average overall expense per person for the whole trip at this time was about 100 florin (Noer 1973).

Mecca (Goksoy 2002). The colonial authorities also barred those who had completed a hajj from entering the colonial civil service and, in 1810, required them to carry a special permit to travel even within Java (Hadler 2009; Goksoy 2002). Fearful that pilgrims would radicalize and convert others to their worldview, the government placed some hajj returnees under surveillance (Goksoy 2002) and forbade them from serving as chiefs or colonial officials in "non-Muslim parts of the outer regions" (Noer 1973, 24). The Dutch regularly arrested Islamic teachers (*kyais* and *ulamas*) suspected of spreading anti-Dutch teachings (Ricklefs 2012).

Snouck Hurgronje, a Dutch scholar of Islam who spent six months in Jedda and six months in Mecca during 1885, distinguished between ordinary pilgrims and politicized Muslims with rebellious aspirations, warning the Dutch government that restricting traffic to Mecca would stoke resentment among Muslims. He suggested instead that the government pay closer attention to the teachings and influence emanating from Saudi Arabia (quoted in Noer 1973, 27–28). On his advice, attempts to restrict hajj traffic ended in 1902. Nevertheless, the prior efforts marginalized *kyais* and hajj pilgrims in the archipelago, creating antagonism among some Muslims toward those who were seen as nominally Muslim and pro-Dutch (Ricklefs 2008).

This distinction between nominal and stricter Muslims was eventually better defined in the twentieth century when nationalist movements emerged in the archipelago.[25] In 1912, four years after the birth of Budi Utomo, an organization that marked the beginning of the national independence movement, Kyai H. Ahmad Dahlan founded Muhammadiyah at the request of several Budi Utomo members (Noer 1973). Muhammadiyah's goals were to spread Islam and improve religious life among Muslims in Indonesia. Influenced by reformist ideas from Egypt, Muhammadiyah opened schools and mosques; published books, newspapers, and periodicals; and established health clinics, residences, and orphanages to serve the poor. In 1926, Nahdlatul Ulama (NU) opened religious schools in Surabaya to increase access to religious education. Whereas Muhammadiyah became the flagship organization

---

[25] Writing about Muslims in Java, Geertz (1976) described nominal *abangan* Muslims as more open to traditional Javanese rituals and more relaxed in their interpretations of Islam. *Santri* Muslims, on the other hand, were more pious in their interpretation and practices of Islam, and were usually trained in Islamic boarding schools (*pesantren*). Other scholars have divided Muslims in Indonesia between reformists and traditionalists; the former group is stricter in their practices, whereas the latter is more open to traditional rituals such as communal feasts (*slametan*), veneration of graves and shrines, and offerings to spirits (Noer 1973, 300–308).

for modernist Muslims, NU represented traditionalist Muslims. Today, the two remain Indonesia's largest Islamic mass organizations.

When Muslims articulated political aspirations in the early twentieth century, this aspiration encompassed all Muslims and was framed as a direct struggle against foreign dominance – that is, as a struggle against the control by the Dutch and the ethnic Chinese in the archipelago. The first group to articulate political aspirations on behalf of Muslims in the archipelago was Sarekat Islam, a broader and more inclusive iteration of its predecessor Sarekat Dagang Islam, which had been an association of Muslim merchants in Indonesia formed to advance Muslims' business interests as they competed against the much more dominant Chinese firms in Java. In 1911, Sarekat Dagang Islam called for boycotts against Chinese merchants and firms, leading to anti-Chinese violence in Surabaya and Surakarta in 1912 and a subsequent ban of the organization by the colonial authorities (Kahin 1970, 67). In September 1912, Sarekat Dagang Islam refashioned itself as Sarekat Islam, with non-merchants and religious figures in its leadership ranks. In 1913, its leader, H. Oemar S. Tjokroaminoto, stated that the group aspired to "build nationalism, get back human rights which have been a grant of God, elevate the inferior position [of the Indonesians and], improve the present unsatisfactory conditions" (quoted in Noer 1973, 112). It called its congresses "national," according to Tjokroaminoto, because the word reflected an attempt to "elevate [oneself] to the level of a nation . . . the first attempt to strive for self-government or at least that Indonesians be given the right to express their voice in political affairs" (quoted in Noer 1973, 112). In 1917, the organization produced a Declaration of Principles and an Action Program, which demanded, among many other things, the establishment of regional councils; transforming the People's Council (Volksraad) in Batavia into a representative legislative body; the right to vote for men aged 21 or older who could read and write and understand Malay; and the termination of *corvée* labor and travel permits (Noer 1973). Because of its national character and political aspirations, it was considered "*the* organization of all Muslims," transcending the reformist–traditionalist divide present in Muslim mass organizations that focused on religious and social issues (Noer 1973, 135).

Muslims were further politically organized in 1937 by the Islamic High Council of Indonesia (MIAI), an umbrella organization that included Nahdlatul Ulama, Muhammadiyah, and other Islamic groups.

In summary, although the use of ethnic and religious identities for political purposes was muted during Dutch rule in Indonesia, we can trace the construction of differences across groups to the colonial administration, decisions, and descriptions of the people of the archipelago. The policies implemented by the VOC and later by the Dutch colonial state not only legitimated local ethnic rulers but also highlighted the European power's religious "otherness," and aligned local Christians and nominal Muslims with the colonizers. Similarly, Dutch suspicions of Muslims who went on hajj pilgrimages and practiced a more reformist manifestation of Islam gave rise to the creation of new organizations representing differing approaches to Islam, which later became politically mobilized.

Japanese Occupation

Japan's takeover of the East Indies was swift and its rule was short. Japan divided the archipelago into three territories. Java was under the control of the 16th army, while Sumatra (and Malaya) was governed by the 25th army, and the remainder of the archipelago was administered by the Japanese navy. During the three years between the troops' initial invasion on January 10, 1942, and their departure in September 1945, Indonesian youths mobilized politically, some local elites saw their fortunes reversed, and relations between *pribumi* and Chinese Indonesians remained tense.

The years of Japanese occupation saw the proliferation of political organizations and military training. To encourage greater support for their war in the Pacific, the Japanese authorities promised greater local participation in governance bodies. The occupation authorities filled civil service positions emptied by departing Dutch officials with *pribumi* civil servants (Mark 2018, 105), and they established a number of mass organizations and military and paramilitary groups that recruited and trained youths to fight.

In March 1943, the occupation formed the mass organization, Pusat Tenaga Rakyat (PUTERA), and recruited four famous Indonesian nationalist activists (Empat Serangkai) – Soekarno, Muhammad Hatta, Ki Hajar Dewantara, and K. H. Mas Mansyur – as its leaders to inspire Indonesians to greater sacrifice to support Japan in the war (Abdullah 2010, 117).[26] To facilitate recruitment of ordinary Indonesians, the occupation encouraged more communication between PUTERA leaders and the masses; it expanded the archipelago's radio towers, networks, and public systems in city squares, and required people to listen

---

[26] Soekarno and Hatta were two prominent nationalist figures who later went on to declare Indonesia's independence together on August 17, 1945. Dewantara was known for his Taman Siswa schools. K. H. Mas Mansyur was former leader of Muhammadiyah.

to regularly scheduled official broadcasts, which included Soekarno's anti-imperialism speeches (Kahin 1970, 108). Though established for Japan's war purposes, PUTERA benefited the nationalists' movement by expanding their reach to many more people across the archipelago.

Shortly after PUTERA was created, the authorities established the voluntary defense army Pembela Tanah Air (PETA) in September 1943 in Java, Bali, and Madura to train youths to fight.[27] In their training sessions, the Japanese instructors of PETA frequently refererred to "independence" (*merdeka*) and told the young cadets that PETA officers would be "future leaders of Indonesia" (Sato 2010b, 133). By 1945, PETA had approximately 37,000 soldiers in Java and 20,000 in Sumatra (Ricklefs 2008, 242). Wary that PUTERA and PETA had become more useful for the Indonesian pro-independence activists' cause than for their own, the occupation then disbanded PUTERA and formed the Himpunan Kebaktian Jawa (the Jawa Hokokai) in March 1944. Unlike its predecessors, the Hokokai was directly supervised by the Japanese commander-in-chief, and it included representation from the Chinese, South Asian, and Eurasian communities (Kahin 1970, 110).

The Japanese applied a similar approach to appeal to Muslims, forming the Majlis Syuro Muslimin Indonesia (Masyumi) in October 1943 and placing NU and Muhammadiyah leaders at its helm (Ricklefs 2008, 242). Fogg (2019, 43) described the creation of Masyumi and the appointment of *ulamas* to various councils as a significant shift, as Muslim religious leaders now were no longer confined to religious spheres of influence but represented in political organizations. In December 1944, Masyumi formed its own militia, the Hizbullah, to staff the Indonesian volunteer army (Buehler 2016).

Japan promised pro-nationalist activists greater involvement in governing Java and created several advisory councils to this end. The Chuo Sangi'in, the Central Advisory Board, was established with Japanese and Indonesian members, led by Soekarno. Initially composed of 23 members, it grew to 60 and incorporated more Indonesians in November 1944. Regional councils, the Shu Shangi-kai, were established in various parts of the archipelago (e.g., Palembang, Lampung, and West Sumatra) with local nationalist activists appointed as leaders (Reid 2005, 417–418).

These various organizations allowed Indonesian leaders to stir nationalist aspirations among the masses, and provided a platform for them to convene, network, and organize as the war neared its end. By the

---

[27] In Sumatra and Sulawesi, the defense army was better known by its Japanese name, the Giyugun or volunteer force (Abdullah 2010, 118).

time the occupation was over, Indonesia had several bodies of trained soldiers in Java, Sumatra, and Sulawesi that could be readily recruited into its national army (Abdullah 2010, 119). PETA soldiers constituted the bulk of the armed body formed at the initiative of the independence preparation committee in August 1945, the Badan Keamanan Rakyat (BKR), and the Indonesian armed forces after independence (Sato 2010a, 201–208).

For the ethnic Chinese in Indonesia, the Japanese occupation began and ended with waves of anti-Chinese violence and looting, along with a series of measures that maintained the alienation of the ethnic Chinese from *pribumi* Indonesians. In early 1942, many parts of Java and Sumatra were under a power vacuum, as the Dutch forces were evacuating, but the Japanese occupation had not established firm control of the archipelago. Retreating Dutch soldiers' "scorched earth" tactics encouraged looters and plunderers to destroy Chinese-owned factories and machines (Claver 2011, 163). Looters targeted Chinese-owned factories, shops, and homes, shouting "eliminate Tjina" or "share with the poor" as they went (Somers Heidhues 2012, 383).[28]

The violence lasted for several weeks before the occupation troops firmly established order in Java. Casualties related to these incidents are unknown, but the looting and rioting costs totaled more than 100 million East Indies dollars (Yang 2001, 43). Similar violence ensued in Sumatra as well (Yang 2001, 43). In 1945, another wave of violence against the ethnic Chinese erupted afresh as Japan retreated and pro-independence youths targeted anyone they suspected of colonial sympathies (Somers Heidhues 2012; Yang 2001).

Antipathy between the Chinese and *pribumi* Indonesians did not lessen during the occupation. Like their predecessor, the new occupier treated the ethnic Chinese as a single entity and largely ignored the distinctions between clans, time of arrival, and extent of assimilation. After the Dutch had officially surrendered, all Chinese residents (and other foreigners) were required to register as aliens (Mark 2018, 113). *Totok* and *peranakan* Chinese were described under a single category, *kakyō* (Yang 2001). Expecting *peranakan* Chinese to be able to speak and recognize Chinese characters, the new administrators humiliated many who could not speak or write the language. Although Dutch schools were promptly shut down after the Japanese troops' arrival, the occupiers kept Chinese schools open, and many *peranakan* Chinese

---

[28] Although these incidents of violence were spontaneous, some reports have suggested that Japanese troops also encouraged *pribumi* Indonesians to loot Chinese-owned shops and properties (Frederick 1978, 351).

enrolled in them. Yang (2001) suggested that these developments brought *totok* and *peranakan* Chinese closer together. The Japanese also relied on quota-mandated rice deliveries, which heavily burdened small farmers in the villages and stoked resentment against Chinese-owned rice milling companies who were perceived to profit from their labor (Sato 2006, 241–242). In its military and political mobilization of youths in Java, the Chinese (as well as Arabs and Indians) were excluded from PUTERA and separated from Indonesian soldiers in the youth paramilitary group Seinendan. The occupiers also created a separate civil defense force for the ethnic Chinese, the Keibotai (Cribb 2010, 110).

These measures aside, the later part of the occupation saw increasing inclusion of ethnic Chinese in efforts and committees preparing for the declaration of independence. Chinese representatives sat in the *pribumi*-dominated Chuo Sangi'in and the Investigating Committee of the People's Economy (Post 2011, 190–191). Many Chinese intellectuals expressed support for an independent Indonesia (Suryadinata 1999), and at this point, many members of the Chinese community spoke Bahasa Indonesia and stopped using Bahasa Melayu Tionghoa (Yang 2001). During the outbursts of violence after Japan's retreat in 1945, in at least one instance ethnic Chinese were spared from violence due to their open support for the republic (Somers Heidhues 2012, 384).

The three and a half years of Japanese occupation in Indonesia did little to ameliorate antipathies between *pribumi* and Chinese Indonesians, as demonstrated by the waves of anti-Chinese violence that bookended the period. Despite the engagement and representation of Chinese communities in the independence movement, the structures that supported this movement revealed the continuing division between *pribumi* and Chinese Indonesians.

In a number of places around the archipelago, the Japanese occupation entailed a reversal of fortunes for local rulers. Distrustful of those with ties to the Dutch, the occupation favored those excluded from power by the prior rulers, believing that these individuals would have stronger anti-Western perspectives (Thorburn 2002). Whereas previously the Dutch colonial authorities had favored Christians and nominal Muslims as local administrators and allies, the Japanese military administration courted Muslim leaders.

In Ambon, for example, the occupation authorities filled civil service positions with Muslim members of the Sarekat Ambon, in place of the *adat* figures previously appointed by the Dutch (Chauvel 1990, 175). In a striking departure from the Dutch colonial preference for Ambonese Christian soldiers to staff its KNIL, the youth organization, Seinendan, predominantly recruited Ambonese Muslims (Chauvel 1990, 189–190).

This preferential treatment was not lost on the Allied forces either. A 1945 Allied report described,

As a class, the Mohammedans appear to have enjoyed better treatment than the Christians, and have not been subjected to the same indignations, but with the sharp decline in standards of living, it is probable that they, too, are now heartily sick of the Japanese. The Christians, who have been strongly anti-Japanese, are enthusiastic over a prospect of the return of the Allies. They strongly accuse the Mohammedans of being collaborators. It is difficult to get independent confirmation of their accusations, and allowance must be made for bias and exaggeration on the part of the Christians, who are very bitter as a rule in their references to the Mohammedans. That collaboration is not all one-sided is evident from the "black list."[29]

Similarly, in the Kei islands the occupation forces imprisoned suspected collaborators, *orang kaya*, and *rat* (Thorburn 2002, 12). Thorburn (2002, 14) has described the approach as follows: "Like the Dutch before them, the Japanese wartime government shifted many village and Ratschaap boundaries, redressing old affronts, rewarding friends or punishing suspected enemies. Their moves often favored Moslem leaders at the expense of Christians, patronizing those they viewed as most strongly anti-Western and anti-colonial." Thirteen Catholic leaders working at the mission were executed soon after Japanese soldiers landed on July 30, 1942, and Protestant and Catholic churches and schools were subsequently destroyed (Laksono 2002, 178–179). Many Kei Catholics and Protestants feared that their Muslim neighbors would report on them to the Japanese authorities (Adhuri 2013, 24).

In West Kalimantan, where Malay sultans had been long-time allies of the Dutch, the Japanese forces arrested and publicly executed whole families of Malay aristocrats on grounds of alleged treasonous efforts from 1943 through 1944, in what became known as the Mandor Affair (Somers Heidhues 2003, 203–207). Claiming that they were involved in a multiethnic conspiracy, the occupiers also arrested and killed wealthy Chinese business owners, journalists, party activists, and others they suspected of any attachment and loyalties to the Dutch. Estimates of the number of deaths vary widely, from approximately 1,000 to nearly 21,000 (Davidson 2008; Somers Heidhues 2003). As Davidson (2008) has demonstrated, this vacuum created by the forced removal of Malay local aristocracies in West Kalimantan enabled new local elites to emerge. In the aftermath of the Japanese occupation, Dayak elites filled this vacuum in West Kalimantan (Davidson 2008, 37–39).

[29] Internal Conditions in Ambon, Ceram, and Adjacent Islands, Secret, App. C. Service Reconnaissance Dept. 1945, p. 5, quoted in Chauvel 1990, pp. 182–183.

This reversal of status of local elites when the Japanese authorities took over sets a precedent that group status and access to power could easily be reversed in moments of power transitions. Local rulers in Ambon, West Kalimantan, and in other places in the archipelago where such reversals happened during the Japanese occupation may have recalled these events 50 years later, when Soeharto was deposed.

1945–1966: Soekarno's Rule

Two days after Japan surrendered on August 15, 1945, Soekarno and Muhammad Hatta read aloud the proclamation of Indonesia's independence on the front lawn of Soekarno's home in Jakarta (Elson 2008). Four years of revolutionary war and diplomatic struggles would ensue before the Dutch officially transferred sovereignty to the federal Republic of United States of Indonesia in 1949. After that, almost two more decades would pass, marked by an experiment with a parliamentary system (1949–1957), the first parliamentary election in 1955, regional rebellions in the 1950s, and a shift toward an autocratic period that Soekarno described as "Guided Democracy" (1957–1966), before the unified, centralized, and uncontested Republic of Indonesia was created. Despite the ups and downs of its political transition, the newly independent Indonesia set out to become an ethnically diverse, politically unified, and strongly unitary state, as demonstrated by its founding documents, national political leaders' rhetoric, and early political decisions.

Chapter 26 of the 1945 Constitution, for example, stipulated that Indonesian citizenship was granted by right to all "native Indonesians" and to "foreigners" as governed by law, thereby implying a pathway to citizenship for foreign citizens living in Indonesia. Chinese and Hadrami Arab residents had the option of obtaining Indonesian citizenship, which many embraced (Elson 2008). Chapter 29 of the Constitution protected freedom of religion while stating that one foundation of the state was a "belief in the one God" (*Ketuhanan yang Maha Esa*) – a broader and more inclusive version than the earlier suggestion of making Islam the foundation of the state. Beittinger-Lee (2010, 37) noted that the final wording was an adjustment of Soekarno's earlier proposal, "belief in God." According to the Political Manifesto (*Manifes Politik*) of 1945, the new republic "entertain[s] no hatred for the Dutch or any other foreign peoples, and certainly none at all towards the Eurasians, the Ambonese, and the Manadonese, who are flesh of our flesh and blood of our blood" (Departemen Penerangan Indonesia 1945, 29). In his speeches, Soekarno repeatedly and consistently articulated the country's emphasis on unity (Elson 2008). The national motto, adopted in 1950, reiterates this value, calling for "Unity in Diversity" (*Bhinneka Tunggal Ika*).

Religious, ethnic, and regional sympathies were discouraged in favor of a more inclusive, secular, and nationalist alternative. Nonetheless, these efforts toward centralization repeatedly encountered challenges from groups who favored a stronger regional role and a more decentralized political structure, a more central position for Islam, and the greater representation of ethnic groups in politics.

The 1945 declaration of independence received support from throughout the archipelago. In Aceh, Daud Beureueh released a statement supporting the independence movement led by "the great leader" Soekarno (quoted in Elson 2008, 117). At its meeting in October 1945, NU released a statement that Indonesia's independence struggle was "an obligatory holy war" (Elson 2008, 117). In Central Java in September 1945, British wing commander T. S. Tull reported that "not a house, not a public building lacked its Indonesian flag" and that "the cohesion of the Indonesians within their own ranks [was] almost one hundred percent" (quoted in Elson 2008, 116–117, 138).

Two days after the proclamation of independence, Indonesia was divided into eight provinces and Soekarno appointed a governor from within each province's population (Kahin 1970).[30] The first cabinet, formed immediately after the declaration of independence, was composed of 16 ministers, most of them Javanese. After the transfer of sovereignty in 1949, Soekarno became the republic's first president with Hatta as vice president. Hatta's selection was perceived, particularly by non-Javanese on the outer islands, as an important symbol of unity and of regional, ethnic, and ideological representation. Hatta hailed from Bukittinggi, West Sumatra, whereas Soekarno was perceived as representing ethnic Javanese and secular nationalists.[31] Five of the 16 members of the federal cabinet led by Hatta from 1949 through 1950 were representatives of states other than the Republic of Indonesia state (Feith 1962).[32] One minister was Hindu, three

---

[30] The eight provinces were West Java, Central Java, East Java, Sumatra, Borneo, Sulawesi, Lesser Sunda islands, and Maluku.

[31] The Soekarno–Hatta leadership duo was known as the *Dwi Tunggal*, or the *duumvirate* in Dutch. See Feith (1962, 364).

[32] The federal Republic of United States of Indonesia (*Republik Indonesia Serikat (RIS)*), which received the transfer of power following the Round Table Conference at The Hague in 1949, was further divided into seven states, nine autonomous regions, and a few smaller entities. The seven states were Republik of Indonesia (which covered Aceh, Yogyakarta, Tapanuli, and Lampung), Negara Indonesia Timur, Negara Pasundan, Negara Jawa Timur, Negara Madura, Negara Sumatra Timur, and Negara Sumatra Selatan; the nine autonomous regions were Jawa Tengah, Kalimantan Barat, Dayak

were Protestant (including one who represented Parkindo, a Christian party), and the remainder were Muslims. Cabinet representation during Soekarno's period was generally allocated along ideological and party lines. All cabinets during the parliamentary period represented the dominant parties at the time, namely the Muslim Masyumi Party and the nationalist Partai Nasional Indonesia (PNI). The country's first parliamentary election took place in September 1955, with more than 20 parties competing. More than 39 million people voted, representing a turnout of 91.5% of registered voters. The PNI won the most votes in this election (22.3%), followed by Masyumi with 20.9%, the NU with 18.4%, and the communist PKI with 16.4% (Ricklefs 2008, 287). These results suggest that the great majority of Indonesian voters identified with nationalist, Islamist, or communist parties.

Symbolic gestures such as a diverse cabinet and rhetoric of inclusion, however, could go only so far in addressing the cleavages that had emerged during the colonial period between those perceived as pro-Dutch and anti-Dutch. In some contexts, this divide fell precisely along ethnic lines. The wording of the 1945 Constitution on granting citizenship rights to "native Indonesians" and "foreigners" indicated clear acknowledgment of a distinction between the two groups. The placement of ethnic Chinese and Arab residents in the "foreigners" category with special processes to follow for obtaining citizenship – even though many of them had intermarried, adopted local customs, been settled in the archipelago for generations, and never intended to return to their ethnic homeland – betrays the implicit assumption among the drafters of the Constitution that Arab and Chinese residents in Indonesia were not Indonesian, or at least not in the same category as their "native" counterparts. The Political Manifesto's mention of ethnic Ambonese, Manadonese, and Eurasians alongside the Dutch who colonized the country reveals a similar sense of division, implying that these groups might have greater attachment and loyalty to the Dutch than to the new, independent state of Indonesia.

Feith (1962) observed that by 1949, Arabs, Chinese, Eurasians, and Europeans were viewed by ordinary Indonesians as, and considered themselves to be, outsiders. Although this perception of otherness was partly related to ethnic loyalties, it can also be attributed to their perceived alignment with the Dutch.[33] This perception helped to cement

Besar, Kalimantan Tenggara, Kalimantan Timur, Banjar, Bangka, Belitung, and Riau; the additional entities were Waringin, Padang, Sabang, and Jakarta.

[33] The common bond of Islam, however, bridged these differences and helped Arabs to assimilate better than the other three "outsider" groups. See Pepinsky (2016) and Federspiel (2001) for discussions of the assimilation of Hadrami Arabs into Indonesian society.

bonds among the remaining groups of ethnically diverse Indonesians, since "the Javanese or the Buginese villager could readily be brought to understand the new idea that he was an Indonesian when this was explained to him in terms of not being Chinese, European, or Arab (or Japanese)" (Feith 1962, 28).

Throughout the early months of the revolution, outbreaks of violence took place against people considered pro-Dutch, many of whom were members of these "outsider" ethnic groups. In 1946, more than a thousand Chinese residents died in a massacre in Tangerang. Hundreds of Eurasians were killed and thousands were sent to internment camps for years in the months following the proclamation of independence (Elson 2008). In some cases, even the common bond of Islam failed to paper over the division between pro- and anti-Dutch supporters. In parts of Sumatra, for example, members of aristocratic families were killed in waves of violence in March 1946 by people who begrudged their close connection to the Dutch (Reid 2013).

On some occasions, the mobilization of ethnic loyalties went beyond targeted violence against other ethnic groups to involve organized demands for alternative political arrangements. In 1949, Darul Islam movement leader S. M. Kartosuwiryo, frustrated that the Republic had not declared itself Islamic, announced the creation of an Islamic state of Negara Islam Indonesia with its own army, Tentara Islam Indonesia. The aim was to "in a tactful way attain local control, succeed in taking power from the Republic, and include [its territory] within the Islamic state" (quoted in Formichi 2010, 142). By 1950, this movement had spread and found support in Aceh, South Sulawesi, and South Kalimantan.[34] Beyond Darul Islam and its efforts to establish an Islamic state, regional rebellions such as the Revolutionary Government of the Republic of Indonesia (PRRI) and Permesta in West Sumatra and South Sulawesi in 1958 emerged to protest against the increasingly communist-friendly, corrupt, authoritarian, and Java-centric Soekarno government. Although neither PRRI nor Permesta demanded a separate ethnic state independent from Indonesia, both groups claimed that Java-based politicians were running the show and that resources were unfairly extracted from the outer islands to fill Jakarta's coffers without an equitable distribution of revenues back to the regions. Accordingly, they demanded stronger autonomy for regional governments as well

---

[34] Archival evidence indicates that Kahar Muzakkar, the movement's leader in South Sulawesi, sent a delegate to the southern Philippines to discuss creating an Islamic state there as well in the early 1950s, demonstrating both the group's aspirations for an international union of Islamic nation-states and its extensive reach (Formichi 2010).

as the creation of a senate in Jakarta designed to advocate for regional interests (Kimura 2013). The rebels also demanded the election of a new president, that the communist PKI be outlawed, and that Hatta and Sultan Hamengkubuwana IX be given the power to form a new cabinet before an election was held (Ricklefs 2008, 298).

Although by many scholars' accounts these regional rebellions posed only a mild challenge to the Republic's armed forces,[35] they had three important political ramifications. First, as Slater (2010) explained, they provided a justification for the military's more dominant political role, both immediately after the rebellions and in subsequent decades under Soeharto's New Order. This was a significant break from the previous period, when civilian politicians played a more visible role in Soekarno's cabinets, much to the dismay of some military officers. Second, they provided a justification for Javanese members of the armed forces to discredit and purge their non-Javanese rivals who were associated with the rebels, and thereby to consolidate their power (Slater 2010). Anderson (1982), quoted in Slater (2010, 112), argued that "the grip of Java-based officers on the high command increased, while Javanese troops became de facto occupiers of much of the Outer Islands." Third, the rebellions discredited a major party, Masyumi, as complicit in the insurgency and even cast unfavorable light on "the parliamentary system more generally as a source of political divisiveness rather than decisiveness" (Slater 2010, 113). Masyumi, which had been one of the most successful parties in the 1955 parliamentary election, was banned in 1960 due to its alleged involvement with the PRRI rebellion. With key politicians from the outer islands discredited, political parties weakened, the parliamentary system undermined, and the military stronger and consolidated after these regional rebellions, Indonesia transitioned to Soekarno's Guided Democracy, and subsequently his New Order regime, in which political parties and ethnic groups were politically demobilized and replaced by autocratic rule and a large role in politics for the military.

Conclusion

This chapter has traced the emergence of ethnic cleavages in the Indonesian archipelago, showing that although ethnic, linguistic, and religious differences are nothing new for the inhabitants of these islands,

---

[35] Slater (2010) pointed out that neither PRRI nor Permesta was particularly violent compared to the country's revolution after 1945 or the anti-communist killings of 1965.

their political relevance depended on which groups were excluded and favored by those in power and the policies that the ruling authorities implemented to manage intergroup relations.

Although the early polities in the archipelago appeared to have a much more fluid conception of identity, the Dutch authorities politicized the distinctions between groups by relying on local ethnic-based rulers to administer their people's affairs, favoring some local rulers over others, and creating separate categories along ethnic lines, and conferring different rights and obligations based on their ethnic identities. Under Dutch colonial rule, distinctions (and tensions) between the ethnic Chinese migrants and indigenous Indonesians, between non-Muslims and Muslims, and between nominal and devout Muslims emerged. Non-Muslims, ethnic Chinese, and nominal Muslims were viewed as allies of the colonial rulers. In their recruitment of soldiers for the colonial army and their choice of allies, the Dutch tended to align with non-Muslims over Muslims, or with nominal Muslims over devout ones. In their census reports and judicial administrations, the Dutch categorized the ethnic Chinese community separately from the rest of the *pribumi* population. Given their role as middlemen and rice millers under the cultivation system, members of the Chinese community were also viewed as close allies of the Dutch who benefited from the suffering of indigenous Indonesians. The tensions were compounded by Dutch policies that alienated Muslims: their restrictions on hajj, suspicious monitoring of those returning from hajj, and the underrepresentation of devout Muslims in the colonial bureaucracy.

These distinctions had powerful implications for the national independence movement and its leaders' ideas about what it meant to be Indonesian. When Indonesia declared independence, the country's leaders aimed to set up a politically unified, ethnically diverse state. This goal was apparent in the country's founding documents and in leaders' rhetoric and policymaking. Yet, even though the country's founders sought to cultivate an independent polity in which different groups were politically represented and meaningfully engaged, the conflicting ideas over how precisely to do politics in an ethnically diverse state caused Indonesia's early years as an independent state to be punctuated by strong political parties, regional uprisings, and challenges to the territorially centralized political model. The weaknesses and failures of Indonesia's early political experiments set the stage – under the country's second powerful leader, Soeharto – for policies that depoliticized the masses and politically excluded those whom Soeharto disfavored.

4   Ethnic Politics in Soeharto's New Order Regime

Multiple ethnic groups have long populated the Indonesian archipelago. As explained in Chapter 3, the distinctions between ethnic groups and the politicization of ethnicity predated Soeharto's New Order regime. Colonial policies sharpened the distinctions between groups, long before the national independence movement and Soekarno's government adopted the understanding of Indonesia as an ethnically diverse but politically unified state where communal loyalties could coexist under an expansive nationalist ideology. Yet, despite Soekarno's rhetoric of diversity and unity and his attempts to cultivate a religiously, ethnically, and ideologically inclusive government, regional unrest erupted in numerous locations, reflecting competing ideas as to how Indonesia should be governed. Revolutionary Government of the Republic of Indonesia (PRRI) and Permesta rebels in Sumatra and Sulawesi sought a more decentralized form of government in which the outer islands would have more autonomy. DI/TII rebels aspired to create an Islamic state. Republik Maluku Selatan (RMS) rebels in Maluku wanted no part of a predominantly Muslim nation that would require them to submit to the will of the central government.

Against this backdrop, mobilizing support from students, academics, and religious groups under the pretext of saving the country from the threat of communism, Soeharto rose to power and successfully installed a military-dominated, territorially unified government. But the politically relevant ethnic cleavages, their capacity to mobilize citizens, and group aspirations did not simply go away. Rather, Soeharto's New Order government had to manage them to cultivate and maintain political stability to avoid a resurgence of regional unrest and challenges to the central government, by focusing on economic development, depoliticizing the masses, accommodating the demands of politically useful groups, and suppressing those who posed a threat. This chapter shows how it did so.

This combined strategy of development, depoliticization, and selective demand accommodation carried important implications for ethnic political mobilization in the New Order. In the first half of his tenure, Soeharto prioritized economic growth and political stability. To that end, he nurtured ties with Chinese Indonesian conglomerates, appointed military personnel to important posts in every branch of government, and staffed his cabinets with Western-educated, Protestant and Catholic technocrats. Despite their small proportion relative to the rest of the population, ethnic Chinese, Protestants, and Catholics were perceived as wielding considerable economic and political influence by virtue of their proximity to the president. In contrast, conservative Muslims were underrepresented in Soeharto's government and restricted from pursuing an Islamist political agenda.

The regime's depoliticization implied that ethnic political mobilization through political parties was not possible, since only approved political parties could compete in elections and the regime took various measures to weaken even those. Furthermore, in the name of maintaining harmony, the regime also forbade discourses that could incite intergroup tension, quelling any uprisings quickly and discouraging public expression of ethnic grievances. In the second half of the New Order period, however, Soeharto sought the support of Islamists and accommodated them in his government. Important bureaucratic, military, and cabinet posts went to representatives of Islamist groups, and fewer minority representatives played a visible role in politics. This Islamic turn was also visible in the membership and recruitment of senior officers for Golongan Karya (hereafter Golkar), the party associated with Soeharto. Whereas in the first half of the New Order period nominal Muslims and Christian generals dominated Golkar's leadership, after 1987 Muslim activists and representatives from Islamist youth and mass organizations began to fill the party's leadership ranks. This political accommodation, however, was not applied with secessionist groups in Aceh, Papua, and East Timor. Those groups' grievances against the regime's injustices and extractive policies in these troubled provinces were answered with more military violence and repression.

The regime's depoliticization of the masses and repressive measures meant that individuals who did not support Soeharto or Golkar would have a difficult time getting their demands met. Although this combination of strategies sustained the regime for some time, eventually it failed as demands for greater accommodation and liberalization led to Soeharto's ouster and the demise of the New Order in 1998, more than 30 years after its birth.

The Birth of the New Order

The New Order regime was born in the wake of a failed coup in 1965 that led to waves of anti-communist killings in Indonesia. The details of who masterminded the coup remain unclear to this day, but the state-endorsed version maintains that a group of PKI supporters who identified themselves as the September 30th Movement (Gerakan 30 September, or G30S) kidnapped and killed six army generals in Jakarta on the evening of September 30, 1965. The movement and its supporters surrounded Merdeka Square in the center of Jakarta and captured the national radio station, using it to announce that it was acting to safeguard Soekarno from a coup plotted by a council of generals in conjunction with the US Central Intelligence Agency (Ricklefs 2008, 319). The coup leaders demanded the replacement of Soekarno's cabinet and the abolition of all army ranks higher than lieutenant colonel (Slater 2010, 141). Nonetheless, the movement failed to mobilize sufficient turnout to be successful. Except for Yogyakarta, where an armed uprising erupted in support of the movement, all other major cities remained quiet. Even the hundreds of supporters who gathered at Merdeka Square in Jakarta were not sufficient to protect the coup leaders (Slater 2010, 141).

In less than 24 hours, Soeharto, a major general in command of the Army Strategic Reserve Command (Kostrad) at the time, regained control of the military. On the evening of October 1, he made a national radio announcement that six generals had been kidnapped by counter revolutionaries, but that he was in charge and would safeguard the president and crush this movement (Ricklefs 2008, 320). In his radio address, Soeharto declared that the rebel movement "must be destroyed down to the very roots. We have no doubt that with the full assistance of the progressive and revolutionary population, the counter-revolutionary September 30th Movement will be crushed to bits" (quoted in Robinson 2018, 148).

This failed coup became a rallying point that unified and mobilized diverse elements of Indonesian society, a pretext for the murder of hundreds of thousands of communist sympathizers in Indonesia, and a precursor of Soekarno's dismissal (Roosa 2006). As a follow-up to Soeharto's October 1 radio message, in the subsequent days the army regularly broadcasted stories about PKI brutality and urged ordinary Indonesians to "crush" and "annihilate" the PKI (Roosa 2016, 284). Rumors spread that the eyes of the slain generals had been gouged out and that some had their genitals cut off. Army reports described members of Gerwani (a PKI-affiliated women's organization) dancing naked and committing sexual acts with the generals, which Wieringa (2011, 548) characterized as "a campaign of sexual slander" that effectively played on conservative Indonesian males' anxieties and imagination. The autopsy results, available to the government but never made public, indicated that the generals had been shot and that their wounds had likely resulted from beatings and being thrown into a well, but that the bodies were intact (Wieringa 2011). The rumors of sexual brutality, however, ignited popular support and aroused protesters to demonstrate against Soekarno and the PKI. Members of groups that otherwise had little in common joined in a chorus to demand Soekarno's resignation and the PKI's complete extermination. Religious organizations framed the struggle against the PKI as a holy war, mobilizing youths and teenage boys in rural areas to execute suspected PKI sympathizers.[1]

Beginning in October 1965, PKI offices and headquarters in various parts of Java and Bali were looted, destroyed, and burned; moreover, sympathizers and members of the PKI were rounded up, detained, and publicly executed.[2] Within the span of just over a year, hundreds of thousands of suspected PKI members and sympathizers across the archipelago were murdered.[3] In some places, the executioners were civilian volunteers acting spontaneously to demonstrate their support for the anti-communist campaign (Cribb 2001a, 237), whereas in other localities "the military did most of the killing" and had a clear chain of command and coordinating role in what it called as the "annihilation operation" (Melvin 2017, 490).

In March 1966, President Soekarno signed a document now known as the Surat Perintah Sebelas Maret (Supersemar), granting Soeharto full authority to restore order. In March 1967, the Provisional People's Consultative Assembly (MPRS) dismissed Soekarno and named Soeharto acting president. Within a year, the same body unanimously appointed him president. Though hitherto relatively unknown, Soeharto had emerged from the 1965 affair as a hero who had saved the country from the threat of communism, with broad-based support from the military, students, religious groups, and the entrepreneurial, professional, and bureaucratic middle

[1] Muhammadiyah declared that exterminating the PKI was an obligatory religious duty (Boland 1982). Nahdlatul Ulama signed an agreement with the army stating that its subgroups Ansor and Banser would provide support in exterminating PKI sympathizers (Wieringa 2011). Similarly, academics, activists, artists, and student groups took to the streets to demand Soekarno's ouster.

[2] Robinson (2018) noted that there was a substantial degree of variation in the timing, form, and intensity of anti-PKI violence throughout the archipelago.

[3] Estimates range from 200,000 to almost a million (Cribb 2001b). In some parts of the archipelago, these killings did not end until 1968 (Robinson 2018).

class, as well as a Westernized intelligentsia (Slater 2010). Masoed (1983) described this unification behind Soeharto's New Order as "a coalition of all religious groups, students and intellectuals. ... Generally it was a grand alliance of those groups long harassed by the aggressive Indonesian Communist Party."[4]

Priorities of the Regime: Order and Development

Soeharto's ascension against this backdrop of the massacre of communist supporters, after years of financial upheavals and political instability, had important implications for how the New Order would be governed and for the regime's priorities. First, the total war against communists provided a warning and a memorable example of what could happen to would-be dissidents and enemies of the regime, and this warning is still regularly reiterated in public discourse. Every Indonesian child learns in school that PKI's murder of the generals constituted a threat to Pancasila – the country's core principle – and that the September 30 movement had to be "crushed" (Roosa 2016, 284). In 1971, Soeharto warned that despite the PKI's physical annihilation as a political organization in Indonesia, supporters of the party "constantly try to mount sabotage, subversive activities and similar actions" (quoted in Elson 2001, 176). Every good citizen, he stated, must constantly be on guard against the "latent threat of communism" (*bahaya laten komunis*) and against those who are "anti-Pancasila" – two terms that in later years of the New Order were frequently used to refer to outspoken critics of the government (Elson 2001, 176). These rhetorical warnings were accompanied by actual repression of protesters of the regime. In 1984, for example, when 1,500 Muslim protesters took to the streets in Tanjung Priok, Jakarta, demanding that four protesters who had been detained a few days prior be released, the military responded with a massacre leading to an estimated 400 deaths and numerous arrests (Subhan and Gunawan 2004).

Second, the army's role in blocking the coup attempt, launching the anti-communist purge, and restoring order gave it a dominant political role in the new government, reinforced further by Soeharto's own military affiliation. Indeed, Soeharto's speeches in the early New Order years acknowledged this. At a ceremony commemorating the anniversary of the paramilitary wing of the armed forces Resimen Para Komando Angkatan Darat (RPKAD) in 1969, he told the audience that "ABRI has become the pioneer of the New Order, and now we must

---

[4] Masoed (1983), quoted in Slater (2010, 180).

become the pioneer of the order of development" (Elson 2001, 174). Mietzner (2018, 85) has described the connection between the anti-communist killings, the military, and Soeharto's regime in even stronger terms:

Without these political massacres, Suharto's "New Order" government would not have been born, and without their shock effects, the regime's institutionalization would not have proceeded so smoothly. Suharto understood the importance of coercion for the consolidation of his rule, leading him to merge the military and civilian state apparatuses into one. To some extent, Suharto's takeover constituted the military's acquisition of the state as a whole.

The sequence of events surrounding the birth of the New Order set the stage for a dominant military.

Third, given the background of years of economic crisis, Soeharto came to power with a clear mandate to rejuvenate Indonesia's economy. The country's GDP (in real terms) in 1967 was about half that of neighboring countries, and lower than its own in 1941.[5] Soeharto began his speech before the Mutual Assistance People's Representative Council (Dewan Perwakilan Rakyat-Gotong Royong) on August 16, 1968, by referring to the stagnant economic growth in the years under his predecessor's rule and specified that his government would focus on economic development. He ended by stressing that Indonesia must pay off its foreign debt: "both that which was squandered by the government of the Old Order, and new loans that we need to implement our stabilization and economic rehabilitation."[6] He succinctly depicted his own government as responsible and development-focused while characterizing Soekarno's rule as financially irresponsible.

Recognizing that the task of economic recovery would require support from donors, Foreign Minister Adam Malik met with US president Lyndon B. Johnson in 1966 to make a case for aid to Indonesia, underscoring that "Indonesia's fundamental task is improvement of the economy" (quoted in Simpson 2008, 225). In 1969, Soeharto introduced his Five-Year Development Plan, wherein he spelled out his development priorities: meeting the basic needs of the population, developing infrastructure, and strengthening agriculture. Every single one of Soeharto's cabinets had the term *Development* in its name

---

[5] In 2005 international dollars, Indonesia's per capita GDP in 1967 was 647 dollars, compared to Singapore's GDP per capita of 5,320, Malaysia's 1,846, Thailand's 1,324, the Philippines' 1,696, India's 809, Ivory Coast's 1,212, and the Democratic Republic of Congo's 709. See Booth (2016, 64).
[6] See Soeharto (1968).

(e.g., First Development Cabinet, Second Development Cabinet, etc.) (Masuhara 2015, 10). This focus on economic development became one of the regime's defining characteristics and its primary source of legitimation.

To stabilize the economy and promote economic growth, the government set out to curb inflation rates and rein in the country's budget deficit. In 1966, the military consumed over 60% of the government budget.[7] By 1969, the budget deficit was brought under control, in part by relying on foreign aid and loans, slashing 25% of military expenditures, and expanding oil revenues and income taxes (Booth 2016, 71). Throughout the oil boom years of the 1970s and early 1980s, oil exports represented a major component of Indonesia's revenues and helped to fund the country's investments in infrastructure.[8] The state took an active role in determining development priorities and managing provision of public goods; only in later years was the provision of some public goods transferred to the private sector (Booth 2016).

Throughout the first 25 years or so of the New Order, economists and engineers in Soeharto's cabinet and bureaucracy prioritized the development of infrastructure, telecommunication, and transportation. Asphalt road networks expanded eightfold from 1968 to 1995, whereas the production of electricity grew 33 fold (Booth 2016, 75). The World Bank reported that Indonesia's GDP growth per capita (based on constant 2010 US dollars) from 1968 through 1982 averaged 4.65% per year, and from 1983 through 1996 it was 4.37% a year. Education and health outcomes improved markedly as well. In 1968, 41.4% of children aged seven to twelve were in primary school. By 1996, this proportion had more than doubled, to over 90%. Infant mortality declined from 145 per thousand live births in 1967 to 47 in 1996 (Booth 2016, 79). The economic gains made during the New Order were irrefutable. Much like its neighbors – Singapore, Malaysia, the Philippines, and Thailand – Indonesia grew rapidly, though some argued that this growth came at the expense of restrictions on civil liberties and democratic development.

Depoliticization of the Masses

Political stability was an important priority for the New Order government (Elson 2001, 175). Wary of the destabilizing effects of party politics and mass mobilization, Soeharto cautioned his listeners in a 1968

---

[7] This breakdown had been consistent since 1959 (Simpson 2008, 225–226).
[8] In 1970, oil exports constituted 26% of the country's revenues; in 1981, they were 70% (Wan 2008, 39).

speech that ideological battles were a "source of tension and contention in earlier periods" (Elson 2001, 175). Comparing political parties to cars on the road, Soeharto expressed the dangers of having too many: "With the one and only road already there, why must we have so many cars, as many as nine? Why must we have wild speeding and collisions? . . . It is not necessary to have so many vehicles. But it is not necessary to have only one. Two or three is fine" (Elson 2001, 189). In an attempt to maintain political stability, the New Order depoliticized the masses by weakening political parties, making elections a performative ritual devoid of real competition, and criminalizing political mobilization outside election periods and political protests. In doing so, the regime raised the costs of political mobilization outside Golkar and de-alignment with the ruling government.

The Weakening Rival Parties

Although the MPRS called for holding an election by July 1968, Soeharto strategically declared in January 1968 that it would be impossible to meet this MPRS deadline, due to "technical problems" such as inadequate preparations and financial strains (Boileau 1983, 49). Another twenty-two months passed before it became clear that an election would actually be held in 1971 (Boileau 1983). At that point, Soeharto decided to "retool" the secretariat of functional groups, Sekber Golkar, into an electoral machine that could ensure his victory in the 1971 election (Boileau 1983, 50–51). The secretariat, by 1968, was a federation of 249 functional groups united by their stance against communism and firmly controlled by the army; almost all its divisions were led by military officers (Bresnan 1993). Established in 1964, it was initially designed to unify diverse groups and reduce the communist PKI party's ability to target them (Boileau 1983). It had little grassroots presence outside Jakarta, and there was not much time to transform it into a political party with a coherent ideology. To improve Golkar's chances of securing victory in 1971, the Department of Defense and Security instructed all local military commanders throughout the country to assist the party in establishing local branches and incorporating local representatives of the Ministry of Home Affairs into the party's leadership ranks (Harjanto 2010). Meanwhile, Lieutenant General Ali Murtopo, Soeharto's personal assistant at the time, was tasked with the responsibility of weakening rival parties' support base.

To weaken the nationalist party Partai Nasional Indonesia (PNI), Murtopo interfered with PNI's general chairman election to ensure that Hadisubeno, the more pro-army leader of the party, would beat his rival, Hardi. PNI delegates passing through Jakarta on the way to Semarang for the party congress in 1970 complained that they had "briefings" with members of Ali Murtopo's Special Operations (Operasi Khusus) organization, who threatened that "the boss wants so-and-so to be general chairman" and "if so-and-so is not elected general chairman, the PNI will have difficulties in surviving" (Crouch 1978, 258). Delegates in East Java were "called by local army commanders, who told them that the president wanted Hadisubeno to be elected" (Crouch 1978, 258). Although Soeharto publicly claimed that the government did not interfere in PNI's internal affairs, many who had initially supported the nongovernment candidate ended up voting for Hadisubeno.

Beyond replacing party leaders with more pro-government figures, the head of the Ministry of Internal Affairs also eroded PNI's support base by encouraging civil servants – many of whom had historically supported PNI – to sign documents stating their "monoloyalty" to the government's electoral machine, Golkar (Boileau 1983, 52–53). Although Amir Machmud, then minister of internal affairs, claimed that civil servants were allowed to belong to political parties, he also said that party membership might make promotion difficult (Crouch 1978). Since Golkar was not officially a political party, it was by definition the only political organization that civil servants could officially join as members. Guntur Soekarnoputra, Soekarno's eldest son, was prohibited from running for a PNI position, due to fear that he would mobilize the party's base (Elson 2001). Local government officials received "quotas" of votes that they had to garner for Golkar in their jurisdiction, regardless of where their true sympathies lay (Crouch 1978, 267).

To weaken rival Islamist parties, the government replaced the newly elected leader of Partai Muslimin Indonesia (Parmusi), the successor of the banned party Masyumi, with a New Order minister of state, Mintareja (Elson 2001; Boileau 1983). Soon afterward, Soeharto issued a presidential decision to establish a new Parmusi board (Crouch 1978, 262). In addition to replacing party leaders with pro-government individuals, Soeharto also used patronage measures to gain favor with *kyais*, who were invited on all-expenses-paid overseas tours, given funds for their religious schools (*pesantrens*), and granted audiences with Soeharto himself (Crouch 1978, 268). Leaders of two Islamist parties, Parmusi and Nahdlatul Ulama (NU), in Central Java were arrested during the election campaign period on grounds of their "involvement in the Communist coup attempt," while leaders of other parties had their homes raided by military officials in search of arms (Crouch 1978, 269).[9]

The first election under the New Order was held on July 5, 1971. Indonesia's 57 million voters could select from among Golkar and nine political parties, which competed for 360 of the 460 seats in the Parliament (Dewan Perwakilan Rakyat (DPR)).[10] The election used a closed-list proportional representation system with provinces as electoral districts. Every administrative district (i.e., kabupaten and kotamadya) was guaranteed a seat, which led to malapportionment since provinces in Java were more densely populated districts and cities than provinces in the outer islands.[11] At the national level, Golkar won a decisive victory with 62.8% of the votes, securing 236 seats in the DPR. Golkar won more than 50% of votes in all provinces except Aceh, Maluku, and Jakarta.[12] This election effectively demoralized Golkar's rivals.[13]

After the 1971 election, the government moved to consolidate political parties and depoliticize the masses. The existing nine political parties were merged into two in 1973, with the United Development Party (Partai Persatuan Pembangunan, or PPP hereafter) formed from four Islamist parties, and the Indonesian Democratic Party (Partai Demokrasi Indonesia, or PDI hereafter) created from a combination of nationalist

---

[9] In response to what Crouch termed "the emasculation of political parties," party leaders launched an anti-Golkar campaign (Crouch 1978, 245–272). The Parmusi-leaning newspaper *Abadi* ran an article criticizing the *kyais* for submitting to the lures of money and flattery. Hadisubeno, the formerly pro-government leader of PNI, campaigned against Golkar and famously claimed that "ten Soehartos, ten [General Abdul Haris] Nasutions, and a cartload of generals don't add up to one Soekarno" (Crouch 1978, 269). He collapsed and died at the end of April, three months before the election. Religious leaders in East Java issued a *fatwa* requiring Muslims to vote for Muslim parties.

[10] The remaining 100 seats were reserved for 75 appointed members from the army, plus 25 from the non-ABRI functional group (Hering and Willis 1973). The nine parties that competed in this election were PNI, NU, Parmusi, Pergerakan Tarbiyah Islamiyah (PERTI), Partai Sarekat Islam Indonesia (PSII), Partai Kristen Indonesia (Parkindo), Partai Murba, Partai Katholik, and Partai Ikatan Pendukung Kemerdekaan Indonesia (IPKI).

[11] For example, as Harjanto (2010, 75–76) observed, South Sulawesi had over two million registered voters and received 23 seats, whereas West Java had more than ten million registered voters and attained 46 seats. Similarly, Jakarta and Irian Barat received nine seats each, even though Jakarta's population was more than five times the size of Irian Barat's.

[12] In Aceh, Muslim parties (i.e., NU, PSII, PERTI, and Parmusi) received 48.9% of the vote. In Maluku, Muslim parties garnered 24.9% and Christian parties (e.g., Parkindo and Partai Katolik) won 22.5% (Hering and Willis 1973, 15c).

[13] PNI attained only 6.9% of the total vote, despite a much stronger showing at 22.3% in the 1955 election. The Islamist party Parmusi won 5.4%; NU performed considerably better with 18.7% (Crouch 1978).

and Christian parties. These two parties and Golkar were the only ones allowed to compete in elections (Masuhara 2015).

Murtopo reportedly introduced the concept of the "floating mass," which maintained that the masses should be "floating" voters (*massa mengambang*) who are not politically organized and mobilized most of the time but are given the chance to express their preferences once every five years during elections (Suryadinata 1982, 26). This concept later was encapsulated in the Political Parties Bill of 1975, which prohibited political activities at the village level except during election campaigns, granted the Ministry of Home Affairs (at the president's direction) the power to supervise political parties, gave the president the right to freeze political parties and Golkar, required civil servants to obtain their supervisors' written consent before joining political parties, and barred parties from establishing branches in the villages, although appointing secretaries and commissioners was allowed (Suryadinata 1982). Later, this bill was amended, and political parties were allowed to send representatives to villages (Crouch 1978). Effectively, the bill restricted both voters' and parties' ability to organize and hold the government accountable in a meaningful way. To further reduce rival political parties' initial appeal to voters, the government required that every political organization pledge its allegiance to Pancasila and subscribe to no other ideology.

Elections in the New Order

In the New Order, elections occurred every five years for the national, provincial, and district legislatures, as voters chose from one of the three legally recognized parties. Elected representatives to the national legislature then elected the president.

But there was little genuine and fair competition in New Order elections. Described elsewhere as more of a "parade of the New Order's invincibility" rather than a true contest, elections disproportionately benefited Golkar and its patron, Soeharto (Aspinall 1997).[14] The official campaign period lasted 60 days in the 1971 and 1977 elections, 45 days in the 1982 election, and 25 days in subsequent elections (King 2010). Since Golkar had established a comprehensive local presence with the aid of the military and the civil service, these increasingly shorter campaign periods did not affect its mobilizational capacity. Golkar could rely on civil servants, who began campaigning for Golkar well before the official

---

[14] Elections were commonly referred to as "democracy festivals" or "democracy parties" (*pesta demokrasi*), alluding to the ceremonial nature of the process (Ufen 2010, 19).

period began under the guise of their official duties (King 2003). For PDI and PPP, on the other hand, these narrowed campaign periods impeded their ability to mobilize support in the villages.

Furthermore, Golkar had abundant financial resources, supported by the required contributions of civil servants to the Yayasan Dana Karya Abadi (or Dakab, hereafter) foundation (Masuhara 2015). Established in 1985 with the sole purpose of supporting Golkar's activities, the Dakab foundation provided at least 200 million rupiah to Golkar and its local branches each month (Masuhara 2015). All PDI and PPP candidates were vetted – a process initially set in place to screen leftist individuals, but one that over time became disproportionately disadvantageous for Golkar's rival parties.[15] Voter intimidation, fraud, and manipulation also biased election results in Golkar's favor. For example, in rural Central Java, alleged communist sympathizers were brought in to military headquarters and encouraged to demonstrate their loyalty to the regime by voting for Golkar (Liddle 1973). In the 1971 election, Golkar won 100% of the votes in the previously PKI-dominated area south of Blitar (Crouch 1978).

Between 1971 and 1997, Golkar won 60% to 75% of the popular vote in each election. Table 4.1 shows Golkar's vote shares and allocations of seats for DPR elections from 1971 through 1997. Given that almost a quarter of the seats in the DPR were reserved for Soeharto-appointed military representatives, Golkar's consistent share of the electoral vote meant that almost 80% of parliamentarians were pro-Soeharto (Masuhara 2015). Soeharto also consistently selected the heads of the DPR, further reinforcing the perception that it was completely under his control and that representatives did little to hold the government accountable. Parliamentarians were described sarcastically as "D4" (*daftar, duit, duduk, diam*, meaning that they "attend, get money, sit down, stay quiet" (Masuhara 2015, 42)). Like elections in the New Order, the lower house was yet another democratic trapping that suggested some superficial semblance of democratic procedure, but with no substance.

Protests in a Depoliticized Setting

These various measures of depoliticization did not totally eliminate opposition mobilization in the New Order. As Aspinall (2005) has persuasively demonstrated, Soeharto's restriction of dissent in the New

---

[15] Before the 1971 election, 735 of 3,800 screened candidates did not make the cut (van Dijk 1992). In 1977, 19% of PDI's candidates were disqualified as a result of the screening process, whereas PPP lost 16% of its candidates and Golkar only 5% (Liddle 1978).

Table 4.1. *Golkar vote shares and seats in DPR elections in Indonesia*

Election	1971	1977	1982	1987	1992	1997
Vote shares (%)	62.8	62.1	64.3	73.2	68.1	74.5
Attained seats in the DPR	236	232	242	299	282	325

Note: The total numbers of DPR seats reserved for elected parliamentarians were 360 for elections from 1971 through 1982, 400 seats for elections in 1987 and 1992, and 425 seats for the 1997 election.
Sources: King (2003). Lembaga Pemilihan Umum (1971, 1978, 1987, 1993, 1997b).

Order was not constant throughout the regime's history, and a variety of expressions of opposition existed at different points. In the late 1960s, Islamist leaders loudly criticized the regime's corruption and sought to ensure judicial independence (Aspinall 2005). The 1970s witnessed two significant episodes of mass unrest, in 1973 and again in 1977, that left observers uncertain about the regime's survival (Aspinall 2005). In the 1980s, "open and organized opposition" was more restricted, and many activists resorted to civil society activism that "avoided direct confrontation with the state" (Aspinall 2005, 25).

The first 15 years of the New Order had much more room for political mobilization and dissent than later years. Students, who contributed greatly to the 1965–1966 protests that helped to bring down Soekarno and legitimate Soeharto's ascension, were again the face of the opposition in the 1970s (Aspinall 2005). In 1970, triggered by the release of a photograph of Ibnu Sutowo, the head of the state oil company Pertamina, posing with a new Rolls Royce car, students took to the streets to protest against gasoline and kerosene price increases and government corruption (Bresnan 1993). Students also protested against Indonesia's first lady Tien Soeharto's development project, the Taman Mini Indonesia Indah (TMII) theme park, which they saw as a wasteful endeavor (Aspinall 2005). Dissatisfied with the government's campaign policies during the 1971 election, students encouraged voters to boycott the election and join their *golput* (golongan putih, or white group) movement.[16]

On January 15, 1974, students again demonstrated against foreign capital during a visit by Japanese prime minister Kakuei Tanaka. Looting and burning of buildings broke out at several locations in Jakarta.

---

[16] The *golput* movement encouraged voters to reject the existing parties' color symbols of green (PPP), yellow (Golkar), and red (PDI) and to opt for white instead as a symbol of moral cleanliness (Aspinall 2005).

At least 8 people died and over 100 were injured during this incident, now known as the Malari riots (Saunders 1998). The government responded quickly and forcefully, arresting more than 700 individuals for alleged involvement in the riots, and banned 11 newspapers (Aspinall 2005).

More protests flared a few years later. Frustrated with economic policies and the armed forces' involvement in politics, students resumed protests after the 1977 parliamentary elections. To nip this growing resentment in the bud, a team of cabinet ministers was sent to campuses for dialogs with student representatives in August 1977. These meetings occasionally turned hostile when student representatives announced impossible "conditions" and shut down the meeting before any real dialog could occur. In January 1978, a publication of the Bandung Institute of Technology student council documented a list of grievances and reasons why they "do not trust and do not want Soeharto to be President of the Republic of Indonesia again." Among other concerns, they criticized the government's lack of "political will" and "deviations and abuses of power by government officials" (Bresnan 1993, 198). The general chairman of the student council was later charged with insulting the head of state. In his defense statement, he claimed that the New Order was a "bureaucratic dictatorship" where all power rested with the president and that Indonesia "had become a nation of beggars and embezzlers, begging for foreign loans and investment, and permitting government 'stooges,' Chinese businessmen, and foreigners to drain the nation of its wealth" (Bresnan 1993, 198).

Following the 1974 and 1978 student demonstrations, the government issued a set of decrees as part of the Campus Life Normalization (Normalisasi Kehidupan Kampus, or NKK) program. These decrees outlawed student political activities and expression on campus, disbanded existing student councils at major universities, and threatened campus administrators with dismissal if student political activities continued (Saunders 1998). Much more stringent curricular requirements were introduced, leaving students with little time for extracurricular activities (Aspinall 2005). As a result of this move to depoliticize campuses, protests largely dissipated in the 1980s.

Ethnic Political Representation and Exclusion

On the surface, the New Order celebrated ethnic diversity as a source of national strength. Soeharto upheld the country's ideology of Pancasila and its national motto "Unity in Diversity," referring to it frequently throughout his career to assert the importance of unity and harmony among Indonesians. The Taman Mini Indonesia Indah theme park, a widely criticized multimillion-dollar project sponsored by First Lady Tien Soeharto, exhibited the traditional homes and costumes of every major island's main ethnic groups, symbolically signaling to visitors the country's respect for ethnic diversity. Public schools offered a local ethnic language as part of their curriculum, to ensure that children would not lose their mother tongue even as they received their education in the national language, Bahasa Indonesia.[17] History textbooks for primary, middle school, and high school children discussed heroes from all major islands in Indonesia and their struggle against Dutch colonial rule, to stress that independence was jointly won. Bank notes bear the faces and names of these heroes, who represent various regions of the archipelago.

But the regime was highly suspicious of group ethnic loyalties and, as a result, prohibited explicitly ethnic political mobilization. There were no ethnic political parties, for example. Even the PPP, designed to appeal to Muslim voters, could not make Islam its governing principle and was required to change its symbol from the Ka'bah to a more generic star, and its politicians touted generic development-focused rhetoric in campaign speeches during the New Order–era elections (Boileau 1983). To avoid communal clashes, in the 1970s the regime introduced the term *SARA*, an acronym for ethnicity (*suku*), religion (*agama*), race (*ras*), and intergroup (*antar-golongan*), which encapsulates sensitive issues related to Indonesians' identity affiliations. In the name of maintaining harmonious and peaceful relations between groups, SARA-related discussions in public were prohibited.[18]

To further deter communal mobilization, one of the government-approved 36 verses on applications of Pancasila, which that every school child in Indonesia must memorize included the call to prioritize Indonesia's unity above one's personal and communal interests.[19]

Nonetheless, in practice the New Order accommodated some groups while repressing and discriminating against others. The following

---

[17] Prior to 1975, local ethnic languages were the primary language of instruction in the early years of school. In the 1975 curriculum, local ethnic languages became a separate course and Bahasa Indonesia became the language of instruction (Rusyana 1999).

[18] For example, when a military priest in West Kalimantan published an opinion piece in a local newspaper in 1971 that criticized the government for not placing more Dayaks in the provincial legislature despite their contribution to Golkar's electoral success, he was put under house arrest for almost a month, until he eventually resigned from his military position. See Tanasaldy (2012, 176–177), and Doera (2003, 301–303).

[19] This verse was found in article 3, verse 1 of the *Pedoman Penghayatan dan Pengamalan Pancasila*, (or P4). P4 was legislated by an MPR bill in 1978 in Ketetapan MPR no. II/MPR/1978.

pages discuss the shift in ethnic representation in Soeharto's national government, before turning to the regime's discriminatory policies toward ethnic Chinese Indonesians and its repression of secessionist groups in Aceh, Papua, and East Timor.

Political Representation

The New Order government of the early 1970s and 1980s had an overrepresentation of military officials and technocrats, with Soeharto at its apex. This tendency started with Soeharto himself, who relied on a small group of trusted military men. The core group of generals around Soeharto in the 1960s and 1970s shared a common military background and years of association with him, but they were relatively heterogeneous in their ethnic and religious backgrounds. In the 1960s–1970s, Soeharto's core group of generals included General Maraden Panggabean, Lt. Gen. Amir Machmud, Lt. Gen. Yoga Sugama, Lt. Gen. Ali Murtopo, Admiral Sudomo, Maj. Gen. Benny Murdani, Lt. Gen. Sudharmono, Lt. Gen. Darjatmo, Lt. Gen. Ibnu Sutowo, Gen. Sumitro, and Lt. Gen. Sutopo Juwono (Jenkins 1984, 20–21).[20] Generals Murdani and Sudomo were Javanese Christians, whereas Panggabean was a Bataknese Christian and Amir Machmud was a Muslim Sundanese. Sudomo and Murdani had known Soeharto since the 1960s (Jenkins 1984).

Many of the Muslim generals in this small circle were perceived as only nominally practicing their faith and saw no difficulty in associating and working with Chinese business figures or Christian activists and academics.[21] General Soedjono Humardani was Soeharto's spiritual adviser in Javanese mystical practice (Jenkins 1984). This small group of generals controlled policymaking and had great influence over intelligence, finance, social welfare, and special affairs (Jenkins 1984; Crouch 1978). Key members assumed formal positions in Soeharto's cabinets as well as leadership roles in intelligence and security agencies, remaining in their posts well beyond the normal term length (Jenkins 1984). Members of the inner core group recognized the need for this "immobility," stating that it was hard "to find someone you can really trust."[22]

---

[20] Machmud, Murdani, and Sugama all became generals later.
[21] Lt. Gen. Ali Murtopo, for example, helped to found the Centre for Strategic and International Studies (CSIS), a Catholic think tank (Sidel 2006).
[22] Quoted in Jenkins (1984, 27).

Many of Soeharto's cabinet members, governors, and legislators also had a military background. In 1977, more than 70% of Indonesia's governors were army officers and more than 50% of the country's 294 district chiefs and mayors came from the military.[23] Military generals were appointed as provincial governors so frequently as to inspire a joke: "Under colonialism, we had a governor-general; now that we're independent, we have general-governors."[24] Military officers occupied up to 80% of mayor, district chief, and governor positions in the early 1970s (Mietzner 2018; Bresnan 1993). Until 1987, 100 of the 460 seats in the Parliament were allocated to military representatives whom Soeharto appointed.[25] Furthermore, almost 50% of heads of civilian departments were filled by military representatives as of 1982 (Bresnan 1993). Military figures were also frequently appointed to lead state-owned enterprises, such as Indonesia's oil company (Pertamina), commodities board (Bulog), and trading firm (Berdikari). Upon retirement, it was common for army generals to join boards of directors of large firms affiliated with the government (Pepinsky 2009; Bresnan 1993).

A similar pattern is recognizable among the leaders of Golkar, Soeharto's political party and main electoral engine. Essentially a creation of the military, Golkar had many members from the armed forces, to the extent that the Golkar–military relationship was described as like that between a parent and child (Masuhara 2015, 172). Particularly in the early years, almost all of Golkar's key leaders were from the military (Boileau 1983). Golkar's Central Executive Board (CEB, hereafter), the body that implemented Golkar's decisions, had heavy military representation.[26]

Because of the military's large political footprint, many observers have described the New Order as a period of military rule (King 1982; Cribb and Coppel 2009). But although the Indonesian military was indeed active and engaged in New Order politics, this engagement was always subject to Soeharto's careful selection or approval of officials. Important appointments occurred only with his blessing, making him the "sole veto player" (Pepinsky 2009, 45).

---

[23] During the New Order, governors of Java were appointed by Soeharto directly, whereas the others were recommended by the Department of Home Affairs and/or the Department of Defense, with Soeharto's final approval (Jenkins 1984, 47).

[24] Quoted in Slater (2010, 186).

[25] This number then declined to 75 through 1997 (Masuhara 2015, 42).

[26] In Bahasa Indonesia, the CEB is known as Dewan Pembina Pusat (DPP). This body was not the real decision-making body. A civilian leader of Golkar in 1978 described its role as that of "approv[ing] a policy which had been made somewhere else" (Suryadinata 1989, 51).

Along with the military, Western-trained technocrats also played an important role in New Order cabinets. Tasked by the MPRS to form a new provisional cabinet, Soeharto formed the Ampera (Cabinet of the People's Suffering), which was described by the US State Department's Bureau of Intelligence and Research (INR) as a "cabinet of technicians."[27] The technocrats whom Soeharto chose to plan and execute Indonesia's economic stabilization and recovery were mostly US-trained economists, sympathetic to the creation of a free-market economy and the reduction of state controls (Simpson 2008, 219). In 1967, US secretary of defense Robert McNamara observed that "all thirteen top members of Soeharto's staff received training in the U.S. under the MAP" (Simpson 2008, 227). Because some of them had been educated at the University of California, Berkeley, this group of advisers was often called the "Berkeley Mafia" (Booth 2016).

Because of the presence and political influence of non-Muslims and nominal Muslims around Soeharto, many Islamists felt marginalized and excluded from politics during the first half of the New Order (Sidel 2006). Not only did the regime take numerous steps to weaken the PPP's political clout, but for the first two decades of the New Order, no one "singularly identified by his or her organizational attachment to Islam" was part of Soeharto's cabinet (Elson 2008, 261). Prominent figures in the 1970s could make derogatory comments about Muslims in public with minimal repercussion.[28] Conservative Muslims took issue with the government's suppression of those who supported the Jakarta Charter, which called for the implementation of Islamic law (sharia) for Muslims and which was deleted from the 1945 Constitution (Hamka 1973), and with the regime's heavy reliance on Western-educated technocrats (Sidel 2006).

Furthermore, Soeharto had championed in 1973 a marriage bill that would have allowed marriages between members of different faiths and would have stipulated that a marriage was valid on the basis of its registration by the state authority rather than religious precepts (Mujiburrahman 2006). It didn't help that the head of the Golkar faction in the MPR at the time was a Catholic (Mujiburrahman 2006). The proposed bill outraged many Islamist public figures, who claimed that it would threaten Islamic family law and Islamic courts, contradict the tenets of Islam, and reduce the number of Muslims, and that Catholics

[27] Quoted in Simpson (2008, 218).
[28] A former PNI leader, Hadisubeno, was quoted warning others in 1970 to be cautious with "the sarong-wearing group," a reference to devout Muslims in Indonesia (Elson 2008).

associated with Golkar and nominally Muslim generals were behind the draft (Mujiburrahman 2006). Renowned Muslim intellectual Hamka (1973, 88) claimed that the bill would "displace sharia and completely destroy Islamic principles" and that Muslims in Indonesia were "in a thoroughly weakened position." There was so much uproar and rumor-mongering about Catholics' access to the president and their influence on the marriage bill draft that Admiral Soedomo, then a Deputy Commander of Security and Order Operations, threatened to revoke press credentials of any entity that published "any news of SARA" (Mujiburrahman 2006, 167). A compromise version that did not diminish the role and authority of Islamic courts or Islamic family law was eventually ratified in 1974.

After two decades of marginalization, however, Muslims' political fortunes began to improve in the 1980s. Faced with the looming retirement of many of his senior-ranking military officers and a growing devotion to Islam among ordinary Indonesians in the 1980s, Soeharto adopted a two-pronged strategy to maintain power: (1) he enticed members of Islamist groups away from PPP to support Golkar, and (2) he revamped Golkar into a political organization that could easily be mobilized nationally to support his development goals (Sudharmono 1997).

To appeal to Muslim voters, Soeharto relaxed the long-contested policy that banned hijabs in public schools (Liddle 1996) and agreed to the systematization of Islamic courts. In June 1991, prior to the 1992 election, Soeharto and his wife went on a much-publicized hajj to Mecca. Moreover, he took his entourage of presidential bodyguards with him and paid for their pilgrimage (Fadillah 2014). Various media outlets featured pictures of Soeharto on hajj and reported stories on how other pilgrims from various countries cheered for him in Mecca (Sutrimo 2013). Later that year, he approved of the creation of Indonesia's first sharia bank, Bank Muamalat Indonesia.

In 1990, Soeharto supported the establishment of an association for middle-class moderate Muslims, the Association of Islamic Intellectuals (Ikatan Cendekiawan Muslim se-Indonesia (ICMI)).[29] ICMI is

---

[29] Concerned that Muslim intellectuals had no official organization, a group of students at Brawijaya University in Malang had come together to call for the creation of an association that would appeal to a broad range of Muslims. They approached Minister of Environment Emily Salim and Minister Bacharuddin Jusuf Habibie for support. Habibie advanced the students' proposal to the president, accompanied by a letter signed by 49 Muslim intellectuals who declared their support for such an association and requested that Habibie be named its chairman (ICMI 2018). On December 7, 1990, ICMI was established in Malang, East Java, with Soeharto's support and with Habibie as its first chairman.

deliberately broad in its membership. Although the organization has the term *intellectuals* in its name, its membership is not limited to scholars, intellectuals, or Islamic religious teachers; any Muslim can join it.[30] The government's sponsorship positioned ICMI to become the prime channel through which Indonesian Muslims could hope to enter politics.

By its second national congress in 1995, ICMI had 1,200 delegates representing 42,000 registered members spread throughout the archipelago (Liddle 1996). ICMI's leaders at the time included prominent Muslims who had kept their distance from the government, as well as government officials and Golkar politicians.[31] Amien Rais, head of Muhammadiyah (Indonesia's second-largest mass organization for Muslims), became chair of ICMI's Council of Experts (Liddle 1996). Several prominent figures from NU, then Indonesia's largest Islamic mass organization, also joined ICMI.

From the government's perspective, ICMI brought in new members and provided a fresh representation of Islam in Golkar. After the 1992 and 1997 elections, 16 ICMI leaders attained seats in the DPR as Golkar representatives (Masuhara 2015, 122). In 1993, Marwah Daud Ibrahim, ICMI's general secretary, became a Golkar representative in Parliament and joined the CEB without any prior party experience (Masuhara 2015, 122). Over time, as Golkar's CEB expanded in size, its members included an increasing number of ICMI affiliates (Masuhara 2015). By 1995, Indonesia's armed forces commander, the army's chief of staff, and Golkar's chairman were all devout Muslims and/or had ties to ICMI.

In addition to making policy concessions that endeared the president to Indonesian Muslims, Soeharto consolidated his rule by reforming Golkar and strengthening its grassroots support. In 1983, he appointed Sudharmono, then state secretary, as Golkar's chairman and gave him the task of transforming the party and recruiting its next generation of

---

[30] On its website, the association specifies that ICMI members do not even need to be university graduates. In its founding document, the term *Muslim intellectual* was defined as "any Muslim who cares for his environment and is constantly increasing in his faith and devotion, intellectual abilities, digging deeper, understanding, and applying knowledge and technology as well as faithful living in his social interactions toward the creation of a prosperous society." See Anggaran Rumah Tangga ICMI, chapter 1 verse 1.

[31] Liddle (1996) listed figures such as Ginandjar Kartasasmita, previously of the defunct political party PNI, and Sumitro Djojohadikusumo, then dean of the faculty of economics at the University of Indonesia and former leader of the Indonesian Socialist party (PSI), as ICMI leaders in 1995. Marwah Daud Ibrahim, who had attained her PhD in the United States in the year before ICMI's establishment and had only recently returned to Indonesia, became the association's general secretary in 1990 (Masuhara 2015).

cadres. Although Golkar had been incredibly effective as an electoral machine, its success rested on various measures of government intervention and manipulation rather than genuine voter support. To build the party's political base, Sudharmono expanded recruitment efforts. When Sudharmono began his reforms in 1983, 32 new members joined Golkar's CEB, the total membership of which was only 42 at that time (Masuhara 2015, 98). Unlike the board's old hands, who had military backgrounds, these new members were young civilian politicians, former student activists, and indigenous (*pribumi*) entrepreneurs who had been disgruntled with Soeharto's reliance on Chinese-Indonesian conglomerates (Masuhara 2015).

In 1984, Sudharmono launched Golkar's individual membership registration program and its cadre cultivation program. By June 1988, an estimated 32 million people were registered as members of Golkar (DPP Golkar 1988b). Each member was required to pay a small membership fee of 100 rupiah per month, which contributed to Golkar's financial war chest (Masuhara 2015, 102). The cadre cultivation program aimed to turn 10% of the residents of every village into Golkar's "village cadres" (Masuhara 2015, 102). These villagers attended training sessions on the 1945 Constitution, Pancasila, Golkar's regulations, public speaking, and political debate. By 1988, Golkar reported having more than eight million members at the village level, in addition to almost one million members of "functional cadres" who represented groups such as youth, women, teachers, and religious leaders at the provincial level (DPP Golkar 1988b, 197–198). Considering that just a decade earlier Golkar had only 28,000 members at the district and municipality levels, this growth was remarkable.

To further widen Golkar's appeal to the everyday Indonesian, Sudharmono and other CEB members embarked on weekend "safaris" to various villages across the country. They visited Islamic boarding schools (*pesantrens*), attended ceremonies, and distributed gifts such as copies of the Koran and substantial funds to help with repairing local mosques (Masuhara 2015, 100). From 1984 to 1987, Golkar reportedly spent more than 1.2 billion rupiah on books and charitable donations to religious foundations, schools, orphanages, and mosques (DPP Golkar 1988a, 2363–2379).

This shift in Golkar's party leadership to incorporate more civilian, moderate, and middle-class Muslims, the party's campaign to broaden its grassroots base, and its concerted efforts to support causes dear to Muslim voters were further bolstered by the party's recruitment of rank-and-file members from Islamic organizations such as NU, Muhammadiyah, and the Islamic student organization Himpunan

Mahasiswa Islam (HMI), which had charters at various universities. Although Golkar was not an ethnic or a religious party, and although Soeharto himself was initially viewed as suspicious of Islam, these efforts created the impression that during the mid-1980s and 1990s, Golkar and Soeharto's New Order regime took an "Islamic turn" (Liddle 1996, 614).

Ethnic Co-optation in Local Administrative Units

Soeharto's strategies to maintain political dominance had repercussions for relations between ethnic groups in districts and municipalities. This subsection will trace the New Order regime's strategies to garner sufficient votes for Golkar at the local level, and their implications on local ethnic political representation and intergroup relations. Like Soeharto's strategy at the national level, his strategies in districts and municipalities also shifted over time. In the first half of the New Order, Golkar relied on local ethnic aristocrats, granting them important positions in district, municipal, or provincial governments. As Soeharto embraced more Muslims into his government in the late 1980s and 1990s, however, the appointments of district chiefs (*bupati*), mayors (*walikota*), and governors (*gubernur*) increasingly favored Muslims with local aristocratic backgrounds and ties to the Muslim organizations ICMI and Himpunan Muslim Indonesia (HMI). Although this shift was unproblematic in regions with overwhelming Muslim majorities, in more religiously mixed areas it received far less welcome.

Upon assuming power in 1967, Soeharto was relatively unknown and Golkar had very little grassroots support. In anticipation of the 1971 election and wary of the popularity of conservative Muslim political parties, Soeharto's military generals tried multiple approaches to ensure Golkar's electoral victory. Based on his research on South Sulawesi, West Nusa Tenggara, and East Kalimantan, Magenda (1989, 937–938) indicated that one main strategy to guarantee Golkar's victory in these regions was to appoint local aristocrats to important local positions to act as a bridge between Jakarta and potentially resistant local voters. Individuals affiliated with local sultanates and kingdoms were installed as district chiefs, mayors, subdistrict heads, district council chairs, and leaders of Golkar's local branches. Examples included, among others, Lalu Ratmadji and Madilaoe ADT in West Nusa Tenggara and Awang Faisal and Awang Badaranie in East Kalimantan (Magenda 1989, 954). Most governors and district chiefs in South Sulawesi during the New Order were aristocrats (Buehler 2014, 168). Many DPR representatives from these provinces and Golkar's provincial leaders had prior experience as civil servants (*pamong praja*); in the outer islands, members of aristocratic families were overrepresented in these positions (Magenda 1989, 920).

This appointment of local aristocrats had historical justifications. First, old sultanates and kingdoms in the outer islands had provided the basis for the creation of administrative units (Fox 2011). For example, Kutai, Gowa, Bone, Soppeng, and Wajo were former sultanates that became districts in the mid-1950s (Magenda 1989, 913).

Second, local aristocrats in the outer islands were usually the few local families who could afford to send their children to the Opeleiding School Voor Inlandsche Ambtenaren (OSVIA) in the 1930s.[32] In South Sulawesi, Kutai, and Sumbawa, OSVIA graduates were very few in number, about ten per region (Magenda 1989). Since the illiteracy rate in eastern Indonesia in 1930 was as high as 90%, these OSVIA graduates automatically became the educated elites in their region (Magenda 1989, 895).

Third, as Magenda (1989, 897) observed, the central government in the 1950s did not have sufficient manpower to run the new country's bureaucracy, particularly in the outer islands. Local aristocrats, with their higher levels of education, prior experience in the colonial bureaucracy, influence and knowledge of the local population became very attractive candidates for the task. Magenda (1989, 898) reported that in the outer islands, "local aristocracies safely put themselves in dominant positions in their own autonomous regions and by virtue of their education, they also controlled the machinery of supra-autonomous region level bureaucracies which had just been created." As such, when autonomous units were dissolved in 1958, many former sultans were absorbed into the unitary state's bureaucracy as district chiefs. For example, Andi Idjo (of the Gowa sultanate) became regent of Gowa, and Andi Mappanjukki (of the Bone kingdom) became regent of Bone (Magenda 1989, 912).

Echoes of Magenda's description can be found in studies of other provinces in the early days of the New Order regime. Amal (1992) described a similar strategy in West Sumatra. Shortly after the 1965 anti-communist purge, Baharuddin Dt. Rangkajo Basja, an ethnic Minang and PNI affiliate with strong leftist sympathies, was removed from his position as governor of West Sumatra. His deputy and acting governor, Saputro Brotodihardjo, was an ethnic Javanese and PNI

---

[32] OSVIA was a school specifically designed to train local students for service in the colonial bureaucracy as *pamong praja* or civil servants.

affiliate whose nomination was strongly opposed by local Islamists and anti-communists. To appease this demand for a "native son," Jakarta appointed Harun Zein, an ethnic Minang academic and rector of the University of Andalas in Padang, who was described as having "one foot in Jakarta and another in West Sumatra" (quoted in Amal 1992, 117). District chief positions in Java and Madura through the early 1970s also went consistently to members of the Javanese aristocracy (Sidel 2006).

Amal (1992, 185) argued that in both West Sumatra and South Sulawesi in the 1970s, Golkar established connections with local ethnic communities and worked closely with local ethnic representatives. In West Sumatra, Harun Zein was the local "native son" who convinced his ethnic community to side with the Jakarta government, while in South Sulawesi Lieutenant Colonel Jusuf, a Bugis aristocrat, was a key person to bridge the local South Sulawesi community to the central government. Both Zein and Jusuf became prominent ministers in Soeharto's cabinets in subsequent years (Amal 1992, 194).

This strategy worked relatively smoothly in more ethnically homogeneous places (e.g., West Sumatra, East Kalimantan, and South Sulawesi) where the local aristocrats were well respected and few alternative ethnic communities were competing for political positions. In more ethnically mixed areas, however, Golkar ended up favoring one ethnic community over others. In West Kalimantan province, for example, where the ethnic Dayaks composed about 40% of the population during Soeharto's rule, Golkar initially liaised with Dayak leaders to mobilize voters and awarded them with local posts, though none ever higher than the subdistrict head level (Davidson 2008). Soejiman, a former governor explained that the size of the Dayak population in West Kalimantan made the ethnic group very important in giving Golkar larger margin of victory there (Davidson 2008, 108). The founder of the Dayak party Partai Persatuan Dayak and Soekarno-era governor of the province, Johanes Chrisostomus Oevaang Oeray, was instrumental in campaigning for Golkar in the 1977 election. Yet, after Oeray was moved to Jakarta to serve as a Golkar representative in Parliament, no other Dayaks rose to political prominence in West Kalimantan during Soeharto's rule. Instead, Muslim ethnic Malays were frequently appointed as local executives and council chairs. Soeharto-era district chiefs in the Dayak-majority in Pontianak district (now Mempawah) in West Kalimantan, for instance, were ethnic Malay until Cornelius Kimha was elected by the local council in 1999 (Davidson 2008, 125). This situation spawned resentment among the Dayak community in

West Kalimantan who felt that they had been faithfully delivering votes for Golkar for decades (Davidson 2008, 115).

In the second half of the New Order, consistent with the shift toward Islamists at the national level, bupatiships and governorships in the outer islands were increasingly assigned to individuals of aristocratic origins with affiliations to Muslim organizations, such as the HMI or ICMI, and with aristocratic origins. For instance, Achmad Amiruddin, an HMI leader and aristocrat, served as governor of South Sulawesi in 1983 and 1988. Lalu Mudjitahid came from a similar aristocratic and HMI background to become bupati of Lombok Barat in 1989 (Magenda 1989, 954). The ascendancy of HMI- and ICMI-affiliated ethnic leaders was also reported in Poso, Central Sulawesi, much to the dismay of local Pamona Christians (Aragon 2007). In these places, by virtue of the identity affiliations of Golkar's local leaders, Golkar increasingly adopted a pro-Islam identity, while PDI, its perceived opposition party, was locally perceived as a party for non-Muslims.

The Chinese Minority: Indonesia's Ethnic "Other"

The distinction between Chinese Indonesians and other Indonesians is not a purely Soeharto-era construct. As Chapter 3 has shown, this perception of ethnic Chinese as foreign dated back to colonial policies that treated them as a separate category. It was maintained and harnessed in the national awakening movement to provide legible boundaries of what it means to be Indonesian, and it was renegotiated again in the 1960s as Indonesia's relations with China turned sour. But not until Soeharto's New Order rule was this political subordination of ethnic Chinese in Indonesia codified and legitimated by the government (Chernov-Hwang and Sadiq 2010).

In 1967, a group of army generals who gathered to discuss the "Chinese problem" decided that the most strategic course of action was to utilize the ethnic Chinese's economic aptitude to bring in revenues for the country, but to require them to assimilate into the preexisting ethnic fabric of Indonesian society.[33] The government launched an "Assimilation Program," targeted only at ethnic Chinese residents. By law, public use of the Chinese language and characters, and celebration of cultural festivals were banned. Chinese-language schools were shut

[33] A memo issued in June 1967 and based on the conversations at this gathering, titled "The Basic Policy for the Solution of the Chinese Problem," was described and translated in Suryadinata (1996, 226–229).

down. Chinese Indonesians were encouraged to adopt Indonesian-sounding names (Chernov-Hwang and Sadiq 2010). This program was designed to remove the group's ethnic identifiers so that they would ultimately be absorbed into the broader fabric of Indonesia's accepted ethnic groups (Hoon 2006).

Ironically, these assimilation measures were coupled with continuous efforts to maintain a clear separation between ethnic Chinese and other Indonesians. Because Chinese Indonesians were required to change their names, the government added a special code on their ID cards to signify their Chinese background (a practice that continued until after Soeharto stepped down). In 1976, a Bank Indonesia memo defined *pribumi* (native) as those who "are not foreign citizens, who do not belong to the category of European or foreign oriental, and who are members of Indonesian indigenous society," but the *non-pribumi* (or non-indigenous) label was applied in practice only to Indonesians with Chinese ancestry.[34] This distinction was also used in official government rhetoric and discourse, and it was not abolished until Soeharto's successor, B. J. Habibie, signed a presidential decree in 1998 (Instruksi President no. 26/1998). Interestingly, the famed TMII display of Indonesia's ethnic diversity never had an exhibit for ethnic Chinese, Arabs, or Eurasians (Siddik 2010).

Along the same lines, the participation of ethnic Chinese individuals in the country's struggle for independence is also missing from government-approved textbooks. John Lie, a member of the Indonesian Navy who worked on arms supplies during Indonesia's independence struggle, was the first and only ethnic Chinese awarded the title of national hero (Pahlawan Nasional) in 2011 (Suryadinata 2015). Only a handful of scholars – many of Chinese lineage themselves – have published popular and academic books on the role of the Chinese in Indonesia's nation building (Tan 2004; Suryadinata 2015).

This distinction between ethnic Chinese and other Indonesians was reinforced through a series of discriminative policies. Unlike other Indonesians, ethnic Chinese had to acquire additional documents as proof of citizenship (SBKRI). Furthermore, ethnic Chinese were subject to cost markups in the processing of official documents; for example, they had to pay twice as much as a *pribumi* for a birth certificate (Chernov-Hwang and Sadiq 2010). Indonesian Chinese also faced discrimination regarding entrance into state-owned universities, public service, and public employment (Heryanto 1999). In most parts

---

[34] See Chernov-Hwang and Sadiq (2010, 195); Bertrand (2004, 45); Pepinsky (2009, 40).

of Indonesia, they were required to apply for work permits to gain employment (Chernov-Hwang and Sadiq 2010).

Fearing the resurgence of communism, the government prohibited Chinese political organizations and permitted only recreational sports and funeral associations (Tan 2004).[35] Prior to Soeharto's assumption of the presidency, Baperki, the organization advocating for the recognition of Chinese Indonesian citizenship during Soekarno's rule, claimed to have 250,000 members (Cribb and Coppel 2009). During the anti-communist purge in 1965–1966, many Baperki leaders and members were killed and the organization itself was outlawed (Purdey 2006).

Without political organizations to champion their demands and aspi-rations during the New Order, ethnic Chinese Indonesians also lacked political representation during this period. In contrast to Soekarno's government, in which a number of ethnic Chinese representatives held positions in various government branches, only one ethnic Chinese ever entered the cabinet: H. Mohammad "Bob" Hasan, a wealthy businessman and Soeharto's golf buddy, who served as Minister of Industry and Trade for the last two months before Soeharto's ouster in 1998 (Simanjuntak 2003; Chernov-Hwang and Sadiq 2010). No ethnic Chinese was ever appointed as a provincial governor during the New Order, and no district, not even those with large concentrations of ethnic Chinese such as Pontianak in West Kalimantan and Tanjung Pinang in Riau, ever had an ethnically Chinese district chief (Arifin, Hasbullah, and Pramono 2017).[36]

Lacking formal political representation, many Chinese entrepreneurs relied instead on close individual connections to Soeharto and the military for their business advancement and political protection. These personal connections – though both economically advantageous and strategically necessary – added a socioeconomic dimension to the ethnic distinction of Chinese Indonesians. In government documents and rhetoric, indigenous Indonesians were often interchangeably described as economically weak and poor (*"golongan ekonomi lemah"*), whereas the Chinese Indonesians were portrayed as wealthy (Chernov-Hwang and Sadiq 2010, 195). The Soeharto government frequently repeated the

[35] Only sports that did not originate in Chinese culture were allowed; thus, for example, lion dancing was banned.
[36] Henk Ngantung, Jakarta's governor from 1964 to 1965 during Soekarno's rule, was a Chinese Christian. He was removed from his position due to his alleged ties to the communist PKI party (IDN Times 2017). No other ethnic Chinese was appointed to governorships in Indonesia until years after Soeharto resigned, when the Chinese Christian Basuki Tjahaja Purnama, vice governor of Jakarta, assumed the province's governor position in 2014, following then-governor Joko Widodo's election as president.

assertion that the Chinese in Indonesia, as in other parts of Southeast Asia, were a "market-dominant minority" (Chua 2003). Although many Chinese in various parts of Indonesia are farmers, petty traders, and day laborers and are by no means wealthy, the widely held perception among Indonesians is that they are a tiny minority group that controls 70% of the country's wealth. A list of the top-20 business figures in Indonesia during Soeharto's tenure showed why this perception prevailed, as all but four of them were ethnically Chinese. Tellingly, three of the four *pribumi* business figures were Soeharto's family members (Pepinsky 2009, 55–56). Although Chinese business conglomerates composed a tiny percentage of Chinese Indonesians overall, the vast amount of wealth they have amassed contributes to this perception.

Along with a set of discriminative policies and a lack of formal political representation, the ethnic Chinese in Indonesia were frequently targeted with violence during Soeharto's rule. The New Order regime was established on the heels of an anti-communist purge that claimed somewhere between 200,000 and almost a million deaths (Cribb 2001b). Many believed that hundreds of thousands of Chinese Indonesians were massacred in the process, though evidence has suggested that this estimate was wildly exaggerated and that the number was closer to 2,000 deaths (Coppel 1983; Cribb and Coppel 2009). During the 32-year New Order regime, a series of attacks on Chinese-owned properties and riots targeting Chinese Indonesians occurred. Riots erupted in 1973 in Bandung; in 1980 in Semarang and Solo; in 1996–1997 in Situbondo, Tasikmalaya, and Rengasdengklok; and in 1998 in the week leading up to Soeharto's resignation in Jakarta, Surabaya, Solo, Lampung, Palembang, and Medan (Purdey 2006; Cribb and Coppel 2009, 458). Contrary to the image of order and stability that the New Order government attempted to project, the regime began and ended, and was frequently punctuated by outbursts of violence against members of ethnic Chinese community in Indonesia.

This combination of discriminative policies, targeted violence against ethnic Chinese Indonesians, and the New Order's blind eye toward (or, at points, active support of) the perpetrators of violence continually reminded Chinese Indonesians of their vulnerability and status as second-class citizens. The anti-Chinese violence surrounding Soeharto's ouster in 1998, as Chinese-owned properties were destroyed, hundreds were killed, and many women were raped and assaulted (Purdey 2006; Jusuf et al. 2007), was so traumatizing that some encouraged ethnic Chinese Indonesians to hide their Chinese identity in the 2000 census (Suryadinata, Arifin, and Ananta 2003, 74).

The ethnic Chinese population in Indonesia was so disenfranchised under Soeharto's rule that one would have expected them to demand greater representation after the autocrat's resignation. One may also wonder why they did not engage in ethnic rioting to articulate their demands. As explained in Chapter 2, one condition of my theory about excluded groups' strategic use of ethnic rioting is that they should perceive a reasonable chance of success in articulating their demands. If *voice* is so costly and other options are tolerable and viable, then disgruntled individuals will not articulate their grievances.

In this case, the state's discriminative policies in most districts had so weakened the ethnic Chinese communities that they lacked organized ethnic communities that could be readily mobilized. In most districts in Indonesia, the proportion of ethnic Chinese community is miniscule.[37] The repeated outbursts of violence against Chinese Indonesians served as warnings of what could befall them in case of (or rather, even despite their lack of) missteps or offenses. Clearly, they could not hope to achieve greater political inclusion by mobilizing violence. The same cannot be said of other politically excluded groups such as the Dayaks in Pontianak (West Kalimantan) and the Christians in Poso (Central Sulawesi) – two locally sizable ethnic groups with strong ethnic institutions.

For the ethnic Chinese Indonesians, using violence to articulate their voice would be too costly and would produce little payoff. Instead, many opted to wait until reforms were well underway and the new rules of allocating political and economic resources were clearer before articulating their demands through formal political means. After the implementation of the direct elections of local executives (Pilkada) in 2005, several administrative units with relatively larger proportions of ethnic Chinese population elected Chinese Indonesian mayors and district chiefs (Arifin, Hasbullah, and Pramono 2017).

Ethnic Mobilization in the Outer Islands

The New Order took a relatively exclusionary approach to ethnic groups with a problematic history. It excluded the ethnic Chinese minority politically, codifying the group's differences from other Indonesians through policy and establishing its reputation as a market-dominant minority, all while keeping the Chinese politically vulnerable and dependent on the patronage of indigenous political leaders. With regard to groups that had articulated sustained secessionist aspirations, such as the Acehnese, East Timorese, and Papuans, the New Order regime was extractive and violent.

---

[37] Arifin, Hasbullah, and Pramono (2017, 323) reported that in most districts, the percentage of ethnic Chinese does not exceed 0.5% of the total population.

The sentiment that Indonesia's government was too Java-centric was nowhere more pronounced during Soeharto's New Order than in Indonesia's three most troubled provinces: Aceh, Irian Jaya (which became Papua in 1998), and East Timor. In all three provinces, secessionist groups have mobilized against the Indonesian government, with varying degrees of success. East Timor and Irian Jaya were coercively integrated into Indonesia at a relatively late date. Irian Jaya did not take part in the independence movement and was not part of the newly independent Indonesia in 1949. Instead, West New Guinea remained under Dutch control until 1963, when Indonesia obtained it from the Dutch through an international agreement. In 1969, 1,025 government-selected tribal leaders participated in the "Act of Free Choice" and, under military intimidation, declared their choice to join Indonesia.[38] Similarly, East Timor was not part of the territory that Soekarno and Hatta claimed in their 1945 declaration of independence. An underpopulated island with few natural resources, Portuguese Timor was of little interest to Indonesia prior to 1975.[39] But when Portugal decolonized in 1974 and the Revolutionary Front of Independent East Timor (hereafter Fretilin) emerged as the dominant political party in Timor, Indonesia became wary of the risk of having a leftist, politically unified, independent neighbor.[40] Within less than two weeks after Fretilin declared Timor's independence on November 28, 1975, Indonesia launched a military operation (Bertrand 2004). The Indonesian-appointed president of the provisional government of East Timor, Lopez da Cruz, estimated a casualty level on the Timor side of 60,000 by February 1976 (Kiernan 2007).[41] East Timor officially became Indonesia's twenty-seventh province on July 17, 1976, under the name Timor Timur.

Aceh, on the other hand, had been part of Indonesia's territory since independence, and the Acehnese had fiercely supported the independence movement (Nessen 2006). Throughout the 1930s and

---

[38] The second Papuan Congress in 2000 later rejected the Act of Free Choice, declaring that it had been presented in a context of "threats, intimidation, sadistic killings, military violence, and amoral deeds that gravely violated humanitarian principles" (quoted in Tadjoeddin 2011, 315).

[39] When Indonesia proclaimed independence in 1945, it claimed the territory previously ruled by the Dutch; however, Portuguese Timor had never been colonized by the Dutch (van Klinken 2012).

[40] Other political parties, the Popular Democratic Association of Timorese (Apodeti) and the Union of Timorese (UDT), wanted integration with Indonesia as an autonomous region or a slower transition period to full independence, but ultimately Fretilin prevailed (Bertrand 2004).

[41] Other accounts estimated that about 100,000 or possibly even 200,000 people (or almost 30% of the total Timor population) died between 1975 and 1979 (van Klinken 2012; McDonald and Tanter 2006).

1940s, the Acehnese believed that their future was firmly intertwined with the liberation of the whole archipelago. Hasan di Tiro, who later proclaimed the Gerakan Aceh Merdeka (GAM) in 1976 and led Aceh's protracted civil war against Indonesia until it ended in 2005, was a pro-Indonesia fighter who fought alongside Javanese soldiers in Java. His close friend Jacoub Djuly described a common perception among Acehnese at the time: "We thought joining Indonesia meant Aceh independence also. Aceh would be independent but part of a larger Indonesian structure."[42] The religious leaders of Aceh in Persatuan Ulama Seluruh Aceh (PUSA) supported the Indonesian central government so fully that they purchased national bonds in 1946 and two aircraft in 1948 and sent hundreds of soldiers to Langkat to confront Dutch troops (Sulaiman 2006). Aceh was so integral to Indonesia's struggle for independence that Indonesia's vice premier, Sjafruddin Prawiranegara, based his office in Aceh for a few months in 1949 (Sulaiman 2006).

Yet even in Aceh, as in Papua and East Timor, secessionist aspirations were strong and durable. Given Timor's predominantly Catholic population, Papua's multitudes of ethnic groups, tribes, and languages, and Aceh's strong Islamist identity, one could argue that these provinces are ethnically and culturally distinct from the rest of Indonesia. However, a number of other provinces in Indonesia also have populations with distinct and strong ethnic identities.[43] While the struggle for independence in Aceh, Timor, and Papua was articulated in terms of achieving freedom for these specific *ethnic* groups, the narratives used by the rebels highlighted Indonesia's marginalization of ethnic groups, repressive violence, and unequal allocation of resources as key reasons for their mobilization. The New Order policies toward these provinces strengthened ethnic identities there and provided secessionist activists, as explained in the following paragraphs, with ample justifications for their claims (Bertrand 2004; Aspinall 2006).

Hasan di Tiro, GAM's leader for many years, stated that Aceh has been "used totally for the benefit of Java and the Javanese."[44] A frequently mentioned notion expressed in pamphlets across Aceh is that if the

---

[42] Quoted in Nessen (2006, 181).

[43] Sulawesi Utara, for example, is a predominantly Protestant province. A number of ethnic groups who live in East Timor can also be found in the neighboring Indonesian province of Eastern Nusa Tenggara.

[44] Quoted in Tadjoeddin (2011), 135. Aceh's earlier rebel movement, Darul Islam, in the 1950s sought to establish an Islamic state and was quickly pacified. Although the centrality of Islam remained prominent in GAM's ideals for political governance, it was not the group's rallying cry.

province were independent, it would be as wealthy as the neighboring oil-rich micro-state Brunei Darussalam (Tadjoeddin 2011).

Because of this perception that "Indonesia is Java," GAM fighters in Aceh targeted Javanese migrants, as well as Indonesian local government officials, military personnel, and the energy infrastructure (Schulze 2006, 230–236).[45] In the mid-1990s, thousands of Javanese migrants in Aceh Utara were terrorized and forced to leave their homes (Barber 2000).

In Aceh and Papua, the dissatisfaction could be traced back to the regime's extractive policies and to military violence in the provinces. In East Timor, the notion of Javanese colonialism in the province had a slightly different political and historical genesis, as further explained later in this chapter. Aceh and Papua's resource wealth substantially enriched Indonesia's national coffers and fueled the country's rapid economic growth during Soeharto's rule. At its peak in the 1980s and 1990s, Aceh's natural gas output brought in more than $2 billion per year in US dollars, while its timber exports reached $450 million per year in value from the 1970s through the 1990s (Sulaiman 2006). Similarly, the government received $22 million in taxes from the Freeport mining company in Papua (Bertrand 2004). Papua's export revenues reached $600 million in 1990. Both provinces' regional GDP per capita (RGDP), which captures revenues earned from natural resource extraction, was significantly higher than the national average, especially during the oil boom in the 1970s (Tadjoeddin 2011). Despite this great economic contribution, however, poverty reduction in the resource-producing provinces was much slower than in resource-poor provinces elsewhere in Indonesia. In fact, Tadjoeddin (2011) found income convergence across provinces from 1976 through 1996, as resource-poor provinces grew much faster than resource-rich ones over the two decades. In 2004, Aceh and Papua were among the provinces with both the highest RGDP per capita and the highest poverty rates in Indonesia (World Bank 2005).

Beyond resource exploitation and unfair distribution of revenues, military occupation and constant violence further alienated the people of Aceh, Papua, and East Timor. At the time of GAM's declaration in 1976, the group was composed of only a few hundred people and had little capacity to mount a significant challenge to the Indonesian government. In response to GAM's founding, the government deployed

---

[45] Javanese migrants were considered "legitimate targets" because GAM viewed them as either working for the Indonesian government or as potential military collaborators (Schulze 2004).

troops to quell the rebellion, and clashes claimed a hundred lives (World Bank 2005, 3–4). When GAM reemerged in 1989, better armed, trained, and organized, the government declared martial law (Daerah Operasi Militer (DOM)), shut the province off from regular visitors and tourists, and regularly stationed soldiers at TNI headquarters in the province. DOM continued from 1989 through 1998, and between 2,000 and 10,000 deaths occurred (World Bank 2005). The entire period of Aceh's civil war from 1976 through 2005 claimed an estimated 15,000 lives (Barron, Engvall, and Morel 2016, 10).

From 1965 through 1999, Papua was under DOM, which granted the military free rein. In 1999, the director of the advocacy group ELSHAM estimated that at least 921 people had died under DOM in Papua. The real figure, according to a Human Rights Watch report published in 2007, may have been several times greater (HRW 2007). Incidents such as the flag-raising ceremony of the separatist group Free Papua Movement (Operasi Papua Merdeka (OPM)) in Papua were met with arrests. Although the specific number of incidents is unknown, the Indonesian military regularly used torture in Aceh, Irian Jaya, and East Timor (Amnesty International 1993; Hernawan 2016; HRW 2007; CAVR 2006). In 1977, when 15,000 people protested against the Indonesian government in Papua, the military responded by dropping napalm on villages in the area (Bertrand 2004). In East Timor, in addition to arrests and execution of Fretilin leaders, the Indonesian military conducted "sweeping" campaigns of villages known to be Fretilin strongholds and burned, bombed, and destroyed food crops to cut off rebel access to food supplies (van Klinken 2012, 7). Local inhabitants were terrorized, beaten, tortured, and forced to relocate to refugee settlements, where they lived in horrid conditions (Taylor 1991). These violent campaigns notwithstanding, Fretilin resistance persisted and gained momentum under Xanana Gusmão, who brought the massacre of peaceful protesters in Dili in 1991 – known as the Santa Cruz massacre – to international attention, galvanizing broad support for Timor's independence.

Table 4.2 shows the aggregated data on casualties during the long secessionist struggles in the three provinces.

Beyond conducting these violent campaigns, the government also implemented development programs to achieve integration in Timor and Papua. Convinced that development efforts would win over Timorese hearts and minds and establish order, the New Order authorities allocated a significant amount of the national budget every year to such programs in East Timor – far greater than what other provinces received (Hill 2000). The government created thirteen administrative districts and

Table 4.2. *Secessionist mobilizations in post-independence Indonesia*

	Aceh	Irian Jaya (Papua)	East Timor
Rebel organization	GAM	OPM	Fretilin
Period of conflict	1976–2005	1965–present	1976–1999
Outcome	Special autonomy	Special autonomy	Independence
Estimated casualties	12,000-15,000	Unknown	102,800

Sources: Barron (2008) and Silva and Ball (2006).

built government offices, schools, and paved roads (van Klinken 2012). The New Order regime widely publicized the fact that it had built "more schools in East Timor between 1975 and 1980 than Portugal had built in the one hundred years prior to 1975" (Lutz 1991). In a 1984 Ministry of Information publication, the government claimed that "establishment of Public Health Service centers, schools, and the construction of roads, etc., have contributed to the speedy restoration of law and order in the community. These activities have served as an effective deterrent against influence and propaganda carried out by a small group of anti-Indonesians."[46] Because of the centralized education system during Soeharto's New Order, schools in Timor followed the same curriculum as in other parts of Indonesia: children received their instruction in Bahasa Indonesia, learned the principles and application of Pancasila, and memorized Indonesia's national history (Bertrand 2004). Timorese students who wished to study outside of the province were given the opportunity to do so, provided that they demonstrated their support for Timor's integration into the country (van Klinken 2012).

These development and integration measures, however, only covered up the alienation that the people of East Timor experienced. Half the flow of development funds was spent on infrastructure to support the government and military apparatus, and the development efforts were construed as helping East Timorese to "think, understand, and act like Indonesians" (Saldanha 1994, 30–31). Although the provincial governors were consistently East Timorese, other government leadership posts and civil service jobs went to migrants from outside the province. In the small business sector, migrants from Sulawesi, Sumatra, and West Timor were more successful than their local counterparts. East Timorese also had no representatives in the central government (Bertrand 2004). The military maintained a commercial monopoly over coffee, forcing

---

[46] Ministry of Information (1984), quoted in Lutz (1991).

local producers to sell their crops at a low price to cooperatives that supplied the military-controlled company (Bertrand 2004).

Furthermore, the continued military violence outweighed any goodwill that these development efforts could have established. When a team of researchers from Gadjah Mada University interviewed Timorese youths and students in the mid-1980s, they found that many were "absolutely committed" to fighting against "the shackles of colonialism" and the "overdose of military" presence in the province.[47] Support for independence remained strong throughout Indonesia's occupation of the territory until Soeharto stepped down in 1998 and his successor, B. J. Habibie, agreed to demands for a referendum on East Timor's independence. In 1999, 78.5% of East Timorese voted in favor of separation from Indonesia. More violence erupted following this referendum, with military-supported militias killing hundreds of civilians and displacing thousands into West Timor and other parts of Indonesia (Robinson 2010; Freedom House 1999). Finally, in 2002, this 27th province of Indonesia formally became a newly independent Timor Leste.

In Aceh, Papua, and East Timor, the New Order's repressive and extractive policies exacerbated underlying ethnic identifications and provided local leaders with justifications for their grievances and reasons to mobilize. Although these were Indonesia's most extreme cases, they illustrate a broader perception that the New Order policies disproportionately benefited the Javanese at the expense of those living elsewhere.

Soeharto's Ouster

Many scholars have analyzed Soeharto's fall, emphasizing either the political or economic factors that led to his regime's demise. Those focusing on economic factors have traced his ouster to the Asian financial crisis of 1997, which led to capital flight, price increases, job losses, confrontations with the International Monetary Fund (IMF), and ultimately the mobilization of protesters who demanded economic and political reforms. On the other hand, political factors included the breakdown of the governing coalition and fragmentation among the ruling elite (Slater 2010; Aspinall 2005; Pepinsky 2009; Mietzner 1999). This section briefly sketches the events that led to Soeharto's fall and Indonesia's subsequent political reforms, with a particular focus on the student protests, opposition figures in the national arena, and the

---

[47] Mubyarto et al. (1991, 43, 61), quoted in van Klinken (2012).

shooting of students and subsequent anti-Chinese riots that preceded the president's resignation.

The economic trigger of the collapse of the New Order was the Asian financial crisis of 1997–1998, which started as what appeared to be a localized currency crisis in Thailand but then reverberated in neighboring Malaysia, Indonesia, and the Philippines before affecting South Korea, Hong Kong, China, and eventually Russia and Argentina. This crisis led to GDP contraction in affected countries for several years, the loss of millions of jobs, and, in both Thailand and Indonesia, the resignation of national leaders.

When the crisis first spread to Indonesia and weakened its currency, few observers imagined that it would topple a decades-old autocratic regime (Wan 2008; Radelet and Sachs 1998). Like Thailand, Indonesia had been growing economically before the crisis. Its average annual real GNP per capita growth rate was 6% from 1985 to 1995, and GDP growth was 8% in 1996 (Rosengard 2004). Soeharto's party, Golkar, had just won another landslide election in May 1997 with more than 74% of the vote, and Golkar's chairman, Harmoko, had declared that Soeharto would be the organization's nominee for president that year. The government's engineering of PDI chairperson Megawati's ouster from her party in 1996, along with its subsequent coercive handling of her supporters, made the possibility of removing Soeharto through the electoral process seem highly unlikely (Robison and Hadiz 2004). With Megawati safely deposed and a government-approved chairperson sitting at PDI's helm, the party that had become the symbol of opposition in the New Order attained a measly 3.04% of the vote in the 1997 elections. Soeharto's regime seemed invincible until the financial crisis hit.

As the rupiah continued to fluctuate and weaken, Soeharto sought aid from the IMF and received a $40 billion bailout package in exchange for a set of reform measures that would "strike at the heart of the politico-business and conglomerate power" (Robison and Rosser 1998, 1600). The first reforms that accompanied the IMF's first rescue package in October 1997 included the closure of sixteen banks, some of which were owned by members of Soeharto's family (Aspinall 2005). Rumors of the seventy-six-year-old president's declining health and uncertainties surrounding his successor led to a further drop in the value of the rupiah.[48] In January 1998, it plunged even further when Soeharto announced an unrealistic budget plan that the IMF criticized as not complying with the agreement (Wan 2008).

---

[48] In December 1997, Soeharto canceled a scheduled trip to Iran and took a ten-day rest. There were also rumors that he had suffered a stroke (Aspinall 2005).

On January 15, 1998, Soeharto signed another bailout agreement with the IMF, which required, among other things, a gradual elimination of subsidies on fuel, gasoline, and electricity and the dismantling of monopolies, some of which were owned by Soeharto's family members and associates (IMF 1998). As a result of this agreement, prices of basic food items jumped, setting off a wave of panicked stockpiling, looting, and protests against IMF-imposed policies (Ressa 1998a). Soeharto's dismissal of Indonesia's central banker and his selection of B. J. Habibie as his vice president in February 1998 were interpreted as defiance of the IMF, prompting the organization to withhold its disbursement of a $3 billion installment.[49]

In a third negotiation in April 1998, the IMF agreed to postpone the withdrawal of subsidies on fuel, gasoline, and electricity until further meetings could be held at the end of June. The economic team representing the Indonesian government understood that if economic recovery was not well on its way by June, fuel price increases would be delayed further (Kartasasmita and Stern 2016). But on May 4, when the IMF disbursed its first installment of the $3 billion package, Soeharto decided to abruptly raise fuel prices, essentially nullifying the last agreement and supporting the IMF's initial request. Gasoline prices increased by 71% and kerosene prices by 25%, which would imply a 100% increase in railway fares, a 60% increase in bus fares, and a 20% increase in electricity costs (Kartasasmita and Stern 2016). The president believed that he had enough political capital to make such a move, and some observers even suggested that he deliberately announced the price increase on the same day as the IMF disbursement to direct popular anger toward the IMF (Sharma 2003). Instead, it mobilized demands for regime change.

Since December 1997, student protests had been taking place on various university campuses across the country, accompanied by emboldened demands from opposition figures. While mostly peaceful, students' messages had evolved from initially criticizing the government's handling of the crisis and the IMF's suggested reforms to calls for increasingly broad political reform. Opinion polls of university students showed that many were opposed to the president's reelection (Aspinall 2005). This turn toward greater opposition mobilization was spurred, in part, by the regime's repressive response to the earlier protests against price increases. In February 1998, Suara Ibu Peduli, a group

---

[49] A *New York Times* article described Habibie as "personifying the kind of crony capitalism and state-directed spending Mr. Suharto had promised to end" (Sanger 1998).

of pro-women activists, defied the military's "Alert-1" warning (*Siaga 1*), which authorized security personnel to shoot demonstrators on the spot, and marched to Bundaran HI in Central Jakarta to criticize the price increases, specifically on powdered milk (Arivia 2007). Protest leaders were subsequently detained, further reinforcing the repressive image of the New Order government and galvanizing the demands for regime change (Aspinall 2005; Budianta 2006). Following the Suara Ibu Peduli protest, students in Yogyakarta, in another public protest, blamed Soeharto for exacerbating the crisis and demanded his resignation, even as the MPR moved to reelect Soeharto for another five-year term. Six students at the University of Gadjah Mada went on a hunger strike, demanding political reforms (Ressa 1998b).

As the protests spread, more public figures began to voice public criticisms of Soeharto and called for political reform, lending greater credibility to the movement. Amien Rais, chairman of Muhammadiyah, became an outspoken opposition voice. In January 1998, he called on the MPR to replace the president with a presidium that would include people representing a broad cross section of society (Aspinall 2005). Given the government's interference in the PDI's internal affairs in 1996 and the subsequent protests and crackdown, Megawati was the default symbol of opposition to Soeharto's coercive rule. Early in 1998, she criticized Soeharto and said she was willing to serve as president (Aspinall 2005). When the government announced price increases on fuel and electricity on May 4, the protests spread to involve non-students, rioting erupted in several cities, and demands for Soeharto's resignation came from even more national figures who had been close allies up to that point, such as ICMI leader Achmad Tirtosudiro, who called for a special session of the MPR. A commission within the DPR called for reversing the price increase (Aspinall 2005).

The momentum for reform took a decisive turn when soldiers killed student protesters at Trisakti University on May 12, 1998. Hundreds of students had been peacefully demonstrating against the price hikes all day and were returning to campus after security officers had prevented them from marching to the Parliament. As they were slowly making their way through the campus gates, shots were fired. The head of the Trisakti University Crisis Center, Adi Andopo Soetjipto, stated that the protesters were "not throwing any rocks and committing any acts of violence" when they "were suddenly shot with sharp bullets, within the campus compounds" (Liputan 6 2013). This shooting led to a public outpouring of grief and support for the student movement. May 12 became a national day of mourning, and the slain students were lauded as "heroes of reform" (*pahlawan reformasi*). Thousands attended the students' burials the following day (Kompas 1998).

Beginning late in the afternoon on May 13 and continuing through the next day, riots erupted almost simultaneously in parts of Jakarta, Medan, Solo, Palembang, Surabaya, and Lampung (Jusuf et al. 2007). Chinese-owned properties were looted, burned, and destroyed, and hundreds of ethnic Chinese were assaulted. A fact-finding team later reported that more than a thousand people died during the riots, and at least 92 women were sexually assaulted in Jakarta, Medan, and Surabaya in the span of two days (Jusuf et al. 2007).[50] Eyewitness accounts described men in military uniforms and boots arriving in trucks and coordinating crowds to attack and loot. Testimonies of rape victims interviewed by the fact-finding team, which was commissioned by the government and composed of members of various government ministries and civil society, further implicated members of the state security apparatus in coordinating, provoking, allowing, and participating in these assaults. In Solo, for example, members of the Special Forces (Kopassus) had arrived as early as 2:00 pm, but remained at the airport for another four hours even as Solo reached its peak of violence (Jusuf et al. 2007).

For months, the government's rhetoric about the financial crisis had become increasingly anti-Chinese. Minister of Home Affairs Syarwan Hamid, for example, attributed the price increase to "rats disloyal to Indonesia" who hoarded goods (Sharma 2003, 157). Thus, when it became clear that riots had occurred practically simultaneously in multiple cities and in a relatively similar fashion, the public began to suspect a deliberate attempt to incite the uprisings (Slater 2010). The killing of university students at Trisakti and the riots that occurred thereafter were politically important because they undermined the regime's projected image as the lone capable enforcer of order. The regime that had legitimated its rule on the grounds of political order and economic prosperity had at best failed to prevent chaos or, at worst, had manipulated violence to lengthen its duration.

After the riots, student demonstrations escalated and demands for Soeharto's resignation came not just from prominent critics of the regime but from his formerly staunch allies. Opposition figures such as Megawati and Amien Rais visited the campus and expressed their

[50] A later study conducted by the Tim Relawan untuk Kemanusiaan Divisi Kekerasan Perempuan reported at least 152 rape victims, 20 of whom died (Yuliawati and Pratiwi 2016).

solidarity with the students. Rais announced the formation of Majelis Amanat Rakyat, which he said was designed to provide "a kind of collective leadership . . . a kind of presidium consisting of all manner of components of the nation."[51] On May 18, 1998, thousands of students arrived in buses and occupied the Parliament complex in Jakarta. On the same day, Golkar chairperson and DPR chairman Harmoko publicly called on the president to step down (Aspinall 2005). To appease these demands, Soeharto appeared on national television on May 19, promising political reforms: "I will not be prepared to be elected any more . . . I have taken the decision as president to implement and lead the national reform immediately" (CNN 1998). The promised reforms included a cabinet reshuffling, new parliamentary elections, and the creation of a reform committee to draft new laws. On May 20, 1998, Harmoko announced that the president had three days to respond before the DPR would initiate the impeachment process. Fourteen cabinet members announced on the same day that they would not join Soeharto's reshuffled cabinet. Nearly 80,000 students had occupied the Parliament grounds throughout the week, receiving broad-based public support (ANTARA 2008).

In contrast to the troops' coercive response at Trisakti one week earlier, this time the military left the students undisturbed, signaling its declining support for Soeharto (Aspinall 2005).[52] On May 21, 1998, Soeharto, flanked by his military chief Wiranto and vice president Habibie, addressed the nation in a televised speech delivered at the Merdeka Palace. Citing "the impossibility of forming the [reform] committee," and taking earnest "consideration [of] the views of the leadership of the People's Consultative Representative Council (Parliament) and the leadership of the factions in it," Soeharto announced that he was stepping down from office and that Habibie would assume the presidency. After more than three decades, his combination of coercion, patronage, and fragmentation of potential challengers to retain power had finally failed him.

---

[51] Quoted in Aspinall (2005, 233).

[52] Many years later, student protesters recalled their fears of a Tiananmen-like suppression (ANTARA 2008; Putra 1998), a concern substantiated by Amien Rais's conversation with members of the armed forces, who informed him that "they were prepared for a 'Tiananmen' solution" (Aspinall 2005, 236). Aspinall observed that military chief Wiranto's refusal to suppress the students' action effectively represented an abandonment of Soeharto, causing the regime to meet its end.

Political Reforms after 1998

The years immediately after Soeharto's resignation were characterized by important political and economic reforms. Of particular interest to this book are the country's electoral reforms and the implementation of a big-bang decentralization that transferred political and fiscal autonomy to districts and municipalities. These reforms not only facilitated genuine political competition but also increased the number of contested seats through the proliferation of administrative units and the implementation of local executive elections. Moreover, they raised the stakes of elections. Whereas voting was essentially performative under the New Order, under *reformasi* and since then, the votes have actually mattered, because democratization meant that voters now had a realistic chance of electing their preferred candidates, with the expectations that elected officials would allocate benefits accordingly.

Electoral reforms in post-Soeharto Indonesia occurred incrementally, through numerous amendments that required debate and negotiation between various stakeholders. Structural changes were made to improve political representation in the legislative bodies. The proportion of elected representatives in the legislature increased gradually until all members were elected by means of an open-list proportional representation (PR) system. In 1999, the size of the Assembly (MPR) was reduced from 1,000 seats to 695, of which 95% were filled by direct or indirect elections (King 2003). The number of seats reserved for appointed military representation was cut in half, from 75 to 38. And in the regional legislatures, military representation dropped from 20% to 10% of the seats (King 2003). By 2004, military appointments to the legislature were completely eliminated and all 550 seats in the Parliament were elected.

To further improve political representation, the Regional Representative Council (Dewan Perwakilan Daerah or DPD) was created in 2004. This council includes four elected representatives from each of Indonesia's provinces (IFES 2014). This body has far more limited powers than the DPR, since it was conceived as an advisory, not a legislative, body.[53] In its early years, members of the DPD included former Golkar affiliates, businesspeople, religious leaders, activists, and academics (Sherlock 2005).

---

[53] The DPD can provide counsel to the DPR on matters regarding regional autonomy, administrative unit creation, natural resource management, and central and regional monetary policy (IFES 2014). It can also propose bills on these matters to the DPR, participate in discussions of bills, and participate in oversight of the implementation of said laws (Sherlock 2005).

Initially, a mixed electoral system was proposed under which 420 of the 495 elected seats in the DPR would be allocated using a plurality system with single-member constituencies, whereas the remaining 75 would be filled using a national-list PR system based on the votes of losing parties (Horowitz 2013). Despite Habibie's support for this proposal, party politicians rebuffed the idea due to fears that they would not be able to compete with Golkar's extensive political machine (Horowitz 2013). Instead, the first post-Soeharto legislative election, in 1999, was conducted using a closed-list proportional representative system at the provincial level, with the additional provision that the specific candidates to receive seats would be determined based on "the relative performance of a party's candidates in each district" (Horowitz 2013, 65–66).

The subsequent legislative elections in 2004, 2009, 2014, and 2019 continued to follow a PR system, though the specifics changed over time. The 2004 legislative election used a more flexible PR system, under which citizens could cast their votes either for a party or for a specific candidate on the list. From 2009 onward, legislative elections used an open-list PR system (Shin 2012). Currently, legislative elections are conducted simultaneously once every five years, as voters elect their representatives for both the Parliament and the provincial and municipal or district assemblies (i.e., the DPR, DPRD Propinsi, and DPRD Kabupaten/Kota), as well as for the DPD. In 2019, the presidential and legislative elections were held on the same day, in a departure from the prior practice under which presidential and legislative elections were a few months apart.

To ensure free and fair elections, the New Order requirement that civil servants must support Golkar was removed. Futhermore, based on Regulation no. 5 of 1999, civil servants who were "members or functionaries of political parties at the moment this regulation takes effect are considered to have relinquished their membership and position."[54] A 2017 regulation, signed by President Joko Widodo, stipulates that civil servants who maintain their roles as party members and functionaries will be dishonorably discharged from their civil service positions.[55] In 2004, when 173 civil servants became party functionaries after the implementation of the government regulations of 1999, 11 were terminated from their civil service positions. Of the 171

---

[54] Peraturan Pemerintah nomor 5/1999, article 7, no. 1, quoted in King (2003), 73. A stricter Peraturan Pemerintah nomor 12/1999 was released soon thereafter. This regulation was later reinforced by Law no. 43/1999 and Regulation no. 11/2017, which ensure the political neutrality of the civil service.

[55] Regulation no. 11/2017, article 255, no. 4, quoted in Afriyadi (2017).

civil servants who ran as legislative candidates in the 2004 legislative elections, 63 were subsequently terminated (Tempo 2004a). In the same vein, active police and military personnel have been forbidden from becoming party members, running as party candidates, and voting in elections since 2004.[56]

Political parties are also now empowered to reflect the ideologies and preferences of their members. In 1999, the DPR passed a law that allowed for the creation of more parties and removed the Soeharto-era requirement that all parties be based on Pancasila (King 2003). This law set relatively easy requirements for a new party to be legally recognized – 50 signatures by citizens over age 21 and registration with a court and the Ministry of Justice – but it requires that political parties must have established offices in nine of the provinces, and in at least half of the municipalities or districts in each of those provinces (King 2003). In a further liberalizing step, this law allowed parties to organize and establish branches all the way down to the village level, and it recognized them as autonomous and free from government interference. This law also limits individual donations to political parties to a maximum of $2,000 per year in US dollars, whereas corporations can donate up to $20,000 per year (King 2003).

In response to these changes, political parties burgeoned after 1998. According to the General Elections Committee, 141 political parties were registered with the Ministry of Law and Human Rights in 1999. Most of these were weak and poorly institutionalized. Tomsa (2014) has shown that most Indonesian political parties lacked enforceable rules and usually had a narrow base of supporters, and that despite the removal of restrictions on political activities below the district level, local party boards are generally inactive outside election cycles. Mietzner (2013) argued that most parties do not even generate enough fees to cover their operations. Only 48 of these parties were eligible to compete in the 1999 election, and of those 48, only 21 managed to place any of their candidates in the DPR (Tan 2015). Tan (2015, 248) observed that many political parties in Indonesia after 1998 were personalistic and patrimonial: "Megawati Soekarnoputri (known as Mother Mega)

---

[56] Despite this requirement and the military and the police reiterating their neutrality in elections regularly (Adri 2018), military presence in politics remains pervasive to this day. Former commander of ABRI, General Wiranto, was a candidate for the 2004 presidential race and a running mate to Jusuf Kalla in the latter's bid for presidency in 2009. He joined Joko Widodo's cabinet in 2016 as coordinating minister for political, legal and security affairs. Prabowo Subianto, Soeharto's son-in-law and former general commander of Indonesia's special force Kopassus, competed in three presidential elections and was appointed as minister of defense for Joko Widodo's cabinet in 2019.

Table 4.3. *Political parties in legislative elections in Indonesia*

Number of political parties	1999	2004	2009	2014	2019
Competed in the DPR election	48	24	38	12	16+
Won more than 5% of total valid votes	5	7	6	10	8 **
Attained seats in the DPR	21	17*	9	12	9

*17 based on actual votes, 16 after the Constitutional Court (MK) settled disputes (Ananta, Arifin, and Suryadinata 2005).
+ 16 national parties competed, plus 4 regional parties compeing in Aceh specifically.
** Parliamentary threshold for 2019 election was 4%. Nine parties attained more than 4% of total valid votes.
Source: General Elections Committee.

is the Partai Demokrasi Indonesia-Perjuangan (PDIP), just as [Partai Demokrat] is known as 'SBY's fan club.' ... What is Gerindra without Prabowo? Hanura without Wiranto?" In her account, only Golkar and PKS were "institutional parties" that "best show professionalization," as demonstrated by their cadre development programs and extensive physical and online organizations outside election cycles (Tan 2015, 249). Table 4.3 shows the fluctuation of the number of parties and their success in gaining representation in the DPR since 1998.

Electoral reform measures also extended to the executive leadership selection process. Whereas during the New Order, elected representatives convened to elect the president, starting in 2004 presidents were directly elected by voters in a majoritarian election. Direct presidential elections in post-Soeharto Indonesia occur every five years, usually in July, three months after legislative elections. To compete in these elections, candidates must be nominated by political parties that gained at least 3% of DPR seats or at least 5% of total votes (Ananta, Arifin, and Suryadinata 2005). This threshold was later adjusted, in 2014, to 25% of votes in legislative elections or 20% of seats in the DPR. Independent candidates cannot enter the direct presidential election without being nominated by a party. Since most political parties cannot meet these support thresholds independently, many have entered into coalitions with other parties to nominate their preferred presidential candidates. If no single candidate and his or her running mate attain an absolute majority of the votes and win at least 20% of votes in over half of the provinces, the two top candidate pairs face each other in a runoff election. Starting in 2014, the Constitutional Court declared that candidates in a two-ticket race must win an absolute majority to win the election.

To date, Indonesian voters have experienced four direct presidential elections. In the first one, in 2004, seven political parties were eligible to nominate candidates, but only five candidate pairs competed in the election.[57] The top-two contenders in the 2004 presidential race were the teams of Megawati and Hasyim Muzadi and Susilo Bambang Yudhoyono and Jusuf Kalla (hereafter SBY-JK). They were narrowly separated by a margin of 7.34% in the first round, but in the runoff SBY-JK received 60.62% of the votes, making SBY the first directly elected president of Indonesia.

In the subsequent presidential elections, the number of candidate pairs dropped to three in 2009 and two in 2014, presumably due in part to the more stringent rules governing parties' ability to nominate candidates. These two elections did not require runoffs. In 2009, incumbent SBY comfortably beat his opponents Megawati and Prabowo, with a large victory margin of 34.01%. The 2014 presidential election was competitive, as Gerindra-backed Prabowo and Hatta Rajasa competed against PDIP's Joko Widodo and Jusuf Kalla; the latter pair won by 6.30%. The same contenders faced each other again in the 2019 presidential election, and Joko Widodo and his running mate, Ma'ruf Amin, defeated Prabowo and his running mate Sandiago Uno by a comfortable margin. Table 4.4 presents basic statistics concerning Indonesia's presidential elections.

Indonesia also implemented drastic changes in the process of selecting provincial, district, and municipal executives. During the New Order period, Soeharto (in consultation with the Ministry of Home Affairs) had appointed all governors, who then appointed district heads (*bupati*) and mayors (*walikota*). These appointees in turn selected the sub district heads (*camat/lurah*) and prescreened and approved the appointments of village heads (Antlov 1994; Tajima, Samphantharak, and Ostwald 2018). Provincial and district executives can serve up to two terms of five years each. After Soeharto's resignation in 1998, local executives partway through their terms were allowed to complete those terms before new elections were conducted. In places where the local executives were nearing the end of their term in 1998, on the other hand, new executives were elected by a majority vote of members of the local legislature, which was itself elected in 1999. Thus, for example,

---

[57] PKS, one of the seven qualified parties, did not submit its own nomination but instead supported PAN's candidate and running mate, Amien Rais and Siswono Yudhohusodo. PKB nominated Abdurrahman Wahid and Marwah Daud, but Wahid failed the Elections Commission's health test and thus could not run (Ananta, Arifin, and Suryadinata 2005).

Table 4.4. *Direct presidential elections in Indonesia*

	2004	2009	2014	2019
Number of candidate pairs	5	3	2	2
Runoff election	Yes	No	No	No
Number of parties eligible to nominate	7	6	10	10
Winning pair	SBY-JK	SBY-Boediono	JW-JK	JW-MA
Winning pair's vote share (%)	60.62*	60.80	53.15	55.32
Margin of votes (%)	21.24*	34.01	6.30	10.64
Winning candidate's party	PD	PD	PDIP	PDIP
Voter turnout (%)	75*	73	70	80

*These data refer to the second-round presidential election. In the first-round presidential election of 2004, the leading candidate pair, SBY and JK, won 33.58% of the vote, and turnout was 78%.
Source: General Elections Committee.

district executives appointed by Soeharto in 1995 were replaced by indirectly elected leaders in 2000; nearly all district executives appointed by Soeharto in 1997 or 1998 did not leave their positions until 2003.[58] Effectively, this arrangement created a semi-exogenously staggered timing of the replacement of local executives through the early years of *reformasi*.

This indirect election of local executives by local legislatures did not last very long, however. In 2005, direct elections of governors, district heads, and mayors began in 226 districts that were due to replace their local executives (Buehler 2016). Law no. 32/2004 on regional government requires that the direct election of local executives, locally known as Pilkada, must follow a plurality system. Law no. 1/2015 sets the electoral threshold for Pilkada elections at 30% of valid votes, calling for a runoff if no candidate meets this threshold.[59] To run in these races, candidates and their running mates originally had to be nominated by political parties that had garnered at least 25% of the votes in the most recent local legislative election or had at least 20% of the seats in the local council. However, the Constitutional Court in 2007 rejected this ban on independent candidates competing in *Pilkada* without party support. This verdict was codified in Law no. 12/2008 on regional government, amending the earlier Law no. 32/2004. According

---

[58] Martinez-Bravo, Mukherjee, and Stegman (2017), appendix A, table S1.
[59] Pilkada elections in Jakarta, the nation's capital, are governed separately under Law no. 29/2007, which requires candidates to attain more than 50% of valid votes to avoid a runoff against the second-place candidate.

to this law, individuals could run as independent candidates as long as they had the support of 3–6.5% of registered voters.[60]

Since 2005, more than 1,200 provinces, districts, and municipalities have held *Pilkada* elections, for an average of about 120 per year across the country (with fewer in the presidential and legislative election years of 2009 and 2014). Starting in 2015, all administrative units due to replace their local executives held their elections on the same day across the country.[61]

These reforms have had significant implications for the political mobilization of Indonesian voters. Because elections are greater in number and much more competitive than during the New Order period, voters actually participate and mobilize. As Table 4.4 showed, turnout in direct presidential elections has been consistently high, especially considering that voting is not compulsory. In the legislative elections of 2009 and 2014, turnout was 71% and 75%, respectively (Aspinall 2014). The 2019 election was the first time the legislative and presidential elections were held simultaneously, and turnout was a record-breaking 80%.

Beyond voter turnout, citizen participation in elections can also be seen in the burgeoning number of candidates competing in elections and individuals participating on campaign "success teams," locally known as *tim sukses*. Members of success teams are responsible for providing information about the candidates to voters in informal settings, organizing events that enable voters to meet candidates, doling out cash to cover voters' transportation expenses, and mobilizing voters on election day. They have become essential parts of candidates' campaigns and a regular feature of Indonesia's elections (Hillman 2017; Aspinall 2014; Simandjuntak 2009). Depending on the size of the district and the candidate's financial resources, success teams are organized in a pattern that mirrors the country's administrative unit hierarchy (i.e., district, subdistrict, village) and can have up to a few thousand members. Although candidates who are also party leaders rely heavily on the party's internal structure to staff their success teams, many candidates also recruit members from outside the party

---

[60] This requirement was later made more stringent in Law no. 8/2015 and Law no. 10/2016, under which aspiring independent candidates must attain the support of at least 6.5–10% of registered voters.

[61] This is described as Pilkada *serentak* or concurrent Pilkada, and it first occurred on December 9, 2015, with 269 elections (9 provincial, 30 mayoral, 224 district) (BBC 2015). The second and third iterations of Pilkada *serentak* were held in February 2017 and June 2018, respectively (ANTARA 2015).

structures (Aspinall 2014). Their profiles vary widely: some success team members are wealthy, landowning financiers who fund the campaign, while others are salaried individuals who coordinate events and run errands (Simandjuntak 2009). This deployment of sizable grassroots campaign teams and their integral role in Indonesia's elections suggests yet another way in which the Indonesian electorate has become far more politically mobilized.

Perhaps the most important indicator of greater citizen participation in politics since Soeharto's ouster is the number of candidates competing in elections. By Aspinall's (2014) count, 180,000 candidates competed for 19,699 seats in the country's national legislature (DPR) and Regional People's Representative Councils in 34 provinces and 491 districts in the 2014 legislative election alone. Toha and Harish (2017) found that the average district election between 2005 and 2013 had five pairs of candidates and running mates vying for the district executive leadership position.

Although these developments have certainly had their own problems – patronage and money politics, the New Order elite's continued presence and control over politics at the national level, and the use of identity politics as a campaign tool among others – they nevertheless suggest a meaningful increase in political participation by citizens in Indonesia.

Conclusion

This chapter has described government measures adopted to manage ethnic loyalties and conflicting ideas of how Indonesia ought to be governed. By focusing on rapid economic development, depoliticizing the masses, and strategically appeasing some groups while repressing others that criticized and posed a threat to the regime, the New Order regime achieved some political stability and apparent intergroup harmony.

These approaches and priorities had implications for the politicization of identity during the New Order regime. First, because voters were depoliticized, Golkar's rival parties were completely weakened, and political mobilization outside election cycles was illegal, those who did not support Soeharto and Golkar had little opportunity to make any demands or claims on the state through formal political means. Those who did articulate their demands and grievances did so by taking to the streets and staging protests on university campuses in the 1970s – an avenue that would also become off limits after Soeharto banned political organizations on campus. Only Golkar was empowered to develop cadres down to the village level, maintain

comprehensive political networks, or construct professional development programs for its members. To carry out any type of political
organization in Soeharto's Indonesia, one had to mobilize within the
permitted confines of the regime, which implied being part of Golkar
and demonstrating overall support for the regime.

From the 1960s through the 1970s, Soeharto surrounded himself
with Western-trained technocrats and nominally Muslim Javanese
military generals. He maintained close ties with a handful of
Chinese Indonesian conglomerates who ran key businesses and became
some of the wealthiest people in the country. Cabinet ministers and
Parliament representatives from this period were frequently Christian,
and for many years no cabinet member was identified specifically as
a representative of Indonesia's devout Muslim communities. Along
with this choice of advisors, Soeharto's policies also earned him a
reputation as anti-Islamic because many of them were perceived as
contradictory to Islam, such as maintaining the policy (an artifact of the
Dutch colonial period) that permitted inter-faith marriages. Soeharto
viewed the extreme left (e.g., communist and PKI sympathizers) and the
extreme right (e.g., observant Muslims, who were labeled as fanatics
and dangerous) as the main enemies of his regime. The politically
favored group during the first half of the New Order regime consisted
of Javanese, nominal Muslims, and Soeharto's allies were Westerners
and ethnic Chinese Indonesians to the extent that they contributed to
Indonesian development and accumulation of capital. On the other
hand, those who claimed to represent political Islam and those with
ties to Soekarno's former secular nationalist PNI party or who had
leftist inclinations, were unwelcome. Those who dared to challenge the
regime directly – the pro-independence fighters in Aceh and Papua –
were met with force and repression.

An important shift occurred in the second half of the New Order,
however. Recognizing that many of his close associates were close to
retirement age, and understanding the potential gains to be achieved by
harnessing Indonesian Muslims' political loyalties, Soeharto began to
accommodate more Muslims in his government and adopted policies
that won him favor among Muslims. Fewer Christians were named
cabinet ministers in this period than during the first half of the New
Order, and the leadership ranks of the armed forces and Golkar
were filled by individuals affiliated with the newly formed Islamic
association, ICMI. From the mid-1980s onward, the New Order regime
appeared much more accommodating of political Islam in Indonesia.

One important implication of these approaches is that the New
Order developed clear ethnic in-groups and out-groups at different

points in time, despite the regime's stated emphasis on inter-ethnic harmony and order, its ban on racially sensitive SARA-related actions and conversations, and its lack of explicitly ethnic political parties.[62] Whichever group Soeharto appeared to favor at a given point in time would have members of their group placed in key positions at all levels of government. This practice would have enormous ramifications in ethnically diverse districts and municipalities, as we will see in the next three chapters.

[62] PPP was the closest thing to an ethnic party under the New Order, because of its appeal to Muslim voters. But because all organizations had to affirm Pancasila as their foundational ideology, PPP (and any other ethnic associations) was prevented from effectively championing the causes and preferences of specific identity groups.

5 Golkar's Dominance and Ethnic Riots

In Chapter 4, I showed that under Soeharto's rule, politicians who did not support him and Golkar faced an uphill battle in getting their demands met, since they were considered potential opponents of the regime. This was particularly true for national-level politicians in Jakarta. At the district level, Golkar's electoral dominance was fueled by a systematic recruiting of local actors who could effectively generate popular support. In ethnically diverse districts, Golkar frequently relied on ethnic and religious networks as both recruitment and mobilization vehicles. Consequently, even though Golkar was not an ethnic party, it targeted constituencies, offered benefits, and excluded people along ethnic lines, just as a explicitly ethnic party would do. As a result, in multiethnic districts, those excluded from Golkar were often members of a minority ethnic group.

In this chapter, I present a quantitative analysis that examines the consequences of such exclusion at the subnational level. My theory predicts that politically excluded actors will tend to mobilize violence during a democratic transition when they perceive that their exclusion is likely to continue under the new regime. As discussed in Chapter 2, political exclusion can take many different forms, among which regime entrenchment is a particularly prevalent one in authoritarian or recently democratized countries. To the extent that candidates and parties associated with the former ruling regime continue to dominate elections even after the democratic transition, those unable to attain electoral success will still feel politically excluded, despite the presence of a macro-level democratic transition. One implication tested in this chapter is that areas where Golkar continued to dominate and where elections remained uncompetitive should have been more prone to ethnic rioting than areas where electoral competition was more intense and Golkar could not assume victory.

Furthermore, if ethnic rioting expresses disappointment over electoral results that signal continued exclusion, a second testable implication is that violence should occur mostly after election results have been announced, rather than before the outcome is known. This implication is the exact opposite of what one would expect if rioting were a strategic campaign tool employed in the run-up to a competitive election. In the latter case, we would expect more rioting just before elections, so as to encourage citizens to vote along ethnic lines.

Third, my theory implies that there should be no association between electoral competition and ethnic riots during the years of Soeharto's authoritarian control, because few would have expected that elections could produce changes in the configuration of power at the local level. Relying on a district-level analysis of Indonesia from 1990 through 2005, I show that districts where Golkar continued to dominate in the first two elections after authoritarian collapse tended to be more riot prone than those where other parties were competitive. My analysis suggests that every percentage point of increase in the competitiveness of elections was associated with a 1% drop in the rate of rioting. Along the same lines, each percentage point of increase in the share of votes captured by Golkar is associated with almost four times more riots. Since ethnic riots are relatively rare events, this effect is substantial.

Empirical Approach and Measurements

To examine these hypotheses statistically, I created an unbalanced panel dataset of districts and municipalities in Indonesia from 1990 through 2005. The analysis was performed at this level of aggregation because the arena of competition of greatest importance for local actors is at the district or municipal level, not the province, subdistrict, or village level (Mancini 2008; Hadiz 2010). Observers had wondered if some provinces would secede after Soeharto's resignation (Emmerson 2000; Rohde 2001), but Jakarta circumvented this possibility by announcing in 1999 a devolution of power under which fiscal and political autonomy would go directly to the districts. As such, local actors knew that district seats would be more politically valuable than provincial ones, because district officers would be receiving sizable revenue transfers from the central government and deciding where the money would go.

I limited my analysis to the period from 1990 through 2005 for both methodological and theoretical reasons. Methodologically, this time range allows for roughly seven years of observations before Soeharto resigned in May 1998 and seven years afterward. This symmetry in the data should capture whatever variation in the degree of violence or political exclusion may exist between the pre- and post-Soeharto years. From a theoretical standpoint, this period encompasses what scholars have identified as Indonesia's years of democratic transition and consolidation, from 1998 to 2004, also referred to as the *Reformasi* period (Tajima 2014). Today, according to most scholarly assessments, Indonesia's democracy is consolidated, despite remaining concerns about its elites' commitment to ensuring the protection of civil rights and the rule of law (Davidson 2009). The total dataset contains 5,371 district-years and does not include districts that seceded and became the independent state of East Timor in 2001.

Measuring Ethnic Riots   To analyze when, where, and why ethnic riots broke out during the country's democratic transition, I use the count of incidents of ethnocommunal violence in districts in a given year as the main outcome of interest. I do not treat ethnic and religious violence as separate categories, so my analysis does not address any differences between religion and ethnicity. In my theory, identity-based groups are considered as networks that can be mobilized to incite violence, and either dimension of identity can function just as effectively as a mobilization tool.

I relied on event-level data collected by Varshney, Tadjoeddin, and Panggabean (2008) and their team of researchers at the United Nations Support for Indonesian Recovery (UNSFIR), who read local newspapers and coded every reported incident of communal violence in fourteen Indonesian provinces from 1990 through 2003. The provinces covered by UNSFIR were Riau, Jakarta, Central Java, West Java, East Java, Banten, Central Kalimantan, West Kalimantan, South Sulawesi, Central Sulawesi, East Nusa Tenggara, West Nusa Tenggara, Maluku, and North Maluku. UNSFIR categorized all reported incidents of communal violence as follows: (1) ethnocommunal (interethnic, inter-religious, and intra-religious); (2) state versus community; (3) economic; or (4) miscellaneous (e.g., lynching, inter-village brawls, election-related clashes, clashes between state agencies, killings of alleged witch doctors, and terrorist violence).[1] Each observation in the dataset comes with a

---

[1] The UNSFIR dataset excludes separatist clashes and crime. Separatist incidents, though a category of collective violence, were excluded because tracking insurgent activities in Aceh and Papua would have posed too great a danger for the research team. Crime was excluded because the dataset does not report violence between two individuals, such as attempted or actual homicide.

description of its trigger event, location, start and end dates, deaths, injuries, and property destruction associated with the event.

Along with UNSFIR, another possible source of data on communal violence in Indonesia is the Village Potential (Potensi Desa, or PODES) surveys collected by the Badan Pusat Statistik. Starting with the 2003 PODES, enumerators asked their respondents, "Has there been any conflict in the village over the past year?" and "If yes, what is the conflict type that has most frequently occurred over the past year?" For the second question, the choices were intergroup fighting, clashes between villagers and security apparatus, student fights, clashes between ethnic groups, and other. These surveys were administered in 60,000 villages during each round and provide fine-grained information on village characteristics. Nevertheless, I did not use this data source for two reasons. First, the questions on communal violence were not asked and reported prior to the 2003 PODES, which means that the years of 1998, 1999, and 2000 and early 2001 were not covered. These are the very years when ethnic rioting increased drastically after the democratic transition began in May 1998. The lack of violence data in these years would severely limit the analysis. Second, the PODES question on types of conflict is unclear and could have been ambiguous for respondents. Given the available options, a typical survey respondent would be hard pressed to determine the proper answer for clashes between religious groups. They could describe such events as intergroup fighting or "other," but they would not describe religious conflicts as occurring between ethnic groups, because in Indonesian the term *ethnic* refers strictly to tribal affiliations (e.g., ethnic Javanese, Sundanese, Bataknese). If they were to answer "intergroup fighting," then their answer would be lumped together with clashes between members of different villages, gang wars, and other kinds of intergroup violence that may or may not have involved ascriptive identities at all. The same lumping would apply if they were to choose "other." For these reasons, I decided to use only the UNSFIR dataset, which coded events based on narrative reports of clashes.

Some limitations of these data must be acknowledged from the outset. First, UNSFIR does not cover provinces, such as Papua and Aceh, where many incidents of violence occurred during the transition years. Because of the exclusion of these provinces, my findings may underreport the true association between political exclusion and violence. Second, UNSFIR data stop at 2003. Although many scholars have used this dataset to make valuable contributions to our understanding of Indonesia's democratic transition, it is unfortunate that the data do not extend for a few more years to provide a fuller picture of violence in Indonesia during the period of democratic transition and before consolidation could emerge.

To address these shortcomings, I sampled Indonesia's national newspaper, *Kompas*, and read every issue of the weekly magazine *Tempo*. *Kompas* provides thorough reporting on important events across the nation (Liddle 1999). Although I would expect *Kompas* to underreport violent events during the New Order, consistent with the regime's desire to project an image of stability, harmony, and order, my primary use of this news source was to capture reports of ethnic riots from 2004 through 2005, after the New Order had collapsed and democracy was well underway.[2] I expected that given the greater freedom of information after Soeharto's ouster, *Kompas* should be a good source of reports on ethnic riots throughout the country in these more recent years.

Prior to its ban in 1994, *Tempo*, a national weekly, had been one of the country's most influential magazines for more than twenty years.[3] It employed rhetorical strategies to reveal the suffering of "victims" of the New Order and thereby to undermine the regime, and it deliberately placed reports on serious incidents in the back of the magazine rather than in the more visible national section to avoid censorship (Steele 2003). The magazine did not resume publication until October 1998, several months after Soeharto had resigned. Assuming that *Tempo* did not change its reporting standards and practices, one can expect the magazine to have reported candidly on conflicts between groups after the New Order had collapsed.

I sampled *Kompas* every eleven days from 1999 through 2005, a sampling interval narrow enough to ensure that any event occurring on the days for which I did not read the papers would be reported on the papers that I did read. Every incident reported to have been triggered by an offense along ethnocommunal lines in the article was coded as an ethnic riot in the dataset for that district-year. For example, an article published in *Kompas* on February 19, 1999, shown below in Figure 5.1, reported that five bombs had exploded in Batumerah and Karangpanjang in Ambon municipality, Maluku, where clashes between Christians and Muslims had erupted from January 19 through

---

[2] According to Steele (2003), news editors during the New Order were frequently warned by government and military officials against releasing reports concerning ethnic, religious, racial, or intergroup issues (popularly expressed in Indonesian by the mnemonic SARA, which stands for "*suku, agama, ras,* and *antar-golongan*"). Varshney, Tadjoeddin, and Panggabean (2008)'s interview of *Kompas* newspaper management confirmed that national media sources were often required to send their reports to the authorities for approval before printing them.

[3] The ban on publication was due to *Tempo*'s cover story on Indonesia's purchase of thirty-nine German warships (McCargo 1999).

Figure 5.1 An example of an article published in *Kompas*, February 19, 1999

January 25. In my dataset, I recorded this event as 1 in my dichotomous variable for ethnic riots, and also as 1 in the counting variable of ethnocommunal riots for Kota Ambon in 1999. The clashes of January 19–25 were inputted as a separate incident of ethnocommunal violence in Ambon. I followed the same procedure in all my review of *Kompas* issues.

I applied a similar approach to my reading of every issue of *Tempo* from January 2002 through December 2005. This period overlaps the UNSFIR dataset by two years and my sampling of *Kompas* by four years. I read *Tempo*'s sections entitled "Cover Story," "National," "Economy," "Law," "Crime," "Environment," and "Events." By reading every issue in my period of observation, I reduced concern for overlooking an event. When entering events reported by *Tempo* into my dataset, I followed the same protocol (described in the Appendix A) employed by Varshney, Tadjoeddin, and Panggabean (2008), recording the event's date, location, type of communal violence, and a summary of the article.

Legend

Riots (% of total)
☐ 0.00–0.00
☐ 0.00–0.60
☐ 0.60–1.79
▨ 1.79–3.87
▧ 3.87–9.97
■ 9.97–49.11

Figure 5.2 Ethnic riots per province, 1990–2005

Second, I further supplemented my analysis with the newly available event-level National Violence Monitoring System (NVMS) data, which record incidents of communal violence reported in local newspapers in Indonesia from 1997 through 2013. Like UNSFIR, NVMS data coverage is not ideal, since the earlier years under Soeharto's rule are not included in the dataset. However, it extends much further into more recent years, enabling analysis of the time period after the consolidation of democracy. Although my main analysis in this chapter relies on the UNSFIR data along with my reading of *Kompas* and *Tempo*, I also present (in the Appendix B) results of regressions using NVMS-based data on ethnic riots, to confirm that my results are not artificially driven by the data sources and coverage.

To measure the frequency of ethnic riots, I constructed a variable to count the occurrence of rioting in every district-year in Indonesia from 1990 through 2005. I also created a variable for the number of deaths associated with a riot. Third, I composed an index variable to capture the severity of violence, ranging from 0 for no incidents of riots in a district-year to 5 where a district-year had more than 500 deaths associated with ethnic rioting. For robustness, I also created a population-weighted variable indicating the number of ethnic riots per 100,000 people in a district-year. Furthermore, I used a dichotomous variable to indicate whether any ethnic riot had occurred in a district-year. In this manner, my analysis tracks whether riots occurred, how many incidents of rioting occurred within a district-year, and the intensity of each event. Using these data, Figures 5.2 and 5.3 depict the spatial and temporal distribution of ethnic riots in Indonesia from 1990 through 2005.

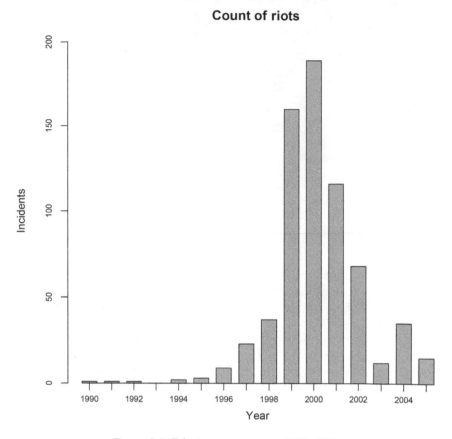

Figure 5.3 Ethnic riots per year, 1990–2005

Figure 5.2 maps the incidents of ethnic rioting that erupted in each province as a proportion of total riots in Indonesia from 1990 through 2005. Although many provinces experienced some violence, only North Maluku, Central Kalimantan, West Kalimantan, and Maluku had more than 3% of all riots in the country, and only Maluku had more than 9.97% of the total. Similarly, according to Varshney, Tadjoeddin, and Panggabean (2008), 85.5% of the riot-related deaths occurred in fifteen districts and municipalities, where only 6.5% of the country's population resided. In other words, though other areas did not completely escape ethnic rioting during Indonesia's democratic transition, most of the fighting was concentrated in a few key areas.

A similar concentration can be observed over time as well. Figure 5.3 shows that rioting increased drastically after 1998, peaked in 2000, and declined steadily thereafter. This variation across time and space is precisely what this book attempts to explain.

Measuring Electoral Competitiveness As noted earlier, a key relationship tested in this chapter is how the perception of continued exclusion correlates with violence during the democratic transition. One way to capture continued political exclusion is to look at the effects of regime entrenchment at the local level on the onset of violence. As a proxy for regime entrenchment, the competitiveness of elections in districts during transition years is a good measure. I use the margin of votes between the winner and runner-up candidates in the district's most recent parliamentary election.[4] From 1977 through 1997, elections were held every five years during Soeharto's rule. Given the time frame of this analysis, the data on electoral competitiveness are based on five elections from 1987 to 2004, with three elections occurring before the country transitioned to democracy in 1998 and two afterward.[5]

In addition to vote margins, I also use the share of votes obtained by Golkar in the most recent election to determine whether challengers faced a significant obstacle in a given district-year. To the extent that Golkar continued to dominate, opposition candidates would interpret this result as continued exclusion. Since a party's decline in popularity does not usually happen overnight, and since local actors would need sufficient information about the political situation to inform their decision whether to riot, I include in my analysis a measure of shifts in Golkar's popularity in the last ten years before 1998. This variable measures the percentage change in Golkar's vote share in the district between the 1987 and 1997 elections.[6] When this measure is negative, it implies that Golkar performed better in 1997 than in 1987 and has thus gained greater support over time. Conversely, a positive value means that Golkar did better in 1987 than in 1997 (just before Soeharto's ouster)

---

[4] Vote margins are coded as follows: $VM_{it} = -1 \times (V1_{it-1} - V2_{it-1})$, where VM_{it} is the vote margin in district i in year t and $V1$ is the vote share of the winner and $V2$ is the vote share of the runner-up in the most recent parliamentary election in the district. I multiply the difference in vote shares between the winner and runner-up candidates by -1 so that larger values of VM_{it} correspond with greater competitiveness.

[5] To compile this data, I photocopied and scanned hard copies of election reports available from the General Elections Committee office in Jakarta, and then inputted the raw data into my dataset manually.

[6] This variable is calculated as: $VSGolkar_i = VSGolkar87_i - VSGolkar97_i$, where $VSGolkar_i$ is the vote share Golkar earned in district i. VSGolkar87 and VSGolkar97 are measures of Golkar's vote share in district i in 1987 and 1997, respectively.

and then lost support over the intervening decade. My theory would predict that districts where support for Golkar waned over time (i.e., where Golkar did better in 1987 than in 1997) would have more riots than districts where support for the party has increased, since waning support would imply that an increasing number of people in the district desired a turnover in political leadership.

If ethnic riots are an expression of protest against continued political exclusion, it should follow that violence would be more likely after an uncompetitive election that signals continued difficulty for challengers aspiring to win office. To determine whether this was actually the case, I include dichotomous variables for an election year, the year before an election, and the year after an election. These variables provide insight into when unrest erupts relative to elections.[7]

Although the dominance of parties and candidates associated with the former authoritarian party is an apt indicator of the electoral challenges that newcomers and opposition candidates may be facing at the onset of democracy, it does not directly capture the political representation of ethnic groups in the districts. Nevertheless, accounts of ethnic elites' cooptation by the New Order regime in ethnically divided districts, as described in Chapter 4, suggest that the distinction between those included and neglected by the New Order regime often fell along ethnic lines.

Controls As described in Chapter 2, a number of other environmental factors may impact the likelihood that ethnic riots will erupt during a political transition. Given my data limitations and the scope of this book, I can account for only some of them: local ethnic composition, prior exposure to violence, and poverty.

The number of ethnic groups in a district and groups' sizes relative to each other can determine the coordination costs and utility of activating ethnic loyalties to mobilize violence along ethnic lines. Among the possible permutations of group compositions in a district, the closer to perfect parity the balance between the largest and second-largest group is, the easier it would be to coordinate and mobilize violence, since very dominant groups would not need to riot and very small ones would expect less payoff from rioting. To control for the effect of local ethnic composition, I created a variable for the ratio of the

---

[7] These measures are coded based on the 1987, 1992, 1997, 1999, 2004, and 2009 parliamentary elections across all districts in Indonesia. The after-election-year variable, for example, assumes the value of 1 for observations in 1993, 1998, 2000, 2005, and 2010, and 0 for other years. The election-year variable is 1 for observations in 1992, 1997, 1999, 2004, and 2009, and 0 for other years.

second-largest group to the largest group in the district. A ratio of one represents perfect parity, whereas a ratio closer to zero signifies greater imbalance between the largest and second-largest groups in a district.

For robustness, I also use several other measures to capture the same concept. In some estimations, I use the difference between the proportion of citizens belonging to the second-largest group and 50%.

In many empirical studies, scholars have used the ethnolinguistic fractionalization (ELF) index as a measure of ethnic diversity.[8] In my robustness checks, I also ran tests using an index for religious and ethnic fractionalization. Since some scholars argue that the fractionalization index has a curvilinear shape, I also included the squared terms of both the religious and ethnic fractionalization indices in my estimations. These measures were calculated from district population data reported in the volumes of the provincial statistical report *Dalam Angka* and in the 2000 census published by the Badan Pusat Statistik.[9]

Earlier research on violence has indicated that prior violence plays an important role in predicting new violence. Prior violence may imply the presence of an abundant supply of fighters ready to be deployed in new clashes (Colombo, D'Aoust, and Sterck 2015). Furthermore, highly violent conflict tends to destroy existing economic and political institutions, thereby lowering the quality of life and potentially increasing the probability of new violence (Collier, Hoeffler, and Soderbom 2008). Beyond enlarging the supply of experienced fighters and weakening institutions, prior incidents of violence can also cement the polarization of ethnic groups and facilitate the onset of new clashes.[10] In my models, I account for the effects of prior violence by creating a one-year lagged variable indicating the number of ethnic riots in the district in the prior year.

The analysis in this chapter focuses on how the exclusion of local elites from politics predicts the onset of ethnic rioting. But elite manipulation is only one part of the causal mechanism, as I have outlined in Chapter 2.

---

[8] The ELF index is constructed based on the Herfindahl concentration index, which is specified as $ELF = 1 - \sum_{i=1}^{N} p_i^2$, where p is the proportion belonging to ethnic group i ($i = 1, 2, \ldots, N$) in a given district-year. A perfectly homogeneous district in which every individual belongs to the same group will have an ELF value of 0, whereas a perfectly ethnically diverse district where every person is from a different ethnic group will have the value of 1.

[9] Because the Indonesian census did not start reporting respondents' tribal affiliation until 2000, my analysis using ethnic fractionalization is limited to observations in the year 2000. The remainder of my estimations rely on religious fractionalization.

[10] In his analysis of Hindu–Muslim violence in South Asia, for example, Brass (1997) has argued that prior riots set in place institutions that perpetually reminded citizens of their ethnic identities and of their difference from other groups.

Elite manipulation of ethnic identities can succeed only to the extent that it effectively rallies individuals to fight. An individual's decision to engage in violence may be driven by many factors, but existing literature has noted that rioters are often unemployed (Becker 1968), poor (Tambiah 1997), or angered by perceived inequality between groups (Tadjoeddin 2013; Mancini 2008). To ensure that these economic variables do not confound my results, I control for logged district GDP per capita, which admittedly is an indirect measure of individuals' disposable income but which, in the aggregate, reflects each district's economic well-being.

State security capacity may also influence whether riots occur (Tajima 2013; Posen 1993). To address this factor, I include a control for district budget spending on security personnel. Adjusted for inflation, the amount of money spent on the salaries of security officers approximately captures the state's capacity to respond to security threats within the district.

I have also added controls for other ecological factors that may be correlated with outbreaks of rioting. Specifically, I include controls for whether a district is urban, logged district population, and district size. Data for these variables are based on the annual provincial *Dalam Angka* volumes.

Regime and regional effects may also be at work in driving levels of ethnic rioting in Indonesia. Authoritarian rule may imply a more capable coercive security capacity that can quickly quell violence before it spreads. Furthermore, under authoritarian rule, news reporting on violence between ethnic groups is usually severely curtailed.[11] Similarly, disparities in development across regions may produce more violence, or they may influence the level of reporting in underdeveloped areas. Infrastructure developments in Java, for example, exceed those on the outer islands (Schwarz 1999; Hadiz 2010). For these reasons, I created binary variables to indicate whether a particular observation took place under Soeharto's authoritarian rule and whether it was located in Java.

To account for any further unobservable district characteristics that may be driving violence, I also use fixed effects in my estimations.

Summary statistics for all the variables in my models are presented in Table B.1 in Appendix B.

---

[11] Former president Soeharto frequently boasted that Indonesia was an orderly, peaceful, and prosperous nation despite its ethnic and religious diversity (Liddle 1999). Reports of skirmishes between groups would have undermined this narrative and were therefore discouraged.

Modeling Choices

My main estimations are based on negative binomial regressions with panel-corrected standard errors. Incidents of violence are rarely independent of each other; ethnic riots in one place can spread to neighboring areas, and prior violence may leave behind such horrible consequences as to foster additional outbreaks in subsequent years (Selway and Templeman 2012). The temporal and spatial distributions portrayed in Figures 5.2 and 5.3 suggest that some element of spatial and temporal dependence was at work, because riots were predominantly concentrated in the years following Soeharto's ouster in 1998 and in a few pockets of Indonesia. Since these events were potentially correlated with each other, a Poisson model that assumes the independence of individual events would not be appropriate for estimating the level of rioting during Indonesia's transition (King 1998). A negative binomial distribution, which relaxes the assumption of independence, is more appropriate for my purposes.[12]

To ensure that my results are not driven by these modeling choices, I also ran my analysis with other models, using alternative dependent variables. I used ordinary least squares (OLS) and Poisson models on the count of ethnic riots, to demonstrate that my main results are not sensitive to modeling choices. In addition, I ran a Firth logit model with a binary dependent variable indicating whether a riot occurred in a given district-year. In this way, I overcome the small sample bias that results from the relative rarity of violence (Williams 2016).[13] I also ran additional estimations with alternative dependent variables: the number of riots per 100,000 people and the index for severity of violence.

Results

The results presented in Table 5.1 confirm the theory's predictions.[14] In columns 1–3, I show the coefficients of negative binomial estimations of the effects of electoral competitiveness on the number of ethnic riots

---

[12] In an earlier work, I included a test of goodness of fit between Poisson, negative binomial, zero-inflated Poisson, and zero-inflated negative binomial models and showed that the negative binomial estimations performed better (Toha 2017).

[13] An alternative approach is to use a rare event logit as proposed by King and Zeng (2001).

[14] This table reports results of estimations using the dataset with missing values. The parentheses show panel-corrected standard errors estimated using Stata's "xtnbreg" command with fixed-effects estimator. I have imputed missing values using Amelia 2 and found that the Amelia-imputed results do not differ meaningfully from those presented in Table 5.1.

Table 5.1. *Electoral competition and ethnic riots*

	DV: Count of ethnic riots				
	Full sample	Full sample	Full sample	New order	Post-Soeharto
Electoral competitiveness	−0.011^			−0.078	−0.013^
	(0.006)			(0.068)	(0.007)
Year after election	0.805***	0.851***	0.659*	2.477***	0.783**
	(0.209)	(0.212)	(0.268)	(0.679)	(0.286)
Golkar vote share		1.577*			
		(0.615)			
% change in Golkar vote share from 1987 to 1997 elections			0.113^		
			(0.060)		
Ratio of second to largest group	✓	✓	✓	✓	✓
Count of riots in prior year	✓	✓	✓	✓	✓
Security expenses	✓	✓	✓	✓	✓
Logged GDP per capita	✓	✓	✓	✓	✓
Logged population	✓	✓	✓	✓	✓
Logged area	✓	✓	✓	✓	✓
Urban dummy	✓	✓	✓	✓	✓
Post-Soeharto dummy	✓	✓	✓		
Fixed effects	✓	✓	✓	✓	✓
Observations	488	488	260	101	225
AIC	491.642	489.115	345.444	74.208	312.670
Log likelihood	−234.821	−233.558	−161.722	−27.104	−146.335

Notes: Dependent variable is count of ethnic riots. Results reported in columns 1–3 are from negative binomial regressions with panel-corrected standard errors. Column 4 reports results of estimation using only pre-1999 observations, whereas column 5 reports results using only post-Soeharto observations. Papua and Aceh observations were excluded from all estimations. ^$p < 0.10$, *$p < 0.05$, **$p < 0.01$, ***$p < 0.001$.

in district-years in Indonesia from 1990 through 2005. These results demonstrate that districts with more competitive elections tended to have fewer outbreaks of ethnic riots. Accounting for other factors that may influence levels of ethnic rioting, the models show that districts with wider electoral margins had higher counts of ethnic riots. The incidence rate ratio (IRR) of the coefficient of the margin of votes suggests that for every 1% increase in competitiveness, the number of riots drops by 1%.[15] In other words, the closer an election was, the less likely it was that a riot would occur in the district. Estimates using alternative measures of ethnic rioting (riot-related deaths or the severity of violence) yielded similar results. Riots claimed far more lives and were more intense when the most recent election in the district was uncompetitive.

The variable of Golkar vote share captures the amount of support for Golkar in the district, and by implication, how difficult it would be for opposition challengers to win. Based on this variable's IRR, the model predicts that a 1% increase in support for Golkar would generate almost four times as many more expected riots in a district while all other variables in the model are held constant.[16]

In Table 5.2, I substitute other parties' vote shares for Golkar's vote share to check whether districts where Partai Demokrasi Indonesia-Perjuangan (PDIP), the perceived opposition party during Soeharto's New Order regime, was dominant tended to have fewer conflicts. Consistent with the theory, I find that districts where PDIP earned a greater percentage of votes had much less violence. The harder it was for non-Golkar candidates to win in district elections, the more violence erupted.

Support for Islamic parties during transition years was positively associated with rioting, although the relationship did not attain the conventional threshold of statistical significance. The combined vote share of all parties other than Golkar in the district's most recent election was associated with a drop in ethnic rioting. The IRR of non-Golkar parties' vote share was 0.21, which suggests that every 1% increase in the combined vote share of parties other than Golkar was associated with a decline by a factor of 0.21 in the expected number of ethnic riots in the district, with all other variables in the model held constant.[17]

The results show some support for the idea that waning Golkar popularity in the years immediately before Soeharto's ouster signaled growing local aspirations for breaking through the barriers to entry. In districts where support for Golkar declined over the last decade prior to 1998, there was more violence than in those where support for Golkar remained stable or increased.

---

[15] The IRRs associated with every variable in columns 1 through 3 are shown in Table B.3 in Appendix B.
[16] See the IRR for the Golkar vote share coefficient in column 2 of Table B.3 in the Appendix B.
[17] The IRRs associated with these estimations are shown in Table B.6 in Appendix B.

Table 5.2. *Party vote shares and rioting*

	DV: Count of ethnic riots			
	(1)	(2)	(3)	(4)
PDI-P vote share	−1.941**	−1.483^		
	(0.678)	(0.757)		
Year after election	0.712***	0.794***	0.793***	0.851***
	(0.199)	(0.209)	(0.210)	(0.212)
Islamic party vote shares (PPP, PKS, PBR, PBB)			0.879	
			(1.497)	
Combined vote share of non-Golkar parties				−1.577*
				(0.615)
Ratio of second to largest group	✓	✓	✓	✓
Count of riots in prior year	✓	✓	✓	✓
Security expenses	✓	✓	✓	✓
Logged GDP per capita	✓	✓	✓	✓
Logged population	✓	✓	✓	✓
Logged area	✓	✓	✓	✓
Urban dummy	✓	✓	✓	✓
Post-Soeharto dummy	✓	✓	✓	✓
Java dummy	✓			
Fixed effects		✓	✓	✓
Observations	1,898	488	488	488
AIC	1027.151	491.645	494.952	489.115
Log likelihood	−499.575	−234.823	−236.476	−233.558

Notes: Dependent variable is count of ethnic riots. Papua and Aceh observations were excluded from all estimations. $^p < 0.10$, $*p < 0.05$, $**p < 0.01$, $***p < 0.001$.

Another implication of my theory is that there should be more violence after uncompetitive elections, since violence serves more as a channel of expressing protest over continued exclusion than as a strategic tool during the preelection campaign period. The results confirm this prediction by showing that years after elections had more clashes than other years.[18]

My theory also predicts that electoral competitiveness should have had no effect on rioting prior to 1998, since there was minimal

---

[18] The IRR for the year-after-election dummy variable in column 1 of Table B.3 implies that the rate of violence was 1.2 times higher in years following an election than in other years.

opportunity to alter the configuration of power under authoritarian rule. Instead, the effects of electoral competitiveness on ethnic rioting should be visible only after 1998, when greater political inclusion became a more achievable goal. Similarly, Golkar's vote share and year-after-election variables should have no relationship with ethnic rioting prior to 1999.

To examine these predictions, I split the sample between pre- and post-democratic transition periods and ran the same analyses. Before Indonesia's transition, the electoral vote margin had no effect on ethnic rioting.[19] The year-after-election dummy variables in columns 4 and 5 are both significant regardless of whether the estimations are done on only New Order observations or only post-Soeharto observations. To consider why this might be the case, note that the year-after-election dummy variable is 1 for district-years in years 1993, 1998, 2000, 2005, and 2010. For the pre-1999 sample, this dummy variable is 1 for district-years that occur in 1993 and 1998. The statistical significance of the year-after-election dummy for the pre-1999 sample is largely driven by the year 1998, since Soeharto resigned in that year and violence was widespread. In separate estimations, I substituted the year-after-election dummy variable with a dummy for the year 1998 to confirm that, indeed, the statistical correlation in the pre-1999 sample is substantially due to violence in 1998. This result is shown in Table B.5 in Appendix B.

Taken together, the results indicate that politically uncompetitive districts where Golkar dominated tended to be more riotous than other districts during Indonesia's democratic transition. This relationship remains robust even after one accounts for the effects of prior violence, ethnic diversity, and poverty, as well as the effects of being outside Java, in a city, and under authoritarian rule. There is also considerable evidence that rioting was more common one year after elections than in other years. This correlation provides support for my argument that ethnic rioting in Indonesia was not generally a campaign tool that politicians use to impact election results, but primarily an angry reaction to perceived barriers to entry that challengers faced during democratic transition.

---

[19] The size of the coefficient of the vote margin in the pre-1999 district regression, shown in column 4 of Table 5.1, is larger than that for the post-1998 regression shown in column 5, but it does not attain the conventional threshold of statistical significance.

Robustness Checks

These results could conceivably be attributable to alternative explanations that would produce similar outcomes, or the associations could be artifacts of modeling choices. To address these possibilities, I took additional steps to check for robustness. First, I checked whether the main results were sensitive to estimation strategies, measures, and sample subsets. To ensure that my results are not dependent on the model specification, I ran the same analysis using OLS and Poisson regressions, both with the same dependent variable of count of ethnic riots and with alternative measures for the dependent variable. In Table B.4 in Appendix B, I show the results of estimations with OLS and Poisson models of the count of ethnic riots in district-years in Indonesia from 1990 through 2005. These results are consistent with the main findings presented in Table 5.1 earlier.

In Table 5.3, I show the results of estimations using alternative measures of ethnic rioting: a binary variable for whether violence occurred, the count of riot-related casualties, the severity of violence index, and the number of riots per 100,000 residents from 1990 through 2005. When using these alternative dependent variables, I can run my estimations using ordinal logit and OLS estimations and demonstrate that my results are not sensitive to the negative binomial model specification.

The OLS results confirm the previously stated findings. The coefficients for electoral competitiveness in columns 4 and 6 are significant at the $p < 0.10$ level and are negative, indicating that greater competition is associated with less violence and fewer deaths per incident. As with electoral competitiveness, the variable for a district's support for Golkar in the prior election yields a similar result in OLS as in negative binomial estimations. Support for Golkar in the previous election is associated with an increase in both the number of riots per 100,000 people and the number of riot-related deaths. The coefficient for Golkar's vote share in column 5 suggests that every 1% increase in this variable is associated with 21 more deaths per incident in a district-year. Similar results appear in ordinal logit estimations, which find that severe rioting was more likely to occur in districts with lower electoral competitiveness and greater support for Golkar.

Next, I show the results of estimations using alternative measures of ethnic diversity. Table 5.4 presents results when the estimations use religious fractionalization and its squared term, the difference between the second-largest group proportion of the population and 0.5, and ethnic (tribal or *suku*) fractionalization. The association between

Table 5.3. Robustness: alternative dependent variables

	DV: Riots dummy			DV: Riots-related deaths		DV: Riots per 100,000 people		DV: Severity of violence		
	(1)	(2)	(3)	(4)	(5)	(6)	(7)	(8)	(9)	(10)
Electoral competitiveness	-0.010* (0.004)			-0.146* (0.072)		-0.002* (0.001)		-0.010* (0.004)		
Year after election	0.705** (0.222)	0.778*** (0.226)	0.332 (0.300)	-0.143 (3.081)	0.255 (3.085)	0.014 (0.051)	0.021 (0.051)	0.689** (0.222)	0.762*** (0.225)	0.286 (0.293)
Golkar vote share		1.595** (0.513)			21.405** (7.921)		0.331* (0.131)		1.608** (0.517)	
% change in Golkar vote share from 1987 to 1997 elections			0.052*** (0.015)							0.047*** (0.014)
Ratio of second to largest group	✓	✓	✓	✓	✓	✓	✓	✓	✓	✓
Count of riots in prior year	✓	✓	✓	✓	✓	✓	✓	✓	✓	✓
Security expenses	✓	✓	✓	✓	✓	✓	✓	✓	✓	✓
Logged GDP per capita	✓	✓	✓	✓	✓	✓	✓	✓	✓	✓
Logged population	✓	✓	✓	✓	✓	✓	✓	✓	✓	✓
Logged area	✓	✓	✓	✓	✓	✓	✓	✓	✓	✓
Urban dummy	✓	✓	✓	✓	✓	✓	✓	✓	✓	✓
Java dummy	✓	✓	✓	✓	✓	✓	✓	✓	✓	✓
Post-Soeharto dummy	✓	✓	✓	✓	✓	✓	✓	✓	✓	✓
Fixed effects	✓	✓	✓	✓	✓	✓	✓	✓	✓	✓
Observations	1,898	1,898	1,043	1,898	1,898	1,898	1,898	1,898	1,898	1,043
AIC	671.081	676.586	435.972	19906.736	19902.311	4328.639	4325.478	982.901	978.443	701.343
Log likelihood	-323.541	-326.293	-205.986	-9943.368	-9941.406	-2155.320	-2153.739	-475.451	-473.221	-334.672

Notes: Models 1–3 are Firth logit estimations. Models 4–7 are OLS with panel-corrected standard errors. Models 8–10 use ordinal logit estimations. Papua and Aceh observations were excluded from all estimations. $^{+}p < 0.10$, $^{*}p < 0.05$, $^{**}p < 0.01$, $^{***}p < 0.001$.

Table 5.4. *Robustness: alternative ethnic diversity measures*

	DV: Count of ethnic riots				
	(1)	(2)	(3)	(4)	(5)
Electoral competitiveness	−0.011*	−0.011^	−0.011^	−0.012	−0.012
	(0.006)	(0.006)	(0.006)	(0.014)	(0.013)
Year after election	0.811***	0.817***	0.799***		
	(0.210)	(0.210)	(0.209)		
Religious fractionalization	−0.009	−3.822			
	(1.406)	(4.345)			
Religious fractionalization squared		5.899			
		(6.348)			
Difference between Group 2's proportion and 0.5			1.107		
			(1.855)		
Ethnic fractionalization				2.182*	4.334
				(1.100)	(3.586)
Ethnic fractionalization squared					−2.584
					(4.078)
Count of riots in prior year	✓	✓	✓	✓	✓
Security expenses	✓	✓	✓	✓	✓
Logged GDP per capita	✓	✓	✓	✓	✓
Logged population	✓	✓	✓	✓	✓
Logged area	✓	✓	✓	✓	✓
Urban dummy	✓	✓	✓	✓	✓
Post-Soeharto dummy	✓	✓	✓		
Fixed effects	✓	✓	✓		
Observations	488	488	488	275	275
AIC	491.737	492.869	491.377	221.899	223.494
Log likelihood	−234.869	−234.434	−234.689	−99.949	−99.747

Notes: Results are based on negative binominal regressions with panel-corrected standard errors. Models 4 and 5 do not use fixed effects because data for ethnic fractionalization are derived only from the 2000 census. Papua and Aceh observations were excluded from all estimations. ^$p < 0.10$, *$p < 0.05$, **$p < 0.01$, *** $p < 0.001$.

electoral competitiveness and ethnic riots remains robust regardless of which ethnic diversity measure is used. As columns 4 and 5 show, the coefficients for electoral competitiveness are not statistically significant when ethnic diversity is measured in terms of ethnic (i.e., tribal or *suku*) fractionalization. Although this particular finding contradicts earlier results, it is based on an estimation with only 275 observations, because data for ethnic fractionalization came only from the 2000 census. The other models shown in Table 5.4 confirm my main result.

Since the additional sources of data (*Tempo* magazine and the *Kompas* newspaper) used to extend the violence data to 2005 may differ systematically in their reporting practices, biases, and standards, it is plausible that the results of estimations using data from these additional sources may be skewed by differences in reporting practices. To check for this possibility, I ran separate regressions using only NVMS-based conflict data and UNSFIR-based conflict data. Because the NVMS dataset coverage ranges from 1997 through 2012, my estimations using NVMS data would overrepresent observations from the post-Soeharto years, and underrepresent those from before democratic transition. The reverse is true for UNSFIR-based data, which cover communal events reported in local newspapers from 1990 through 2003.

Table 5.5 presents the results of regressions with observations based on UNSFIR data, on a variety of dependent variables and model estimations.

The vote margin variable is not statistically significant in these estimations, although the variable for the vote share won by Golkar is. The period covered by UNSFIR data ranges from 1990 through 2003, thereby providing vote margins for three elections under the New Order regime (1987, 1992, 1997) and one election afterward (1999). As established earlier, the competitiveness of elections under the New Order regime was not expected to have any effect on ethnic rioting. Only post-Soeharto elections should show this relationship. But the fact that the UNSFIR data cover only one round of elections after the beginning of the democratic transition could explain the lack of statistical significance. That the Golkar vote share variable remains statistically significant despite the smaller number of observations and elections included in the data is consistent with the findings presented in Table 5.1.

Using NVMS-based conflict data from 1997 through 2012, the variable for Golkar's vote share in the district's most recent election is positively associated with the count of ethnic riots, even after controlling for a host of possible correlates (see Table B.7 in Appendix B). This finding is consistent with my main results. The coefficients for the vote margins

Table 5.5. *Robustness: only UNSFIR-based data*

	DV: Count of ethnic riots			DV: Riots per 100,000 people		DV: Riots dummy			DV: Severity of violence		
	(1)	(2)	(3)	(4)	(5)	(6)	(7)	(8)	(9)	(10)	(11)
Electoral competitiveness	−0.010			−0.004*		−0.006			−0.005		
	(0.006)			(0.002)		(0.005)			(0.005)		
Year after election	0.819***	0.873***	0.632*	0.020	0.035	0.860***	0.901***	0.509	0.812***	0.851***	0.423
	(0.217)	(0.221)	(0.269)	(0.084)	(0.085)	(0.242)	(0.244)	(0.330)	(0.240)	(0.242)	(0.321)
Golkar vote share		1.611^			0.561*		1.145^			1.114^	
		(0.682)			(0.245)		(0.651)			(0.656)	
Δ Golkar vote share from 1987 to 1997			0.113^					0.021			0.011
			(0.060)					(0.019)			(0.018)
Ratio of second to largest group	✓	✓	✓	✓	✓	✓	✓	✓	✓	✓	✓
Count of riots in prior year	✓	✓	✓	✓	✓	✓	✓	✓	✓	✓	✓
Security expenses	✓	✓	✓	✓	✓	✓	✓	✓	✓	✓	✓
Logged GDP per capita	✓	✓	✓	✓	✓	✓	✓	✓	✓	✓	✓
Logged population	✓	✓	✓	✓	✓	✓	✓	✓	✓	✓	✓
Logged area	✓	✓	✓	✓	✓	✓	✓	✓	✓	✓	✓
Urban dummy	✓	✓	✓	✓	✓	✓	✓	✓	✓	✓	✓
Java dummy	✓	✓	✓	✓	✓	✓	✓	✓	✓	✓	✓
Post-Soeharto dummy	✓	✓	✓	✓	✓	✓	✓	✓	✓	✓	✓
Fixed effects	✓	✓	✓	✓	✓	✓	✓	✓	✓	✓	✓
Observations	395	395	192	1118	1118	1118	1118	608	1118	1118	608
AIC	433.464	430.634	294.557	3121.681	3119.990	491.754	499.798	308.690	785.268	783.451	554.062
Log likelihood	−205.732	−204.317	−136.279	−1551.840	−1550.995	−233.877	−237.899	−142.345	−376.634	−375.725	−261.031

Notes: Results reported in columns 1–3 are from negative binomial regressions with panel-corrected standard errors. Columns 4–5 report OLS results with panel-corrected standard errors; whereas columns 6–8 report results using Firth logit. Columns 9–11 are results of ordinal logit estimations. Papua and Aceh observations were excluded from all estimations. ^p < 0.10, *p < 0.05, **p < 0.01, ***p < 0.001.

variable, on the other hand, lose their statistical significance and change signs depending on whether the estimation was using a negative binomial (column 2 in Table B.7 in Appendix B) or an OLS (column 4) model.

Conclusion

This chapter has examined some of the observable implications of my theory of ethnic rioting, as developed in earlier chapters, by testing them against available data. Relying on subnational data on districts in Indonesia from 1990 through 2005, along with data collected from my review of *Tempo* and *Kompas*, I have shown that districts where regime entrenchment and electoral barriers to entry remained after democratic transition were more prone to outbreaks of ethnic violence. Specifically, I have demonstrated that every 1% increase in Golkar's vote shares in the district was associated with almost four times as much violence, after controlling for a variety of other correlates. Furthermore, districts with uncompetitive elections were associated with more violence than those where the vote margin was not as wide. In terms of the sequence of events, riots tended to follow rather than to precede elections, lending support to the notion that ethnic rioting was an expression of frustration over election results, not a strategic campaign tool designed to cause voters to vote along ethnic lines.

Although these findings support the notion that uncompetitive areas are more prone to rioting during a democratic transition, the link between lack of competition, Golkar dominance, and ethnic political exclusion at the district level is much less direct. Golkar's vote share and vote margin effectively capture the theoretical construct of regime entrenchment, but they say little about ethnic political configurations at the district level, since neither Golkar nor its counterparts were ethnic parties. Without a measure of ethnic political configurations at the district level, the theory that political exclusion of ethnic elites drives violence would need support from other sources of information.

Accordingly, in Chapter 6, I turn from broad patterns and associations between Golkar dominance and riots, as unearthed by statistical tests, to my case studies conducted in the provinces of Maluku and Central Sulawesi. I will trace the development of conflict in two pairs of cities, seeking to determine whether individuals engaged in rioting around the time of democratic transition were more likely to be representatives or leaders of ethnic communities. I also consider whether Jakarta's disregard of their demands was a motivating factor in their rioting and whether violence ended once the previously excluded groups saw members of their ethnic group elected to executive positions.

6   Micro Dynamics of Exclusion and Riots

We have seen that continued regime entrenchment and opposition candidates' difficulty in winning elections tended to go hand in hand with violent mobilization during Indonesia's democratic transition. Why this association exists, however, remains unclear. My central argument is that local elites claiming to represent the majority of the district's population mobilize violence when they feel threatened. To properly identify the mechanism that may link political exclusion and violence, I need finer-grained data than those presented in Chapter 5.

In this chapter, to explore the mechanisms that underlie this broad pattern, I trace the development of conflicts in Ambon and Maluku Tenggara, Maluku province and in Poso and Banggai, Central Sulawesi province. I compare the local political configuration of ethnic groups across the four districts, identify which groups were politically excluded or included, and trace how disgruntled local elites used existing ethnic or religious identities to manipulate violence. Although all four districts are diverse along ethnic and religious lines and are located in outer island provinces with relatively similar levels of development, only Ambon and Poso experienced high levels of violence, whereas Banggai and Maluku Tenggara had minor skirmishes that quickly dissipated.

My interview data demonstrate that local elites were involved in shaping the narrative and in mobilizing and coordinating violence in Ambon and Poso, and that many of these individuals were also closely connected with local ethnic institutions and networks. In Maluku Tenggara and Banggai, on the other hand, skirmishes and triggering events did not escalate into widespread ethnocommunal rioting as they did in Ambon and Poso. One key reason is that in Maluku Tenggara and Banggai, local ethnic and religious leaders were more concerned with using their influence to quell violence and to rally for alternative causes. The contrasting experiences of these four communities provide further evidence that local elites' political interests influence whether existing identities become weaponized during a democratic transition.

I begin this chapter by discussing the cases, methodological approach, and limitations of my fieldwork. Then, after a brief overview of the Central Sulawesi and Maluku political landscape, I examine the four specific cases. Each case study scrutinizes voters' initial political preferences based on Indonesia's first democratic election in 1955, the political configuration of the district at the time of democratic transition, and local elites' actions during the conflict. I conclude by considering the implications of these four case studies for the dynamics of political exclusion, local elite grievances, and the production of violence during a democratic transition.

Case Selection and Methodological Approach

Case Selection

To identify the mechanism that links political exclusion to levels of rioting, I selected districts that are relatively similar in terms of ethnic and religious diversity, geographical proximity to Jakarta, and degree of economic development but vary with regard to the main dependent and independent variables in my study. In this way, I can effectively control for other factors that may also be driving violence by keeping them constant across the different units. Ambon and Poso experienced some of the greatest and longest-lasting violence between Christians and Muslims during Indonesia's democratic transition. Their neighboring districts, Maluku Tenggara and Banggai, remained relatively quiescent by comparison.

All four districts are located on Indonesia's outer islands and are geographically distant from Jakarta, so they could be expected to suffer from comparably poor security capacity and response during a political transition. All four districts' GDPs rely heavily on the agricultural sector, with the result that jobs in the state bureaucracy may promise greater upward mobility than other forms of employment. The districts are also religiously and ethnically diverse, with presumably similar exposure to the problems that accompany diversity.

For the purpose of drawing inferences, the four cases I study in this chapter should ideally be similar along more dimensions that could influence the onset of riots between Christians and Muslims so I could truly isolate the effects of local elites' desire to enter politics. For example, the strength of individuals' loyalties to other identity-based communities may condition the effects of local elites' efforts to mobilize violence along religious lines (Laitin 1986). In the context of these specific districts in this chapter, it is entirely plausible that individuals in some of the units had much stronger ties to their tribal or ethnic communities and did not view their religious ties as politically relevant. In such a setting, the demographic balance between religious groups, political configuration between religious communities, and local elites' mobilization efforts may not work as well. Furthermore, new research on ethnic rioting has also highlighted the importance of social networks in influencing individuals' decision to participate in violence (Scacco 2010). These factors, however, are not easily detectable and evaluated *ex ante*, based on secondary sources prior to my commencing my fieldwork. To the best of my knowledge, there were no existing studies or data that reported the strength of individuals' attachment to ethnic versus religious communities at the district or municipal level at the time. Similarly, to my knowledge there was no available study that compared the density of social networks and communities' abilities to informally regulate their members' behaviors in terms of participating in riots across districts and municipalities in Indonesia at the time.

Without hard data that I can rely on to select my cases and to control for variation along these factors, I rely on a next-best strategy, which is to select administrative units that appear equally likely to have residents with a strong or stronger attachments to alternative identity-based communities. In Ambon, ethnic Ambonese were roughly evenly split between Christians and Muslims, which means that Ambonese Christians and Muslims can bridge the religious divide and identify solely on the basis of their shared ethnic Ambon identity. Muslims in Ambon were also comprised of other ethnic groups, such as ethnic Bugis, Makassar, and Buton migrants from South Sulawesi. This also implies that Muslims in Ambon could view initial triggers as primarily assaults on migrant ethnic groups, not on Muslims in Ambon more broadly. In Maluku Tenggara, a majority of the population identified as ethnic Kei, even as they were evenly divided between Muslims, Catholics, and Protestants. The 2000 census reported that approximately 25% of the population in Maluku Tenggara were ethnic Aru (who were also predominantly Christian), and about 1% Javanese. Since both the majority local ethnic groups in both Ambon and Maluku Tenggara were relatively evenly divided between Christians and Muslims, I am assuming that in both Ambon and Maluku Tenggara, residents could have strong attachments to their ethnic communities, relative to their religious groups. In Poso, many Muslims are ethnically Tojo, Bungku, Gorontalo, and Buginese, whereas the Christians are ethnic Pamona. Unlike in Ambon and Maluku Tenggara, in Poso there was not much cross-cutting between the religious and ethnic groupings. The Pamonas were almost exclusively Protestants, whereas ethnic Tojos and Bungkus

Table 6.1. *Poso and Banggai in numbers*

	Poso	Banggai	Central Sulawesi
Demography			
% of Muslim population in 2000	56	75.9	78.4
% of Christian population in 2000	40.2	16.2	17.2
Religious fractionalization	0.53	0.39	0.36
Population in 2000	186,414	270,728	2,012,393
Christian–Muslim riots (1998–2012)			
Incidents	307	7	499
Deaths	553	0	625
Injuries	446	2	900
Economy			
GDP per capita in 2000	1.71	2.36	4.18
% of GDP from agriculture in 2000	42.76	50.87	38
% poor in 1999	31.22	32.44	24.88*

Notes: Religious fractionalization was calculated using the Herfindahl–Taylor index, as described in my analysis in Chapter 5. GDP figures are in million rupiah, excluding oil and gas revenues, in constant prices.

* The poverty rate figure for Central Sulawesi was from 2002, since the Indonesia Database for Policy and Economic Research (DAPOER) did not report earlier figures.

Sources: Violence data are based on National Violence Monitoring System (NVMS); economy-related data are based on DAPOER; demography data came from the 2000 census.

were typically Muslim.[1] Similarly, in Banggai district, ethnic Banggai were consistently Muslim. This implies that at least in the Banggai–Poso comparison, I cannot rule out based on the selection of cases the influence of attachments to alternative groups, and I would need to pay careful attention to whether strength of attachments to alternative groups may also be driving the mobilization of violence.

The balance between the Christian and Muslim population in Poso in 2000 was even greater than that in Banggai for the same year (see Table 6.1). Approximately 40% of Poso's population was Christian in 2000, while 56% was Muslim. In Banggai, 16% of the population was Christian and 75% was Muslim. In Maluku, Maluku Tenggara was 61% Christian and 38% Muslim, whereas Ambon was 73% Christian and 26% Muslim (see Table 6.7).

Ideally, I would have liked to select cases that were more similar in their Christian–Muslim balance. Given the differences in composition

[1] Aragon (2007, 50) observed that the ethnic Tojo group is a relatively new construct. In the 1980s, the Tojo were still subsumed within the broader ethnic Pamona group.

between the two populations in Banggai and Poso, one could claim that Banggai had less violence than Poso because of its smaller percentage of Christians while in Poso Christians represented almost half the population. Helpfully, however, the differences in demographic balance between districts run in the opposite direction in Maluku, where Ambon (the district with more rioting) had a less evenly split population than Maluku Tenggara. If demographic balance had been the primary determinant of violence in these districts, Maluku Tenggara should have had more violence than Ambon. The fact that the Poso–Banggai pair exhibited violence in the more evenly split district, but the Ambon–Maluku Tenggara pair did not, suggests that other factors were more influential in producing ethnic riots.

Diversity alone does not automatically predict violence during a democratic transition. Instead, the important considerations are whether the differences between groups are politicized by the exclusion of groups from local political positions, and whether excluded elites manipulate loyalties to provoke violence as a way to articulate their demand for greater inclusion in politics. Helpfully, between the two more evenly split districts (Poso and Maluku Tenggara), only Poso had excluded ethnic elites and higher levels of violence. Between the two less evenly balanced districts (Banggai and Ambon), Ambon had these two features and Banggai did not. Because of this distribution of features, the paired comparisons between Maluku Tenggara and Ambon and between Banggai and Poso allow us to identify the mechanisms linking political exclusion and levels of violence.

Another important aspect of the cases examined in this chapter is that the clashes that erupted in Maluku and Central Sulawesi provinces pitted two religious groups, Christians and Muslims. Even though in both Maluku and Central Sulawesi, violence could have mobilized groups along ethnic lines, and in the case of Ambon early clashes had ethnic undertones (Schulze 2017), the framing of the violence in the two provinces was mostly religious, not ethnic (Al Qurtuby 2016). The selection of cases examined in this chapter that involved only religious violence could be seen as problematic in view of the possible differences in determinants, processes, and outcomes between the politicization of ethnic and religious identity. For instance, the arrival of external militias to aid fellow co-religionists in Poso presumably would not have happened had the clashes been framed as Tojo-versus-Pamona riots. However, as discussed in Chapter 2, my theory treats the various dimensions of ascriptive identity (religion, ethnicity, tribe, and race) as essentially the same; they are affiliations that can be mobilized for political purposes, and their members' loyalty to and affection for their group wax and wane depending on the context. For the purpose of identifying the mechanisms linking political exclusion, the politicization of identity, and the mobilization of violence – my goal in this chapter – I believe that this assumption is appropriate. It makes little difference whether locally excluded groups were defined along ethnic or religious lines, as long as some groups were excluded and local elites mobilized group loyalties to provoke violence.

Furthermore, the alternative approach of comparing pairs of cases where one pair had religiously motivated conflict and the other involved ethnic-based clashes could introduce an additional confounding factor. By focusing only on clashes between religious groups, I can control for differences that may exist between the two types of appeals and associated politicization processes.

The main variation between the four districts, aside from their level of violence, concerned which dimension of identity (i.e., ethnic or religious) was politicized in 1998 and the local elites' responses to trigger events. Therefore, Ambon, Maluku Tenggara, Poso, and Banggai serve as excellent cases for examining my theory.

Methodological Approach

My task in this chapter is to consider whether a link exists between the exclusion of local ethnic groups and the excluded elites' mobilization of violence. To this end, as explained in this section, I evaluated the degree of exclusion of local ethnic groups, local elites' coordination and mobilization of violence, and subsequent outbursts of violence in each case. Some methodological questions arise here: How could I determine which groups were excluded and which were not in each district? And how should I discern whether local elites in a given district deliberately manipulated identity loyalties to provoke violence?

To identify which groups were excluded in each district, I used three types of information. The first was the size of ethnic groups relative to each other. For each administrative unit, I compiled the names and relative sizes of ethnic and religious groups at the time of Indonesia's democratic transition. I assumed that disgruntled local elites would turn to ethnic networks to the extent that these networks existed within their districts, and if they believed that mobilizing said networks would have a reasonable chance of success. A relatively small minority group would not be viable as a vehicle for political mobilization. Conversely, a numerically dominant group should not need to use violence to articulate its demands because it is well represented already. I assumed that if a group constituted at least 10% of the district's total population, it had the capacity to coordinate activities aimed at achieving greater ethnic representation in local politics. If there was a sizable ethnic group in the district that consistently lacked political representation, I interpreted this situation as an indicator of local political exclusion.

The second information source used to identify whether groups were excluded in the district was the (mis)match between voters' expressed preferences for ethnic parties and the New Order district leaders' identity affiliations. Since the New Order regime took great pains to ensure that Golkar was electorally dominant (as explained in Chapter 4), and because Islamist parties in the New Order and post-Soeharto years were the closest thing to ethnic parties in Indonesia, I looked at the district-level vote results in the 1955 parliamentary election as an indicator of voters' initial political preferences regarding ethnic representation in politics. The 1955 election was the country's first national democratic election, and at least 30 political parties (including ethnic ones) and independent candidates competed for voters' support (King 2003, 16).[2] Where the 1955 election results indicate popular support for ethnic parties, I interpret this result as indicating that voters in these districts wanted greater ethnic representation in politics in their districts. To the extent that the affiliations of local political leaders (e.g., district chiefs/mayors and vice regents/vice mayors, council chairs and vice chairs, and secretaries) in the New Order mirrored the popularity of ethnic parties in the district in the 1955 elections, this result would imply that ethnic groups within the district were politically included. If, on the other hand, the 1955 election results in a district showed a strong support for ethnic parties and yet subsequent local leaders in the district did not come from the ethnic parties popular in that district, this would mean that voter preferences in that district were not well accommodated in local politics during the Soeharto era and that local elites claiming to represent this particular ethnic group may have been disgruntled at the time of Indonesia's democratic transition.

This strategy of relying on the 1955 election results as an indicator of voters' early preferences has obvious limitations. Many who voted in 1998 were not voters in 1955. Even without population influxes due to both migration and natural causes, the voters who supported ethnic parties in 1955 may have had vastly different preferences in 1998. As detailed below, the districts examined in this chapter have received a large number of migrants from other parts of Indonesia, and these

[2] In 1955, voters elected 260 representatives to Parliament on September 29 and 520 members of the Constituent Assembly on December 15 (Feith 1962).

newcomers' political preferences may not be consistent with those of the districts' local residents. Although some scholars have noted important similarities and continuities between the 1955 and 1999 election results in Indonesia (King 2003, 133–134), the large time gap between the two elections makes noteworthy differences inevitable.

Another important limitation is the scarcity of ethnic parties that championed tribal or ethnic causes in 1955. Although many political parties competed in that year, the seven highest-ranking parties in terms of total vote share were the secular-nationalist Partai Nasional Indonesia (PNI); Islamist parties Masyumi, Nahdlatul Ulama (NU), and Partai Sarekat Islam Indonesia (PSII); the communist party PKI; and Christian parties Parkindo and Partai Katolik (Feith 1962, 122–142). There were local ethnic parties in some districts, such as the United Dayak Party (Partai Persatuan Dayak) in West Kalimantan, the Sunda Election Movement (Gerakan Pilihan Sunda) in West Java, and Gerinda in Yogyakarta, along with smaller parties that appealed to specific identity-based groups such as the Consultative Council on Indonesian Citizenship (Badan Permusyawaratan Kewarganegaraan Indonesia, or Baperki) for Indonesians of Chinese descent,[3] but most of these gained little electoral support (Hillman 2012).[4] As for the ethnic groups in Ambon, Maluku Tenggara, Banggai, and Poso, no explicitly ethnic Pamonese, Ambonese, or Buginese political party competed in 1955. If religion was the only dimension of identity to be politicized in the districts examined here, this list of political parties competing in 1955 is not problematic. But if ethnicity or tribe were the politicized dimension of identity in the district, then the vote shares of religiously based parties in 1955 would not reveal much information about voters' early political preferences (since no tribe-based parties were marketing themselves directly to the specific ethnic groups in the districts) and voters from one ethnic group may support different religious-based parties depending on their affiliations. Despite these limitations, I chose to use the 1955 election results to indicate voters' likely preferences and demands for ethnic representation in politics because, to my knowledge, alternative information directly measuring voters' preferences for ethnic representation during Soeharto's rule and shortly after 1998 does not exist.

---

[3] Baperki, though a separate organization, was considered closely affiliated with the communist party PKI (Cribb and Coppel 2009). Baperki claimed to have 250,000 members shortly before the anti-communist coup.

[4] Of the parties mentioned here, the United Dayak Party, Baperki, and Gerinda each attained one seat in the Parliament (Feith 1962, 435).

The third source of information about political exclusion in each district was my interviewees' comments. I paid particular attention to how they described the clashes (if any) that occurred in their districts, the ethnic and religious groups in their districts, and their district's politics. To the extent that the interviewees mentioned particular groups in their descriptions of local politics, I considered these groups politically relevant. If a group was never mentioned by any interviewee, I concluded that it was not politically relevant. Explicit comments (presented in subsequent sections of this chapter) about groups' resentment of their lack of access to political and economic resources were interpreted as a sign of those groups' exclusion from politics.

To identify which groups were *not* politically excluded, I listened for the specific ways in which my interviewees described their local leaders. Did they depict the district chiefs or mayors in terms of their religion, ethnicity, or neither? As I show in this chapter, in Ambon and Poso incumbents and contenders for district political posts were frequently described by their religious affiliation. In Banggai and Maluku Tenggara, on the other hand, my interviewees explicitly described their district chiefs in terms of their ethnic Banggai/Kei identity. I interpreted this finding as indicating that, in the latter two districts, ethnic identity was more politically important than religious identity and that the ethnic Banggai group was not politically excluded.

To evaluate the role of local elites in framing, mobilizing, and coordinating violence, I relied on my interviewees' descriptions of clashes and the roles that various people played in them. I supplemented the informants' comments with existing rich accounts from other scholars, NGO reports, and newspaper articles. Where specific individuals (or organizations) were described in these accounts as funding, recruiting, providing information to, coordinating deployment of, and giving shelter to fighters, I concluded that the relevant individuals and the groups they represented were actively engaged in mobilizing and escalating violence. Using the same sources, I also took note of individuals, groups, and organizations who were leading initiatives to reduce the violence and restore communication between groups, communities, and neighborhoods, and I interpreted these behaviors as indicators of groups' attempts to reduce violence.

I conducted my interviews in two waves. While working for the Social Development Unit at the World Bank's Jakarta office in 2003 and 2004, I interviewed more than fifty individuals in Ambon and Maluku Tenggara in Maluku, and in Palu and Poso in Central Sulawesi. These early interviews provided useful background and gave me initial contacts for my dissertation fieldwork, which I conducted in stages from February through December 2009.

To reach my interviewees, I used the snowball sampling technique. I began by approaching development workers and NGO activists who were working and living in each town. I also sought out community leaders – youth, religious, traditional, ethnic, and party leaders – in each province, as well as government bureaucrats and conflict participants from each of the two warring factions. Since the riots in Maluku and Central Sulawesi pitted Christians against Muslims, I spoke with a roughly equal number of community leaders on each side. My interviews were open ended, lasting anywhere from thirty minutes to three hours. All interviews were conducted in Bahasa Indonesia, without the aid of a translator since both my interviewees and I were fluent in that language. The interview locations were selected by the interviewees, and included public spaces (e.g., coffee shops or small kiosks), as well as private homes and offices.

My interview questions primarily aimed to obtain the interviewees' perception of how and why violence occurred, the relevant community leaders within the district, the roles of various parties involved, and how the violence impacted their lives. In reconstructing and presenting what I learned, I have narrowed my analysis to events during the early stages of violence – between late 1998 and early 2001 – that other observers considered ethnocommunal. The latter years of violence – from 2002 onwards – in both Ambon and Poso involved external militias and saw forms of violent activity (e.g., terrorist attacks) that were not ethnocommunal and that lie outside the scope of this research.

Some limitations must be acknowledged, starting with my positioning as a researcher conducting interviews in a post-conflict setting. As others have noted, researchers' gender, race, ethnicity, sexual orientation, class, and suggested preferences can affect their research in a variety of ways (Guillemin and Gillam 2004). In my fieldwork, I was introduced and accompanied by local contacts who were themselves well connected and respected in the community by virtue of their development and/or advocacy work. My face and manner of speech betray my Indonesian, and specifically Jakarta, background. This impression granted me insider access to some extent, since some interviewees assumed that they would not have to explain the broader Indonesian political context and that I would understand their expressions, spoken and otherwise. My respondents were mostly generous, comfortable, and eager to share their stories and time with me. A few did ask why I was interested in asking such questions or what my own religious and ethnic affiliations were, and two inquired whether I had any ties with the US government once they learned that I was a PhD candidate at an American research university. Though none explicitly expressed suspicion or withdrew from the conversation, these questions indicated some measure of discomfort or at least curiosity that may have shaped their interactions with me.

The second limitation concerns the large time gap between the riots and my interviews. By the time I arrived in 2003, and certainly in 2009, the clashes had occurred many years ago. Many of the conflict participants had fled, and in 2009 the country was in the throes of elections and the creation of new administrative units (colloquially termed *pemekaran*). This coincidence may have been particularly relevant for my conversations in Banggai, where most of the people I interviewed were primarily concerned about the ongoing issue of district splintering and the location of the new district's capital. For this reason, I supplemented and cross-checked my interviews with secondary sources written by those who either were present or had conducted and finished their fieldwork much closer to the actual time of the riots.

The third limitation revolves around the limits of using individuals' affiliation as an indicator of representation and inclusion. This chapter presents evidence of group political representation, based on available information about the religious affiliations of individuals in key executive positions in the districts. This approach risks lumping people into analytical categories, flattening the diversity of attachments and experiences of individuals that may overlap and cut across group boundaries, and assuming that mere affiliation with a group implies overall support for the group's interests and concerns. A more fine-grained picture of a group's political inclusion in local politics would include details on the kinds of policies, decisions, and groups that were championed during a person's tenure in office. Although I was able to incorporate this discussion in some cases for political figures in more recent years, I was not able to do this across the board.

Central Sulawesi Province

Today, Central Sulawesi is one of six provinces in Sulawesi, a vast and mountainous K-shaped island between Kalimantan and the Moluccas. In 1945, when Soekarno and Hatta proclaimed the country's independence, all of Sulawesi was one large province. In 1960, it was split into three provinces: North, Central, and South Sulawesi. In 1963, Southeast Sulawesi splintered from South Sulawesi to become a separate province. More recently, the provinces of Gorontalo and West Sulawesi were created in 2000 and 2004, respectively. Throughout the New Order, Central Sulawesi had five districts and municipalities, until new administrative units were formed after 1998.[5] When Soeharto resigned in 1998, Central Sulawesi had slightly more than two million people, or approximately 1% of the country's total population of 205 million.[6] The province's GDP per capita in 1998 was around four million rupiah, and approximately 24% of its population lived below the poverty line as of 2002.[7] Central Sulawesi's main revenue source was the agricultural sector, which exported palm oil, copra, cloves, and cacao (Hasurullah 2009). In 1997, shortly before ethnocommunal violence erupted in Central Sulawesi, the agricultural sector contributed 38% of the province's overall regional GDP.[8] Other services, the hotel and restaurant sector, and the construction sector were the next-largest contributors, whereas mining ranked second from the bottom as of 1997.[9] In 1998, 41.21% of the province's population had access to clean water and 61.96% to electricity, and 27% of eligible youth were enrolled in senior secondary schools.

The province is considerably diverse along ethnic and religious lines. Though historically Muslims have remained mostly along the coasts and Christians in the interior, the development of the Trans-Sulawesi highway, the government's migration program, and the appointment of civil servants have led to greater Muslim migration into the province's interior areas (Aragon 2007). According to the 2000 census, the ethnic groups in the province included the Kaili (20.5%), Bugis (14.39%), Javanese (8.25%), Banggai (5.43%), Buol (4.53%), Balinese (4.4%), and a combination of miscellaneous groups (34.37%).[10] In terms of religious composition, Central Sulawesi was predominantly Muslim (78%), with 16% Christians, 3.8% Hindus, and 0.2% Buddhists.[11] Compared to its overwhelmingly Muslim neighboring provinces, Gorontalo

---

[5] Poso, Banggai, Donggala, Buol Toli-Toli, and Kota Palu were the administrative units in this province throughout Soeharto's rule.

[6] Data come from the World Bank and the Indonesia Database for Policy and Economic Research (DAPOER) for 1998

[7] The GDP per capita figure is based on constant prices, inclusive of oil and gas revenues.

[8] This figure was calculated based on Central Sulawesi's GDP excluding oil and gas, in constant prices in millions of rupiah, as reported in DAPOER.

[9] Mining and quarrying represented 2.1% of the province's GDP (excluding oil and gas) in 1997, whereas other services contributed 16.9%, the trade, hotel and restaurant sector contributed 13.6%, and construction 8.1% in 1997. This ranking of sectors in their contribution to the province's GDP has remained relatively consistent, based on the figures reported in DAPOER in 2012.

[10] The 2000 census was the first one since the colonial count in 1930, in which respondents were asked to identify their ethnic/tribal affiliations. Prior censuses during the New Order did not report population breakdown by ethnic or tribal affiliations.

[11] These data also came from the 2000 census.

(97% Muslim) to the north and South Sulawesi (89%) to the south, Central Sulawesi has a more religiously mixed population.[12]

Like most of Indonesia during the New Order, Central Sulawesi had relatively few reported incidents of ethnocommunal rioting. Although skirmishes between youths, students, and villagers occurred, they never escalated to the point of widespread clashes that claimed hundreds of lives.[13] During the country's democratic transition, however, Central Sulawesi became a site of severe, long-running conflict. According to the National Violence Monitoring System (NVMS) data, 5,847 incidents of ethnocommunal rioting erupted in Central Sulawesi between 1998 and 2012. These clashes led to 1,297 fatalities (Barron, Jaffrey, and Varshney 2016). These numbers place Central Sulawesi among "high-conflict" provinces, alongside West Kalimantan, Central Kalimantan, Maluku, North Maluku, Aceh, Papua, and West Papua (Barron, Jaffrey, and Varshney 2016, 196, 216) (Figure 6.1).

Despite the staggeringly high number of clashes in Central Sulawesi province overall, there was considerable variation across its districts. According to NVMS reports of ethnocommunal incidents from 1998 through 2007, Poso had by far the highest number with 268 incidents, followed by Palu with 51 and Morowali and Parigi Moutong with 16 each. The rest of the province either remained peaceful or had very few violent incidents. When one considers the casualty figures, the concentration of violence within a narrow area becomes even more obvious, as 538 of 599 deaths reported in Central Sulawesi from 1998 through 2007 occurred in Poso. No other district had more than 17 deaths during that time period, and four districts (i.e., Banggai Kepulauan, Banggai, Toli-Toli, and Buol) had no reported casualties due to ethnocommunal violence.

Given this wide variation in levels of violence during Indonesia's democratic transition, I selected Poso and Banggai as my two primary fieldwork sites in Central Sulawesi. The two districts are relatively similar in geographical terrain, demographic composition, and economy. Before the splintering of new districts from Poso in 1999 and 2003,

---

[12] The population breakdown for South Sulawesi was based on the 2000 census; data for the religious composition of the Gorontalo province came from the 2010 census since the 2000 census did not report figures for this newly created province.

[13] In 1988, a fight between a Christian Toraja police officer and Muslim Bugis vendors erupted at a market in Palu. The police officer stepped on a Quran, angering Muslims in the community. That same night, a church was burned down. Life returned to normal the following day (Aragon 2000). In 1995, a brawl erupted between Christian youths from Madale and Muslim youths from Tegalrejo in Poso, leading to the burning of one house in Madale. This clash was quelled quickly without any further escalation (Lasahido et al. 2003, 40).

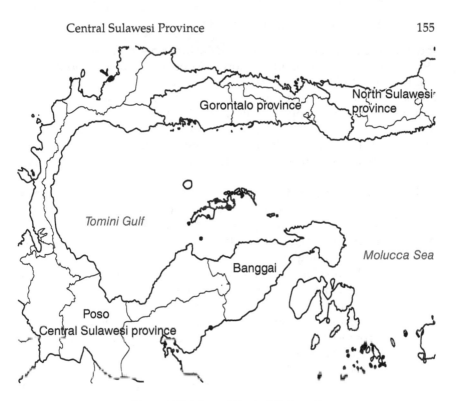

Figure 6.1 Map of Central Sulawesi

Poso and Banggai were neighbors.[14] Both districts rely on agriculture, have hilly and mountainous topographies with access to bodies of water, and are similarly religiously diverse. Table 6.1 showcases these comparisons. Despite these similarities, Poso was a hotbed of violence during Indonesia's democratic transition, while Banggai was peaceful. In the following sections, I compare these two cases to highlight the importance of local ethnic elites' accommodation or exclusion from politics in accounting for the diverging patterns of violence during the country's democratic transition.

District 1: Poso

The first case, Poso in Central Sulawesi, was an instance of rioting prompted by local elites' politicization of communal loyalties. Before

---

[14] Morowali split from Poso and became a new district in 1999; Tojo Una-Una followed suit in 2003.

the first eruption of the Christian–Muslim riots there in December 1998, Poso was a town of little renown. Approximately a six-hour drive from Central Sulawesi's capital Palu, Poso is a regency at the mouth of the Tomini gulf. It had an area of over 28,000 square kilometers and a population of approximately 400,000 before losing parts of its territory when Morowali, and then Tojo Una-Una, broke away. Poso's main claims to fame were its being a midway point between South and North Sulawesi provinces and a large producer of ebony (KONTRAS 2004).

Religious and ethnic diversity predated the establishment of Poso as an administrative unit, and even the establishment of Central Sulawesi province and the independent state of Indonesia. Poso's coastal population reportedly embraced Islam as early as the sixteenth century, when the coastal Bungku fiefdom was part of the Ternate sultanate in North Maluku (Mahid, Saliadi, and Darsono 2012).[15] Islam spread along the coasts, in part thanks to the efforts of a Hadrami cleric, Idrus bin Salim Al-Juffrie, who founded Al Khaerat, which became the largest Islamic organization in eastern Indonesia, boasting 18 million members across 12 provinces (Tempo 2010). The nearby hinterlands, on the other hand, did not embrace world religions until Dutch missionaries arrived and established a post in Poso in 1892 (Van Randwijck 1981). Tentena, a town near the Poso lake, became the site of one of the largest Christian churches in Central Sulawesi, Gereja Kristen Sulawesi Tengah (GKST).

The overall Poso population composition shifted with the influx of migrants from South Sulawesi, Java, Bali, and North Sulawesi over the course of the New Order regime, with the most drastic change occurring in some Christian-majority subdistricts in the highlands.[16] Ethnically, Poso residents are divided between the To Pamona, To Mori, To Napu, To Behoa, and To Bada in the highlands who are predominantly Christian, and the To Ampana and To Bungku along the coasts who are predominantly Muslim (KONTRAS 2004).

The Local Political Configuration in Poso In Indonesia's first democratic election in 1955, Poso voters displayed a very strong preference for religious parties. In the 1955 constitutional assembly election, Islamist parties PSII, NU, and Masyumi won 61% of all votes, while the Christian party Parkindo received 25% (PemiluAsia 2018).

---

[15] Since 2000, Bungku has been in Morowali district.
[16] Pamona Selatan, for example, saw an increase in its Muslim population, from 3.44% of the subdistrict's total population in 1972 to 22.87% of the total population in 1996 (KONTRAS 2004).

Table 6.2. *Soeharto-era party vote shares for local council (DPRD II) elections in Poso, Central Sulawesi (1971–1997)*

Election	PPP	Golkar	PDI	Non-Golkar (combined)
1971	n/a	90.40	n/a	9.60
1982	7.02	92.35	0.63	7.65
1987	4.45	94.32	1.22	5.68
1992	6.16	86.80	7.04	13.20
1997	6.78	87.93	5.29	12.07

Notes: Figures are in percentages (%). In 1971, PPP and PDI were not yet created. Instead nine other parties competed alongside Golkar. These parties' vote shares are reflected in the "Non-Golkar (combined)" column. *Source:* Adapted from Haliadi (2004, 84–93).

The same parties won almost exactly the same vote shares in the legislative election that same year (61% and 26%, respectively).

This initial preference, however, was not reflected in elections under the New Order. In the first New Order election in 1971, in which ten parties competed, 90% of the votes went to Golkar, while PSII, NU, and Masyumi combined to win only 7.2%. The Catholic party and Parkindo together received just 2.04% (Hering and Willis 1973). In every New Order election since 1971, Golkar won more than 80% of the votes in Poso; its main opponents, PPP and PDI, together never claimed more than 15%. Table 6.2 reports the vote shares of Golkar and other parties in district council (DPRD II) elections in Poso from 1971 through 1997.

These vote results enabled Golkar and military representatives to dominate the local legislatures in Poso. Golkar representatives occupied more than 70% of seats in local councils during Soeharto's rule, while appointed military representatives held an average of 17% of the seats.[17]

Golkar's dominance carried implications for the representation of religious groups in important government posts. In the early years, Golkar selected more council members and chairs who identified as Protestant. After 1971, however, Golkar stocked the councils with more Muslim representatives, averaging about 54% Muslim to 45% Christian representatives.[18] This pattern was also mirrored in Golkar's selection of council chairs in Poso, as shown in Table 6.3.

---

[17] These figures are based on the number of seats allotted to each party in the Poso local assemblies in 1971, 1982, 1992, and 1997, as reported in Haliadi (2004, 84–96).

[18] I calculated these averages based on the numbers of Poso local council representatives by religious affiliation, as reported by Haliadi (2004).

Table 6.3. *Chairs of regional councils (DPRD) in Poso,*
Central Sulawesi (1961–1999)

Election	Name	Party	Religion
1961	B. L. Sallata	PNI	Protestant
1964	J. M. Lengkong	Golkar-military	Protestant
1971	J. M. Lengkong	Golkar-military	Protestant
1977	Roessali	Golkar-military	Muslim
1982	Roessali	Golkar-military	Muslim
1987	Said Fuady	Golkar-military	Muslim
1990	Miradj Safa	Golkar-military	Muslim
1997	Mulyadi	Golkar-military	Unknown
1999	Akram Kamaruddin	Golkar	Muslim

Note: In Haliadi's 2004 report, B. L. Sallata was listed as "ex-officio" but
Aditjondro (2001) documented that Sallata was a PNI politician.
Source: Haliadi (2004, 196–205).

Other than the assembly chairs and members, the most important
posts in Poso were in the executive branch. District regents, secretaries,
and heads of planning wielded considerable influence over civil service
hiring; the allocation of development contracts, licenses, and permits;
and the delivery of public services. Consequently, these positions
were highly coveted, and Poso residents paid close attention to which
communities were represented.

A recurring theme I heard in my interviews in Poso and Palu was
that elites' struggle for local government posts influenced the riots in
Poso in the late 1990s and early 2000s. One person who had remained in
Palu throughout the conflict described it as "essentially an elite conflict,
fought by ordinary people who had their private grievances that they
had suppressed for a long time."[19]

A Poso-based NGO activist specifically pointed to a growing perception of unfairness in the allocation of posts between Christians and
Muslims in Poso as a sore point:

Poso is very old, at least 100 years old. We never had violence of this scale.
But our political composition really did shift drastically recently. During the
Dutch rule, Poso was 70% Christian and 30% Muslim. More recently, Muslims
are playing greater roles in politics while Christians are not. In Poso, we have
a "power-sharing" agreement. When the regent is Muslim, then the vice regent

[19] Interviewee 2, journalist, April 5, 2009.

Table 6.4. *Soeharto-era district chiefs in Poso, Central Sulawesi (1967–1998)*

Name	Term	Religion	Military?	Born in C. Sulawesi?
Ghalib Lasahido	1967–1973	Muslim	Yes	Yes
R. P. M. Koeswandi	1973–1984	Protestant	Yes	No
Soegiono	1984–1988	Unknown	Yes	No
J. W. Sarapang	1988–1989	Protestant	No	No
Arief Patanga	1989–1995	Muslim	No	Yes
Arief Patanga	1995–1999	Muslim	No	Yes

Notes: Italicized names are caretaker, interim district chiefs. Military affiliations are identified based on the use of military titles in secondary sources.

Sources: The list of district chief names is based on the Poso district government website. See www.posokab.go.id/sejarah-kabupaten-poso/. Religious, military, and party affiliations of the chiefs from 1973 through 2005 are based on Aditjondro (2004).

or the district secretary would be Christian. This has gone on for many years. This was how we maintained balance.[20]

Beyond this agreed-upon sharing of power between Christians and Muslims, several people referred to an implicit rotation agreement, under which Christians and Muslims took turns placing their co-religionists in the main executive leadership position.[21] Table 6.4 demonstrates some rotation of representation between Muslim and Christian communities in the first few rounds of district chief appointments.

The first district chief appointed by Soeharto, Ghalib Lasahido, was a Muslim of Una-Una descent who served as *bupati* for six years. R. P. M. Koeswandi, a Protestant Javanese, succeeded him and was district chief of Poso for more than ten years, followed by Soegiono, another outsider, who served until 1988.[22]

The configuration of local leaders in Poso had a tangible impact on ordinary Poso residents, especially during Arief Patanga's term. An ethnic Tojo Muslim and head of the Poso branch of Ikatan Cendekiawan Muslim se-Indonesia (ICMI), Patanga was an affiliate

---

[20] Interviewee 13, NGO activist, April 6, 2009.

[21] Interviewee 7, journalist, November 13, 2009.

[22] The claim of a power-sharing arrangement between district chiefs and secretaries in the earlier years is harder to verify, however. I do not have access to the full list of Poso district secretaries over the years, and could compile only the most recent ones (i.e., from 1990 onwards). More recent district secretaries have generally had religious affiliations different from those of the district chiefs. van Klinken (2005, 84) argued that this was in fact a recent practice that began in Arief Patanga's term.

of Muhammadiyah. Accordingly, his rise to district leadership was emblematic of the Muslim political ascendancy in Poso, and of the decline of Protestant influence in politics. His affiliations with ICMI, Muhammadiyah, and Golkar meant that he had the "winning political package of the late 1980s and 1990s," as ICMI and modernist Muslims affiliated with Muhammadiyah were generally on the rise in Soeharto's government in these later years (Aragon 2007, 52). The fact that Patanga allegedly had bribed various people within the provincial bureaucracy to support his nomination did not help the situation.

According to Christian sources, Patanga received the governor's blessing only with the explicit instruction that he must "groom a would-be successor from the Christian community" (Aditjondro 2004, 17). During his term as district chief, Patanga installed his family members in strategic government posts and amassed great wealth.[23] He and his relatives exercised considerable control over district government resources and doled them out to people within their networks.

One Muslim NGO worker emphasized the importance of local elites' dissatisfaction with Patanga as follows:

Patanga had ruled for two terms already. This had clear repercussions for the local economic distribution. Only people of a certain religious background enjoyed the economic distribution. Power sharing did not work; only people close to Patanga could enjoy the economic sharing that came from proximity to the ruler.[24]

When Soeharto resigned in May 1998, Patanga was near the end of his term. Anticipation of his departure raised speculations as to who would succeed him. For disgruntled Poso residents, Soeharto's departure, the overall regime change, and the advent of new procedures for selecting local leaders presented an opportunity to correct the perceived injustices.

A Muslim religious leader in Palu drew a direct link between Poso elites' electoral interests and the riots:

Golkar had enjoyed a clear single majority before *reformasi*. Then, when the system changed and it was clear that there would be an indirect election, both Christians and Muslims in Poso began to prepare their desired candidates. For Poso Christians, it was clear that Patanga's successor would have to be a Christian. But suddenly, Golkar dropped in a candidate whom neither the

---

[23] His wife, Rahmah Patanga-Patilewa, was deputy secretary and then promoted to head of the Civil Service Corps in Poso, in charge of hiring, promotion, and firing civil servants in Poso. His brother, Agfar Patanga, became head of district construction (Aragon 2007, 52–54).
[24] Interviewee 13, NGO activist, April 5, 2009.

Christians nor the Muslims in Poso liked. This was Golkar's big blunder, and it alienated a lot of people. Abdul Muin Pusadan, this dropped-in candidate, was Muslim. According to the power sharing agreement, his vice regent and/or secretary should have been a Christian. But to make matters worse, he picked an Arab Muslim as his secretary. The chair of the local council, was also Muslim! Everything got worse as a result. That's why I said that this is all about political interests.[25]

The importance of Poso elites' demanding greater representation in local government as a factor that shaped the outbreak of violence becomes even clearer when one considers their roles in framing, coordinating, mobilizing, and sustaining violence, as discussed next.

Christian–Muslim Violence in Poso The Christian–Muslim riots in Poso were among the most intense, bloodiest, and longest ethnic riots that occurred anywhere in Indonesia during the country's democratic transition. From 1998 through 2012, according to NVMS data, at least 553 people died and 446 were injured.

Violence between Christian and Muslim communities in Poso spanned so many years, involving external militias and adopting a variety of forms, that prior studies have analyzed it in phases.[26] The clashes began in December 1998 and were not declared over until 2007. In this section, I limit my analysis to the early stages of violence, from December 1998 through July 2001, to highlight how politically excluded local elites took advantage of otherwise banal trigger events to reframe the narrative and mobilize violence along communal lines to serve their political purposes. In these early years, the fighting was indeed communal in nature, as the actors involved were civilians and villagers armed with homemade weapons, not trained fighters and militia members. The later phases, on the other hand, involved sniper attacks and bomb blasts carried out by trained militias, who used army weapons clearly imported from elsewhere (Aragon 2007).

In Poso, violence began in 1998 with a knife fight between a Christian and a Muslim youth on Christmas eve, which that year also happened to

---

[25] Interviewee 3, Muslim religious leader, November 12, 2009.
[26] McRae (2013, 7), in his excellent analysis of Poso violence, for example, divided the years of conflict into four phases: the urban riots phase from December 1998 to April 2000; the widespread killings from May to June 2000; a protracted two-sided conflict phase from June 2000 to December 2001, and then again in August 2002; and the bombings and sniper attacks from 2002 to 2007. In another example, Sangaji (2007, 258) described the conflict in five phases. For Sangaji, Phase 1 began with the first outburst of violence in December 1998 and lasted for a few days. After eighteen months of quiet, the second phase of violence erupted in April 2000. Phase 3 took place from May to June 2001, Phase 4 occurred in July 2001, and Phase 5 from November 2001 to 2007.

fall during the Muslim fasting month of Ramadan.[27] Religious leaders from both communities met and declared publicly that the incident was a result of alcohol abuse: They called for the banning of alcohol sales and consumption for the rest of Ramadan. The police then went on raids to seize alcohol from Chinese-owned shops throughout Poso and, in the process, civilians took it upon themselves to assist by destroying (Christian) Chinese-owned properties (Aragon 2001, 61). Before long, rumors spread that Christian churches were being burned. Young men armed with homemade weapons from both communities arrived in trucks and burned homes of the opposing groups. This first outburst of violence lasted a few days, injuring 200 people and destroying 400 houses (Aragon 2001). No one died, and Poso remained peaceful afterward for 18 months.

One person I interviewed who had witnessed the outbreak described his recollection of the event thus:

> Initially in 1998 the targets were karaokes, discotheques, and places that sold alcohol. Those places were burned down first. The alcohol was also burned. The restaurants selling alcohol and liquor were also burned. But this [violence] lasted briefly, and things calmed down almost immediately. The big conflict was not until May 2000.[28]

A knife fight between youths is not an uncommon occurrence in many parts of Indonesia. How did a seemingly trivial incident precipitate such a protracted outbreak of communal violence in Poso? This incident, like others in the early stage of violence there, was a by-product of Poso local elites' concerted efforts to produce violence.

As early as August 1998, after Patanga announced that he would not seek reelection when his term as district chief ended, both Christians and Muslims in Poso began rallying on behalf of their preferred coreligionist candidates. Christians threw their support behind Yahya Patiro, then district secretary and a Golkar affiliate who was popular among PDI voters. Poso Muslims lobbied for Damsyik Ladjalani, a Golkar-affiliated Muslim who was first assistant to the district secretary. Leaflets, banners, and graffiti slandering the Christian-backed Patiro appeared in public spaces and increased in number immediately following the knife fight.

---

[27] Here, the details vary. In Poso Muslim accounts of this incident, a Christian man knifed a Muslim inside a mosque (Hasurullah 2009, 24). Christian accounts, on the other hand, maintain that the two youths got into a fight, after which a Christian man knifed a Muslim, who then escaped to a local mosque and broadcast from the mosque speakers that a Muslim youth had been slain in the mosque (Damanik 2003, 14–15).

[28] Interviewee 13, NGO activist, April 5, 2009.

A banner demanding the hanging of Patiro and his close supporter, Herman Parimo, had been on display in a mosque in the predominantly Muslim Kayamanya neighborhood since November 1998 (Aragon 2001). On December 28, an anti-Christian message appeared at a major intersection, just two hours before clashes erupted in Poso. These leaflets and fliers did not appear on their own. Christian sources maintained that Ladjalani had been spotted distributing incendiary fliers that accused ten Christian government officials – including his direct rival, Patiro – of planning to assassinate Patanga, the district chief (Damanik 2003). Police forensic results later linked the fliers back to Agfar Patanga, brother of the incumbent district chief and major supporter of the Muslim candidate, Ladjalani.

Local elite involvement went well beyond these actions of framing the upcoming election in religious terms, by circulating rumors, incendiary fliers, and threats. Eyewitness reports maintain that Parimo, a strong supporter of the Christian candidate Patiro, and his sons were spotted mobilizing the crowd during the December 1998 riots (Lasahido et al. 2003). Parimo, who was a member of the now defunct local youth group Gerakan Pemuda Sulawesi Tengah (GPST), had approached the regent to ask if he could revive the GPST and recruit Protestant youths to maintain peace in Poso (Aragon 2013). Although Patanga flatly refused, on December 26, 1999, Parimo toured villages and asked village chiefs to send their Christian youth and offered money in exchange for their support (Aragon 2013).

On the Muslim side, Ladjalani allegedly not only urged, but paid, crowds on March 20, 1999 to attack a hotel where Patiro had been staying (Damanik 2003; Budi SP, Setiawan, and Muhamad 2000). Parimo was arrested on charges of organizing riots by Pamona youth and mobilizing the masses; and he was sentenced to fourteen years in prison. He appealed but became ill and died at a hospital in Makassar in April 2000. Patiro, the Christian regent hopeful, was exonerated and assigned to a post in the provincial government office in Palu (van Klinken 2007). Agfar Patanga was convicted of doctoring the fliers and sentenced to a two-year jail term, while his brother Arief (the incumbent district chief), was removed from office before the end of his term without explanation. For their involvement in the violence, both Patiro and Ladjalani were disqualified as district chief candidates.

In June 1999, Indonesians voted in their first national legislative election after Soeharto's resignation. Golkar won easily in Poso, securing an overall majority in the local council. In October 1999, when Poso representatives voted for a district chief, the Golkar-backed candidate who had been "dropped in" from Palu, Abdul Muin Pusadan, comfortably beat his Christian rival Eddy Bungkudapu and Muslim rival Ismail Kassim (Lasahido et al. 2003).

Further evidence of local elite involvement in sustaining and stirring violence was apparent during the district secretary selection process, which occurred in April and May 2000. Central Sulawesi governor H. Bandjela Paliudju appointed a Muslim from Bungku, Malik Syahadat, for the job. This appointment disappointed both Poso Christians and Muslims, as both groups felt that their preferred candidate had lost. Chaelani Umar, a PPP provincial assembly member, released a warning statement: "If the people's aspirations are neglected, that is, the aspiration calling for drs. Damsyik Ladjalani to become Secretary of Poso, the riots of 1998 which had so afflicted this district will recur, and their scale will be even greater."[29] This statement was printed in the local newspaper on April 15, 2000, with the headline "Poso Will Have More Violence" (Suyono and Madjowa 2000). The day after this statement appeared, the second phase of violence began. Although this publicized warning may have in fact unleashed the tensions that had been bubbling up until that point, its content suggests that more violence had been in the works for some time.

A less ambiguous case of elite involvement involved A. L. Lateka, a former head of the supervision and control division of the Regional Investment Coordinating Board (BKPMD). After a series of killings of Muslims in villages in late May 2000 in Poso,[30] Lateka called the police and admitted that he had sponsored recent anti-Muslim attacks and paid 30 million rupiah for a team of Christian "outsiders" to come in and wreak havoc (Damanik 2003, 61). His admission was printed in *Jawa Pos* on May 30, 2000. In subsequent skirmishes, Lateka was shot and killed and his body delivered to the house of a religious leader affiliated with Al-Khaerat.

One female village resident arrested for her participation in the May attacks on Muslim-dominated villages provided further evidence of

[29] Harian Mercu Suar, Palu, April 15, 2000, cited in Damanik (2003, 23).
[30] On May 23, 2000, ninja-clad men gunned down a Muslim police officer and two Muslim civilians in Moengko, before a riot subsequently erupted in Sayo (Human Rights Watch 2002, 17). Five days later, on May 28, 2000, a group of Christian men, led by Fabianus Tibo, a Catholic plantation worker from Flores, East Nusa Tenggara, launched attacks on several Muslim villages in Poso, including the brutal incidents at Sintuwu Lemba village, near Kilo Nine, where some women were subjected to sexual violence and men hiding in the Wali Songo pesantren were gunned down despite having surrendered. Days after the Kilo Nine killings, three mass graves with thirty-nine bodies were discovered (Human Rights Watch 2002, 17).

local elites' involvement in mobilizing violence. Despite not knowing that there were going to be attacks on Muslim villages, she described how "someone just handed us black clothes and a red headband, and told us to get into a car" (Budi SP, Setiawan, and Muhamad 2000). When pressed for details on the identity of the person who provided her the clothes and instructions, she claimed that it was A. L. Lateka. Another Christian village resident echoed this story. He said that he had little clue of what the problem was, but "a masked man" came to his house and "we were told to attack" (Budi SP, Setiawan, and Muhamad 2000).

The involvement of religious leaders was visible in Poso. One Muslim community leader I interviewed testified in court against a Protestant affiliated with the GKST. He claimed, without naming any names: The people involved in mobilizing the violence were actually GKST people. I testified about this in court. One GKST commander was leading the fighters. I saw him in the field with my own eyes. Because of my testimony in court, he ended in jail.[31]

Rinaldy Damanik, a well-known and loved GKST pastor, was brought to trial in June 2003 on account of his possession of weapons in August 2002. When the car Damanik was driving was stopped by the police in Peleru, Morowali, the police found seven homemade long-barreled firearms, four short barrel guns, and 144 rounds of ammunition (Tempo 2003). Although 14 of the 21 witnesses testified that they saw the weapons brought out of Damanik's car, the reverend insisted that they were not his. His supporters claimed that the security apparatus was trying to frame him. Damanik was sentenced to three years in prison (Tempo 2003) but was released by November 2004 (Tempo 2004b).

On the Muslim side, one source interviewed by the Human Rights Watch claimed he had attended a Muslim gathering at Al Khaerat's headquarters in Palu shortly after Tibo's May attack on Kilo Nine and Kasiguncu. I quote below his recollection of an Al Khaerat leader's appeal at this meeting: Muslims of Palu, at this time our brothers in Poso will be surrounded by the Christian *kafirs*. Let us together go and help them. If we die in war it is not in vain. We struggle in the path of Allah. Allah has promised heaven for those of his people who fight the *kafirs*.[32]

One Muslim interviewee told me that he posted an open call on the Internet for fellow Muslims in Indonesia to aid their struggle in the conflict:

[31] Interviewee 3, Muslim religious leader, November 12, 2009.
[32] See Human Rights Watch (2002, 19).

Because of these incidents [of violence against Muslims], I wrote a letter on the internet, calling for all the laskar [fighters] to come to Poso . . . . I felt that things had gone too far and must come to an end. So I invited everyone and declared on the internet that come 1 Syawal [the Islamic new year], I want to perform the Ied prayer in Tentena.[33]

This call for Muslim fighters across Indonesia to assist Poso Muslims reinforced the religious framing of the conflict. As local and external jihad militias emerged, the clashes extended well beyond the initial conflict between local elites that had defined the early stages of violence.[34]

The early incidents of violence in Poso were consistently described as an "elites' conflict." It is important to note, however, that many community figures had pushed for an end to violence during its early stages. One way they had tried to establish peace was to respond to the immediate needs of the victims.

Reluctant to answer any of my direct questions about why and how violence in Poso unfolded, a Muslim entrepreneur in Palu stressed that one factor that sustained the violence in Poso was that far too many people kept debating about who was responsible for specific acts of violence. Such discussions, he believed, were futile and could potentially lead to more violence. Instead, he claimed that the path to peace lies in grassroots initiatives to care for the victims of violence. He proceeded to recount his team's efforts to that end in Poso and Palu:

A lot of people already expressed their opinions on [the conflict]. I don't want to think about why conflict erupted and who did what. I am only concerned about the victims who needed immediate help. So, when other community figures of Central Sulawesi asked me to lead the Muslim victims finding team, I agreed. I only want to find the victims, and if I can help, I will help them . . . . So if we found [the victims] in the form of corpses, our immediate response was to evacuate them so they could be buried properly. If we found live victims needing medications, I coordinated their transfer to Palu, and sometimes even to Makassar, where they could receive proper care. That's it. These kinds of conversations run the risk of being misunderstood, and of potentially creating even more problems. Just one misspoken word, people could get really angry and fight again. This is why I think it is crucial that there is at least one team who works without thinking about the causes of violence. We shouldn't look backward. In my reading of the situation at the time, the first thing that can calm people's emotions is if they see that their dead receiving proper burials. We treated everyone who was ill and injured, and we supported those who

---

[33] Interviewee 3, Muslim religious leader, November 12, 2009.

[34] Schulze (2019) provided excellent discussions of the militias' involvement in Poso conflict.

are still alive and who had lost their families. I brought children who have lost parents to Poso and sought donors and foster families for them. We fed the ones who came and stayed with us. This helped reduce the tension and normalize the situation a bit.[35]

Since the team was not government funded or initiated, I asked how he managed it and raised the necessary support. He elaborated that many Poso and Palu residents took it upon themselves to contribute.

We relied on donations from the community. For example, if today my team from the field tells me that we need 50 shrouds to bury the dead, I will call my friends and inform them of our needs. Within one day, almost always, we get exactly what we need. I have done this for shrouds, gloves, ropes. We needed a lot of ropes because many corpses were thrown off the cliffs.[36]

These efforts, while mostly aimed at rescuing Muslim victims, were not exclusively carried out by Muslims. Some Christian volunteers joined and the team saved victims, both Christian and Muslim, as they were encountered:

I didn't think at the time, whether the victims were Christian or Muslim. I just went. My friends were also the same. I think if this is a person, then her heart is probably like mine. I never felt that if someone is Christian, that I had to be more careful. I never thought much about that. If fate would have you harm me, then I would just accept that as my fate . . . .. Some Christian friends joined me at the time, because my friends came from both groups.[37]

In the later phases of the violence, local religious leaders' appeals to end it also bolstered these community-driven efforts. One interviewee described Al Khaerat leaders' powerful influence on Muslim Poso and Palu residents and their effectiveness in guiding their co-religionists to refrain from violence:

The Laskar fighters came from outside to cultivate people here who were still angry and vengeful. They had quite a number of followers. That was their attempt to spread the violence from Poso to Palu. They bombed the local police headquarter, a pig farm, and a kindergarten. But why did these attempts not work? Because apparently, Palu residents' resilience and resistance to trigger events is quite strong. Why? Because they had seen what happened in Poso due to provocation. Second, Al Khaerat actively campaigned broadly everywhere to caution people not to be easily triggered and influenced. They were very

---

[35] Interviewee 16, April 4, 2009.
[36] Interviewee 16, Muslim entrepreneur, April 4, 2009
[37] Interviewee 16, Muslim entrepreneur, April 4, 2009.

effective. Al Khaerat is extremely respected as one of the oldest and largest Muslim organization in eastern Indonesia.[38]

This chapter's point that local elites mobilized violence as a way of leveraging their demands for inclusion does not preclude other motivations that were driving people's participation in violence. A number of interviewees also stressed the importance of inequality, grassroots resentment, and the security apparatus' slow and half-hearted responses.

When I asked why people would participate in violence, one interviewee said, "The clash started because there was so much imbalance between the poor and the wealthy. Now that the poor are living better, the encouragement to do negative things will have less of a draw."[39]

Asked the same question, another person traced the worsening of violence to the authorities' slow response: "Because people have died already. If the authorities had dealt with these clashes at the beginning, they would not have escalated. But what we saw instead, there was a tendency to allow things to unfold and worsen. Not until people started dying were these things handled more seriously."[40]

There was also a widespread perception among my interviewees that the state security forces were either incapable of dealing with the threat of violence or complicit in allowing it to unfold. One Muslim religious leader in Poso described his experience in the early 2000s as follows:

We had heard that Poso would be attacked by people from the north. Toward nightfall, the entire Poso town was already aware of an imminent attack. We had even put up a blockade. We had machetes ready to welcome its arrival. At the time, the district chief had instructed all subdistrict heads (*camat*) to advise whether an attack was coming to Poso. The answer that came back was that no, there was no attack. All the *camats* in all the subdistricts said no, no attacks. So at 10:00 p.m., the district chief and chief of police went around town and instructed people to open the blockade, saying that it was not true that there would be an attack, and that this was just an issue spread by provocateurs. But at exactly 1:00 a.m., the attack came. This was when I began to think that there was some element of design at work. How could they not know?[41]

This same person described an encounter he had with a group of fighters and soldiers in May 1999:

---

[38] Interviewee 2, local journalist, November 12, 2009.
[39] Interviewee 16, Muslim entrepreneur, April 4, 2009.
[40] Interviewee 13, NGO activist, April 5, 2009.
[41] Interviewee 3, Muslim religious leader, November 12, 2009.

I was on my way back from Makassar in 1999, a few days before the May 1999 violence erupted . . . . I boarded the bus dressed in a *habib* [Islamic] outfit. The bus driver told me: "change your outfit, sir. There is a riot in Tentena." On the road, our bus was stopped. There were people all dressed in black with red headbands. Right next to them were soldiers, in their uniforms and with their gears. The people stopped our bus and went inside. They entered with their machetes and were ready to kill us all, but then I heard a loud bang. Apparently one of the soldiers had fired a shot. And I heard one of them said, "Let the public transportation go" . . . . After that, the people let us go . . . . The interesting thing to me was that with the soldiers' presence, [violence] was actually stoppable.[42]

This event signified to this interviewee that the security personnel could have prevented the escalation of violence in Poso had they truly wanted to do so.

The clashes between Christians and Muslims in Poso were triggered by banal events such as fights between youths from different religious communities. These clashes, however, occurred after months of intense rumor-mongering, distribution of incendiary fliers and leaflets decrying specific religious communities, and threats against community leaders, during the run-up to a much-anticipated election for Poso district chief. The events described in this section suggest that local elites from Christian and Muslim communities in Poso framed the contested election in religious terms. The candidates themselves, Ladjalani and Patiro, engaged actively in politicizing religious loyalties, coordinating riotous supporters, and mobilizing violence. Also significantly, clashes in the early stage of Poso violence occurred around important moments where district government posts would be allocated – first, after the incumbent Patanga announced his departure and during the communities' efforts to rally support for their candidates in December 1998, and then again in 2000 around the time of the district secretary's selection. Although these clashes began before important elections and, therefore, may seem to contradict one implication of my theory, the fact that violence continued to escalate and spread well beyond the elections – such that many scholars describe the Poso conflict in stages – indicates that elite politicization of identity for electoral purposes before elections could not have been the only driver of violence. The case of Poso lends support to the overall argument that local elites' demand for political accommodation drove the mobilization of violence during Indonesia's democratic transition.

---

[42] Interviewee 3, Muslim religious leader, November 12, 2009.

District 2: Banggai

Banggai district lies on the eastern tip of Central Sulawesi province, on the coast of the Tomini gulf. Its capital, Luwuk, is 610 kilometers (or a 16-hour drive) from Palu, Central Sulawesi's provincial capital. Prior to Indonesia's independence, inland Banggai, Luwuk, and the archipelagic Banggai islands were subsumed under the Poso *afdeling* (district), under the jurisdiction of the governor of Grote Oost (the Great East) (Tirtosudarmo 2008). When Central Sulawesi province was created in the early 1960s and the provincial capital was placed in Palu, many Banggai-born local figures who contributed to the republic's efforts to quell the Kahar Muzakar rebellion in southern Sulawesi felt slighted.[43] They demanded a separate province, East Sulawesi, with Poso as the capital (Tirtosudarmo 2008). This request was ignored.

In 1990, Banggai was an expansive district covering over 11,000 square kilometers, with a population of 225,453. But the district would experience two splits: first in 1999, when the island Banggai Kepulauan district was created, and then again in 2012 when the new Banggai Laut district split from Banggai Kepulauan. Today, the district covers more than 9,000 square kilometers and is home to more than 350,000 people (Banggai 2015).

In 2016, more than a quarter of Banggai's local GDP came from the processing industry, with another quarter from the agricultural, fisheries, and forestry sectors. However, the fastest-growing sector in the district's local GDP was mining, thanks to the presence of natural gas, nickel, gold, iron, and granite in the district. At the time of Indonesia's transition to democracy, Banggai's GDP per capita was slightly higher than Poso's, at 2.36 million rupiah per person in 2000 (compared to Poso's 1.71 million rupiah). As in Poso, according to the Indonesia Database for Policy and Economic Research (DAPOER) data, roughly 30% of residents were living below the poverty line in 1999.

Banggai is religiously diverse, with 75% of its population identifying as Muslim and 16% as Protestant or Catholic as of the 2010 census. The Christian percentage dropped after Banggai Kepulauan, which was 30% Christian in the 2010 census, became a separate district in 1999. In terms of ethnic composition, Banggai is also considerably fractionalized, with 26% of its population identifying as ethnic Saluan, 19% as Javanese, 9% as Gorontalo, 8% as Balinese, and 7% as Bugis. Like Poso, Banggai was a designated transmigration area in the Soeharto era, and it has received a large influx of migrants from Bali and Java over the years.

---

[43] For a thorough review of this rebellion, see Harvey (1974).

The Local Political Configuration Religion is not an important factor in political representation in Banggai. Instead, its residents and local government officials highlight the importance of the district's lineage to the kingdom of Banggai. This focus is evident in the religious affiliations of the district chiefs and the formal discourse presented by the district government on its official website; it was reinforced in many of my interviews.

It is difficult to ascertain Banggai voters' political identification along party lines before the New Order. Until 1960, the district was subsumed under Poso, which in turn was part of North Sulawesi province until Central Sulawesi province was created. Hence, when Indonesia conducted its first free and fair national elections in 1955, Banggai voters' political preferences were aggregated with those of other voters in the Poso district. In the 1971 national election, the last one before Soeharto streamlined ten political parties into PPP, Golkar, and PDI, 87.7% of Banggai voters chose Golkar, nearly identical to the 90% of voters in Poso who supported Golkar in the same election (Hering and Willis 1973). The Islamist parties PSII, NU, and Masyumi together garnered 9.6% of Banggai's votes in 1971, while the Christian party Parkindo and the Catholic party received a combined 2.3% (Hering and Willis 1973). In every election after 1971, Banggai voters cast their votes overwhelmingly in support of Golkar.

Since the district's inception in 1959, 12 district chiefs have been appointed to lead it, and all of them have identified as Muslim (Table 6.5).

Table 6.5. *Soeharto-era district chiefs in Banggai, Central Sulawesi (1967–1998)*

Name	Term	Religion
Drs. F. S. Simak	1969–1973	Muslim
Drs. A. Aziz Larekeng	1973	Muslim
Drs. Eddy Singgih	1973–1978	Muslim
Drs. Malaga	1978–1980	Muslim
Joesoep Soepardjan	1980–1986	Muslim
Drs. H. M. Junus	1986–1996	Muslim
Drs. H. Sudarto SH	1996–2001	Muslim

Source: The list of district chiefs' names is taken from the Banggai district government website. See http://beranda.banggaikab.go.id/sejarah/ Data on religious affiliations of district chiefs are collated from online profiles and conversations with interviewees.

When I asked some of my interviewees whether Banggai ever had an informal power-sharing agreement akin to that in Poso and Ambon, where individuals representing different religious communities would either be paired together in district leadership positions in the same term or take turns occupying key posts across terms, I received this reply:

Banggai is not like Poso. I think the selection of bupati and secretary was really unfair in Poso, since Christians in Poso used to have a lot more land and influence in Poso, whereas towards the end [of Soeharto's rule], Muslims were quite dominant in the bureaucracy. In Banggai, there are some Christians, but not that many, and historically this entire area was under the Banggai kingdom. To this day, people are very loyal to the king of Banggai. The kingdom has always been Muslim.[44]

In this individual's perspective, because the district emerged out of the kingdom of Banggai that had been historically Muslim, it is perfectly acceptable to have Muslims in important seats in government.[45]

The importance of the Banggai kingdom is also reflected on the official district government website, where the first sentence in the historical overview section traces the district's lineage to the kingdom. The section begins: "Before the administrative district of Banggai was created, Banggai was part of the kingdom of Banggai, based in Banggai island." It describes the district's creation in 1959 as follows: "On December 12, 1959, there was a handover of power from the last king of Banggai kingdom, Syukuran Aminuddin Amir who was at the time the caretaker of Banggai in Luwuk, to Bidin, the first regent of Banggai district."[46]

Given the emphasis on Banggai's historical lineage, the dimension of identity that appears to be most relevant in discourses on political representation in Banggai is that of ethnicity or, specifically, tribal affiliation (suku). The Banggai kingdom historically was composed of three main ethnic groups: Banggai, Balantak, and Saluan. In describing the elected district leaders in Banggai and the districts that have broken off from it, Banggai Kepulauan and Banggai Laut, one of my respondents was quick to add that the recently elected district chiefs were "native Banggai" (asli Banggai).[47] In an analysis of the composition of Banggai Kepulauan leadership, Warsito (2007, 84) highlighted how Ali Hamid,

---

[44] Interviewee 29, customary leader, July 2, 2009.
[45] Twenty-one kings had ruled Banggai since its inception in the early sixteenth century. Every Banggai king since 1872 had a Muslim name (Wacana 2015).
[46] See http://beranda.banggaikab.go.id/sejarah/.
[47] Interviewee 30, party activist, February 7, 2009.

the district regent indirectly elected by the local council in 1999, was "an ethnic Banggai and direct descendant of kings of Banggai."

This rhetoric emphasizing the current political authorities' ties to the ancestral kings of Banggai is unique and, upon reflection, noticeably missing in Poso. Relative to Banggai, the only dimension of identity that mattered at the time of my visit and in my interviews with respondents in Poso was religion. In Banggai, on the other hand, my interviewees frequently and spontaneously mentioned the kingdom of Banggai, the importance of the king, and the customary laws.

Clashes in Banggai Although relatively similar to Poso in terms of its demography, economy, and geography, Banggai had a mostly peaceful transition to democracy. Between 1998 and 2001, while Poso was experiencing its worst bouts of communal violence, Banggai had two ethnocommunal incidents, but both were short-lived and did not result in any casualties. In November 1998, a clash erupted when twenty residents of Boluang in Bunta subdistrict attacked and burned down the home of A. Khum, a local resident of Chinese descent, and ended within a day without any intervention by the authorities (per NVMS). The district had no further incidents of ethnocommunal rioting for the next 18 months (NVMS). But on July 6, 2000, clashes between Christians and Muslims that erupted in various parts of Poso district spilled over to Sepe village in Balantak Selatan, Banggai. A group of men, wearing red headbands armed with machetes and homemade weapons, stopped public buses and searched passengers. No casualties were reported in this specific incident. Although crime, student brawls, and protests occurred in Banggai during these initial years after democratic transition, it had relatively few incidents of clashes between Christians and Muslims.

When I arrived in Luwuk in 2009, the few incidents of Christian–Muslim conflict were so distant in my interviewees' minds that one of them referred to such clashes as the "Poso conflict."[48] One customary leader mentioned, "We had some incidents, but that was because our people became emotional after hearing stories of what happened in Poso. Banggai is like a mini-Indonesia. You can find any kind of person here, and we get along fine."[49]

Instead, the main threat of local violence arose from the proposal to create a new Sulawesi Timur province, which would entail the creation of new districts and the selection of these new district capitals.

[48] Interviewee 28, village chief, February 5, 2009.
[49] Interviewee 29, customary leader, February 7, 2009.

In January 2000, a group of senior bureaucrats in Central Sulawesi put forth a proposal advocating for the creation of a new province, Sulawesi Timur. According to their proposal, it would incorporate Poso, Banggai, Banggai Kepulauan, Luwuk, and Tojo Una-Una, plus the newly proposed districts of Pamona and Parigi Moutong (Tirtosudarmo 2008). Although the new province would be 70% Muslim and would comprise an ethnically diverse population, religion and ethnicity would not become causes of mobilization in the discourse around its creation (Tirtosudarmo 2008). Rather, advocates stressed the economic benefits, pointing out that 70% of Central Sulawesi's current revenues come from areas that would be part of the new province (Sangaji 2006).

When Banggai Kepulauan was formed in 1999, a dispute emerged over where the new district capital would go. Residents of Banggai island demanded that it be there, as opposed to Salakan on Peling island, as had been legislated by Law 61, 1999 (Kompas 2008). In February 2007, a clash erupted after thousands of Banggai residents took to the streets and occupied the Banggai Kepulauan regent's office upon the announcement that the capital would be moved from Banggai to Salakan (AntaraNews 2007). Four people died and a dozen were injured as a result of this clash (Liputan 6 2007).

Those who supported the capital's relocation claimed that it was in accordance with the law, pointing out that the relocation had been delayed (Liputan 6 2007). Appealing to history and customary laws, supporters of keeping the capital on Banggai island claimed that the Banggai kingdom had been based there and that this historical kingdom continued to command the loyalty of residents of contemporary Luwuk and nearby islands, including Peling, where their counterparts wanted to place the new capital.[50] One person claimed that placing the new capital in Salakan in Peling would be akin to "honoring the child before the parent."[51] Beyond history and tradition, supporters of Banggai claimed that Banggai's infrastructure was far more developed and could better support the workings of a district capital. One of my interviewees declared, "Go to Salakan. You will see that there is no way it is ready. Electricity is available for only six hours a day. There is no water. There is one bank, BNI. People live miserably there. In Banggai, everything is ready."[52] This conflict was eventually resolved, when another district, Banggai Laut, was formed in 2012 and Banggai island formed the bulk of the land territory of the new district.

---

[50] Interviewee 30, political party activist, February 7, 2009.
[51] Interviewee 30, political party activist, February 7, 2009.
[52] Interviewee 29, customary leader, February 7, 2009.

This reliance on customary laws and traditions suggests that the strength of attachment to an ethnic (i.e., Saluan) community may be sufficiently strong that it pacifies the effects of the mobilization of violence along religious lines. My interviewees' comments show little trace of concerns over religious representation within their district. Instead, based on the references to customary laws and the kingdom of Banggai as the historical ancestor of the district, I infer that political legitimacy depends on ties to the kingdom of Banggai for my Banggai interviewees. Their preoccupation with the splintering of a new district and the new capital's location seems to further support the idea that governance and political arrangements need to be in line with Banggai's ethnic customs. The strength of attachment to the ethnic community may have shaped the kinds of issues that became relevant, the demands that people made, and the lack of violence around religion. To the extent that Banggai political leaders conform to expectations based on customs – both in terms of their profiles and in terms of their practices – there was little reason for Banggai local elites to mobilize violence along religious lines to agitate for change.

Maluku Province

Long before independent Indonesia came into existence, the Moluccas' spice production inspired the spice trade and drew merchants, soldiers, and missionaries alike. In 2014, the archipelagic province of Maluku was among Indonesia's poorest, as measured by its very low GDP per capita and 18% of Maluku residents living in poverty.[53] In 1997, shortly before Soeharto resigned, 40.75% of all households in Maluku had access to clean water, 62.20% of households had electricity, and only 7.71% of eligible students were enrolled in senior secondary schools. van Klinken (2007) described Maluku as one of the most "state-dependent" in the country, noting that a very large portion of the urban population was employed in the civil service.[54] In 1999, North Maluku was carved out of Maluku to form a new province, with Ternate as its capital.

With an area of over 850,000 square kilometers and at least 1,208 islands, Maluku is a vast and sparsely populated province. Water covers most of its territory. In 1971, it was more than half Christian, but because

---

[53] DAPOER reported that Maluku's GDP per capita in 2011 (without oil and gas, in constant price) was at 2.8 million rupiah per person, only slightly higher than the Indonesian province with the lowest GDP per capita, Nusa Tenggara Timur.

[54] van Klinken (2007, 90) stated that in 1990, Maluku had 55,000 civil servants, more than the number of civil servants in East Java, a province with a population seventeen times larger.

of the government transmigration program of the 1970s and 1980s, this demographic composition gradually changed. By the 2000 census, 49% of the province's population was Muslims and 50% was Protestants or Catholics. The province is home to a number of small ethnic groups, both migrant and local. According to the 2000 census, Maluku's population was 10% ethnic Ambonese, 10% Butonese, and 10% Kei.[55] The largest category reported was "others," representing a combination of many small, unidentified ethnic groups, that constituted 42% of Maluku's population in 2000.

Relative to other Indonesians living in the Dutch East Indies, historically a larger proportion of Ambonese Christians were well educated and employed in the colonial bureaucracy.[56] By the 1930s, many Ambonese Christians worked as clerks or as soldiers in the Royal Dutch Indies Colonial Army (Chauvel 1990; Aritonang and Steenbrink 2008). This pattern continued into the post-independence bureaucracy as well; through the 1980s, the Ambonese civil service was dominated by Christians (van Klinken 2007). When Muslims began to enter and rise through the ranks of the civil service in Ambon in the 1990s, their ascendancy was interpreted as a threat to Ambonese Christians' access to economic and political resources (van Klinken 2007). This perception of declining status resonated even more widely after 1992, when a Muslim became governor; within four years, all district chiefs in Maluku were Muslims (Tadjoeddin 2013). Among ordinary Ambonese Christians, the rise of Muslim bureaucrats in Ambon coincided with increased unemployment and greater difficulties attaining elite positions within the civil service (van Klinken 2007).

There was very little party politics and cadre development at the local level in Maluku during Soeharto's regime. Only Golkar had extensive local party branches at the district and subdistrict levels, and even Golkar's political mobilization was limited to campaign periods, when the party would hold parades and rallies frequented by local celebrities and performers.

The largest nongovernment organization is the Maluku synod, Gereja Protestan Maluku (GPM) (van Klinken 2007). Established in 1935, the GPM has hundreds of congregations throughout the province, and its youth wing, Angkatan Pemuda Gereja Protestan Maluku (AM-GPM), has thousands of members. Much like other large Protestant synods in

---

[55] BPS (2000, 37–38, 73–74).

[56] The same has been said of ethnic Minahasans in Northern Sulawesi who, like the Ambonese, also converted to Christianity and occupied posts in the colonial and post-independence civil service in higher numbers than non-Minahasan Sulawesi residents (Henley 1996).

Indonesia, GPM organizes its vertical hierarchy to mirror that of the government (van Klinken 2007). Through a series of ministry and social activities, the church provides a large social network for Maluku youths and equips them with leadership and organizational training. GPM provides a ready-made structure and a supply of activists who can be easily mobilized. Many politically prominent Protestant Maluku figures are also GPM activists and leaders (van Klinken 2007).

Muslims in Maluku are not as politically or centrally organized. Although local offices of national Islamist mass organizations such as Nahdlatul Ulama and Muhammadiyah do exist, they are not very strong (van Klinken 2007). Likewise, the national council of ulamas, Majelis Ulama Indonesia (MUI), has failed to organize Muslims in Maluku. A Muslim Ambonese remarked, "While Ambonese Christians [i.e., Protestants] were well organized under the command of church and synod, Muslims had no organization. At the time, MUI did not function. It was only a place to put things. It was just a name!" (Al Qurtuby 2016, 51). van Klinken (2007, 92) summarized the situation succinctly: "In Ambon Muslims had no equivalent of the Protestant GPM."

Table 6.6 lists the religious affiliations of all Maluku governors during the New Order period. With the exception of G. J. Latumahina and Soekoso, all self-identified as religiously Muslim. In contrast, Christians predominated among Maluku secretaries, as five of seven secretaries between 1965 and 1998 identified as Protestant. Provincial council chairs between 1971 and 1997, on the other hand, were all Muslim (Pieris 2004, 223–224). In this light, it appears that Maluku provincial government

Table 6.6. *Soeharto-era Governors in Maluku (1965–1998)*

Governors	Term	Religion	Secretaries	Term	Religion
G. J. Latumahina	1965–1968	Protestant	J. J. G. Sahetapy	1965–1971	Protestant
Soemitro	1968–1973	Muslim	M. K. Soulissa	1971–1976	Muslim
Soemeru	1973–1976	Muslim	G. A. Engko	1976–1983	Protestant
Hasan Slamet	1976–1987	Muslim	J. M. E. Soukotta	1983–1987	Protestant
Soekoso	1987–1992	Catholic	M. Akib Latuconsina	1987–1991	Muslim
M. Akib Latuconsina	1992–1997	Muslim	L. H. Tanasale	1991–1995	Protestant
M. Saleh Latuconsina	1997–2002	Muslim	Akyuwen	1995–1999	Protestant

Notes: Italicized names are interim (*pejabat*) governors.

Sources: Names and terms of governors and secretaries are based on BPS (2016b, 61); governors' and secretaries' religious affiliations are based on Pieris (2004, 223).

positions were allocated with consideration of religious representation during the New Order, with the governor position more frequently allocated to Muslims.

The appointment of Muslim governors in the 1990s led to what many Ambonese Christians considered the "Islamization" of government in Maluku (Pieris 2004, 175–176). Bertrand (2004) described a similar scenario in the context of education and teacher hiring in Ambon.

In January 1999, Maluku suffered one of the country's deadliest outbursts of ethnocommunal violence. Christian–Muslim clashes in Ambon, the provincial capital, broke out just a few weeks after a similar riot in Poso, Central Sulawesi. From Ambon, clashes spread to the neighboring districts of Maluku Tengah, Maluku Tenggara, and Buru, claiming at least 5,000 lives and forcing at least 500,000 people to leave their homes (ICG 2000).[57] Existing accounts generally concur that the forms of violence shifted from 1999 and most of 2000, when the combatants were large crowds of local civilians using homemade weapons, to late December 2000 and afterward, when communal warfare dissipated and was replaced by shootouts, bomb attacks, and assassinations (Al Qurtuby 2016).

Although representatives of Christian and Muslim Ambonese signed the Malino II peace accord in 2002, low-level skirmishes continued to occur through 2005 (Tajima 2014). The ripple effects of violence in Ambon were felt in North Maluku – a new province carved out of Maluku in 1999 – where Christians and Muslims battled each other in Ternate, Tidore, and Halmahera from August 1999 through December 2000.[58] Even though the clashes in Maluku were widespread and the death toll was high, not every district in the province witnessed the same level and intensity of violence; there was relatively little violence in Kei and Aru, for example.[59]

Table 6.7 presents the demographic and socioeconomic characteristics of Ambon and Maluku Tenggara. These administrative units are relatively similar with regard to their GDP per capita and the contribution of the agricultural sector. Demographically, both Ambon and Maluku Tenggara had a sizable Christian population and a fairly similar

---

[57] Estimates vary based on sources. The International Crisis Group reported in 2000 that a death toll of 5,000 was accepted by most observers. NVMS reported at least 2,796 casualties in Maluku.

[58] According to NVMS data, at least 3,273 people died in clashes in North Maluku.

[59] Clashes in Maluku were so widespread that Sidel (2006, 168) described them as "province-wide," in contrast to the more localized ethnocommunal violence in other provinces.

Table 6.7. *Ambon and Maluku Tenggara in numbers*

	Ambon	Maluku Tenggara	Maluku Province
Demography in 2000			
% of Muslim population	26.20	38.70	49.10
% of Christian population	73.70	61.20	50.20
Religious fractionalization	0.432	0.659	0.573
Ethnic fractionalization	0.732	0.540	0.769
Population in 2000	186,911	183,958	1,149,899
Christian–Muslim riots (1998–2012)			
Incidents	609	20	953
Deaths	1,410	200	2,796
Injuries	3,327	339	5,389
Economy			
GDP per capita in 2000	5.47	0.71	2.29
% of GDP from agriculture in 2000	23.51	42.77	28.25*
% poor in 2002	7.46	39.29	34.78

Notes: Religious fractionalization was calculated using the Herfindahl–Taylor index, as described in my analysis in Chapter 5 GDP figures are excluding oil and gas revenues, in millions of rupiah, constant prices. *Data on percentage of GDP from agriculture for Maluku province are for 1997, since 2000 figures were not available.

Sources: Violence data are from NVMS; economy-related data are from DAPOER; demographic data are based on the 2000 census.

level of fractionalization along religious lines.[60] These similarities notwithstanding, NVMS reported 609 incidents of Christian–Muslim clashes in Ambon between 1998 and 2012, which claimed 1,410 lives and injured 3,327. These clashes were among the most violent and deadly in the country. In the same time period, 20 incidents occurred in Maluku Tenggara, and 200 people died and 339 were injured as a result of ethnocommunal violence (NVMS). This divergence is particularly striking in view of these districts' similarities on various socioeconomic and demographic indicators. In the subsequent sections, I examine the role of local elites and examine why Ambon was engulfed in violence whereas Tual, which at the time was part of Maluku Tenggara district, was relatively quiet (Figure 6.2).

---

[60] The demographic data presented in Table 6.7 are based on the 2000 census. For pre-conflict figures, the ICG (2002, 1–2) cited figures from the Bureau of Statistics and reported that in 1997, 51.92% of the population identified themselves as Protestant, 5.55% as Catholic, and 42.38% as Muslim. Maluku Tenggara in that same year was 54.6% Protestant, 23.08% Catholic, and 22.13% Muslim.

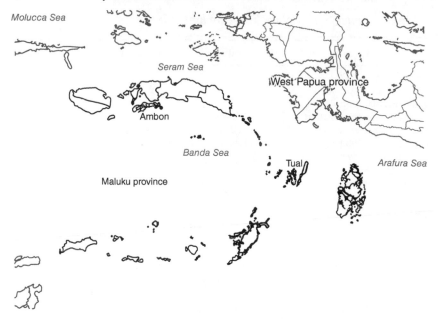

Figure 6.2 Map of Maluku

District 3: Kota Ambon

As the capital of Maluku province, located on an island that shares the city's name, Ambon is a bustling community that covers about 40% of the island. The administrative focal point of the entire Maluku province, it is located off the Ambon gulf. With approximately 200,000 residents prior to the 1990s violence, the city had become increasingly overcrowded. It was the target destination for many migrants who relocated to assume positions in the bureaucracy and other sectors. Although Ambon remained majority-Protestant until 1997, the proportion of Protestants had been slowly declining over the previous years.

Intervillage brawls are common in Maluku, and antagonism between Muslims and Christians was recorded as early as the Portuguese colonial period (Aritonang and Steenbrink 2008). One interviewee explained that in the 1980s, news of "a Muslim murdering a Christian family, or Christians murdering Muslims [was] "frequent, but it never raised a huge uproar and became a 'religious' problem."[61] In Ambon specifically, clashes between the Protestant-majority Mardika

[61] Interviewee 18, November 8, 2009, Ambon.

community and members of the predominantly Muslim Batumerah neighborhood were common in the Soeharto years. When these clashes occurred, though, they were usually resolved quickly by the local police, community elders, and religious leaders (Al Qurtuby 2016). Ambon was an example of religious harmony and integration (Tajima 2014). The city has a tradition called *pela gandong* that bonds pairs of villages – often dominated by members of differing religious communities – in ancestral pacts to assist each other in times of crisis such as famine and warfare. *Pela gandong* also provides a mechanism for residents to strengthen ties between villages through exogamy (Bartels 1978).

The Local Political Configuration Ambon's political configuration has fluctuated over time. In the constitutional assembly election of 1955, the Christian party Parkindo won 46% of the votes, followed by Masyumi with 28% (van Klinken 2006). In the legislative election later that year, Parkindo won 49% and Masyumi 24%. This early preference for religious parties continued even in the 1971 New Order election, in which ten parties competed. Although in most parts of the country Golkar won the lion's share of the votes, in Ambon Golkar captured only 32.3%, trailing Parkindo's 34.5%, with Masyumi getting 16.7% (Hering and Willis 1973). These election results indicate that religious political parties enjoyed strong support among Ambonese voters, despite Golkar's growing electoral dominance in the city, as it consistently won about 70% of the vote in later years (van Klinken 2006).

As for representation in key government positions in Ambon, the principle of power sharing described in Poso seems to have applied here as well, as illustrated by the affiliations of individuals appointed to mayor, secretary, council chair, and vice council positions in the city throughout the New Order. Table 6.8 lists the names of council chairs and vice chairs in Ambon from 1982 through 1998, along with their religious affiliations.

Generally, when the chair of the local council was Muslim, one of the vice chairs would represent the Christian community and vice versa. The same was true of mayors and secretaries in Ambon during this time period. As Table 6.9 shows, a Christian and a Muslim were generally paired in these two appointments. Most Soeharto-appointed mayors in Ambon were Protestant, while the city secretaries were more roughly split between Protestants and Muslims.

These appointments notwithstanding, there was a widespread perception that Christians were becoming increasingly marginalized in politics. The Ambon mayoral selection in 1996 was particularly

Table 6.8. *Soeharto-era local council (DPRD) chairs and vice chairs in Ambon (1982–1998)*

Council chairs	Term	Religion	Vice chairs	Religion
Th. Soplanit	1982–1987	Protestant	J. Gantong	Protestant
			Hi. A. W. Rahawarin, SH	Muslim
Hi. A. W. Rahawarin, SH	1987–1992	Muslim	F. Sinanu	Protestant
			Hi. Ismael Hatuwe	Muslim
Hi. A. W. Rahawarin, SH	1992–1997	Muslim	Suratno	Muslim
			John Mailoa	Protestant
			Hi. Umar Tuasamu	Muslim
Letkol Inf. Suratno	1997–1999	Muslim	J. J. Apituley	Protestant
			Hi. Umar Tuasamu	Muslim

Sources: Data of names of council chairs and vice chairs are based on BPS (2003, 33); data of religious affiliations are based on online profiles and interviewees' comments.

Table 6.9. *Mayors and secretaries of Ambon (1966–1998)*

Mayors	Term	Religion	Secretaries	Term	Religion
Ahmad Malawat	1966–1969	Muslim	N. E. Syauta	1966–1969	Protestant
Matheos Manuputty	1969–1975	Protestant	N. E. Syauta	1969–1971	Protestant
S. Assagaf	1975	Muslim	Z. J. Tauran	1971–1980	Muslim
Alberth Porwayla	1975–1986	Protestant	Abd. Fatah Syah Doa	1980–1987	Muslim
J. D. Wattimena	1985–1990	Protestant	J. Tamtelahitu	1987–1992	Protestant
Johanes Sudijono	1990–1996	Catholic	H. Apono	1992–1996	Muslim
Chris Tanasale	1996–2001	Protestant	H. Apono	1996–2001	Muslim

Sources: Mayors' and secretaries' names and terms are based on BPS (2012) volume. Religious identification of mayors and secretaries is based on biographical information available online.

contentious. Against the backdrop of a Muslim (Saleh Latuconsina) succeeding an incumbent Muslim governor (Akib Latuconsina) in Maluku the previous year, and with regents in all other districts within the province being Muslim, the decision on the next mayor of Ambon was interpreted as a harbinger of the likely future status of Ambonese Protestants. Against the municipal council's recommendation to reappoint the incumbent Javanese Catholic Sudijono as mayor, then-governor Latuconsina nominated a Muslim military candidate. Ambonese Protestants strongly resisted this choice and insisted that the successor come from the Ambonese Protestant community (Bertrand 2004). Latuconsina eventually relented and appointed Protestant Chris

Tanasale instead. He was the last New Order mayor of Ambon before his successor, another Protestant, was indirectly elected by the local council in 2001 (Bertrand 2002).

When Soeharto resigned, there was much speculation in Ambon about the new local political configuration. Golkar's hegemony was no longer assured. The date of the upcoming election was announced in December 1998, just one month before the first outburst of violence in Ambon. Muslims feared that Christians were gearing up for the election and that they would expel Muslims – particularly migrant Muslims of Buton, Bugis, and Makassar descent – from the island to remove voters who would vote against the Partai Demokrasi Indonesia-Perjuangan (PDIP) (Tianlean 2005). Although the PDI is officially a secular nationalist party, in Ambon it was predominantly associated with Protestants (van Klinken 2007).

PDIP campaign teams in Ambon were members of the GPM church's youth wing, AM-GPM.[62] Shortly before the first post-Soeharto election in 1999, church ministers encouraged their congregations to vote for the PDIP (van Klinken 2007). Inasmuch as PDIP was the anti–New Order party at the national level, it was also the Christian opposition party in Maluku (van Klinken 2007). Christian Ambonese were hoping for a reversal of fortunes in local government and believed that PDIP was the vehicle. When the results were announced in July 1999, PDIP had won 53% of the votes, while all the Islamist parties won a combined total of 21%. Consistent with its local Christian identification, all but one of PDIP's representatives on the Ambon local council were Protestants (van Klinken 2006).

Christian–Muslim Violence in Ambon The ethnocommunal riots between Christians and Muslims in Ambon were one of the bloodiest, longest, and most complicated episodes of violence during Indonesia's democratic transition. This section highlights how religious politicization, narrative reframing, and coordinated attacks escalated into bloody violence that spread throughout almost the entire province.

The trigger event seemed innocent enough: a brawl between Christian and Muslim youths in the late afternoon of January 19, 1999, which was Idul Fitri, a Muslim holiday.[63] The details about how this initial

---

[62] The reverse was not necessarily true, since some church leaders were active members of Golkar (van Klinken 2007).

[63] The consensus amongst narrative accounts of Christian–Muslim violence in Ambon is that violence began on January 19, 1999. But some accounts maintain that Christians had attacked and destroyed homes of migrant Muslims in Hative Besar, Teluk Baguala, on December 13, 1998 (Tianlean 2005, 90–91).

brawl led to widespread rioting remain sketchy, as both Christians and Muslims claimed that the other side struck first.[64] Both communities did appear to act simultaneously, as rioters from one majority-Christian neighborhood attacked a Muslim neighborhood while Muslim rioters attacked predominantly Christian areas. A Human Rights Watch (1999) report described the two events as occurring within thirty minutes of each other. van Klinken (2007, 98) wrote that "both groups of attackers kept coming back repeatedly, for hours throughout the night."

The fighting spread across the city and continued sporadically through February 1999, involving mostly local Ambonese using home-made weapons, knives, and machetes (ICG 2000). By this point, clashes had spread beyond Ambon to nearby islands, but they had not prompted the arrival of Muslim militias from Java to fight in solidarity with their co-religionists. The months of March through June 1999 were peaceful, and the 1999 election occurred without a hitch.[65] Fighting resumed in Ambon in July 1999 and continued regularly throughout the rest of the year. By August, the clashes had spread to North Maluku province; by December, at least 500 Muslims had been killed in Tobelo, on Halmahera island in North Maluku, and more than 10,000 Muslims had fled the island (ICG 2000). The particularly brutal killings in Tobelo led to widespread outcries against the massacre of Muslims and the government's lack of a firm response. At least 100,000 protesters marched in the streets in Jakarta in January 2000, and a "sword-carrying procession in white robes through the streets in Jakarta" in April 2000 demanded strong action from President Wahid (ICG 2000, 8–9). By May 2000, 3,000 men identified as members of a group called Laskar Jihad had left for Maluku to help the local Muslims battle the Christians. Armed with automatic weapons, these men reached Maluku without any intervention from military or government personnel, despite President Wahid's earlier threats to arrest them (ICG 2000, 9).

The president declared a civil emergency in Maluku and North Maluku provinces on June 27, 2000, and placed a Hindu brigadier general, I Made Yasa, in charge in place of Christian Brigadier General Max Tamaela to ensure military neutrality. Nevertheless, despite the declaration of a civil emergency, the two provinces remained engulfed

---

[64] For Christian accounts of the riots in 1999, see Waileruny et al. (1999); Pieris (2004). For Muslim accounts, see Kastor (2000).

[65] The ICG (2000) reported that voting did not take place in a few districts in Maluku. A number of observers interpreted this lull in fighting as an evidence of elite involvement and a "grand design" to provoke violence (Tianlean 2005, 62).

in violence throughout 2000 and 2001, as the militias continued fighting and driving people from their homes.

Almost no one in Ambon believed that the clashes were spontaneous. While there were differing views on who mobilized violence, to what end, and why ordinary Ambonese participated in the clashes, I was consistently told in many conversations that the clashes in Ambon were cultivated, mobilized, and sustained.

For example, for months prior to the first outburst in January 1999, residents of Ambon had been bombarded with streams of news and a series of events that politicized religion. In October 1998, an anonymous leaflet was widely circulated, claiming that "all 38" top positions in the civil service would be vacated and filled with Muslims (van Klinken 2006, 139). This leaflet politicized religion in Ambon amid the considerable speculation surrounding the post-Soeharto selection process for local representatives and executives.

In late November 1998 in Ketapang, an ethnically diverse neighborhood in Jakarta, after an altercation between local Muslims and a group of Christian Ambonese street thugs (*preman*) who manned a parking lot attached to a church, rumors spread that the Christian Ambonese *preman* had burned a local mosque.[66] A photo journalist's assistant who had captured an image from the Ketapang clash said, "The *preman* were said to have attacked people while they were praying . . . two glass windows at the mosque were broken. But there was this widespread rumor that the mosque had been burned down. Muslims will immediately get emotional when they hear something like that" (Wargadiredja 2018). Clashes intensified over night and led to fourteen deaths. Churches and Christian schools in the same area were burned shortly thereafter, and in retaliation, some Muslims in Kupang West Nusa Tenggara were murdered in December 1998 (van Klinken 2007).

The authorities did not intervene in time to stop the unfolding violence, but shortly after the clash, they sent Ambonese in Jakarta, without proper government-issued IDs listing Jakarta as their official residence, to Ambon. A researcher for Human Rights Watch attributed this decision to the economic uncertainties at the time: "Because business in Jakarta was uncertain, the Ambonese gangsters couldn't feed themselves . . . . It's simple thinking: send them back to Ambon" (Wargadiredja 2018).

---

[66] The term *preman* refers to a member of an organized gang or street level criminal, often contracted to do illegal dealings. The term was derived from an older Dutch term "vrijman" or "free man," which historically referred to "non-contract overseer or a coolie day-laborer, thus still in the employ of the company, though not legally bound to it" (Ryter 2001).

But in Ambon, their arrival stirred anxiety and wariness among local residents. Describing local residents' reaction to this shipment of fighters, one local NGO activist said, "Indeed after Ketapang erupted in 1998, the preman [thugs] were shipped back here to create chaos."[67]

Another NGO activist echoed this observation, attributing the violence that erupted in Ambon in early January 1999 to the arrival of these men:

There was a strong indication that in the Ketapang 1998 incident, sons of Ambon, both Christian and Muslim, were contracted and deliberately sent back to stir trouble in Ambon. I can say this because I think it is strange that they seemed to know before anyone else that the Al Fatah mosque was burned down, even though at the time no one had any cell phones, technology then was not like what it is today. They came with weapons, carrying them everywhere in public. It wasn't easy to get weapons. They must have gotten their supplies from somewhere.[68]

The local government also took measures that further escalated anxiety. The governor's office sent delegations to visit communities across Maluku, telling them to be wary of "provocateurs" and to "listen to their religious leaders" (van Klinken 2007, 97). The governor also instructed mosques to set up telephones so that they could receive information from the large Al Fatah mosque in Ambon. van Klinken (2007) observed that these measures, though perhaps well intentioned, also gave local religious leaders a platform to circulate news rapidly. Abdul Wahab Polpoke, an Ambon-based ulama affiliated with Nahdlatul Ulama and affectionately known as Ustad Polpoke, was one local religious leader who circulated warnings to local residents. Having received information that Ambonese Muslim communities would be attacked on Idul Fitri by supporters of the now-defunct, mostly Christian separatist group Republik Maluku Selatan (RMS), Polpoke announced via a mosque's loudspeakers in advance of the January 19 riots, "Muslim communities [in Ambon] are obliged to prepare with guns, because on the day of Idul Fitri, vast attacks will be committed by RMS. If you die in the warfare you will become a martyr, but if you are not involved in the war and then you die, you will become an infidel" (quoted in Al Qurtuby (2016, 47)). Several interviewees told me that it was well known that the sound of the clanging of a stick hit repeatedly against lamp poles on the street was a signal of an imminent attack.[69]

---

[67] Interviewee 17, Ambon NGO activist, November 7, 2009.
[68] Interviewee 19, Ambon NGO activist, November 7, 2009.
[69] Interviewee 20, academic, November 7, 2009; Interviewee 17, local NGO activist, November 8, 2009; Interviewee 25, local NGO activist, November 6, 2009.

These rumors, preparations, and warnings heightened the salience of religion and primed residents to interpret everyday events, such as fights between Muslim and Christian youths, through a religious lens.

Granted, some of the people I interviewed recognized that these rumors, warnings, and leaflets were not unusual. One NGO activist indicated that such items had appeared in Maluku as far back as the early 1980s. He recalled,

> I remember, even in 1985, when I was in high school, a few times I received in Tidore leaflets that were very provocative. There were so many; we had names for them. Black leaflets, white leaflets, red letters, etc. The claim was about rumors of "Christianization" in the government. But nothing ever came of them.[70]

For many casual observers I interviewed in Ambon, rumormongerers in 1998 were usually *preman*. A Muslim Butonese kiosk owner in Ambon told me: "The tip about the fight between the Butonese and Kailolo, a *preman* said it, I heard. A drunken *preman* said that there was a plan to attack people from Buton."[71]

One person, who spoke on condition of anonymity, told me the names of specific *preman* believed to be responsible for inciting and mobilizing crowds:

> Agus Watimena was the provocateur from the Christian side; on the Sangadji [Muslim] side, there are Ongen Sangaji [and] Basri Sangaji. Agus Watimena died in a clash, Basri is also dead, but the rest of these preman are still alive and well today. Berti was imprisoned, but he was released and is now in Jakarta. He did not want to get out of prison without Munir's [a human rights activist] protection. Ongen Sangaji is still around. Femi Souisa is also still around. These preman were used by the government, and now they are rewarded with projects.[72]

For this person, the fact that *preman* were only lightly penalized for their involvement in violence and could enjoy normal life after the conflict suggests that they must have had links to members of the political elites in either Ambon or Jakarta. Indeed, a Human Rights Watch report named some of the same people and indicated that they had ties to Soeharto's son Bambang Soeharto and daughter Siti Hardianti Rukmana (Human Rights Watch 1999).

---

[70] Interviewee 18, local NGO activist, November 8, 2009.
[71] Interviewee 23, Butonese shopkeeper in Ambon, November 7, 2009.
[72] Interviewee XX, November 7, 2009.

According to one village imam I interviewed, the clashes he witnessed in Ambon "mostly involved youths. Not adults. If adults were ever involved [in a clash], there usually would be a solution."[73]

The initial brawl that set off the riots in Ambon was not much different from other fights that had occurred between youths in Ambon. van Klinken (2007) reported that passers-by barely noticed this initial clash when it occurred on January 19, 1999. One Muslim imam in Ambon told me: "When the first clash erupted, we thought nothing of it. It seemed that it was just a fight between irresponsible youths, and we expected it to die out. But then as the days went on, we kept hearing more and more things."[74]

Instead, many in Ambon believe that these clashes were planned, organized, and deliberately sustained to serve some people's interests. One regional council member in Ambon stressed,

It is normal that Ambonese fight over cloves. Fights between fellow Christians or fellow Muslims, and between Christians and Muslims, are all common. Only within a few months usually everything is normal again. But this last time, it was deliberately provoked and escalated. There were attempts to incite religious fanaticism, such that people could only think about how to remain alive.[75]

One reason why many people believe that these clashes were planned was the coordination and targeting of violence that emphasized religion rather than other dimensions of identity. In the first few days of violence in Ambon, the targets were non-Ambonese Muslim migrants of Buton, Bugis, and Makassar (BBM) descent. Schulze (2017, 2104) reported that in the early days of the conflict, there were "calls for the BBM to leave Maluku, as well as anti-BBM banners and slogans." A Christian former mayor of Ambon, Dicky Wattimena, was reportedly seen giving instructions and telling BBM migrants to go home during the riot (Schulze 2017). Yet despite the initial targeting of migrant Muslims in the early days of the riots, very quickly the events adopted religious undertones given the targeting, coordination, and other attributes of the violence that followed.

In its description of Ambonese Christians' burning of kiosks and pedicabs (becak) owned by BBM migrants on January 19, the Human Rights Watch (1999, 13) wrote,

Christians gathered at the GPM church on Anthony Rebok Avenue about 10:00 p.m. and burned a few kiosks at the edge of the street before going after the

---

[73] Interviewee 28, village religious leader, November 6, 2009.
[74] Interviewee 26, Muslim preacher, November 6, 2009.
[75] Interviewee 44, Ambon local council member, January 20, 2004.

pedicabs (*becak*) owned largely by Butonese and Bugis. They piled the becaks into a huge stack, then set the stack alight. Muslims who lived around the al-Fatah mosque then joined forces with the Muslims already on the street. Christians and Muslims forces faced off around Avenue A.M. Sangaji, one of Ambon's main streets.

Along those streets, Muslims were handing out white armbands and headbands to other Muslims so that they would be able to identify each other. Nur Wenno, head of the information post (*posko*) at the al-Fatah mosque, told the Human Rights Watch that from about 7:00 p.m. on the evening of January 19, he ordered people at the mosque to wear a white cloth on their right wrist during the day and on their left at night.

Another NGO activist said that the shift happened subtly, but there was a clear departure from the initial clashes:

At first it was the clash between Yopie and Syamsul. Yopie is Ambonese, and Syamsul is Butonese. But that was just a simple clash, between Butonese and Ambonese. We didn't really care much since it was just [an] ethnic [clash]. So it didn't escalate. When the Butonese were being killed, Ambonese Muslims didn't feel frightened or threatened, since the target was clearly Butonese migrants. But then, the Silo church was burned. The Al Fatah mosque was burned. And [the killing] kept on, so eventually they said how come so many Muslims are dying.[76]

Even in these early days, the participants in violence were already identifying themselves along religious lines. Muslim fighters identified themselves with white armbands and headbands; Christians wore red ones.

Ambonese Christians and Muslims alike describe the conflict as a "holy war," consistent with the religious symbols and inscriptions, rallying cries, and pre-battle rites that accompanied these clashes (Al Qurtuby 2016, 75). Al Qurtuby (2016, 47, 54, 75) recounted that Muslim fighters were adorned in white and frequently shouted "Allahu Akbar," while Christian rioters went into battle singing hymns, after saying prayers and receiving blessings from church ministers, many of whom were themselves fighters. In Muslim homes ransacked and looted by Christians, messages reading "Jesus" or "I love Jesus" were inscribed on the walls, further demonstrating the use of religion in mobilizing rioters (Ecip 1999, 100).

Beyond religious attributes and rhetoric, religious buildings were the primary targets and coordination posts during the riots. Although

---

[76] Interviewee 17, local NGO activist, November 7, 2009.

there was no evidence that the GPM synod or the Catholic diocese of Ambon provided institutional support for Christian combatants, many of them were activists in AM-GPM, the youth wing of the GPM synod (Al Qurtuby 2016; van Klinken 2007). One of Ambon's main churches, Maranatha, became the site of a communications office that coordinated battle information and disseminated it to other churches in Maluku. Al Fatah, Ambon's main mosque, served a similar purpose for Muslim combatants (van Klinken 2007). Those who died in battle were hailed as martyrs by their respective communities.

Commenting on the targets of violence in Ambon, one interviewee described how the conflict shifted from initially targeting BBM migrants to targeting religious groups:

Conflict in Ambon began because the PDIP was about to go up [compete] in the election. In Maluku, the PDIP is a Christian party. There were skirmishes of violence targeted against BBM migrants at the beginning of the conflict. The homes of BBM migrants were burned down. However, this issue was not strong enough to push people out, so the issues were reshaped to be about religion. The Al Fatah mosque and the Silo church were attacked, to anger both Muslims and Christian Ambonese.[77]

These interviewees' comments indicate that aggrieved local elites took an active part not only in shaping the narrative of the conflict but also in the coordination, mobilization, and production of violence in Ambon from 1998 through 2001.

Still, for one Christian NGO activist I interviewed, the involvement of local religious leaders during the conflict was not strategic but driven by peer pressure:

Ambonese Christians are generally churchgoers. So during the conflict, whether they wanted to or not, pastors also had to get involved. It's a lie if anyone said they weren't involved; as long as they didn't flee Ambon, they were involved. Everyone gathered at church before the fight. Before every fight, we all prayed at church. At that time, everyone was very emotional and angry. No one could say, "do not fight." They would be killed.[78]

One Christian reverend echoed this overwhelming power of social pressure:

At that point, it was very hard to calm the people. Muslims fled to a mosque and were barricaded by soldiers. I tried to stop the people from bombing and setting the mosque on fire, but they yelled that we will be the first they killed

---

[77] Interviewee 19, local NGO activist, November 7, 2009.
[78] Interviewee 17, local NGO activist, November 7, 2009.

if we "betray them by protecting the Muslims." It was very hard to stop that movement.[79]

These interviewees' comments indicate that aggrieved local elites took an active part not only in shaping the narrative of the conflict, but also in the coordination, mobilization, and production of violence in Ambon from 1998 through 2001. Once the wheels were set in motion and violence was unfolding, it appears that there was simply too much pressure not to participate.

District 4: Maluku Tenggara

Maluku Tenggara – a district with hundreds of islands lying more than 600 kilometers southeast of Ambon – rarely captured media attention before 1999. At the time, Maluku Tenggara had three main archipelagos: the Kei islands, Tanimbar islands, and Aru islands. The district lost a substantial portion of its territory, population, and natural resources when Maluku Tenggara Barat, the Aru islands, and Tual splintered in 1999, 2003, and 2008, respectively, to form separate administrative units. By 2015, the district was home to 98,684 people and covered an expanse of over 4,000 square kilometers (BPS 2016a, 10,64).

Historically, Maluku Tenggara was one of the poorest districts in Maluku. In 1986, there were only five wells serving 13,000 people in Tual, the main town in the Kei islands (Laksono 2002). In 1996, only 51% of households in Maluku Tenggara had access to clean water, and just 37% of homes were electrified (DAPOER data). In 2002, 39% of the district's population lived in poverty. These islands are so remote that as of March 1999, there were only twelve policemen in Tual (ICG 2000). In 2000, its regional GDP per capita was at 700,000 rupiah.[80]

The population of Maluku Tenggara is religiously diverse but ethnically more homogeneous than Ambon's. In the 2000 census, 38.97% of the district's population identified as Muslim, 25.82% as Catholic, and 35.34% as Protestant. With this demographic composition, Maluku Tenggara had a slightly higher level of religious fractionalization than Ambon, albeit with a different dominant religious group. In terms of ethnic composition, the 2000 census reported that 61% of the district's population identified as ethnic Kei, 25.67% as ethnic Aru, and about 1% as Javanese. When Laksono (2002) conducted his fieldwork in Kei in 1986, he observed that almost everyone there spoke the native

---

[79] Interviewee 43, local pastor, February 6, 2009.
[80] This figure is based on the district's total GDP excluding oil and gas (in millions of rupiah), in constant prices, as reported by DAPOER.

language and that the population was overwhelmingly ethnically Kei. Based on the 2000 census data for Maluku Tenggara, the district's overall ethnic fractionalization score was 0.54, only slightly less than Ambon's 0.73.

The islands of Maluku Tenggara have been home to multiple faith communities for a long time. When Jesuit missionaries arrived in Tual in 1888, they discovered that most of its residents were Muslim. Elat, a city on the neighboring island of Kei Besar, was already an important hub for Protestant missionaries. By the 1920s, Kei's residents were 34% Muslim, 28% Catholic, and 18% Protestant. Much like communities in other parts of Maluku, however, these groups were generally separated into religious enclaves; each village was either predominantly Muslim, Protestant, or Catholic (Aritonang and Steenbrink 2008). In villages where more than one religion is represented, communities of faith self-segregate into different quarters within the village (Thorburn 2002).

The Local Political Configuration The early political preferences of Maluku Tenggara voters are reflected in the 1955 election results. Parkindo received 43% of the votes, the Catholic party 21%, and Masyumi 20% in the constitutional election. A similar breakdown (40%, 21%, and 21%, respectively, for the three parties) can be found in the results of the 1955 legislative election. Taken together, more than 80% of votes went to religious parties in Maluku Tenggara in 1955. In the 1971 election, Golkar won 58.9%, Parkindo and Catholic parties received a combined 30.1%, and Islamist parties PSII, NU, and Masyumi won 7.6% (Hering and Willis 1973, 126).

Yet by 1998, even though local politics in Maluku Tenggara mirrored that in Ambon, religion was far less politicized. The religious identification of officials appointed to key posts in the district indicates a power-sharing arrangement in the local government between Muslims, Catholics, and Protestants. When the district chief was Muslim, the accompanying secretary would come from the Protestant or Catholic community, and vice versa. In general, the council chairs of Maluku Tenggara since 1977 have been Muslim while the council vice chairs have been a mix of Catholics, Muslims, and Protestants. Maluku Tenggara's regents were mostly Catholics or Protestants until the very last one prior to Soeharto's resignation, Hi. H. A. Rahayaan (regent from 1991 through 2002).

More than religion, the dimension of identity that determines access to local political posts in the Kei islands is one's status within the customary *adat* system. The Kei customary law, Hukum Larwul Ngabal, holds an important role in the islands. The words "Larwul Ngabal" are in the district official emblem, on the uniforms of district civil servants, and on government buildings (Hooe 2012, 201). One observer stated that the Larwul Ngabal has "come to define what it is to be Keiese" (Thorburn 2008, 116). Rahayaan, the former regent of Maluku Tenggara, said, "When we speak of law in Kei, we mean first and foremost Hukum Larwul Ngabal. After that there is the religious law of the al-Quran and the Bible, and thirdly the formal law of the Republic of Indonesia" (quoted in Thorburn (2002, 1)). Thorburn (2002, 5) found this sentiment echoed by many of the informants he interviewed during his fieldwork in Kei in 1997–1998, concluding that "the bonds of family and adat were far more important, and far stronger, than any differences between imported religions."

The *adat* laws divide the Keiese people into three segments: the *mel-mel* (nobility), *ren-ren* (commoners), and *iri-iri* (slaves) (van Klinken 2006; Hooe 2012). Of the three groups, the *mel-mel* dominate Maluku Tenggara's bureaucracy (Madubun 1997; van Klinken 2007). In his field research in the 1990s, Hooe (2012) learned that many of his *ren-ren* and *iri-iri* interviewees could not get government jobs despite their college degrees, because membership in the higher rank of *mel-mel* was a more important requirement (Hooe 2012, 156–157). Whatever screening process that district officials conducted was intended to ensure that only individuals of *mel-mel* rank were appointed to village chief positions (Hooe 2012). Similarly, van Klinken (2006, 138) noted that "membership of the aristocracy is the first (but unwritten!) rule governing participation in the local governing elite."

The local bureaucracy in Maluku Tenggara, while relatively diverse in terms of religion, is relatively homogeneous in terms of *adat* ranks. High-ranking officials in the local government are generally also *adat* nobility.

Violence in Maluku Tenggara Although fights were not unheard of before the 1999 riots between Christians and Muslims in Maluku Tenggara, the eruption of ethnocommunal conflict there came as a complete surprise.[81] A few days before serious violence began in Kei in March 1999, a Kei *adat* leader commented publicly at a national convention of customary law leaders in Jakarta, that the Christian–Muslim violence in Ambon "cannot happen in Kei; our family ties and *adat* traditions are far more important to us than any religious differences" (quoted in Hooe, 2012, 237).

---

[81] Hooe (2012) provides a thorough overview of recent conflicts in Kei before the 1999 violence. See Hooe (2012, 211–233).

Compared to the clashes in Ambon, ethnocommunal violence between Christians and Muslims in Maluku Tenggara was less intense and shorter in duration. After a small outburst of violence in Dobo, in the Aru islands, in January 1999, violence began in earnest in Maluku Tenggara at the end of March 1999. After months of hearing news and updates about violence in Ambon and in other parts of Maluku, Kei residents had their own experience of ethnocommunal violence after a Christian youth spray-painted insulting graffiti on a wall in Tual on March 29, 1999, a couple of days after the Muslim holiday Idul Adha (Thorburn 2002, 1). The offending youth was arrested but subsequently released by the police (then headed by a Catholic) on the grounds that he was legally a minor (ICG 2007, 4). This action angered many Muslims, who viewed the treatment as too lenient. Rumors swirled that Christians would attack Tual Muslims, and people began erecting barriers in their neighborhoods to protect themselves against attacks (ICG 2007, 5). One leader of a Muslim youth organization explained, "In Tual, the potential for conflict came from external actors. People from Ambon arrived with various information, which made our people emotional and angry."[82]

When fighting did erupt, villagers donned themselves with red or white headbands to mark their religious identification. Armed with machetes, spears, bows, and bamboo cannons, Christian fighters gathered at a church to pray before moving en masse to attack predominantly Muslim villages. Christian fighters subsequently launched additional offensives, attacking mosques on April 2, 1999, as Muslims were gathered for Friday prayers (Ecip 1999, 121–126). Fighting spread across the Kei islands for the following two months, claiming at least 200 lives and displacing one-quarter of the islands' residents (Thorburn 2002, 2).

Eyewitness accounts of the clashes in Kei noted that some high-ranking local government bureaucrats (and their relatives) were seen directing crowds and coordinating attacks (Ecip 1999, 123). Two of the villages involved in the early rounds of fighting on April 2, 1999, were those of the Protestant district secretary and Muslim regent (Thorburn 2002, 2). Thorburn (2008) observed that the villages involved in the conflict from April through June 1999 were those with a high number of civil servants and government officials. Although this information suggests that some local elites were involved in coordinating and mobilizing violence in the Kei islands, their efforts were overshadowed by local customary leaders' efforts to quell the disturbances.

Fighting in the Kei islands ceased in June 1999, approximately three months after it began. Compared to clashes in other parts of Maluku,

[82] Interviewee 47, leader of Muslim youth organization, January 25, 2004.

violence in Maluku Tenggara was shorter and much more contained. When clashes erupted, customary leaders from Kei Besar and Kei Kecil sent letters to the village chiefs in their jurisdiction, stressing that, "according to *adat*, we can engage in war in only two circumstances: if the honor of our women is violated, or if others encroach on our territory. These situations are not part of the current conflict. Therefore we cannot fight one another because there is no reason or excuse to fight" (quoted in Hooe, 2012, 245).

There were other appeals to the customary law to stop violence. One *raja* in Tual described the *adat* leaders' response to the clashes in this way:

There are twelve main *rajas* in Kei Kecil and Kei Besar. This group of rajas traveled throughout the villages – six in Kei Kecil and six in Kei Besar – to explain that we should not be attacking each other anymore. We did not have much money, but we have authority over the customary laws. We declared a sanction that whichever village resumes violence, then all other villages will unite and attack that village. We traveled across the villages for one month.[83]

One leader of a Muslim youth organization in Tual confirmed the importance of customary leaders' role in restoring order after the 1999 conflicts:

Here, conflict ended much more quickly than in Ambon because of the exemplary involvement of the *bapa raja* and religious leaders. I also think our people are generally still more cohesive and tightly knit. The issues that made people angry were stuff that were imported from Ambon. We just received their ripples. In Ambon there are so many problems, and the *adat* leaders are not consistent; they themselves often violated *adat* rules. In Maluku Tenggara, *adat* is much stronger. In Ambon, *pela gandong* is a mere ritual.[84]

A survey of 100 respondents in the Kei islands confirmed this sentiment, with 75% of survey respondents reporting their belief that violence in Maluku Tenggara was started by people who fled Ambon.[85]

Other local efforts to restore peace began almost immediately in June 1999. *Adat* ceremonies stressing the common bond across the different religious groups were performed for the reopening of churches and mosques, the return of refugees, and the building of *adat* monuments in affected villages (Hooe 2012, 246–247). In March 2000, 1,500 *adat*, government, and religious leaders from Maluku gathered in Langgur, in Kei Kecil, for a conference on the revitalization of *adat* for peace and

---

[83] Interviewee 45, Tual customary leader, January 28, 2004.
[84] Interviewee 47, leader of Muslim youth organization, January 25, 2004.
[85] Uar (2005), quoted in ICG (2007, 4).

reconciliation (Hooe 2012, 247). Although the incorporation of appeals to customary laws in peace and reconciliation efforts has occurred elsewhere as well, nowhere else was it as successful as in Maluku Tenggara.

One possible reason for this difference, as Hooe (2012) has highlighted, is the dominance of the *mel-mel*, Kei aristocrats, in the district bureaucracy. Because many of the ethnic Kei aristocrats and customary leaders were already part of the state's local apparatus, it was in their interest to stop the spread of violence and restore order. Kei ethnic leaders were not interested in fighting battles that they viewed had come from Ambon.

Another possible reason, as suggested by my interviewee's comments, is that ethnic institutions and residents' attachment to their ethnic groups in Maluku Tenggara are far stronger than in Ambon or in other areas where violence escalated and adopted a religious framing despite initial ethnic undertones. In Ambon, as well as in Kei, local customary leaders made statements and appeals to stop violence. Yet, the effectiveness of Kei ethnic leaders' appeals and efforts to quell it indicate that residents in Kei were willing to listen to their ethnic leaders, who had sought to stop violence. The appeals that had fallen on deaf ears in other places had worked well in Maluku Tenggara. This suggests that, in addition to the political accommodation of local elites, conflict may be avoided in Maluku Tenggara in part due to the strength of the residents' attachment to their ethnic community, leaders, and institutions.

Conclusion

The four cases examined in this chapter, Ambon and Maluku Tenggara in Maluku province and Poso and Banggai in Central Sulawesi province, highlight the importance of excluded local elites in framing, mobilizing, and organizing violence during the democratic transition in Indonesia. Although the four districts were similar in their levels of religious and ethnic diversity, measures of economic development and dependence on the state, and geographical distance from Jakarta, Ambon and Poso had some of the heaviest, most protracted ethnocommunal violence in the country. Their neighboring districts, Maluku Tenggara and Banggai, on the other hand, were relatively peaceful in comparison. Banggai had hardly any incidents of conflict between Christians and Muslims during the transition years, and Maluku Tenggara experienced relatively limited fighting for three months. In this chapter, I have shown that the diverging outcomes across the four districts can be traced to the districts' local political configuration at the time of the democratic transition, and to the local elites' actions and responses to trigger events.

At the time of the democratic transition, religion was already politicized in Ambon and Poso. My interviewees consistently stressed the importance of power sharing between Christians and Muslims in the bureaucracy, and many commented on how Christians in their districts had felt increasingly marginalized during the later years of Soeharto's rule. District regents, secretaries, and council chairs regularly represented different religious communities during a particular term. The PDI, the New Order's perceived opposition party, had a religious dimension in Poso and Ambon, since many PDI party activists were simultaneously Christian community leaders. The first bouts of fighting in Poso and Ambon erupted within months before the district elections in which local executive and legislative seats would be at stake for the first time. One widely circulated rumor in Ambon during November and December 1998 was that Muslims would be attacked and driven off the island to ensure that the PDI would win the 1999 election.

In contrast, religion was not as politicized in Banggai and Maluku Tenggara. Instead, the dimension of identity that mattered more was ethnicity. In Banggai, the customary leaders of the Banggai ethnic community were well accommodated in the local government and in a position to shape the rhetoric and priorities of the district. In Maluku Tenggara, Kei aristocrats of *mel-mel* rank have dominated local leadership positions.

In response to a trigger event, religious elites in Ambon and Poso quickly mobilized along religious lines – setting up coordination posts in mosques and churches, marching with fighters and singing religious hymns after prayers and blessings, and describing the conflict as a holy war. In Banggai, on the other hand, local elites explicitly labeled an initial clash involving Christians and Muslims as a spillover from Poso, implying that local Banggai residents should have no role in these external conflicts. In Maluku Tenggara, although clashes did erupt and pit Christians against Muslims for three months, the customary local leaders swiftly took various measures to appeal to their communities to stop the violence. As in Banggai, the initial fights between Christians and Muslims in Maluku Tenggara were also a ripple effect from Ambon, and the *rajas* of Maluku Tenggara reminded their people of the *adat* bond that united them. Whereas local elites in Ambon and Poso reframed banal fights between Christian and Muslim youths and escalated them into more intense violence, in Maluku Tenggara and Banggai they worked hard to quell violence by appealing to the people's common bonds of customary laws and history. These appeals were effective, indicating both that local elites were committed to stopping violence and that their co-ethnic residents valued their attachment to their ethnic communities sufficiently to abide by the expectations of the groups' leaders.

This chapter has shown that local elites' interests in local positions influenced their reactions to trigger events. Their demand for a new local political arrangement influenced whether or not they framed trigger events in ways that would allow violence to escalate or dissipate. Although in both Maluku and Central Sulawesi violence began in advance of the 1999 national election, it is important to note that these clashes escalated and widened well beyond elections in ways that earlier theories focused on elites' electoral incentives as a predictor of violence cannot sufficiently explain. Violence continued to the extent that local elites found it useful to leverage their demands for a more favorable local political arrangement. In Chapter 7, I show that when a new arrangement of local power sharing – largely through the creation of new administrative units – successfully appeases local elites' concerns, violence dissipates.

7   How Riots Dissipated

Ambon today bears little trace of its past violence. In contrast to my first visits half a decade earlier, in 2009 the city was no longer full of damaged buildings with anti-Muslim or anti-Christian graffiti written on their walls. Many of the neighborhoods abandoned as residents fled from violence are now inhabited again, albeit in some cases by new groups of people. When I visited in 2009, the city was preparing to welcome and install the World Peace Gong, having been selected by the United Nations Committee on World Peace as the thirty-fourth site to receive this landmark (Kompas 2009).[1] Except for this big gong, I saw few physical reminders of past violence at prominent spots in the city. The billboards that dotted Ambon's streets – campaign slogans, advertisements, and public service announcements – looked remarkably similar to those found in cities that had remained peaceful during Indonesia's transition years.

A local NGO activist who had remained in Ambon throughout the years of severe conflict described the striking difference:

Between 1999 and 2002, nobody dared enter this [Christian] area. [Name redacted] and I risked lives every day to enter Christian neighborhoods to exchange information and basic supplies; I had to take off my *jilbab* [hijab]. Nowadays, we can come in and out of neighborhoods easily. Back then, nobody uttered the word "peace" because it could anger people and risk your life. Now, we have the World Peace Gong coming to Ambon.[2]

Despite the hundreds of lives lost and the protracted fighting between Christians and Muslims during Indonesia's transition years, Ambon

---

[1] The gong, which displays the flags of hundreds of countries and symbols of the world's major religions, now sits in Ambon's central park, Taman Pelita, where it was installed in a November 2009 ceremony by President Soesilo Bambang Yudhoyono. Ambon is one of three Indonesian cities with a World Peace Gong (Tempo 2011). The other two, Yogyakarta and Kupang, were also affected by rioting during Indonesia's democratic transition and have made similar strides in reestablishing peace.
[2] Interviewee 24, local NGO activist, November 6, 2009.

today appears to have mostly recovered from violence. Although occasional youth brawls after drunken revelries in the city were reported as recently as of March 2018, these clashes did not escalate into full-blown ethnic riots or interreligious strife like those that claimed hundreds of lives nearly two decades earlier (Pamanawa News 2018).

This decline in ethnic rioting reflects a common pattern across Indonesia (Barron, Jaffrey, and Varshney 2016). At its peak in 1999, ethnic riots directly caused 2,102 deaths in Indonesia; by 2004, there were only 22. High-conflict provinces such as West Kalimantan, Central Sulawesi, and North Maluku experienced sharp drops in violence. Figure 7.1 shows the pattern over time of incidents of ethnic rioting and resulting deaths and injuries in the high-conflict areas of West Kalimantan, Central Kalimantan, Central Sulawesi, Maluku, and North Maluku.

These charts demonstrate that the riots had largely ended by 2004. Although Maluku and North Maluku saw some recurrence of rioting in 2011, it never approached the severity of 1999 and 2000 (Barron, Jaffrey, and Varshney 2016).[3]

Indonesia's relatively quick decline in violence is unusual for areas affected by clashes between ethnic groups. Typically, locations that have been exposed to violent conflict experience additional clashes for a longer period of time (Walter 2004). Collier, Hoeffler, and Soderbom (2008) have described this continuity of violence as the "conflict trap," from which bitterly divided countries can escape only with great difficulty. Even if the intensity of recurring violence may not be the same, post-conflict areas are usually vulnerable to other forms of violence (Fortna 2008; Boyle 2014). Some students of civil wars have argued that ethnic wars tend to last longer than non-ethnic wars (Fearon 2004; Montalvo and Reynal-Querol 2010).[4] These insights from other parts of the world would suggest that Indonesia's outbursts of ethnocommunal violence during political transition should have lasted much longer than they did. Yet, within five years of the first eruption of ethnic rioting after Soeharto's ouster, violence had virtually disappeared even in the highest-conflict provinces.

What accounts for this decline? One implication of my theory is that once political exclusion has been ameliorated, violence should diminish. Some precedents suggest such a relationship. In a recent study

---

[3] This decline in the level and severity of violence characterized other types of communal violence in Indonesia as well (Barron, Jaffrey, and Varshney 2016).

[4] Others disagree with this claim, however, contending that the length of ethnic civil wars has less to do with ethnicity directly and is more linked to the governments' relationship with ethnic groups (Wucherpfennig et al. 2012).

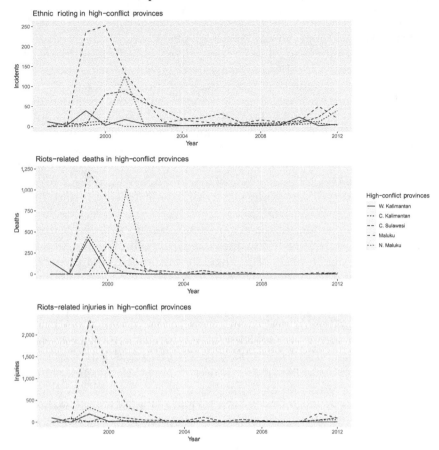

Figure 7.1 Declining violence in high-conflict provinces

of ethnic civil wars, Cederman, Gleditsch, and Wucherpfennig (2017) demonstrated that ethnic civil wars around the world declined in the mid-1990s, in part because governments implemented more accommodating and inclusive policies toward excluded groups. Typically, greater political inclusion would imply, at a minimum, an increase in the political representation of marginalized communities. Ethnic quotas in legislative positions are one common way to achieve this goal.

For recently transitioned countries, there is another possible, though not heavily studied, institutional solution to demands for political inclusion: the creation of new administrative units. Carving out new local governments from existing ones increases the number of administrative positions, elected seats, and local agencies involved in the daily tasks of local government. Although this action effectively expands the size of government and may have negative fiscal effects, it also means more opportunities for those who aspire to government positions and can thus help to accommodate previously excluded groups.

In this chapter, I test whether violence declines once excluded local actors are accommodated in local politics. If, as I have proposed, local-level political exclusion motivates the mobilization of ethnic riots during political transition, then accommodating the excluded groups should cause violence to dissipate. To evaluate hypotheses 8a and 8b from Chapter 2, this chapter analyzes whether districts with a prior history of ethnic riots that have experienced a turnover of leadership and/or an increase in electoral competition are more likely to witness a decline in violence. Since political inclusion can be achieved by exiting the district and creating a separate administrative unit, hypothesis 9 suggests that districts with higher levels of political exclusion during a democratic transition should be more likely to split. By the same logic, hypothesis 10 predicts that districts with higher levels of ethnic rioting during a political transition should be more likely to split than districts that remained peaceful.

Furthermore, this theory also has implications for the characteristics of newly partitioned or "child" districts. If it is true that district splits are driven in part by excluded ethnic groups' desire to attain better political inclusion in the new child districts, then the newly partitioned districts in conflict-affected provinces should be more ethnically homogeneous than their parent districts (hypothesis 11a). Also, newly partitioned districts in conflict areas should have a majority population that is ethnically different from that of their parent districts (hypothesis 11b). Lastly, partitioned districts in conflict areas should elect leaders whose ethnic affiliations reflect those of the district's population with greater frequency after the split (hypothesis 11c).

To examine these hypotheses, I first investigate the statistical relationship between declines in political exclusion and in violence in riot-affected districts. Second, I consider whether exclusive districts are more likely to be partitioned than others. Third, I seek to identify the unique characteristics of newly partitioned districts, which should follow the pattern outlined above if district splitting is motivated at least in part by excluded groups' desires to carve out separate units for themselves. To test hypotheses 8a, 8b, 9, and 10, I rely on statistical analyses of an unbalanced panel of districts and municipalities in Indonesia from 1999 through 2012. To examine hypotheses 11a, 11b, and 11c, I compare relevant district indicators.

The next section discusses the prevalence of subnational administrative unit proliferations around the world, along with their determinants, procedures, and consequences as observed in earlier studies. Then, I describe how Indonesia's implementation of decentralization after Soeharto's ouster has enabled greater local autonomy, political competition, and the creation of new districts. In the subsequent section, I discuss the methodological approach and data used to examine the implications of my theory. After that, I present the results of my quantitative analysis, followed by a summary of the chapter's findings.

Administrative Unit Proliferation around the World

The proliferation of administrative units, broadly defined as the creation of new units within a state's territory, has been common in developing and post-communist countries (Swianiewicz 2010).[5] Some have specified further that administrative unit proliferation is particularly common when countries are transitioning from authoritarian rule to a multiparty system (Boone 2003; Hassan 2016).

Geographically, this trend is particularly prevalent in sub-Saharan Africa, where 29 countries saw an increase of at least 20% in their number of administrative units between 1990 and 2012 (Blom-Hansen et al. 2016).[6] Ghana nearly doubled its number of districts from 110 to 216 in the span of 12 years (Resnick 2017). Zambia added almost 30 new districts "nearly doubled" between 2011 and 2016 (Resnick 2017), and Kenya's districts between 1992 and 2002 (Hassan 2016, 510). Unit proliferation has also been quite common on other continents. Vietnam's number of provinces grew from 40 in 1988 to 64 in 2004 (Malesky 2009). Similarly, Hungary and Czechoslovakia experienced a 50% increase in

---

[5] The term *administrative unit proliferation* is often used interchangeably with *district splits* (Pierskalla 2016), *government fragmentation* (Billing 2019), and *district creation* (Hassan 2016), even though the proliferation of units can also happen at a higher (e.g., state, province) or lower (e.g., ward, commune, village, subdistrict) tier of government. The partitioning of districts to create more units is also different from gerrymandering, which involves redrawing electoral district boundaries so that the group creating the new lines is virtually assured of victory (Groffman 1985; Malesky 2009). Often gerrymandering also implies discrimination against certain voters along party and racial lines (Marelius 2005). The total number of administrative units does not change as a result of gerrymandering.

[6] This trend of administrative subdivision of units runs counter to the trend of amalgamation of units in developed countries since 1950 (Blom-Hansen et al. 2016). In Sweden, for example, the number of municipalities has shrunk from 2,281 in 1951 (Lidstrom 2010) to just 278 in 1975 (Hinnerich 2009). Similar trends have occurred in the Netherlands (Allers and Geertsma 2016), Germany (Blesse and Baskaran 2016), and Japan (Nakazawa 2013) among others.

municipalities between 1989 and 1993 (Grossman and Lewis 2014). In Brazil, the number of municipalities grew from 4,491 to 5,561 between 1991 and 2001 (Lima and Neto 2018).

Frequently implemented as part of countries' decentralization reforms, the creation of new, smaller administrative units is designed to reduce the distance between governments and citizens and thereby improve service provision (Bardhan 2002). Politicians typically justify splitting districts by claiming that it will bring local governments closer to the people. South Sudan president Salva Kiir, for example, stated that the purpose of creating new states was to "decentralize power, placing resources closer to the rural population while at the same time reducing the size of the national government" (Resnick 2017, 48).

Many politicians are so convinced of both the effectiveness and the popularity of creating new districts that they are not shy about taking credit for them. For example, K. Chandrashekhar Rao, chief minister of India's Telangana state, claimed at a gathering in Narayanpet in advance of the state's assembly election in December 2018, "I take 100% responsibility of making Narayanpet a district. The earlier CMs [chief ministers] didn't create a single district, but with your blessings I created 31 districts; it won't be difficult for me to make Narayanpet the 32nd district"(The News Minute 2018). When he pushed for the creation of 31 districts in 2014, Rao contended that the new districts would enable better governance (The News Minute 2018). International financial institutions and donors have enthusiastically supported these reforms on the same grounds (Hassan and Sheely 2016).

The implementation of administrative unit proliferation varies across countries. In some Sub-Saharan African countries, incumbent presidents may create new administrative units without needing approval from either the legislature or an independent commission (Resnick 2017; Prempeh 2008). In Kenya, for example, executives can unilaterally create new units (Hassan 2016). Sometimes, the central government may not necessarily desire unit proliferation but implements it anyway because international donors want to showcase this reform as part of a larger package of decentralization actions. For example, Englebert and Sangare (2010, 17) reported that there was little local demand for the creation of new units in Burkina Faso, and that the government implemented the reform simply "because donors wanted it."

Other countries, meanwhile, have adopted a more bottom-up and consultative approach to district creation. In India, after the announcement of the schedule for creating new districts in Telangana, the state government encouraged district collectors to submit proposals for new districts, in advance of consultations with the state's representatives.

A draft would be made publicly available after a conference with district collectors, and citizens would then have one month to provide feedback (The Times of India 2016).[7] Similarly, in Uganda, existing local district councils must pass a motion to approve the secession of a portion of its territory and then forward the request to the Ministry of Local Government. If that ministry approves, the proposal proceeds to the Parliament for further deliberation (Grossman and Lewis 2014).

In theory, smaller administrative units offer a lot to like. They should give local governments better information about local preferences and needs than the central government (Oates 1972), and this better information should result in efficiency gains. Moreover, smaller units should also imply greater accountability and transparency of government officials. And smaller units make it easier for citizens to move between administrative units as a signal of dissatisfaction with their local government, thereby pressing government officials to improve their performance (Tiebout 1956).

In practice, however, the creation of new administrative units around the world has generally been driven by considerations other than improving government performance and services. Some scholars have argued that national-level political elites partition local administrative units to enlarge their political support base and weaken opposition candidates (Green 2010; Kraxberger 2004). In Kenya, Hassan (2016) has shown that incumbent executive leaders strategically created new units in anticipation of a competitive election where voters in the new units may be more readily persuaded to vote for the incumbents in the upcoming election. In Uganda, for example, newly formed units provided incumbent president Museveni with an additional 2.5% to 3% of the vote (Grossman and Lewis 2014). In countries plagued by threats of secession and civil war, local administrative unit partitioning is a way to appease demands for greater autonomy without relinquishing control of the national government altogether (Lake and Rothchild 2005; Hechter 2000). The Soviet Union's creation of local autonomous units and indigenization (*korenizatsiya*) of the local government's bureaucracy was an example of this strategy, although some have argued that it backfired since it only fueled even greater demands for autonomy (Roeder 1991, 203–204). Pierskalla (2016) has shown that the creation of new administrative units in Indonesia was motivated by residents' desire for greater ethnic homogeneity.

---

[7] District collectors are members of the civil service responsible for, among other things, supervising district governance activities, such as the collection of taxes and provision of public services.

The effects of administrative unit breakup on governance are also ambiguous. In India, villages in newly created states witnessed an improvement in nighttime lighting and education outcomes (Asher and Novosad 2017). In a study of Malawi, Nigeria, and Uganda, Grossman, Pierskalla, and Dean (2017) demonstrated that fragmented regions had better health-care outcomes. On the other hand, Lima and Neto (2018) found that partitioned municipalities in Brazil experienced an increase in per capita public expenditures, due to reduced economies of scale and rent-seeking behavior. In Burkina Faso, Billing (2018) indicated that communities in splinter units have poorer access to public services than those in units that did not split.

I will now examine how the creation of new districts helped to accommodate the demands of excluded ethnic groups in Indonesia and reduced overall levels of violence.

Administrative Unit Proliferation in Indonesia

In Indonesia, district splits were part of the country's big-bang decentralization. Faced with growing demands for more regional autonomy in resource-rich areas, the Indonesian government passed decentralization laws in 1999 and implemented decentralizing reforms in 2001. With Laws no. 22 and 25 of 1999, the central government devolved political and fiscal autonomy to districts and municipalities. This devolution marked a change from the New Order, under which Indonesia was a centralized, unitary state in which most important decisions were determined at the national level. Provincial and district governments functioned as local coordinators and representatives of the central government, which meant in practice that the provincial and district executives had little say over decisions concerning service provision and distribution (Hadiz 2010; Antlov 2003).[8] Through decentralization, the central government granted autonomy over the provision of services such as education, health, and infrastructure to local governments, keeping only fiscal and monetary policies, foreign policies, and defense issues under its direct control.

The central government also distributes general and earmarked fiscal transfers to equip local governments to carry out their responsibilities and to address regional disparities (Tadjoeddin 2011). Funds actually

---

[8] Antlov (2003, 143) reported that in the New Order regime, "priorities and initiatives were determined from atop and seldom in line with local demands .... Budget allocations were not based on performance or need, but rather on how close local governments were with the central government and how well local elites could lobby decision-makers in Jakarta."

generated by local governments, or *Pendapatan Asli Daerah*, represent only 7% of their total revenues on average (Hoffman et al. 2006).[9] An average district in Indonesia therefore receives more than 90% of its total revenues from central government fiscal transfers (Bazzi and Gudgeon 2021). These transfers, known as *Dana Perimbangan*, are comprised of a general grant (*Dana Alokasi Umum*, or DAU), special allocation funds (*Dana Alokasi Khusus*, or DAK), shared taxes (*Dana Bagi Hasil Pajak*, or DBH Pajak), and shared revenues from natural resources (*Dana Bagi Hasil Sumber Daya Alam*, or DBH SDA). Their amounts are calculated by a formula that takes into consideration a district's fiscal need and capacity.[10] Local officials have discretion over how the funds are used and allocated once they have been transferred to the district level (Bazzi and Gudgeon 2021).

Another aspect of Indonesia's decentralization is the election of local executive leaders. Under the New Order, mayors, district chiefs, and governors were appointed directly by Soeharto. They frequently came from the civil service or the military, and every single appointed executive in the New Order was affiliated with Golkar. In post-Soeharto Indonesia, the method of selecting local leaders was reformed to increase leaders' accountability to the local electorate (Mietzner 2010). From 1999 through 2004, local executive leaders were selected by a vote of local council members, who themselves were elected in a closed-list proportional representation legislative election (Rasyid 2003; Fitrani, Hoffman, and Kaiser 2005). Then, with Law no. 32 of 2004, the system shifted further so that mayors, district chiefs, and governors are now directly elected, in what is called *Pilkada* or *Pemilihan Kepala Daerah*.[11]

The first batch of *Pilkada* elections happened in 2005 in units where the Soeharto-appointed executives' terms were coming to an end.[12] All other districts had their first wave of *Pilkada* by 2010. *Pilkada* occurs every five years as candidates run in pairs, either with party support or as independent candidates. Until 2015, a candidate had to garner at least 30% of the vote to be named the winner; if no candidate reached

---

[9] By some scholars' count, in 2009 only 8% of total revenues originated from taxes and user fees (Sjahrir, Kis-Katos, and Schulze 2013).

[10] The formula for calculating the size of these transfers has varied slightly over time, but the key factors are each district's population size, area, human development index, cost of construction index, and GDP per capita. The main components of a district's fiscal capacity include original revenue, shared taxes, and shared natural resource revenue (Ministry of Finance 2016).

[11] Some also use the term *Pemilukada* to refer to these direct elections of local executives.

[12] Approximately 40% of all district leaders were directly elected in 2005 (Sjahrir, Kis-Katos, and Schulze 2013).

this percentage, the top two vote getters would then compete in a runoff election.[13]

The third manifestation of Indonesia's decentralization is the possibility of creating new administrative units. As elsewhere, proponents of district splits argue that they will make local governments closer to the people, help them respond more readily to their constituents' needs, and improve service provision and economic development (Fitrani, Hoffman, and Kaiser 2005). Implementation procedures have been designed to ensure that new administrative units achieve these desired goals. The creation of new administrative units entails the multiplication of political seats, allocation of state resources, and ostensibly greater political autonomy over local governance issues.

By law, the creation of a new administrative unit follows a bottom-up process that takes into consideration the readiness and viability of the proposed new districts.[14] The process begins with the majority of the village councils in villages that would form the new unit expressing their desire for the split. The parent district's legislature and district chief may support or kill this initiative, based on the local evaluation team's report on the readiness of the proposed unit.[15] If approved, the proposal then goes to the governor, who in turn can either support or reject it. If the governor supports the initiative, the proposal is submitted to the provincial legislature, which may also support or reject it. If the parent district chief and legislature, governor, and provincial legislature all approve, the governor then forwards the proposal to the Ministry of Home Affairs. The ministry responds by sending an evaluation team to analyze the feasibility of the new unit and to draft a report for the Dewan Pertimbangan Otonomi Daerah (DPOD), a regional autonomy evaluation committee at the national level. The DPOD, composed of key ministers, representatives of the Local Government Association, and selected local legislators, can then decide, if it wishes, to send its own evaluation team to conduct further research on the readiness of the proposed new unit before it drafts its recommendation memo for the president (Bratakusumah and Solihin 2001). The president has the final word on whether to approve the district's creation.

---

[13] In Jakarta, candidates must get at least 50% of the votes to win. Since 2015, *Pilkada* elections have been held simultaneously in all units holding elections, with no runoffs; instead, the leading vote getter is declared the winner (Thornley 2015).

[14] This process is governed by Regulation no. 78 of 2007, which replaced the earlier Government Regulation no. 129 of 2000.

[15] The assessment of readiness considers, among other factors, the proposed district's population, fiscal capacity, and revenue-generating potential (Government Regulation no. 78 of 2007, ch. 6).

In actual practice, however, despite this appearance of evaluative rigor, district creation does not depend heavily on the proposed district's readiness. Many districts were created before they met the minimum requirements, and political considerations often override economic viability or preparedness (Kompas 2015). New units may be carved out to maximize control over revenues from natural resources (Fitrani, Hoffman, and Kaiser 2005) or fiscal transfers from the central government (Booth 2011; Fitrani, Hoffman, and Kaiser 2005). Some poorer units may desire to split so that they can receive more state support per person than they would have received if it subsumed within their parent district. In areas with low levels of economic activity, civil service jobs are so highly coveted that the multiplication of local state agency offices is valued for creating new jobs for the better-educated but underemployed segment of the population (Tadjoeddin 2011). The capacity of the advocates advancing a particular proposal for new districts may also influence whether a new district is created (Pierskalla 2016).

As a result of these forces, the number of administrative units in Indonesia increased drastically after 1999.[16] The number of districts and municipalities (excluding East Timor, which seceded in 2001) grew from 298 in 1998 to 497 in 2012. Figure 7.2 displays the drastic increase in the number of tier 2 administrative units in Indonesia since 1999.

As Figure 7.2 demonstrates, the greatest increases occurred between 1998 and 2004. The proliferation halted between 2004 and 2006 and again from 2008 through 2012 due to moratoria set in place by the central government. Djohermansyah Djohan, who was the director general of regional autonomy at the Ministry of Home Affairs, lamented that "80% of the 205 new administrative units that were created in the Reformasi years failed to perform . . . . The government implemented a moratorium

---

[16] Some creation of new administrative units had occurred prior to decentralization as well. The territorial organization of administrative units in Indonesia dates back to the Dutch colonial government. Shortly after the passage of the 1922 Government Reform Act, the Dutch created three provinces in Java (Booth 2011). Outside Java, however, provinces were not created until after 1945. Sumatra was carved into three provinces in 1950, while several islands – Kalimantan, Sulawesi, Maluku, and Nusa Tenggara – each became a separate province (Booth 2011). Not until 1957 did the central government grant provincial status to Aceh, Riau, Jambi, Bali, East Nusa Tenggara, West Nusa Tenggara, and four provinces in Kalimantan and two in Sulawesi, in response to rebellions in Sulawesi and Sumatra (Booth 2011; Kahin 1999). By 1961, there were 22 provinces and 259 districts and municipalities in Indonesia, excluding districts and municipalities in Irian Jaya, which at the time was still under Dutch control (Booth 2011). By 1998, when Soeharto resigned, Indonesia had 27 provinces and 298 districts and municipalities. Thus, while certainly not nonexistent, district creation was relatively limited in scope during Soeharto's rule.

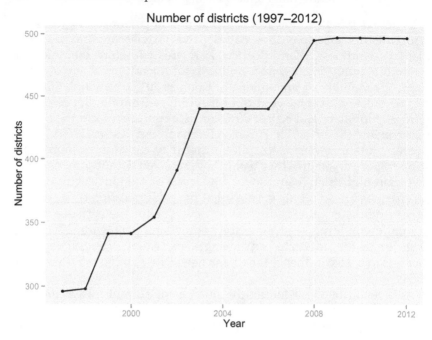

Figure 7.2 Number of districts and municipalities, 1997–2012

on district splitting since many of the proposed units were considered unprepared to separate from their parent districts" (Tribune 2016).

In 2014, to further quell the tide of district proliferation, laws containing more stringent requirements for new units were passed. In 2016, Vice President Jusuf Kalla emphasized that due to the fiscal burden on the national budget that district proliferation had imposed, the government would not consider further splits until the country had achieved a growth rate of 7% (Tempo 2016). Even so, the Ministry of Home Affairs reported that between 2009 and 2014, 87 proposals were still pending or unprocessed, and as of April 2016, 199 more proposals had arrived for consideration (Tempo 2016).

Geographically, the increases in the number of administrative units were greatest outside Java. As Figure 7.3 shows, Sumatra had the largest extent of unit creation, adding 77 districts and municipalities. Papua added 30 districts and municipalities in the same time period, while Kalimantan had 25 more districts and municipalities in 2012 than in 1997. In contrast, Java added only 10 new districts and municipalities during the same time period.

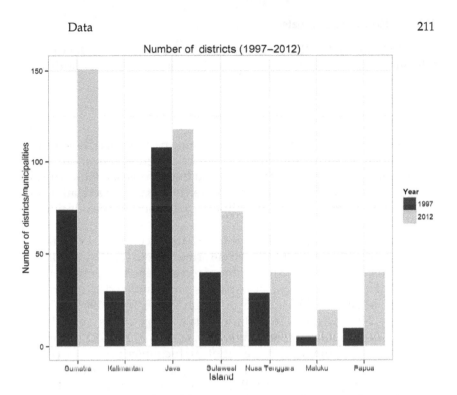

Figure 7.3 Number of districts and municipalities on Indonesia's major
Islands, 1997–2012

These data indicate that boundary change has been primarily a
post-Soeharto and non-Java phenomenon. In the subsequent sections,
I demonstrate that the pattern of unit creation aligns well with trends
in the occurrence and decline of local ethnic conflict.

Data

As noted earlier in this chapter, my analysis examines three issues:
(1) whether districts affected by ethnic rioting during the political
transition witnessed a decline in rioting in conjunction with increased
electoral competition; (2) what district-specific characteristics predicted
a split into multiple administrative units; and (3) the ethnic makeup
and electoral decisions of new child districts partitioned from conflict-
affected districts, as compared to the prior parent district.

The first and second parts of my analysis utilize an unbalanced
panel dataset in which every observation is a district-year in Indonesia

from 1998 through 2012. I discuss the attributes of these data in the following section. My third analysis relies on comparisons of district characteristics.

Measuring Change in Ethnic Rioting

Whereas my goal in Chapter 5 was to examine patterns of riots across all districts in Indonesia during the country's democratic transition, here I pay specific attention to districts that had high levels of conflict during the democratic transition, seeking to determine whether a relationship exists between a reduction of political exclusion and the decline in rioting.

I relied on the World Bank's event-level data on communal violence in Indonesia, the National Violence Monitoring System (National Violence Monitoring System (NVMS)). A team of researchers read through more than 120 local and national newspapers and hand-coded reports on incidents of communal violence in 16 provinces from 1998 through 2014. The NVMS covers 16 of Indonesia's 34 provinces and 53% of the country's population (Barron, Jaffrey, and Varshney 2016). Among those covered in the dataset are eight high-conflict provinces (Aceh, Maluku, North Maluku, Central Sulawesi, Central Kalimantan, West Kalimantan, Papua, and West Papua). The other eight – East Java, North Sumatra, Lampung, East Nusa Tenggara, West Nusa Tenggara, South Sulawesi, North Sulawesi, and Jakarta and its surrounding areas (Jabotabek) – are considered low-conflict provinces.[17] The dataset contains information on the date, location, deaths, injuries, and property damage for individual incidents of violence, as well as the identity of the actors involved, the type of weapons used, and the state security interventions that occurred in response. The incidents of communal violence reported in the NVMS are categorized as follows: crime, domestic violence, violence during law enforcement, resource conflict, governance conflict, election conflict, identity-based conflict, separatist conflict, popular justice conflict, and other conflict.

To date, the NVMS provides the broadest coverage of newspaper-based data on communal violence in Indonesia. As Bazzi and Gudgeon (2021, 39) have observed, the NVMS contains 4,795 additional district-months of incidents relative to those in the Uppsala Conflict Data

---

[17] For more details on the NVMS's temporal and spatial coverage, see Barron, Jaffrey, and Varshney (2016).

Program (UCDP) Georeferenced Event Data (GED) dataset. Compared to the Village Potential (Potensi Desa or PODES) surveys, which ask village chiefs every three years about incidents of violence in the preceding three years, the NVMS covers a broader time period and does not suffer from the self-reporting biases that plague survey data. Finally, compared to the United Nations Support for Indonesian Recovery (UNSFIR) data on communal violence in Indonesia from 1990 through 2003, the NVMS dataset records violent events well beyond Indonesia's democratic transition. The dataset that I compiled and used for the analysis in Chapter 5 stops at 2005 and thus is not as helpful for analyzing the decline of violence in more recent years.

Nevertheless, two limitations of the NVMS dataset must be acknowledged. As noted above, it covers only half of Indonesia's provinces, and this coverage is disproportionately focused on the eight high-conflict provinces. These are the only eight with complete data from 1998 to 2014; the eight low-conflict provinces have data only from 2005 onward. Second, the dataset relies on provincial newspapers, often with headquarters based in bigger cities and thus may systematically underreport events in more remote places. Nevertheless, this dataset offers the fullest insight into patterns of communal violence across Indonesia.

Using the NVMS's original coding of "identity-based conflict," which the dataset defines as violence triggered by group identity (e.g., religion, ethnicity, tribe), I created variables for the number of incidents, injuries, and deaths related to ethnic riots, a binary variable for whether an ethnic riot occurred in a district year, and lagged variables for each of these items.[18]

---

[18] My count of ethnic riots captures events categorized in the NVMS as identity-based conflict, which includes events coded by NVMS as (the description of each category was quoted verbatim from NVMS' original wording): 88884 for "Violence triggered by group identity (religion, ethnicity, tribe, etc.)," 4402 for "Violence triggered by identity of other groups," 4403 for "Violence triggered by ethnic/tribal dispute (regarding cultural attributes or symbols of diaspora, language and so forth)," 4404 for "Violence triggered by disputes between members of different religious groups," 4405 for "Violence triggered by disputes over interpretation within a religion (e.g. between sects)," 4406 for "Violence triggered by issues pertaining to migration/diaspora/refugees," 4407 for "Violence triggered by issues pertaining to migration/diaspora/refugees as well as ethnicity/tribalism," and 4408 for "Violence triggered by long-standing enmity between residents of particular villages/neighborhoods." I excluded events categorized under codes 4409, "Violence triggered by gender-related issues (including LGBT)"; 4410, "Violence triggered by issues between supporters of different sports clubs/teams"; and 4411, "clashes between student groups," because these are not related to ascriptive identity.

To capture the change in the level of rioting in conflict-affected districts, I calculated the change in the number of riots between each year and the preceding one.[19] A positive value for this variable indicates more incidents in the current district-year than in the same district during the prior year, suggesting an increase of violence; conversely, a negative value represents a decline in violence. In 1999, the year with the greatest ethnocommunal violence in Indonesia, an average district in high-conflict provinces experienced 9.58 more incidents than in the prior year. Ten years later in 2009, the average district in the same provinces had 0.033 fewer incidents than during the prior year.

Measuring Changes in Levels of Political Exclusion

Turnover By turnover, I mean a change in elected officials from one election to the next. Given the context of Indonesia's democratic transition, I coded the turnover variable in terms of turnover away from Golkar to any other party. This dichotomous variable assumes the value of 1 if a party other than Golkar won election in a district where Golkar had won the prior election and 0 otherwise. I coded this variable based on election reports released by the General Elections Committee on legislative elections from 1997 through 2005.

In my estimations, I included the variables of whether the districts had a turnover away from Golkar in the 1999 election, and whether the districts had a turnover from Golkar in the 2004 election.

Electoral Competitiveness To measure change in the competitiveness of elections from one election cycle to the next, I created a delta vote margin variable, which captures the difference in vote margin between the most recent and the previous election in the district.[20] If a district's elections become increasingly competitive over time, the variable, delta vote margin, would have larger, positive values. My theory would predict a negative association between delta vote margin

---

[19] This variable, delta violence, is constructed as follows: $\Delta\ Violence_{it} = Violence_{it} - Violence_{it-1}$, where $Violence_{it}$ is the number of ethnic riots in district i in year t and $Violence_{it-1}$ is the number of ethnic riots lagged by one year.

[20] As described in Chapter 5, the variable vote margin is calculated as $VM_{it} = -1 \times (V1_{it-1} - V2_{it-1})$, where VM_{it} is the vote margin in district i and year t, and $V1$ is the vote share of the winner and $V2$ the vote share of the runner-up in the most recent parliamentary election in the district. This measure is multiplied by -1 so that larger values on this variable indicate more competitiveness. Correspondingly, this variable delta vote margin is calculated in this manner: $\Delta\ VM_{it} = VM_{it} - VM_{it-1}$, where VM_{it} is the margin of votes in the most recent legislative elections in district i and year t, and VM_{it-1} is the same variable lagged by one year.

and the number of ethnic riots, along with a positive association between delta vote margin and the change in the level of violence from one year to the next.

Since the statistical analysis presented in this chapter covers district-years after Soeharto had resigned in 1998, the delta vote margin variable calculates the difference in vote margin in the district from the 1999 to the 2004 election.

Directly Elected Executive Leader To measure whether a district had an executive leader who was chosen through the local direct *Pilkada* elections, I created a binary variable of lagged elected leader. This variable takes the value of 1 when a district had a directly elected executive in the most recent election and 0 otherwise. This variable was coded by Pierskalla (2016), who compiled the information based on the Ministry of Home Affairs' list of *Pilkada* election dates in all units in Indonesia.

Split To measure where and when a district split occurred, I used the Ministry of Home Affairs' list of the date when each administrative unit was formed and created a dummy variable, "split," which takes the value of 1 in the year when a district lost territory to form a new unit and 0 otherwise. Correspondingly, I created binary variables called "parent" for any district that was subdivided to create new units and "child" for districts carved from existing units from 1999 through 2014. I also added another binary variable, "nosplit," for districts that never experienced any splitting. Furthermore, I recorded each district's age as the difference between the current year and the year of the district's birth.

Control Variables To account for possible confounding factors, I included controls for variables that may influence the onset of violence. In particular, I controlled for district logged GDP per capita (including oil), area in square kilometers, population size, religious fractionalization, and percentage of population in poverty. I used various measures of district revenues: logged natural resource revenues per capita, logged transfers per capita, logged personnel expenditure per capita, and logged original revenues (*Pendapatan Asli Daerah,* or PAD).

These measures were based on data reported by the DAPOER, which represents an aggregation of household and village-level surveys conducted on a regular basis. The measures of district religious fractionalization and Golkar dominance were the same indicators as those used in Chapter 6, although for robustness I also ran my estimations using district religious fractionalization and proportion of villages won by Golkar as determined from the data used in Pierskalla (2016).[21]

My estimations relied on OLS, logit, and negative binomial models depending on the dependent variables. I used a logit model to examine the correlates of district splits, and I used negative binomial and OLS models to examine the predictors of change in the level of violence and the number of ethnic riots in Indonesia.

Although it would be ideal to include district-specific and year-specific fixed effects, the main results shown in this chapter do not utilize them because clashes were concentrated in a few key places in the country. To check for robustness, I used alternative measures and ran the tests on subsamples of the data using different models.

Results

Turnover and Decline in Violence

My first analysis examines the association between turnover in favor of opposition candidates, increased electoral competition, and decline in Golkar's electoral dominance, and changes in levels of ethnic rioting in conflict-affected areas. Table 7.1 shows the results based on OLS regressions of conflict-affected districts in Indonesia from 1997 through 2012.[22]

As Table 7.1 indicates, turnover from Golkar in 1999 (i.e., districts where parties other than Golkar won the 1999 election) was associated with less change in the number of ethnic riots in a district. A smaller value in the change of levels of violence means in a given district-year, violence is less than what the district experienced in the prior year. That is, turnover away from Golkar in 1999 was correlated with a greater decline in violence. This correlation is statistically significant even after accounting for the district's amount of violence in the prior year and

---

[21] Unlike my initial measure of district fractionalization, which was based on my calculation of population data by religion as reported in the *Dalam Angka* volumes, Pierskalla (2016)'s measure of district fractionalization was based on census data.

[22] Conflict-affected districts in my analysis are coded as districts with at least one incident of ethnic rioting between 1998 and 2012 according to NVMS. I ran a similar examination using the ethnic riot data that I collected based on a sampling of *Tempo* and *Kompas* and appended with UNSFIR data. The results of this particular inquiry were presented in table 2 of Toha (2017, 643) and are generally consistent with the results contained in this chapter.

Table 7.1. *Turnover and change in the levels of violence in conflict districts*

	(1)	(2)	(3)
0/1 turnover to opposition in 1999 election?	−0.759**		
	(0.259)		
L.count of ethnic riots	−0.593***	−0.596***	−0.598***
	(0.064)	(0.065)	(0.065)
Religious fractionalization	1.342*	1.369^	1.341^
	(0.674)	(0.751)	(0.722)
0/1 turnover to opposition in 2004 election?		0.411	
		(0.378)	
Change in vote margin from the 1999 to 2004 election			0.010
			(0.008)
Logged GDP per capita (with oil)	✓	✓	✓
Logged population	✓	✓	✓
Logged area	✓	✓	✓
Poverty rate	✓	✓	✓
Observations	476	476	476
AIC	2172.600	2181.216	2180.741
Log likelihood	−1078.300	−1082.608	−1082.371

Notes: The dependent variable in these models is the change in the count of ethnocommunal violence in a district from one year to the next. Conflict districts are those that experienced ethnocommunal violence from 1997 through 2012. Coefficients are based on OLS regressions with robust standard errors. $^{\wedge}p < 0.10$, $^*p < 0.05$, $^{**}p < 0.01$, $^{***}p < 0.001$.

other likely correlates of violence, and it is consistent in estimations using various subsamples of the data.[23]

Turnover to non-Golkar parties in 2004, however, was not correlated with changes in the level of ethnic rioting. In various estimations and subsamples, this variable was consistently not statistically significant, suggesting that the key electoral factor impacting the prevalence of ethnic rioting was whether a district voted for a party other than Golkar at the peak of the democratic transition, in the 1999 election. This was the election that signaled to excluded political actors whether they

[23] For robustness, I also ran the same estimations on various subsamples (e.g., conflict districts that gave birth to new districts since 1999, child districts partitioned from conflict-affected districts, and the full sample of all districts in Indonesia) and found consistent results with regard to the correlation between change in violence and turnover away from Golkar in the 1999 election. These results are shown in Appendix B.

would remain excluded under the new government. If turnover away from Golkar occurred in a district in the 1999 election, excluded local elites in conflict-ridden districts would conclude that challengers had a reasonable chance of attaining local posts in the new government.

Only in child districts in conflict areas was the turnover away from Golkar in 2004 still positively correlated with the change in the count of riots. In districts where Golkar lost power in the 2004 election, the number of riots in a given child district in a year was more likely to be higher than the number of riots in the same child district in the previous year. Although this result does not conform to my theory's empirical expectation and suggests that child districts may be vulnerable to violence because of other factors related to Golkar's loss of power in 2004, I would interpret it with caution, however, since there are only 94 observations in these estimations. (See Table B.13 in Appendix B.)

For robustness, I ran the same estimations with the count of ethnic riots in a given year as the dependent variable, to trace the association between turnover from Golkar in the 1999 election and overall levels of violence (i.e., not the change in violence). The results were consistent: again, turnover from Golkar in 1999 predicted a lower incidence of ethnic riots in conflict-affected districts (see Table B.14 in Appendix B). Turnover away from Golkar in the 2004 elections was generally statistically not significant, except in the estimation using only parent districts in conflict areas. In this particular estimation (see column 8 in Table B.14 in Appendix B), turnover away from Golkar in 2004 was positively associated with the number of riots, indicating that parent districts in conflict areas that voted for parties other than Golkar in 2004 experienced higher levels of violence than their counterparts. Again, however, this result should be interpreted with caution, since for the most part this variable bears no statistical significance except with regard to this particular subsample.

Taken together, these results suggest that the data on district-level ethnic riots from 1999 through 2012 in Indonesia conform to the expectation outlined in hypothesis 8a, that districts that experienced prior violence would see a decline in rioting after an electoral turnover.

There was no association between change in vote margin and change in the level of rioting from 1999 onward. The change in a district's vote margin from 1999 to 2004 captured the shift in the competitiveness of elections during the first few years of democracy. Across various model specifications and subsamples, this variable was statistically not significant.[24] These statistical results based on changes in vote margin

---

[24] In my negative binomial regressions with the number of ethnic riots as the dependent variable, the variable of change in vote margin continued to lack statistical significance.

between the 1999 and 2004 district legislative elections provide little support for hypothesis 8b. Increasing electoral competitiveness from 1999 to 2004 does not seem to have lowered violence in conflict areas over time.

Determinants of District Splits

The results of the second part of my analysis – an investigation of the determinants of district splits – lend support to the idea that districts with greater barriers to entry for opposition candidates and prior exposure to violence were more likely to partition than others.

I used the same unbalanced panel data from 1999 through 2012. Table 7.2 presents the results.

The coefficients reported in that table indicate that Golkar's vote share in the district in the most recent legislative election was positively associated with the occurrence of a split in a given year in that district. The greater the district's support for Golkar, the more likely it was to split, after accounting for district socioeconomic and demographic characteristics and the district's level and severity of violence in the prior year. The predicted probability of a split when all other variables in Model 1 are held at their means, and when Golkar's vote share shifts from the 25th to the 75th percentile, increases by 0.0149.[25]

The Golkar vote share variable used in these estimations is not available for years after 2005, since it was constructed from legislative elections in 1997, 1999, and 2004. Although this limitation may not be problematic, since almost 66% of unit splits in this dataset occurred between 1998 and 2004, the results could conceivably be skewed due to this incomplete time coverage.

To check for robustness, I ran the same estimations using an alternative measure of Golkar's strength, namely the proportion of villages in the district that voted for Golkar in the last election.[26] The full results appear in Table B.10 in Appendix B. Consistent with my main findings, the coefficients in Table B.10 indicate that the probability of a split increases where more villages in a district support Golkar.

The only exception was in the estimation using only child districts in conflict areas. See Table B.14 in Appendix B.

[25] To calculate this figure, I reran the regressions using "xtlogit" and calculated the predicted probability of split with CLARIFY.

[26] This measure was coded and aggregated based on PODES village surveys in Pierskalla (2016) and covers observations from 2001 through 2012, with varying extent of missing data for each year.

Table 7.2. Determinants of district splits

	(1)	(2)	(3)	(4)	(5)	(6)	(7)	(8)
Golkar vote share	2.733*	2.518*	2.918*	2.495*	3.619*	3.619*	3.685*	3.676*
	(1.365)	(1.414)	(1.303)	(1.256)	(1.510)	(1.510)	(1.483)	(1.476)
L.count of ethnic riots	0.030***	0.032***	0.027**	0.025**	0.059***	0.059***		
	(0.008)	(0.011)	(0.010)	(0.009)	(0.017)	(0.017)		
Logged PAD revenues	0.692***							
	(0.175)							
Religious fractionalization	-1.023	-2.688*	-1.182	-0.763	-1.862	-1.862	-1.371	-1.265
	(1.228)	(1.500)	(1.104)	(1.118)	(1.269)	(1.269)	(1.281)	(1.309)
Logged area	0.784***	0.746**	0.834***	0.709***	0.970***	0.970***	0.924***	0.908***
	(0.161)	(0.236)	(0.207)	(0.163)	(0.238)	(0.238)	(0.231)	(0.226)
Logged population	-0.409	2.240***	-0.038	-0.019	-0.029	-0.029	-0.016	-0.018
	(0.324)	(0.570)	(0.647)	(0.350)	(0.315)	(0.315)	(0.311)	(0.308)
Logged DAU transfer per capita		3.784***						
		(0.767)						
Logged staff expenditure per capita			-.044					
			(1.196)					
Logged natural resource revenues per capita				0.083				
				(0.076)				
Poverty rate (% of population)					0.002	0.002	0.007	0.007
					(0.030)	(0.030)	(0.031)	(0.031)
L.death ethnic riots							0.026**	
							(0.008)	
L.injuries ethnic riots								0.016**
								(0.006)
Observations	1136	1126	876	1064	801	801	801	801
AIC	188.539	164.182	183.336	184.786	173.083	173.083	175.365	176.083
Log likelihood	-87.269	-75.091	-84.668	-85.393	-79.541	-79.541	-80.683	-81.041

Notes: The dependent variable is a dummy variable for a split occurring in a district-year. Papua and Aceh observations were excluded from all estimations. Coefficients are based on logit models with robust standard errors. ^ $p < 0.10$, * $p < 0.05$, ** $p < 0.01$, *** $p < 0.001$.

I also checked whether Golkar's electoral dominance had differential effects on district splits in different time periods. In Tables B.11 and B.12 in Appendix B, I present the results of logit regressions on subsamples of the data. The results of estimations using the 1999–2005 sample are consistent with those of estimations with the full sample, although the statistical significance of the variable denoting the share of villages in the district where Golkar had won in the previous election is considerably weaker.

In estimations using district-years after 2005, the results differ in significant ways. First, the variables for the share of Golkar-supporting villages in the district, lagged ethnic riots, and religious fractionalization are not statistically significant. Second, the coefficients for the share of villages backing Golkar are not significant, with signs changing in some estimations. Third, the lagged number of ethnic riots is negatively associated with districts splitting after 2005. Fourth, unlike in all other estimations on district splits, in the estimations using only observations after 2005, the religious fractionalization variable is positively correlated with splits. These differences suggest that the variables used in the models are sensitive and that the results found thus far are not robust. While this may be true, it is also possible that the importance of Golkar's electoral dominance and prior exposure to violence dissipates as more demands for greater political representation are met.

The coefficient signs of lagged riots and deaths and injuries related to ethnic riots are positive, implying that more exposure to violence in the previous year increases the likelihood of splitting, but this association is sensitive to other parameters in the models.[27] Substantively, this suggests that although conflict-affected districts are more likely to partition than peaceful ones, the effects of prior rioting may not be as strong as was hypothesized.

In summary, the findings in this analysis support hypotheses 9 and 10, which predicted that districts that experienced ethnic rioting during Indonesia's political transition and those where non-Golkar candidates had a difficult time winning an election would be more likely to partition than their counterparts.

---

[27] In the estimations using the alternative measure of Golkar's electoral dominance, namely the share of villages in the district where Golkar won in the prior election, the variables of lagged number of riots, injuries, and deaths related to ethnic riots are not statistically significant. See Table B.10 in Appendix B.

New Districts in High-Conflict Provinces

Does the splitting of a district tend to create more homogeneous units, with leaders who represent the ethnic identity of the majority of the district's population? One implication of my argument is that newly created child districts should be ethnically more homogeneous than and distinct from their parents, because partitioning occurs at least in part to resolve exclusion in the parent district. In this section, I discuss the differences between child and parent districts in high-conflict provinces, so as to evaluate hypotheses 11a, 11b, and 11c.

To this end, I compared districts in Central Sulawesi, North Maluku, and Maluku, where clashes had occurred between Christians and Muslims from the late 1990s through the early 2000s.[28]

Here, parent districts are those administrative units from which new units were created between 1998 and 2014; child districts are new administrative units (i.e., districts and municipalities) carved from existing units after 1998. Child districts can further subdivide and become parent districts themselves, so it is possible for the same district to be both child and parent. Non-splitting units are those that existed before Soeharto's resignation in 1998 and were never partitioned.

For my analysis in this section, I concentrate on high-conflict provinces with prior clashes between Christians and Muslims, for two reasons. First, to compare the demographic composition within the districts before and after the democratic transition, I need pre-transition, district-level population data. For years before 1998, district population data by religion are available. Population data by ethnicity and tribe, on the other hand, were reported only in the 2000 census and thereafter. Beyond data availability, a second reason for focusing on districts with prior Christian–Muslim clashes is that it is simpler to compare two groups' composition across parent, child, and non-splitting districts than to compare many more groups across districts that may have as many as ten politically relevant ethnic groups within their borders.[29]

---

[28] North Maluku province was carved out of Maluku province in 1999. In this section of the chapter, 1997 data for the administrative units refers to the ten units that were subsumed under Maluku and Central Sulawesi provinces in 1997.

[29] There are five officially recognized religions in Indonesia and more than 300 ethnic groups. Distinctiveness in ethnic identity between parent and child districts would imply that the parent district is predominantly populated by one ethnic or religious group while the child is predominantly of another. Given the numerous possible permutations of the composition of those 300 ethnic groups within a district, it seemed much simpler to compare the two dominant religious groups in parent-versus-child districts in conflict-affected areas.

Table 7.3. *Proportions of non-Muslims in 1997 and 2010 in Central Sulawesi, Maluku, and North Maluku provinces*

Type	# of units	Mean 1997	Mean 2010	Difference
Parent districts created before 1999 that subdivided	8	0.301	0.367	0.066
Child districts that further subdivided	3	(0.301)	0.567	0.266
Child districts that never subdivided	18	(0.301)	0.283	0.018
Non-splitting districts that were created before 1999	2	0.312	0.378	0.066

Note: Numbers in parentheses refer to the 1997 figures of the parent districts from which child districts were partitioned.

Sources: Demographic information are from the 2010 census, 2000 census, and 1997 Dalam Angka volumes; district status as parent, child, and non-splitting units is based on the Ministry of Home Affairs' full list of administrative units in 2014. Non-Muslim figures for Palu and Halmahera Tengah before the split are based on the 2000 census.

Table 7.3 compares the proportion of non-Muslims in parent, child, and non splitting districts in three high-conflict provinces.

In these high-conflict provinces where clashes pitted Christians against Muslims during Indonesia's democratic transition, there were 10 administrative units in 1997 and 31 in 2010, together comprising a total of 41 district-years. Between 1997 and 2010, 21 districts split from existing units in these provinces. Of these 21 new districts, 3 further split to create new units, whereas 18 did not subdivide further. Of the 10 districts that existed in Central Sulawesi and Maluku in 1997,[30] 8 were partitioned; 2 remained intact and are considered non-splitting units.[31] Although this is a small sample of districts in Indonesia, these are the districts with the heaviest fighting in the country during the democratic transition (Barron, Jaffrey, and Varshney 2016). If the logic of district subdivision as a means of escaping political exclusion was at work, one would expect to find it here.

[30] The province of North Maluku was not created until 1999.
[31] Information on these administrative units' date of establishment and their initial parent units (if any) is based on my coding of the Ministry of Home Affairs' full list of Indonesia's administrative units in 2014. District creations after 2014 are not included here.

Partitioning in these provinces occurred mostly from 1999 through 2003.[32] To compare the pre- and post-split averages of the proportions of non-Muslims in the districts, I used district population data from 1997 and 2010. The change in districts' average non-Muslim population from 1997 to 2010 was consistent between districts in existence prior to 1999 that had birthed new units and those that were never partitioned. Both sets of districts saw an increase of 0.066 in their average non-Muslim population between 1997 and 2010. In terms of groups' relative size, parent districts that had existed prior to 1999 and then subdivided had 36.7% non-Muslims in 2010, whereas non-splitting districts that had existed prior to 1999 had 37.8% non-Muslims.

Child districts that were carved from older districts but never subdivided further, however, saw a decline in their non-Muslim population from 30.1% (when they were still subsumed in their parent districts) to 28.3%. This difference between 1997 and 2010 suggests that new, child districts created in high-conflict provinces had higher proportions of Muslims in 2010, after they had split from their parents, than when they were still part of their parent districts in 1997. These child districts that remained intact after partitioning had 22.8% fewer non-Muslims than their parent districts in 2010.

Child districts that seceded and then further subdivided to create more new units had the highest increase in the proportion of non-Muslims from 1997 to 2010. The average proportion of non-Muslims in these districts in 2010 was 56.7% of the total population, nearly double the percentage in 1997 when they were subsumed in their parent units. On the other hand, child districts that seceded but subsequently remained intact had a *decline* of 5.9% in their proportion of non-Muslim population from 1997 to 2010. These figures suggest that partitioning may be making the districts more homogeneous over time, as parent districts became more predominantly non-Muslim, child districts that never subdivided became more predominantly Muslim, and children districts that further split into multiple new units became more predominantly non-Muslim.

These numbers, though admittedly descriptive and anecdotal, are consistent with the predictions outlined in hypothesis 11a that newly carved districts should be more ethnically homogeneous than their parents.[33]

---

[32] Five districts in these provinces – Sigi, Maluku Barat Daya, Buru Selatan, Kota Tual, and Pulau Morotai – were created in 2007 and 2008.

[33] These figures are also consistent with the broader findings reported by Pierskalla (2016), which suggest that partitioned districts had lower levels of ethnic fractionalization. Comparing the average ethnic fractionalization in parent, children, and

Table 7.4. *Districts with co-ethnic executives in provinces with Christian–Muslim riots*

Co-ethnic exec?	All districts in 1997 (%)	All districts in 2010 (%)
No	20	6.45
Yes	80	93.55

Notes: This table includes all districts in Maluku, North Maluku, and Central Sulawesi. There are 10 districts in 1997. There are 31 districts in 2010, which include parent, child, and non-splitting districts.

One central argument of this book is that district partitioning may be a way for excluded ethnic groups to exit exclusionary districts and may be driven partially by their desire for better representation in local politics. One implication of this argument for newly carved districts is that elected officials in newly carved districts should be more likely to share the ethnic affiliations of the district's majority population. To examine hypothesis 11b, I coded the religious affiliations of district chiefs and mayors in 41 districts in Maluku and Central Sulawesi in 1997 and of district chiefs and mayors in Maluku, North Maluku, and Central Sulawesi provinces in 2010. To compile information on executives' names and religious affiliations, I relied on district governments' official websites, online biographies, and print and online news reports about incumbent executives in these administrative units in 1997 and 2010.

Tables 7.4 and 7.5 compare the proportion of districts with co-ethnic executives in Maluku, North Maluku, and Central Sulawesi, across all (i.e., parent, child, and non-splitting), child, and non-splitting units.

In 1997, the average proportion of non-Muslims in each district across the three provinces was 30% of the district's population. All but two of the ten administrative units in these provinces in 1997 were predominantly (i.e., more than 50%) Muslim.[34] Furthermore, I treated an administrative unit as having a co-ethnic executive when its executive leader in a given year shared the religious affiliation of the predominant

---

non-splitting districts in Indonesia between 2000 and 2010, Pierskalla noted that whereas parent districts had an average ethnic fractionalization score of 0.622 in 2000, after district partitioning their ethnic fractionalization score in 2010 had dropped to 0.554. New administrative units averaged at 0.518 on the fractionalization index. In other words, new districts were more homogeneous than their parents (Pierskalla 2016).

[34] In 1997, only Ambon and Maluku Tenggara had more than 50% non-Muslims. If a district had a non-Muslim population of at least 30% but less than 50%, I refer to that percentage as sizable.

Table 7.5. *Child districts with co-ethnic executives in provinces with Christian–Muslim riots*

Co-ethnic exec?	Child districts in 1997 (%)	Child districts 2010 (%)
No	(28.57)	4.76
Yes	(71.43)	95.24

Note: Figures in parentheses refer to the percentages of child districts that had co-ethnic executives when they were part of their parent districts. Child districts in this table are districts in Maluku, North Maluku, and Central Sulawesi that were created after 1999.

population in the district.[35] For example, in 1997, Maluku Tengah district had a 31.8% non-Muslim population and a regent who identified as Protestant (Rudolf Rukka). I coded Maluku Tengah as not having a co-ethnic executive in 1997 since the majority population of the district was Muslim. Poso, a district with a similarly sizable proportion of non-Muslims (38%) in 1997, had a Muslim district chief (Arief Patanga) in 1997; I therefore coded Poso as having a co-ethnic executive.

Applying these parameters, I found that eight of the ten units (80%) in the high-conflict provinces that I examined had co-ethnic executives in 1997. In 2010, 29 of 31 units had co-ethnic executives (93%). In other words, the splintering of administrative units produced not only a greater number of units within the provinces but also an increase in the percentage of co-ethnic executives.

As Table 7.5 demonstrates, concerning whether the child districts had co-ethnic executives in 1997 based on their 2010 demographic composition, one finds that 6 of 21 (28.57%) had executives who did *not* share their religious identifications when they were part of their parent districts. For example, in 2010, Seram Bagian Timur district had a population that was more than 95% Muslim. In 2010, its district executive, Abdullah Vanath, was Muslim. But when it was still part of Maluku Tengah in 1997, the Muslim residents of today's Seram Bagian Timur district had an executive, Rudolf Rukka, who was not their co-religionist. By 2010, the percentage of child districts with executives who did not share the religious affiliation of the majority of the district population had dropped to just 4.76% across the three provinces.

---

[35] I coded only the religious affiliation of the executives, not the elected vice regents or vice mayors, even though candidates often choose running mates whose ethnic identity broadens their voter support base. I did this because far less information is available on the religious affiliation of vice regents and vice mayors prior to 1998.

Of the 21 child districts in North Maluku, Maluku, and Central Sulawesi, 10 would have had non-co-religionist executives in 2010 had they remained part of their parent units and had the 2010 election outcomes been the same. For example, Tojo Una-Una district (more than 90% Muslim) had split from Poso, a district which by 2010 was 63% non-Muslim. In 2010, Tojo Una-Una's regent was Damsyik Ladjalani, a Muslim and thus a co-religionist of the majority of the district's population. Had Tojo Una-Una remained part of Poso, in 2010 the Muslim population of Tojo Una-Una would not have a district executive who shared their religious affiliation.

These numbers are descriptive and reflect aggregate trends in high-conflict provinces that may not resemble those in other parts of Indonesia. However, others have identified similar patterns elsewhere in the country. The split of Bengkayang district from Sambas in West Kalimantan provides one example. Before the partitioning, Sambas was 15.3% Dayak, 52.7% Malay, and 16.5% Chinese. The creation of Bengkayang took most of the Dayak population out of Sambas. After the split, Sambas became 3.4% Dayak, 79.9% Malay, and 10.8% Chinese. Bengkayang was 52.4% Dayak, 18.7% Malay, and 9.4% Chinese (Tanasaldy 2012). In other words, Sambas became more predominantly Malay and Bengkayang predominantly Dayak. In the first local executive election in Bengkayang, every contending pair of candidates had a member of a Dayak community on the ticket. Yacobus Lunda and Suryatman Gidot, both of whom are ethnically Dayak and affiliated with the Partai Demokrasi Indonesia-Perjuangan (PDIP) party, won the election (Subianto 2009).

In similar separation, the predominantly Chinese Kota Singkawang municipality split from the predominantly Dayak district of Bengkayang in 2001 (Arifin, Hasbullah, and Pramono 2017). In 2015, the municipality was 36.5% ethnically Chinese. In 2007, Singkawang staged its first *Pilkada* elections and voters elected their first Chinese (Christian) mayor, Hasan Karman (La Ode 2012). Hasan Karman and his running mate, Edy R. Yacoub, defeated four other candidate pairs, all of which included an ethnic Chinese on the ticket (La Ode 2012, 115). In 2015, Singkawang voters elected another ethnic Chinese mayor, Tjhai Chui Mie, the city's first female Chinese mayor and a practicing Tao Buddhist, who has kept her Chinese name (in contrast to the practice of many Chinese Indonesians in the country, who adopt Indonesian-sounding names). She and her running mate, H. Irwan, received 42.6% of the votes, defeating three other candidate pairs: incumbent deputy mayor Abdul Muthalib and his running mate Muhammadin with 26.7%; Andi Syarif and his running mate Nurmansyah with 17.13%; and lastly,

Tjhai Nyit Khim (another female Chinese candidate and wife of the incumbent mayor, Awang Ishak) and Suriyadi with 13.5% of the votes (Endi 2017). Although Singkawang voters had also elected the ethnically Malay Awang Ishak (whose running mate was another Muslim Malay, Abdul Muthalib) in 2012 and thus cannot be considered as resistant to non-co-ethnic local leaders, the popularity (and subsequent victory) of ethnic Chinese candidates in the town suggests that a desire for a more ethnically homogeneous administrative unit and a co-ethnic executive leader may have motivated the creation of this municipality.

These accounts, along with the quantitative findings presented in this chapter, indicate a pattern in which administrative units that were previously marked by violence subdivided into smaller units to create more ethnically homogeneous territories. After the splits, the new units almost invariably elected an executive of the majority ethnic or religious group. Administrative unit proliferation seems to function as a means to place co-ethnics in power, creating new units where the majority of the electorate is more likely to vote along ethnic lines. In many multiethnic units, local executive election candidates have strategically partnered with running mates who represented a different ethnic or religious community from their own, thereby expanding their reach along ethnic lines. In this manner, many locally sizable ethnic groups easily find their representation in different candidate-pairs. This strategy may preemptively avoid any perceived need to use violence to leverage demands, as local politicians seem to already recognize that excluding representatives from larger identity-based groups would be political suicide.

Conclusion

This chapter began with the observation that ethnic rioting declined relatively quickly in Indonesia. Since conflict tends to perpetuate itself in most settings, it was curious that the scourge of ethnic riots in Indonesia dissipated almost as quickly as it arose. In this book, I have proposed that barriers to participation in local governments prompted the onset of violence during a democratic transition as excluded actors mobilized violence to intensify their demands. One implication of this argument is that once these demands for political inclusion are met, violence should decline.

Indonesia presents an interesting opportunity for analysis not only because the violence generally declined almost as quickly as it started but also because its implementation of decentralization offered an alternative channel to address political exclusion at the local level.

In Hirschman's parlance, the splitting of administrative units can function as a means of exiting from politically exclusionary districts. Once excluded local actors have their own units, where presumably they can elect their people to important positions, the use of rioting as a form of voice is no longer necessary and should therefore decline.

In this chapter, I established a statistical relationship between declines in political exclusion and in violence in riot-affected districts. I also showed that exclusive districts were more likely to be partitioned than their counterparts, when controlling for various potentially confounding factors. Finally, I demonstrated that the unique characteristics of newly partitioned districts in high-conflict provinces conformed to my expectations, in that they were more ethnically homogeneous and elected executives from the majority group.

8   Conclusion

Let us remember that what look like religious conflicts are normally the product of political or geostrategic manipulation, or proxies for other antagonisms. There are endless examples of different religious groups living together peacefully for centuries, despite their differences. Today's artificial divides, therefore, can and must be overcome, based on respect for the independence and territorial integrity of the countries concerned.

Antonio Guterres (2018)

When Secretary-General António Guterres addressed the United Nations Security Council in June 2018, he knew not to depict ethnic clashes as inevitable as US president George H. W. Bush seemed to do when he described the Balkan wars in 1992 as "a complex, convoluted conflict that grows out of age-old animosities" (Rosenthal 1992). In 2015, US president Barack Obama, while visiting Kenya, gave a speech that lauded that country's progress, but cautioned that "old tribal divisions and ethnic divisions can still be stirred up" (Obama 2015). Like these world leaders, the community of scholars has a much more nuanced understanding of why clashes between ethnic groups erupt today than it did many years ago.

Although we recognize that violence is not an unavoidable outcome of intergroup differences, we know less about why some areas seem much more resilient to triggers of violence and why, even when violence did occur, in some places violence ended relatively quickly while in others it dragged on.

Why did ethnic riots erupt in some parts of a multiethnic country undergoing political transition and not others? If an entire country is experiencing transition, then transition-specific factors should apply universally across the entire country. Across the areas that experienced violence, some also recovered much faster, while others remained embattled for much longer. The subnational variations in both the geographical distribution of riots and the timing of their rise and decline indicate that a focus on national-level factors is insufficient. To explain why some regions remained quiescent when others went up in flames, one must pay close attention to local characteristics.

Recap of the Argument and Findings

Existing explanations of ethnocommunal violence have typically focused on state security capacity, societal factors (e.g., inequality, group competition, intergroup association, ancient hatred), and electoral incentives that compel politicians to mobilize voters along ethnic lines and provoke violence in the process. These analyses, however, were largely based on cases in South Asia, the United States, and Europe, and generally on countries with mature institutions and stable democracies, not ones undergoing political transition.

Scholars who have examined incidents of violence during political transition in Indonesia have highlighted the transition period's character as a "critical juncture," wherein groups struggled to protect their interests and status in the new government. Most of these studies either focused on national political actors' machinations and how they shaped violence or zeroed in on a very limited number of cases where highly violent clashes erupted. These works have offered rich analyses of highly violent conflicts during Indonesia's transition, but given the range of cases examined, they do not explain the broader geographical and temporal variations, or the differences in intensity of violence and speed, in the rise and decline of ethnic riots across municipalities and districts in Indonesia.

I have sought to address these gaps by studying the patterns of ethnic rioting across administrative units in Indonesia during the country's transition to democracy in the late 1990s and early 2000s. Across the hundreds of administrative units in the archipelago, only a handful of them experienced intense ethnic rioting during power transfer, and some of them recovered much faster than others. Using a combination of methods, including in-depth interviews with local community leaders, econometrics, and controlled comparison of cases, I have offered an analysis that both identifies broad patterns across a large section of administrative units over many years and is sensitive to the local dynamics that cannot be quantified with available data through my controlled comparison of administrative units in Indonesia. Although I cannot wholly overcome the reporting bias that comes from using only certain kinds of data (e.g., events reported in national media outlets such as Kompas and Tempo, government-published statistics for municipalities and districts), I hope that this deliberate mixed-methods approach has ameliorated some of the potential problems.

Applying Hirschman's framework of exit, voice, and loyalty, I have argued in this book that when faced with continued exclusion in local politics despite countrywide democratization, local elites can either turn to ethnocommunal violence to leverage their demands for greater representation in politics (i.e., voice) and/or carve out separate administrative units for themselves (i.e., exit). I have shown that violence tended to occur in areas with continued exclusion in the initial years after democratic transition, and that it declined when exclusion was ameliorated, either by increasing openness to challengers (e.g., turnover and increasing levels of competition) or by the creation of new administrative units. This focus on the importance of political exclusion as a key determinant of violence during power transfers carries a number of implications. Among others, it suggests that ethnic diversity alone is not a sufficient condition for predicting the outburst of violence, and that ethnic identities must become politicized before they can rally members of ethnic groups to violence.

In Chapter 3, I traced the development of ethnic communities as politically relevant cleavages over the course of Indonesia's history. The archipelago we now know as Indonesia has had a high exposure to ethnic, linguistic, and religious diversity for a very long time. Ethnic identities gained political relevance during colonial rule, as the Dutch categorized and governed their subjects differentially along ethnic lines. When the Japanese took over control of the archipelago, their administration also politicized people along ethnic lines by reversing the status of some local ethnic elites and granting favor to others who were excluded in the Dutch period. During Soekarno's rule, despite the founders' best attempts to create a multiethnic, unified state, many groups mobilized violently as they felt that their demands were ignored. Chapter 3 demonstrated that ethnic diversity does not automatically produce violence and that ethnic mobilization occurred when government policies highlighted the differences between groups and chose winners and losers among them.

Chapter 5 examined the implications of my theory across Indonesian districts and municipalities during the democratic transition. Relying on my sampling of coded national media reports, I developed a new dataset on ethnocommunal violence in Indonesia from 1990 through 2005, extending the event-level data on communal violence from 1998 through 2003 collected by UNSFIR research team. I collected district-level voting data from parliamentary elections both in the New Order (from 1987 through 1997) and in the transition years (from 1999 through 2005), and I coded data on district socioeconomic indicators from provincial *Dalam Angka* volumes and censuses. Using this new district-level dataset,

I showed that ethnic riots were more common in politically exclusionary and ethnically diverse areas after Soeharto's ouster.

Chapter 6 turned to the mechanisms and considered my theory's expectations on how local elites would react to trigger events, based on their political exclusion, district's composition, and the supply of groups available for mobilizational purposes. Ambon and Maluku Tenggara (Maluku province) and Poso and Banggai (Central Sulawesi province) are similar in important ways; they are located in high-conflict provinces, at similar stages of economic development, relatively equally ethnically diverse, and reliant on state resources. At the point of democratic transition, excluded ethnic elites in Ambon and Poso utilized their ethnic networks, reframed trigger events in ethnic terms, and coordinated and mobilized violence. In contrast, local elites in Banggai and Maluku Tenggara, who were not politically excluded from local governments, responded differently to trigger events, with the result that riots did not escalate to the same levels as in Ambon and Poso.

A key implication of my argument is that rioting should decline when the demands that motivated unrest are met. In the context of Indonesia's political transition, the accommodation of these demands could happen in two ways: through turnover in district-level leadership (facilitated by increased political competition within a district) or through the creation of new districts that enabled previously excluded groups to be better represented. Chapter 7 used a new event-level dataset from the World Bank's NVMS to demonstrate that district splits were more common in districts with greater levels of political exclusion and higher levels of violence during the democratic transition. Chapter 7 also showed that the newly created districts in conflict areas tended to be more ethnically homogeneous than their parent districts, and that elected district executives in the child districts were more likely to share the majority ethnic or religious affiliation of their district than before the split.

Threats of Violence, Demands, and Power Sharing in Indonesia Today

Beyond the specific case of ethnic rioting during power transfers in multiethnic settings, this book's argument also has broader implications for the relationship between demand making and group mobilization. One implication deals directly with policymakers' worries about the precedents that accommodation creates for future mobilization of violence. Would accommodation of demands expressed through violent mobilization incentivize more violence in the future?

In Indonesia today, more than twenty years after Soeharto resigned, the practice of turning to group mobilization to leverage demands continues. Although ethnic rioting appears to have declined as local elites have been mostly accommodated through the creation of new administrative units, direct local executive elections, and increased local autonomy, group mobilization, particularly around executive elections, remains relatively common. The overall levels of violence around elections remain relatively low after transition years (Toha and Harish 2020), but some politicians have repeatedly relied on the threat of violent mobilization to get what they want.

Though my argument deals specifically with how local ethnic elites use violence to leverage demands after formal political channels prove disappointing and ineffective, a decision to present demands via group mobilization requires simply a readily mobilizable community, a demand, weak and ineffective structures, and a reasonable chance of success. In the following pages, I consider two noteworthy examples, one from the 2017 governor election in Jakarta and another from the 2019 presidential election.

Commonly believed as the stepping stone to presidential candidacies, the position of Jakarta governor race has consistently been in the spotlight.[1] When Joko Widodo (popularly known as Jokowi) ran for this seat in 2012 with a Chinese Christian running mate, Basuki Tjahaja Purnama (or Ahok, as many call him), some hard-line Muslim groups protested against having a non-Muslim leader. After Jokowi became president in 2014, many worried that Ahok, who assumed the governor seat his former running mate had vacated, would be next in line for the highest office in Indonesia.

In the 2017 election, Ahok and his running mate, Djarot Saiful Hidayat, competed against Anies Baswedan and Sandiaga Uno. Even though Ahok had enjoyed high approval ratings earlier in June 2016, at least 30% of polled respondents had already said that they would not support him because of his religion (Setijadi 2017, 4). This was not the only deterrent, however. Sumaktoyo (2019) suggested that ethnic sentiments and Ahok's ethnic Chinese identity were more influential in pushing voters' support away from him than religion. Furthermore, Ahok's forced relocation of residents in north and east Jakarta was highly unpopular among the poor (Wilson 2017), and many found his

---

[1] For news articles and op-eds on how the Jakarta governor race is predictive of candidates' presidential ambitions, see Kompas (2016), The Jakarta Post (2018), and Kompasiana (2012).

harsh and unfiltered speech rude (Setijadi 2017, 5). Ahok remained a strong contender for the seat, but certainly not without opposition.

The election took a decisive turn toward identity-based politics when a recorded video of Ahok addressing a small gathering of voters in North Jakarta went viral on Facebook in September 2016, leading to unprecedented levels of mass mobilizations around Islam during a local executive election. In the video, Ahok warned voters not to be "duped" by religious leaders who used the Quranic verse (Al Maidah 51) that cautions Muslims against having an unbelieving leader. In response, hard-line Muslim groups demanded that Ahok be brought to trial for blasphemy and insulting Islam. Waves of protests began occupying prime spots in Jakarta from November 2016 on an almost monthly basis, calling for Ahok to be arrested, tried, and removed from his position. Hundreds of thousands, many from outside of Jakarta or even outside of Java, gathered to protest, pray, and express their grievances (Fealy 2016). They labeled their actions as the Defense of Islam Act (Aksi Bela Islam), and Habib Rizieq Shihab, the Islamist organization Front Pembela Islam (FPI)'s leader, insisted that the protests would not cease until Ahok was arrested (CNN 2019).

This religious framing of the anti-Ahok protests was very effective, as the movement attracted many participants and maintained its momentum until the government acquiesced. When protesters demonstrated in front of the presidential palace and demanded an audience with the president, he did not meet with them directly, but the vice president, Jusuf Kalla, and then coordinating minster for political, legal, and security affairs, Wiranto, did. Still angry, some protesters clashed with security personnel and burned a police truck and car (Amelia 2016). That same night, the president appeared on television and gave a five-minute statement promising that Ahok would be investigated. Ahok was named a suspect the very next day.

At the movement's second protest, on December 2, 2016, 500,000 to 3 million people assembled in central Jakarta to demand that Ahok be arrested immediately. President Jokowi made a surprise appearance and participated in the group's prayer. Hendardi, chairman of the Setara Institute for Democracy and Peace, echoed a sentiment many analysts felt in Indonesia when he lamented the president's decision to appear there, suggesting that "it legitimates people who for a long time have insulted him, undermined him and caused chaos, ... and gives the impression that the pressure from the masses can become law, that the law on its own does not work" (Lamb 2016). After this highly publicized protest, the movement adopted the name of the 212 Movement, for December 2. Ahok's trial began within a couple of weeks after the protest. Ahok lost the election decisively in April 2017, and he was found guilty and sentenced to two years in prison in May 2017.

Ahok's fall demonstrates not only the mobilizational capacity of Islamist groups in impressing their demands on those in power but also the government's accommodating response. Whereas the earlier chapters of this book have examined how local politicians can use mobilization and violence to demand entry into local politics, the waves of anti-Ahok protests offer an example of how similar mobilization and threats of violence can keep unwanted people out of politics. Before the Al Maidah video went viral, nearly 60% of Jakartans said they would want Ahok to be reelected; by November 2016, more than 50% of respondents said that they would not support his candidacy (Setijadi 2017, 3–4). In a 2018 national survey, most Muslim respondents reported that they believed that Ahok was guilty of blasphemy and that they supported the interpretation of the Al Maidah verse to mean that a non-Muslim "should never have been governor in the first place" (Mietzner and Muhtadi 2018, 159).

The effectiveness of mass mobilization was once again displayed in 2019, when a mostly peaceful presidential election campaign was followed by one of the worst bouts of post-election violence in recent history. In this election, old rivals from the 2014 presidential election, Jokowi and Prabowo Subianto, faced each other again.

In 2014, Jokowi and his running mate, Jusuf Kalla, defeated Prabowo Subianto and Hatta Rajasa, by a margin of approximately eight million votes (53.15–46.85%). At the time, Jokowi promised reform and greater inclusion for non-typical elites, whereas Prabowo was viewed as a representative of the old ways, given his close ties to Soeharto and his history of human rights abuses. Prabowo refused to acknowledge defeat, accused the General Elections Committee of not investigating massive fraud, and insisted on challenging the results before the Constitutional Court (Kwok 2014). The court rejected his complaint in August 2014 (Kompas 2014).

In 2019, a similar sequence of events transpired, but this time accompanied by a two-day riot after the announcement of the election results. Jokowi ran a campaign touting his prior performance in infrastructure development, while Prabowo presented himself as a capable leader and promised to fight corruption and improve welfare (Nathalia 2019). These official campaign platforms notwithstanding, the 2019 election saw a rise in Islamist mass mobilization and politicization of identity. Jokowi's supporters framed the election as a battle between those who desire an inclusive, secular, tolerant Indonesia and Prabowo and his supporters, who they claimed would introduce an Islamic caliphate (Nathalia 2019). Prabowo's camp, with support from the 212 Movement activists, called Jokowi a bad Muslim, an atheist, a communist, and a Christian at various points during the election campaign.

Although the election itself went smoothly, for weeks between the voting day and the official announcement of the results, Prabowo and his allies claimed that the election was fraudulent (Aditya and Salna 2019) and encouraged voters to launch a "people power movement" (CNN Indonesia 2019a). They submitted a complaint to the Bawaslu (the country's election monitoring agency), asserting that Jokowi's camp had committed "structured, systematic and massive" campaign violations (Ramadhani 2019).[2]

Within hours of the official announcement of results on May 22, 2019, protests erupted in front of the Bawaslu office in central Jakarta, escalating into a two-day riot that led to 700 people injured and 10 deaths.

While Prabowo's camp fiercely denied involvement in the riots (CNN Indonesia 2019a), many believed that they had been involved. Authorities stated that the riots were "not a spontaneous incident, but … something by design" (Kapoor and Ardiansyah 2019). The police seized an ambulance with Prabowo's Gerindra party logo on it, carrying rocks, tools, and envelopes stuffed with cash, which were to be distributed to rioters (Human Rights Watch 2019), indicating that violence was purposefully orchestrated (Kapoor and Ardiansyah 2019). There were reports that former members of Prabowo's group, Tim Mawar in the Kopassus forces, were seen participating in the riots (CNN Indonesia 2019b).

On May 22, Jokowi's campaign spokesperson Arya Sinulingga said that "Prabowo-Sandiaga must take responsibility for the May 22 riots. No matter what, the protests occurred because Prabowo refused to admit defeat" (Nathaniel 2019). He encouraged Prabowo to address his supporters to stop further violence.[3] A group of activists submitted a police report against Prabowo and his campaign team on May 30, calling them responsible for the riots (Nathalia 2019).

In September 2019, the court sentenced six of the arrested rioters, three of whom were Prabowo supporters who had traveled from West Nusa Tenggara province to Jakarta to participate in the protests and riots. One of them, Randy Lolo, was arrested with US$2,760 in his pocket

---

[2] This complaint was rejected one day before the election results were announced.
[3] Prabowo eventually made a statement to this effect (Putri 2019).

(Wijaya 2019). They were represented in court by a Gerindra-affiliated advocacy team, Advokat Cinta Tanah Air (ACTA) (Nathalia 2019).

Despite these indications of Prabowo's role in inspiring the May 2019 post-election violence, just a few months later, in October 2019, Jokowi named him as Defense Minister in his coalition cabinet.[4] Alongside Prabowo, another Gerindra politician, Edhy Prabowo, was appointed as Minister of Maritime Affairs and Fisheries in the cabinet (Gorbiano 2019). With other representatives from NasDem, Partai Demokrasi Indonesia-Perjuangan (PDIP), Golkar, PKB, and PPP in the cabinet, Jokowi's second term has incorporated nearly all of the major parties in Indonesia. With only SBY's Democrat party and the Islamist parties PKS and PAN remaining outside, Jokowi's government has been described as a "fat coalition" (Amindoni 2019), as it controls nearly 70% of the seats in the Dewan Perwakilan Rakyat (DPR). Clearly, Jokowi placed a heavy premium in ensuring that he would face no quarrels from national party elites.

These two cases of group mobilization around executive elections in Indonesia suggests that long after political transition is over, politicians can and do effectively use the threat of violence to pressure ruling authorities into accommodating their demands. These two cases did not witness a resurgence of ethnic rioting, but the politicization of religion was rampant and effective in mobilizing protesters.

Beyond Indonesia

A cursory look at violent mobilizations in other parts of the world suggests that this relationship between local actors' mobilization of ethnic-based loyalties to gain entry into politics and outbursts of violence may apply more broadly in other weakly institutionalized settings. As examples, I consider the election-related ethnic violence in Kenya and the riots in Osh, Kyrgyzstan.

Kenya

Kenya, like Indonesia, is a multiethnic and newly democratic country. After the country transitioned to a multiparty system in 1991, elections in Kenya were rife with violent mobilizations, pitting ethnic groups who backed competing candidates against each other.

---

[4] This is an incredibly important position since according to the 1945 Constitution, the sitting defense minister would carry out the tasks of the president alongside the foreign and home affairs ministers if the president and vice president were to die, quit, be impeached, or otherwise become unable to carry out their duties.

With more than 50 million people from over 40 tribes, Kenya is a diverse society. The five largest ethnic groups – the Kikuyu, Luo, Luhya, Kamba, and Kalenjin – represent about 70% of the country's population. Kenya is also home to migrant communities such as Arabs and South Asians, most of whom have Kenyan citizenship. Linguistically, ethnic groups in Kenya can be categorized into three large language groups: the Bantu, Nilotic, and Cushite. Swahili and English are widely used as the lingua franca. In terms of religion, Kenyan citizens are nearly 80% Christian and 11% Muslim.

The Kikuyus, who comprise about 20% of the population and form the largest ethnic group in the country, have historically been well represented in politics since the country gained independence in 1963 (Nellis 1974). During the first 15 years after independence, President Jomo Kenyatta (a Kikuyu) and his party, the Kenya African National Union (KANU), tried to broaden ethnic representation by appointing individuals from different ethnic groups to his government.

When Kenyatta died in 1978, he was succeeded by his vice president, Daniel arap Moi, an ethnic Kalenjin. Moi consolidated his position by criminalizing opposition parties and promoting Kalenjin politicians to positions of power, much to the Kikuyus' dismay. During Moi's rule, demands for a federal system that would grant autonomy to local ethnic groups (*majimbo*) were reinvigorated (Maxon 2016). Ethnic groups who had been marginalized under Kikuyu dominance and felt that the Kikuyus had taken over their lands were particularly in favor of the *majimbo* system. The Kikuyus, on the other hand, worried that a federal system would imply forced evictions from their homes and lands along with ethnic cleansing. The politicization of ethnic identities intensified during this period, and it grew worse as Kenya shifted to a multiparty system.

In 1991, opposition parties were decriminalized amidst pressures for political and economic reforms. Moi won the country's multiparty presidential election in 1992, which was marred by accusations of electoral fraud and ethnic violence.[5] Similar violence accompanied the 1997 election, as the opposition candidate Kibaki (a Kikuyu)'s Kikuyu base was targeted with intimidation and violence. The UN Office of the High Commissioner on Human Rights (OHCHR) reported that violent attacks were centrally organized, and that perpetrators were allegedly given immunity, and that in 2007, hundreds of thousands of Kenyans were still displaced from their homes (OHCHR 2008).

---

[5] Moi won 36% of the votes, while the runner-up, Kenneth Matiba, won 26% of votes, and Mwai Kibaki placed third with 19% (EISA 2010b).

In the 2002 election, Moi was constitutionally barred from running in the election after 24 years of rule. His favored candidate, Uhuru Kenyatta, also son of the country's first president, lost to Kibaki and Raila Odinga, who led the multiethnic opposition coalition, the National Rainbow Coalition (NaRC). Kibaki had promised during his campaign that if elected, he would serve for one term only and would introduce a new constitution creating the office of prime minister, to which Odinga, a Luo, would be appointed (Maxon 2016). Despite being confined to a hospital after a car accident and a minor stroke weeks before the election, Kibaki won by a landslide and was sworn in on December 29, 2002, thanks to Odinga who had masterminded and carried on the campaign while Kibaki was hospitalized (Cheeseman 2008).[6] This was the first time a ruling party had been defeated in Kenya since 1963. This coalition soon fell apart, however, when it became clear that Kibaki would not honor his commitment to making Odinga prime minister and when he delayed and eventually put forth a watered-down version of a draft constitution in 2005 (Human Rights Watch 2008). Odinga resigned, and Kibaki stacked his government with many former technocrats, ministers, and elites from the Kenyatta regime, most of whom were Kikuyu (Murunga and Nasong'o 2006).

The December 2007 election occurred against the backdrop of these disappointments. Despite his promise to serve only one term, Kibaki decided to run again, with the support of the Party of National Unity (PNU) and also of many politicians affiliated with Moi and Kenyatta, his 2002 opponent. Kibaki competed against his former ally, Odinga, who was backed by the Orange Democratic Movement (ODM) this time. Intimidation and outbursts of violence marked the whole election campaign period.[7]

Although the voting on election day went smoothly, suspicions of irregularities grew as the votes were counted (OHCHR 2008). Odinga's initial lead of over a million votes "evaporated under opaque and highly irregular proceedings," and despite objections by Odinga's camp and European Union election observers, the Electoral Commission of Kenya (ECK) did not investigate these claims and instead declared Kibaki the winner by a narrow margin (Human Rights Watch 2008, 22). The ECK announced that Kibaki won approximately 4.5 million votes and Odinga 4.3 million (Cheeseman 2008, 176). Although citizens voted in

---

[6] Kibaki won more than 62% of the votes, while Kenyatta won 31% (EISA 2010a).

[7] Human Rights Watch (2008) reported that the weeks from August through December 2007 saw up to 200 deaths and 70,000 people displaced due to tensions between ethnic groups supporting different candidates.

both the presidential and parliamentary elections simultaneously, there was a wide discrepancy between the parliamentary and presidential election results. In the parliamentary election, the ODM won 99 seats and Kibaki's party won only 43 (Human Rights Watch 2008, 22). This discrepancy, among others, suggests vote tampering to favor Kibaki in the presidential race. By Cheeseman (2008)'s account, many Kenyan voters believed that Odinga had in fact won the election by a much wider margin. Within an hour after the official election results were announced on December 30, 2007, Kibaki was hastily sworn in at the State House, even as violence began in various parts of the country.

The fighting would continue for about two months, through late February 2008. Overall, the clashes killed over 1,000 people and displaced more than 500,000 people from their homes (Cheeseman 2008). Although the clashes involved different ethnic groups and took various forms in different parts of the country, and some had occurred in the months leading up to the election, the waves of violence related to the 2007 election in Kenya were motivated by ODM's supporters' sense of years of exclusion and their fear that they would again lose another election (Cheeseman 2008).

The hostilities ended only when both parties signed on February 28, 2008, a power-sharing agreement, the National Accord and Reconciliation Act. This pact outlined the creation of the office of prime minister, who would have the authority to supervise and coordinate executive functions of the government. According to this agreement, the government would be composed of the president, vice president, prime minister, two deputy prime ministers (each nominated by a member of the coalition), and cabinet ministers. The document also stipulated that the act would be incorporated into the country's constitution.

To implement this agreement, the government amended the constitution in 2010 and implemented a series of institutional reforms, which granted local autonomy and established 47 counties before the 2013 election (Elfversson and Sjögren 2020, 50). The county boundaries were designed to subdivide all major ethnic groups into different counties, so as to encourage multiethnic coalition building (Elfversson and Sjögren 2020, 50). According to the 2010 constitution, presidential candidates must win more than 50% of the votes, including 25% or more in at least 24 counties, to win the presidential election. This requirement was added to ensure that presidential candidates would broaden their appeal to multiple ethnic groups.

Although there has been some violence in later elections, Kenya's power-sharing arrangement has generally been considered successful, and other countries in Africa have implemented arrangements modeled after Kenya's (Cheeseman and Tendi 2010, 204).[8]

Certainly, important distinctions exist between the ethnopolitical landscapes in Indonesia and in Kenya. The violence around the 2007 election in Kenya came after the waves of election-related violence in 1992 and 1997, when thousands died and more than 300,000 people were displaced, and perpetrators of violence enjoyed impunity (Human Rights Watch 2008). Clashes erupted afresh in 2017, though not to the same degree of severity (Human Rights Watch 2017). The violence occurring in 2017 suggests that there is more to violence in Kenya than demands for inclusion and representation. Furthermore, whereas political parties in Indonesia have not explicitly championed specific ethnic groups' causes at the exclusion of others, political parties in Kenya have been described as "vehicles of ethnic nativism" (Mutua 2008, 22). Nonetheless, these distinctions notwithstanding, Kenya's election-related communal violence shows how groups' concerns over being shut out from important positions have motivated them to turn to violence and that a power-sharing arrangement was the solution of choice to address the problem.

Kyrgyzstan

Another example of ethnic riots as a result of continued exclusion during a national political transition was the 1990 and 2010 riots in Osh, a province in the southern region of Kyrgyzstan, a former Soviet republic.[9]

Kyrgyzstan, which declared its independence in August 1991, is no stranger to political transitions. Beyond perestroika and the country's journey to independence, Kyrgyzstan has also had two mass mobilizations that led to the ouster of its presidents. Perestroika introduced political and economic reforms, including the March 1989 national election, which saw contests over parliamentary seats and collectives' greater independence in nominating candidates (Huskey 1995). Although the 1989 national election still benefited the established apparatus in Kyrgyzstan and many of the seats were uncontested,

---

[8] Cheeseman and Tendi (2010, 204) noted that Angola, the Democratic Republic of Congo, Djibouti, Liberia, Mali, Senegal, Somalia, South Africa, and Sudan, among others, have implemented similar arrangements.

[9] Osh is a province in the Fergana Valley, which borders with Uzbekistan. Osh city, the provincial capital, is the country's second largest city and was a major hub of the Silk Road.

the elected members of the Kyrgyzstan Supreme Soviet subsequently passed legislation that allowed for more contests in local elections (Huskey 1995).

Within two months of the country's declaration of independence, in October 1991, Askar Akaev was elected as president with more than 95% of the vote. He served as president for 15 years, until he was overthrown in what his successor, Kurmanbek Bakiev, liked to describe as the "March 2005 events" (Marat 2008, 231) instead of the more pro-democracy term that many international observers used, the "tulip revolution" (Bond and Koch 2010, 538). Bakiev ruled for four years before he was ousted in April 2010. A provisional government assumed power immediately after Bakiev's departure and was in the process of preparing for an election when the second Osh riot erupted in June 2010.

The Kyrgyz, Slavs, and Uzbeks comprise a large segment of the population in southern Kyrgyzstan.[10] Historically, Uzbeks and Kyrgyz have coexisted peacefully for many years in the Fergana Valley, often intermarrying between groups (Human Rights Watch 2010).

The Kyrgyz ethnic group is further subdivided into three broader categories, each of which has many clans (Bond and Koch 2010). Some observers have noted a regional divide between the northern and southern Kyrgyz clans, as historically the northern clans were more willing to cooperate with the Russians than their southern counterparts, who supported the Kokan Khanate (Bond and Koch 2010, 536).

In the Osh province specifically, a third of the population is Uzbek, many of whom live in the capital city, also called Osh.[11] The Kyrgyz have worked primarily in cattle breeding, while Uzbeks have mostly engaged in agriculture and trade (Commercio 2018).

During Soviet rule, Uzbeks in Osh enjoyed economic dominance but were underrepresented in politics and administration, while the Krygyz suffered the opposite burden. They were well represented in administrative and bureaucratic positions, but many felt economically marginalized. According to Amelin (1993), two-thirds of the members of the regional People's Deputies executive committee was Kyrgyz. The republic's first secretary from 1961 through 1985, Turdakun Usubaliev, an ethnic Kyrgyz, appointed his relatives and fellow Kyrgyz to administrative posts (McGlinchey 2014). In 1990, more than 80%

---

[10] In 1989, the population breakdown in Kyrgyzstan was 52% Kyrgyz, 21.5% Slav, and 13% Uzbek (Commercio 2018, 767).

[11] According to Commercio (2018, 767), by 2009, 79% of the Osh urban population was Uzbek and 17% Kyrgyz, whereas in the rural areas of Osh, the balance was roughly the opposite: 73% Kyrgyz and 24% Uzbek.

of positions in the city's department of internal affairs were filled by Kyrgyz individuals (McGlinchey 2014). The same was true for the police forces. Northern Kyrgyz clans were better represented among low- and middle-level appointments in the bureaucracy than their counterparts (Bond and Koch 2010, 536). Not until 1985, when Absamat Masaliev, a southern Kyrgyz, became Kyrgyzstan's party leader did southern Kyrgyz gain access to government positions (Bond and Koch 2010, 536).

Osh Uzbeks, on the other hand, were hardly represented in administration and bureaucracy but enjoyed economic privileges relative to their Kyrgyz neighbors. Only 4% of the members in the party leadership bodies were Uzbek (McGlinchey 2014). In the regional People's Deputies executive committee, only 5% were Uzbek (Amelin 1993). But in terms of wealth, the Uzbeks were better off, occupying nearly 71% of the trade, commerce, and agricultural sectors (Commercio 2018; Tishkov 1995). The out-migration of many Slavs during perestroika shifted the balance to a larger proportion of Uzbeks in the Osh province. The collapse of the collective farms caused many Kyrgyz who had previously lived in rural areas to migrate to the city for employment opportunities. As Megoran (2013, 901) stated, "To an incoming Kyrgyz, it seemed as if Uzbeks had some of the best land, the wealthiest businesses, and the best houses in the best locations – that the Kyrgyz were second class citizens in their own state." Since Uzbeks had dominated the urban economy, they had better access to land and housing in Osh than the Kyrgyz, many of whom were recent arrivals in the city (Liu 2012).

For Uzbeks, perestroika enabled the group's political mobilization along ethnic lines. After a Supreme Court decision in November 1989 decreed the replacement of Russian with Kyrgyz as the official language in the Kyrgyz Soviet Republic, an Uzbek rights group, Adolat, emerged (Human Rights Watch 2010). This organization demanded state recognition of the Uzbek language, the right to receive higher education in Uzbek, the creation of autonomous Uzbek administrative units (*oblast*) (Commercio 2018), and the secession of territory to join neighboring Uzbekistan (Minorities at Risk Project 2004).

These demands for an autonomous administrative unit specifically for Uzbeks agitated the Kyrgyz counterpart organization, the recently established Osh-Aymaghi, which in turn demanded that the authorities address the land and housing shortages afflicting the Kyrgyz who had migrated into the city in recent years as Russians left (Razakov 2011, 121).

Against this long backdrop of resentment over continued economic marginalization of the Kyrgyz and political alienation of the Uzbeks, riots broke out on June 4, 1990 (Human Rights Watch 2010). When the predominantly Kyrgyz authorities decided to allocate plots of land for housing projects from land owned by an Uzbek-dominated collective farm, Uzbeks protested and were confronted by Kyrgyz counter-protesters.

Although clashes began in the city, they subsequently spread over the next few days to Uzgen and 30 nearby villages, until the violence dissipated when Soviet troops arrived to restore order (Tishkov 1995). More than 300 people died (Human Rights Watch 2010). Incidents of violence continued for the next few months. The state of emergency declared at the onset of the violence remained in effect until November.

In the Soviet press, Kyrgyz leaders were vilified (McGlinchey 2014). Kremlin officials attributed the 1990 riots to Osh Kyrgyz leaders' "incompetence" and "corruption" (McGlinchey 2014). Although Kyrgyzstan was not the only territory in the Soviet Union to experience outbursts of ethnocommunal violence at this time, or the only one in Central Asia, the 1990 Osh riot was the only riot that led to trials in the Soviet Union (McGlinchey 2014).

The collapse of the Soviet Union did not improve Osh Uzbeks' political fortunes. With the 1990 riots still fresh in people's memory, the newly elected president Akaev promised a modestly inclusive government that would protect the languages and cultures of minority groups, including the Uzbeks (Akaev 1993).[12] He created the Assembly of the People of Kyrgyzstan, which included Russian and Uzbek representatives, and he established two Uzbek higher education institutions in Osh (Liu 2012).

Despite these developments, Akaev did not elevate Uzbek to the status of an official language, nor did he establish a separate *oblast* for them. He understood that an Uzbek brain drain would be unlikely, as life in Uzbekistan is perceived as harder than in Kyrgyzstan (Matveeva 2007). In 1990, the prime minister of Uzbekistan also rejected calls for Uzbek-dominated areas in Kyrgyzstan to secede and join Uzbekistan (Minorities at Risk Project 2004), leaving the Uzbeks of Kyrgyzstan no real exit option.

Instead, Akaev stacked his government with fellow northern Kyrgyz, much to the dismay of southern Kyrgyz, who felt sidelined during Akaev's 15-year reign (Bond and Koch 2010). Southern Kyrgyz launched various demands for greater southern representation in government, such as the relocation of some government ministries and parliament to

---

[12] His slogan was "Kyrgyzstan – Our Common Home" (Commercio 2018), and in his inaugural speech he promised to develop the Kyrgyz language, culture, and history while ensuring the "protection of the national interests, languages, and cultures of everyone: Kyrgyz, Russians, Uzbeks . . . " (Akaev 1993, 33–34).

Osh (Bond and Koch 2010). The ethnic Uzbeks, meanwhile, had no voice at all as this government was effectively entirely Kyrgyz (Liu 2012).

When Akaev was ousted and succeeded by Kurmanbek Bakiev in 2005, the southern Kyrgyz found an ally, as Bakiev hails from Jalal-Abad in southern Kyrgyzstan and enjoys extensive support in the south (McGlinchey 2011). But Bakiev's rule did not improve the position of Osh Uzbeks. His government denied Uzbeks political representation in key positions, refused to grant the Uzbek language official status, and instead promoted nationalist Kyrgyz politicians (Bond and Koch 2010).

Uzbeks also continued to feel discriminated against by the police and authorities in property disputes. In July 2006, 200 Kyrgyz families in Jalal-Abad forcibly squatted on farmland and properties owned by an Uzbek parliament member and entrepreneur, Kadyrjan Batyrov. The police did not intervene and instead encouraged Batyrov to take the case to court, where he failed to win at both the district and regional levels. The matter dragged on for a year before it was finally settled in the Supreme Court. Azimzhon Askarov, a human rights activist, stated, "The Batyrov case that drags on for almost a year is a clear indication of discrimination against the Uzbeks. When Uzbeks seize Kyrgyz-owned lands, the authorities respond very quickly" (Rotar 2007). Fifty-nine percent of urban Uzbek respondents in Kyrgyzstan indicated in a 2007 survey that they felt that their ethnic identity limited their rights (Hierman 2015).

An opportunity for greater Uzbek inclusion emerged after Bakiev's ouster in April 2010, when Roza Otunbayeva, who led the interim government, dissolved Bakiev's national parliament and solicited the support of Uzbek leaders to restore its authority. After pro-Bakiev Kyrgyz attacked government offices in Batken, Osh, and Jalal-Abad protesting Bakiev's removal, Uzbek leader Kadyrjan Batyrov was allegedly involved in an arson attack on Bakiev's compound near Jalal-Abad on May 14 (Khamidov 2010). Many believed that Batyrov did this in exchange for a promise of greater Uzbek representation in the new government.

For ethnic Kyrgyz in southern Kyrgyzstan, however, this demand, along with the dissolution of the prior regime's parliament, signaled an attempt to wrangle power from their hands and to promote Uzbek interests (McGlinchey 2011). A Kyrgyz respondent commented, "Uzbeks have control over the bazaars and property in valued spots. They have a lot of money. And now they want political power. They have to curb their appetites and behave moderately. This is a Kyrgyz country, after all" (Khamidov 2010).

Twenty years after the initial outburst of violence between Uzbeks and Kyrgyz in Osh, a similar episode of violence between the same two groups erupted afresh in the same city on June 10–14. Triggered by a casino brawl between Uzbek and Kyrgyz men and escalated by rumors of the rape of Kyrgyz women, riots started in Osh city and spread to nearby towns. As a result of this violence, 350 people died and more than 100,000 people were displaced from their homes (McGlinchey 2011).[13] Thousands of buildings were destroyed in Osh, Jalal-Abad, and Bazar-Kurgan during the violence (Human Rights Watch 2010, 4). Although in the initial stage of the riots many Uzbeks reportedly attacked and killed Kyrgyz men and women, by the end of the violence most of the buildings destroyed were Uzbek-owned properties (Human Rights Watch 2010). Riots began to dissipate only after the authorities empowered security officers with a "shoot-to-kill" policy on June 12, after several days of what many witnesses described as troops' ineffective and reluctant intervention to stop the violence (Human Rights Watch 2010).[14]

In the aftermath of the conflict, the Organization for Security and Cooperation in Europe (OSCE) High Commissioner on National Minorities encouraged Kyrgyzstan authorities to devise with a power-sharing arrangement that would incorporate representatives of Uzbek and other national minorities in various institutions (Lewis and Sagnayeva 2020). This proposal was met with protests in Kyrgyzstan, as protesters believed that this plan would embolden Uzbeks' demands for secession (Lewis and Sagnayeva 2020).

The new president, Almazbek Atambayev, led a broad-based reconciliation initiative and produced a document in April 2013 that attempted to appease both the nationalists and marginalized citizens through stressing the importance of unity where citizens will be "multilingual, educated and open to innovation and contacts" (Galdini 2014). Despite this rhetoric, the document lacked concrete plans on how to improve Uzbek rights after the 2010 violence. The police and justice departments did not bring to justice those who perpetrated violence in the 2010 riots. Instead, most of the criminal charges were directed toward the Uzbek community, who bore most of the burden of property losses and

---

[13] According to the Human Rights Watch (2010, 7) report, the authorities confirmed 356 deaths related to this violence, but the report also mentioned an alternative plausible estimate of 900 deaths associated with this violence.

[14] According to Human Rights Watch (2010), the police and security officers seemed less concerned about stopping the violence committed by ethnic Kyrgyz individuals, and more focused on disarming Uzbek men. In some areas, some witnesses claimed that the security forces had abetted Kyrgyz attacks on Uzbek neighborhoods.

casualties (Galdini 2014). In short, the government did little to address the roots of the problems.

The series of violent episodes between ethnic Kyrgyz and Uzbek groups in southern Kyrgyzstan at various points of transition has demonstrated that political transitions created opportunities for disenchanted groups to articulate their demands and to try to shift the balance of power in their favor. Although these windows of opportunity do not by themselves inevitably lead to violence, in Kyrgyzstan in 1990 and in 2010, both Uzbek and Kyrgyz groups perceived that their claims would be ignored unless they mobilized. Though both Osh Kyrgyz and Uzbek groups had had a long history of economic and political alienation, not until the provisional government courted Uzbek community leaders for their support in 2010 did Osh Kyrgyz feel threatened and decide to mobilize to assert themselves and their claims.

Broader Implications

The cases reviewed above illustrate that the mobilization of violence between ethnic groups during political transitions is not unique to Indonesia but is in fact quite common in many parts of the world. Indonesia is not a unique case. The Kenya and Kyrgyzstan cases reviewed here highlight the applicability of my argument and suggest some avenues for future research.

Broadly, the story of groups' violent mobilization as a tool for political engagement after disappointment with formal channels such as elections finds support in these cases. In Kenya, the bulk of the riots occurred after Odinga supposedly lost the election and there was a widespread perception of election fraud. This election came after Odinga and his supporters were denied a promised power-sharing arrangement despite their role in helping Kibaki win the 2002 election. The turn to violence was a last resort. Similarly, in Kyrgyzstan, the 1990 riots were provoked by protests against the government's decision to allocate land to the Kyrgyz, whereas the 2010 riots were fueled by the ethnic Kyrgyz' wariness of Uzbeks' demands for more representation and Uzbeks' frustration with their continued political exclusion.

These cases also lend credence to another implication of my argument, about accommodation and dissipation of violence. In 2007, the intergroup violence following the election in Kenya continued for weeks and ceased only when the warring parties signed a power-sharing agreement in February 2008. The 2010 constitution that embodied the principles of this power-sharing agreement further assuaged worries about exclusion in the new government. In addition, the creation of new counties also multiplied the number of seats and provided more venues for local actors to attain coveted positions. In Kyrgyzstan, on the other hand, a mutually acceptable arrangement between Uzbeks and Kyrgyz has not been reached since the country's independence; as a result, unsurprisingly, the tension between the two groups reached its boiling point during subsequent political transitions.

Ethnocommunal violence in Kenya and Kyrgyzstan and its resolution (or the lack thereof, in the latter case) also points to several avenues for future research. The experience of Kyrgyzstan in particular illustrates a pattern in which the dominant group resents the forms of accommodation that an excluded group appears to be gaining after its mobilization. When the provisional government solicited Uzbeks' assistance to restore order in exchange for a greater role in the new government, southern Kyrgyz resented this move and fought back. The 2010 riot in Osh was largely prompted by the Kyrgyz refusal to relinquish power in the face of a rising "ethnic competitor" (Wachtel 2013). What prompts accommodation in some cases and resistance in others? Why do we see power-sharing agreements in many countries in sub-Saharan Africa, but not in Kyrgyzstan?

Furthermore, if accommodation does not happen, will violence continue? This book shows that when demands are accommodated, groups no longer need to use violence as a strategy for making demands, so the violence dissipates. Conversely, the same logic implies that when demands are not accommodated, fighting continues. As chapters 5–7 have demonstrated, accommodation in Indonesia worked as local elections became more competitive and allowed the incorporation of new players into politics. Beyond the increased electoral competitiveness, accommodation also occurred through administrative unit partitioning, which provided disgruntled local actors with an exit option from their home administrative units and effectively multiplied the number of seats available for local actors. In Kenya, a similar arrangement occurred, through the creation of new counties and the granting of broader autonomy to local governments. In Kyrgyzstan, meanwhile, the Uzbek demands were never accommodated, and Kyrgyz–Uzbek relations have remained tense over the decades. The Uzbek minority group did not enjoy the benefit of a viable exit option. Migrating to Uzbekistan was not an attractive solution for many Uzbeks in Kyrgyzstan, since they knew their lives there would be harder (Commercio 2018). The request for a separate autonomous *oblast* was also consistently denied, and Uzbekistan also refused to annex the Uzbek-majority regions in Kyrgyzstan. The lack of accommodation of demands voiced and the lack of an exit option here imply that violence should continue. But the

Fergana Valley had long periods of relative peace as well. What, then, accounted for the absence of fighting, if neither accommodation nor exit was available for the Uzbek minority group? Could the relative peace be a function of the third element of Hirschman's framework, loyalty, where individuals become resigned to a sub-optimal arrangement simply because both exit and voice are too costly and ineffective?

Finally, other kinds of violence have also occurred in the countries that have experienced the ethnocommunal riots descried in this book. Since Soeharto's ouster in 1998, Indonesia has witnessed anti-Chinese violence, violence around the secession of East Timor, ongoing secessionist mobilization and violence in Papua, periodic terrorist attacks, and low-level violence around local executive elections. Kenya is not new to ethnic violence, and since 2007 it has also suffered terrorist attacks. Similarly, Kyrgyzstan has had to deal with border disputes with its neighbors since independence, and it is wary of Uzbeks' support for Uzbekistan and the challenge they may pose to its sovereignty. Although this book has deliberately focused on only one kind of violence, it would be naive to assert that other kinds of violence have no influence over the onset of riots and the government's responses to ethnic rioting. The interaction between these different kinds of violence and their precise relationship with ethnocommunal violence still await delineation.

Appendix A   Data Collection Protocol

Data Collection Protocol for Kompas Data

The data collection protocol for Kompas and TEMPO follow closely the protocol outlined in Wilkinson and Varshney's data collection protocol for their Hindu–Muslim riots data (Wilkinson 2004; Varshney 2002). This data collection protocol was originally published as part of Toha (2017)'s online appendix, and is printed in full, with slight modifications, here.

Source

To collect additional data on ethnocommunal violence in Indonesia, I read *Kompas*, a national-level newspaper based in Jakarta, Indonesia. The bulk of this data collection work was done in the archives of the National Library in Jakarta in the summer of 2004. The remaining portion of the data was collected during a visit to the Asia Library at Cornell University, where I read through the pages of *Kompas* microforms. These visits and data collection were made possible through the generous support of the UCLA Graduate Mentorship Program.

Time Period

The time period covered by this data is from 1999 to 2005. I deliberately limited my data collection to this period for two reasons: (1) to extend the United Nations Support for Indonesian Recovery (UNSFIR) coverage from 1990 to 2003, to include 2004 and 2005; and (2) to have some years of overlap between the *Kompas* and UNSFIR data to examine how the two correlate with each other.

Sampling Procedure

I read the newspapers every eleven days from 1999 to 2005. With this method, I do not waste time reading every *Kompas* paper ever published during my period of interest, and simultaneously avoid possible bias from selecting days that are more conducive to conflict. Admittedly, eleven days is a long period that events occurring on Day 1 may have become old news on Day 11 that the Day 11 paper would not report it. Regardless, I assume that the conflicts that I am interested in are of national political interest (and hence they would be reported in the national newspaper) and that due to its political implications it would at least be mentioned in the papers even eleven days after the event occurred. If for whatever reason the paper is not published on the day that it is supposed to be read, I read the paper from one day before or after the scheduled date as a substitute. To avoid potential bias, I substitute public holidays with the day before and after alternately.

Data Entry

I recorded incidents reported in the paper as having been triggered by an offense along ethnic lines or, more broadly, incidents fought by communities defined by ethnic identities. For Indonesia between 1999 and 2005, this includes anti-Chinese violence; clashes between Christians and Muslims in Central Sulawesi, Maluku, and North Maluku; and clashes between Dayaks and Madurese in Central and West Kalimantan. Separatist clashes, street justice violence, terrorist violence, criminal attacks, gang fights, and student brawls, though communal in nature are not fought along ethnic lines and are consequently excluded from this dataset.

In entering the data into my dataset, I recorded the event's location (e.g., province, district, subdistrict, and village name) and date. This information is later recoded into both a count variable (i.e., count of clashes that occurred in a district-year) and a binary variable (i.e., whether communal clashes occurred in a given district-year. 1s are for when clashes did occur, and 0s if otherwise).

The specific procedure for data entry is as follows:

Source Date Enter the date in which the violence is reported in the following format: month/day/year.
Village(s) Enter when given. If the violence occurs in multiple villages, enter all the villages as reported, separated by commas. For example: village A, village B, village C, etc.
Town(s) Enter when given. If the violence occurs across several towns, enter all towns as reported, separated by commas. For example: town A, town B, town C, etc.
Subdistrict(s) Enter when given. If the violence occurs in multiple villages and/or towns that are part of different subdistricts, list the subdistricts following the same sequence as the list of villages/towns. For example, if village A (part of subdistrict X) and village B (part of subdistrict Y) are listed as "village A, village B" in the Village column, then the Subdistrict column should read subdistrict X, subdistrict Y.

Thus, readers would know the subdistrict to which each village belongs.

District(s) Enter when given. If violence occurs across multiple districts, list the district following the same sequence as the list of villages/towns/subdistricts.

Province(s) Enter name of province. If violence occurs across multiple provinces, list all of them.

Year Enter year of observation.

Conflict Write 1 if conflict was reported to have been triggered by an offense along ethnic lines, involved multiple people on both the perpetrator and victim sides, and the groups involved were separated along ethnic lines.

Data Collection Protocol for Tempo Data

Source
To supplement *Kompas* data, which may have suffered from censorship and underreporting, I rely on news reports of a national weekly magazine, *Tempo*. Archives of this magazine were accessible at the *Tempo* office in Jakarta, Indonesia.

Time Period
For the purpose of this research, I read through every edition published from 2002 through 2005. By reading through these four years, I was able to collect 2004 and 2005 data that were not included in the UNSFIR dataset, provide violence data gleaned from a national publication other than *Kompas*, and have enough years of overlap to estimate the correlation between *Kompas*, *Tempo*, and UNSFIR datasets.

Data Collection Protocol
I read every weekly edition of *Tempo* from 2002 through 2005, with approximately 50 editions per year and approximately 200 editions for the entire four years. I read closely the "Laporan Utama" (cover story), "Hukum" (law), "Kriminalitas" (crime), "Lingkungan" (environment), "Nasional" (national reports), and "Perisitiwa" (events) sections, and skimmed the rest (e.g., religion, education, interviews).

Following closely the data collection protocol of the UN team (Varshney et al. 2008), I recorded incidents of collective violence that fall under the following categories: ethnocommunal clashes between groups, collective violence against the state (or members of state apparatus), collective violence driven by economic concerns/demands, and other miscellaneous forms of collective violence. Examples of clashes that fall under ethnocommunal category include clashes between ethnic groups, clashes between religious groups, and sectarian violence between members of a religious community.

Given the definitional scope of this project, I do not include separatist clashes and demonstrations under the "state" collective action category. Instead, this category refers to mass demonstrations against state policies, group attacks on state properties, and clashes between civilians and police/military officers motivated by reasons other than separatist demands.

Economic-related collective violence refers to clashes, protests, and demonstrations motivated by struggle over land use, laborer relations with their employers and companies, use of natural resources, and others.

Incidents that fall under the "Miscellaneous" category range from killings of alleged witch doctors in Java, clashes between party supporters during election campaigns, brawls between villagers, terrorist bombings and attacks, killings of petty criminals commonly known as street or popular justice, clashes and shootings between status agencies (military and police officers), and others.

Data Entry

In collecting the data, I recorded the event's location (e.g., province, district, subdistrict, and village name), category of violence, narrative of event, and date. This information is later recoded into both a count variable (i.e., count of clashes that occurred in a district-year) and a binary variable (i.e., whether communal clashes occurred in a given district-year; 1s are for when clashes did occur, and 0s if otherwise) in my dissertation dataset.

The specific procedure for data entry is as follows:

Source Date Enter the date in which the violence is reported in the following format: month/day/year.
Source Title Enter the title of the article in which this event was reported.
Village(s) Enter when given. If the violence occurs in multiple villages, enter all the villages as reported, separated by commas. For example: village A, village B, village C, etc.
Town(s) Enter when given. If the violence occurs across several towns, enter all towns as reported, separated by commas. For example: town A, town B, town C, etc.
Subdistrict(s) Enter when given. If the violence occurs in multiple villages and/or towns that are part of different subdistricts, list the subdistricts following the same sequence as the list of villages/towns. For example, if village A (part of subdistrict X) and village B (part

of subdistrict Y) are listed as "village A, village B" in the Village column, then the Subdistrict column should read: subdistrict X, subdistrict Y. Thus, readers would know the subdistrict to which each village belongs.

District(s) Enter when given. If violence occurs across multiple districts, list the incident in the other districts as separate incidents.

Province(s) Enter name of province.

Year Enter year of incident.

Month Enter month of incident.

Date Enter specific date of incident, in mm/dd/yyyy format. Multiple incidents in one day and occurring in one district are counted as ONE incident. Events in different days in the same district are counted as separate incidents.

Category of violence Enter whether the incident reported falls under ethnocommunal, state, economic, or other category of violence.

Description of incident Write as much as possible of the description of the incidents.

Trigger event Write as much as possible of the triggers of the incident (e.g., gambling, drunken brawl, fights between individuals).

Casualties Enter number of people killed in a given incident.

Injuries Enter number of people injured in a given incident.

Property damage List types and number of property damaged in a given incident.

Weapon used List types of weapons used, if any, during the incident.

Law enforcement response Write whether there was any response from military or police or government apparatus, and if so, what.

Appendix B   Additional Tables and Figures

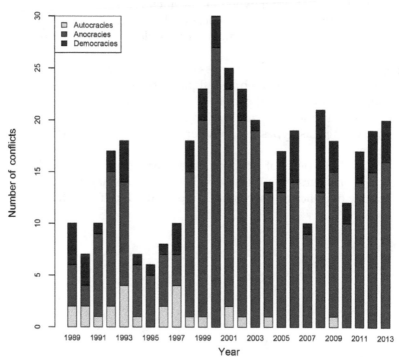

Figure B.1 Global distribution of communal conflicts

Notes: To construct this figure, I matched the location of each communal conflict within a country-year reported in the UCDP dataset with the country's corresponding Polity IV score for the "polity2" variable at the onset of violence. Polity IV scores countries on a scale from −10 (for strongly autocratic) to 10 (for strongly democratic), and democracies are assigned a score of 6 and above. This figure was originally included in the online appendices of Toha (2017).

Table B.1. *Summary statistics of variables in Chapter 5*

	Mean	sd	min	max	Count
Count of riots	0.13	1.71	0	59	5,371
Riots-related death	1.84	39.14	0	1,384	5,371
Count of riots per 100,000 people	0.04	0.72	0	29	5,210
Severity of violence	0.06	0.39	0	5	5,371
0/1 for ethnic riots	0.04	0.19	0	1	5,371
Electoral competitiveness	−41.73	29.45	−100	−0	5,363
Year after election	0.26	0.44	0	1	5,371
Ratio of second to largest religious group	0.13	0.20	0	1	3,003
Count of riots in prior year	0.13	1.79	0	59	4,842
Security spending	152.63	990.83	0	45,928	3,404
GDP per capita (logged)	1.08	1.08	−3	6	5,127
Population (logged)	12.90	0.95	8	15	5,210
Area (logged)	7.43	1.80	2	13	5,371
Urban (y/n)	0.21	0.41	0	1	5,371
After 1998 (y/n)	0.51	0.50	0	1	5,371
Golkar voteshare	0.56	0.27	0	1	5,363
% change in Golkar voteshare from 1987 to 1997 elections	−3.43	12.50	−79	24	2,164
Delta vote margins	17.13	26.93	−59	94	4,054
Turnover in favor of opposition	0.05	0.22	0	1	5,371
PDIP voteshare	0.19	0.17	0	1	5,363
Islamic party voteshare (PPP, PKS, PBR, PBB)	0.15	0.12	0	1	5,363
Voteshare of non-Golkar parties	0.44	0.27	0	1	5,363
Ethnic fractionalization	0.38	0.28	0	1	334
Ethnic fractionalization squared	0.23	0.23	0	1	334
Religious fractionalization	0.17	0.17	0	1	2,951
Religious fractionalization squared	0.06	0.09	0	1	2,951

Table B.2. *Summary statistics of variables in Chapter 7*

	Mean	sd	min	max	Count
Count of ethnic riots (NVMS)	0.42	4.11	0	171	6,729
0/1 turnover to opposition in 1999 election?	0.49	0.50	0	1	6,729
Injuries related to ethnic riots (NVMS)	1.38	26.00	0	1,685	6,729
Deaths related to ethnic riots (NVMS)	0.82	17.36	0	845	6,729
Religious fractionalization	0.15	0.17	0	1	3,187
Poverty rate (% of population)	17.59	10.63	1	111	5,178
Logged GDP per capita with oil and gas, in constant price	1.66	0.74	−1	6	5,596
Logged area	7.43	1.67	2	12	3,938
Logged population	12.70	1.02	9	16	6,442
0/1 turnover to opposition in 2004 election?	0.14	0.34	0	1	6,729
Change in vote margins from the 1999 to 2004 election	5.95	17.56	−46	61	6,729
Districts with ethnic riots (1997–2012)	0.25	0.43	0	1	6,729
Parent * conflict district	0.11	0.32	0	1	6,729
Child * conflict district	0.07	0.25	0	1	6,729
Delta violence	0.06	3.37	−66	170	6,252
0/1 for whether a split occurred this year	0.02	0.15	0	1	6,729
Logged natural resource revenues per capita	9.05	2.74	0	18	5,675
Logged dau transfer per capita	13.15	1.34	6	17	6,006
Logged PAD revenues	23.47	1.32	15	28	6,067
Logged staff expenditure per capita	13.33	0.81	8	16	4,584
Golkar_share_all	0.24	0.13	0	1	3,367

Table B.3. *Incidence rate ratios of electoral competitiveness*

	DV: Count of ethnic riots				
	Full sample	Full sample	Full sample	New order	Post-Soeharto
Electoral competitiveness	0.989^			0.925	0.987^
	(0.006)			(0.063)	(0.007)
Year after election	2.237***	2.343***	1.933*	11.903***	2.188**
	(0.467)	(0.496)	(0.518)	(8.082)	(0.626)
Golkar vote share		4.841*			
		(2.977)			
% change in Golkar vote share from 1987 to 1997 elections			1.120^		
			(0.067)		
Ratio of second to largest group	✓	✓	✓	✓	✓
Count of riots in prior year	✓	✓	✓	✓	✓
Security expenses	✓	✓	✓	✓	✓
Logged GDP per capita	✓	✓	✓	✓	✓
Logged population	✓	✓	✓	✓	✓
Logged area	✓	✓	✓	✓	✓
Urban dummy	✓	✓	✓	✓	✓
Post-Soeharto dummy	✓	✓	✓		
Fixed effects	✓	✓	✓	✓	✓
Observations	488	488	260	101	225
AIC	491.642	489.115	345.444	74.208	312.670
Log likelihood	−234.821	−233.558	−161.722	−27.104	−146.335

Notes: Dependent variable is count of ethnic riots. Papua and Aceh observations were excluded from all estimations. ^$p < 0.10$, *$p < 0.05$, **$p < 0.01$, ***$p < 0.001$.

259

Table B.4. *Robustness: alternative modeling choices*

	OLS		Poisson	
	(1)	(2)	(3)	(4)
Electoral competitiveness	−0.007*		−0.026***	
	(0.003)		(0.004)	
Year after election	0.091	0.108	0.730***	0.663***
	(0.119)	(0.119)	(0.147)	(0.143)
Golkar vote share		0.955**		3.583***
		(0.306)		(0.376)
Ratio of second to largest group	✓	✓	✓	✓
Count of riots in prior year	✓	✓	✓	✓
Security expenses	✓	✓	✓	✓
Logged GDP per capita	✓	✓	✓	✓
Logged population	✓	✓	✓	✓
Logged area	✓	✓	✓	✓
Urban dummy	✓	✓		
Post-Soeharto dummy	✓	✓	✓	✓
Fixed effects	✓	✓	✓	✓
Observations	1,898	1,898	488	488
AIC	7561.696	7556.516	681.921	636.067
Log likelihood	−3770.848	−3768.258	−331.961	−309.033

Notes: Dependent variable is count of ethnic riots. All estimations are using the full sample of district-years from 1990 through 2005. Papua and Aceh observations were excluded from all estimations. Columns 1–2 are results from OLS estimations with "xtreg"; columns 3–4 are results based on Poisson models with "xtpoisson" in Stata. $\hat{}p < 0.10$, *$p < 0.05$, ** $p < 0.01$, ***$p < 0.001$.

Table B.5. *Prior to 1999 observations*

	DV: Count of ethnic riots					
	New order	Post-Soeharto	New order	Post-Soeharto	New order	New order
Electoral	−0.078	−0.013ˆ			−0.078	
competitiveness	(0.068)	(0.007)			(0.068)	
Year after election	2.477***	0.783**	2.073**	0.835**		
	(0.679)	(0.286)	(0.701)	(0.291)		
Golkar voteshare			18.639	1.424*		18.639
			(13.813)	(0.701)		(13.813)
Year 1998 dummy					2.477***	2.073**
					(0.679)	(0.701)
Controls	✓	✓	✓	✓	✓	✓
Fixed effects	✓	✓	✓	✓	✓	✓
Observations	101	225	101	225	101	101
AIC	74.208	312.670	73.508	312.154	74.208	73.508
Log likelihood	−27.104	−146.335	−6.754	−146.077	−27.104	−26.754

Notes: Dependent variable count of ethnic riots. Papua and Aceh observations were excluded from all estimations. $ˆp < 0.10$, $*p < 0.05$, $**p < 0.01$, $***p < 0.001$.

Table B.6. *Incidence rate ratios of party vote shares*

	DV: Count of ethnic riots			
	(1)	(2)	(3)	(4)
PDIP voteshare	0.143**	0.227ˆ		
	(0.097)	(0.172)		
Year after election	2.039***	2.212***	2.210***	2.343***
	(0.407)	(0.463)	(0.463)	(0.496)
Islamic party voteshare			2.409	
(PPP, PKS, PBR, PBB)			(3.606)	
Voteshare of				0.207*
non-Golkar parties				(0.127)
Controls	✓	✓	✓	✓
Fixed effects		✓	✓	✓
Observations	1,898	488	488	488
AIC	1027.151	491.645	494.952	489.115
Log likelihood	−499.575	−234.823	−236.476	−233.558

Notes: Dependent variable is count of ethnic riots. Papua and Aceh observations were excluded from all estimations. $ˆp < 0.10$, $*p < 0.05$, $**p < 0.01$, $***p < 0.001$.

Table B.7. *Robustness: main results using NVMS data*

	(1)	(2)	(3)	(4)
Golkar vote share	1.641*		0.397	
	(0.834)		(0.742)	
Year after election	0.678***	0.595***	0.384^	0.398^
	(0.174)	(0.170)	(0.213)	(0.213)
Electoral competitiveness		0.007		−0.006
		(0.008)		(0.006)
Ratio of second to largest group	✓	✓	✓	✓
Count of riots in prior year	✓	✓	✓	✓
Logged GDP per capita (with oil)	✓	✓	✓	✓
Logged population	✓	✓	✓	✓
Logged area	✓	✓	✓	✓
Urban dummy	✓	✓	✓	✓
Observations	1,246	1,246	1,246	1,246
AIC	938.505	941.548	.	.
Log likelihood	−458.252	−459.774		

Notes: Dependent variable is count of ethnic riots. Papua and Aceh observations were excluded from all estimations. Columns 1–2 are results from negative binomial estimations; columns 3–4 are from OLS regresions. Columns 2 and 4 present results of estimations using only district-years after 1998 (i.e., post-Soeharto observations). $^{\wedge}p < 0.10$, $^*p < 0.05$, $^{**}p < 0.01$, $^{***}p < 0.001$.

Table B.8. *Robustness: party vote share with NVMS data*

	DV: Count of ethnic riots		
	(1)	(2)	(3)
PDIP voteshare	−0.575		
	(0.795)		
Year after election	0.600***	0.601***	0.678***
	(0.181)	(0.167)	(0.174)
Islamic party voteshare (PPP, PKS, PBR, PBB)		1.990	
		(1.519)	
Voteshare of non-Golkar parties			−1.641*
			(0.834)
Ratio of second to largest group	✓	✓	✓
Count of riots in prior year	✓	✓	✓
Logged GDP per capita (with oil)	✓	✓	✓
Logged population	✓	✓	✓
Logged area	✓	✓	✓
Urban dummy	✓	✓	✓
Post-Soeharto dummy	✓	✓	✓
Java dummy	✓		
Observations	1,246	1,246	1,246
AIC	925.362	940.504	938.505
Log likelihood	−450.681	−459.252	−458.252

Notes: Dependent variable is count of ethnic riots. Papua and Aceh observations were excluded from all estimations. $\hat{}p < 0.10$, $*p < 0.05$, $**p < 0.01$, $***p < 0.001$.

Table B.9. *Robustness: alternative modeling choices with NVMS*

	DV: Count of ethnic riots			
	(1)	(2)	(3)	(4)
Main				
Electoral competitiveness	−0.006		−0.010***	
	(0.006)		(0.003)	
Year after election	0.398^	0.384^	0.433***	0.455***
	(0.213)	(0.213)	(0.072)	(0.073)
Golkar voteshare		0.397		2.000***
		(0.742)		(0.274)
Ratio of second to largest group	✓	✓	✓	✓
Count of riots in prior year	✓	✓	✓	✓
Logged GDP per capita (with oil)	✓	✓	✓	✓
Logged population	✓	✓	✓	✓
Logged area	✓	✓	✓	✓
Urban dummy	✓	✓	✓	✓
Post-Soeharto dummy	✓	✓	✓	✓
Observations	1,246	1,246	1,246	1,246
AIC	6800.687	6801.481	2576.083	2541.968
Log likelihood	−3391.343	−3391.741	−1279.041	−1261.984

Notes: Dependent variable is count of ethnic riots. All estimations are using the full sample of district-years from 1990 through 2005. Papua and Aceh observations were excluded from all estimations. Columns 1–2 are results from OLS estimations with "reg"; columns 3–4 are results based on Poisson models with "poisson" in Stata. ^$p < 0.10$, *$p < 0.05$, **$p < 0.01$, *** $p < 0.001$.

Table B.10. *Robustness: alternative Golkar dominance and fractionalization measures (full sample)*

	(1)	(2)	(3)	(4)	(5)	(6)	(7)	(8)
Golkar_share_all	1.596*	2.539**	2.367**	1.427`	1.264	2.043**	1.654*	1.642*
	(0.804)	(0.831)	(0.792)	(0.838)	(0.820)	(0.753)	(0.801)	(0.802)
L.count of ethnic riots	0.014	0.023	0.017	0.016	0.012	0.016		
	(0.011)	(0.022)	(0.012)	(0.011)	(0.012)	(0.011)		
Religious fractionalization	-0.272	-0.265	-0.494	-0.436	-0.836	-0.178	-0.061	-0.187
	(0.966)	(1.087)	(1.029)	(1.018)	(1.078)	(0.966)	(0.933)	(0.940)
Logged PAD revenues	-0.236`						-0.264*	-0.249`
	(0.129)						(0.128)	(0.127)
Logged area	1.021***	0.985***	1.000***	1.027***	1.245***	0.985***	1.024***	1.006***
	(0.121)	(0.127)	(0.122)	(0.122)	(0.158)	(0.112)	(0.123)	(0.120)
Logged population	0.194	0.010	0.614*	-0.033	-0.031	0.126	0.220	0.196
	(0.221)	(0.220)	(0.259)	(0.261)	(0.253)	(0.202)	(0.220)	(0.221)
Poverty rate (% of population)		0.033*						
		(0.016)						
Logged DAU transfer per capita			0.757**					
			(0.279)					
Logged staff expenditure per capita				-0.171				
				(0.271)				
Logged natural resource revenues per capita					-0.155**			
					(0.049)			
L.injuries ethnic riots							-0.007	
							(0.007)	
L.death ethnic riots								0.003`
								(0.002)
Observations	2,164	1,978	2,175	2,032	2,058	2,246	2,164	2,164
AIC	510.648	460.232	523.281	489.349	485.434	540.613	511.167	509.948
Log likelihood	-248.324	-223.116	-254.640	-237.675	-235.717	-264.307	-248.583	-247.974

Notes: Dependent variable is a binary variable for whether or not a split occurred within a district-year. Aceh and Papua observations were excluded from the model. Coefficients are based on logit models with standard errors corrected for panel datasets. `p < 0.10, *p < 0.05, **p < 0.01, ***p < 0.001.

265

Table B.11. *Robustness: alternative Golkar dominance and fractionalization measures (1999–2005 sample)*

	(1)	(2)	(3)	(4)	(5)	(6)
Golkar_share_all	1.530^	2.484*	1.384	1.449	1.004	1.746*
	(0.916)	(0.990)	(1.011)	(0.915)	(1.016)	(0.874)
L.count of ethnic riots	0.017	0.026	0.011	0.016	0.014	0.018
	(0.012)	(0.022)	(0.013)	(0.012)	(0.012)	(0.012)
Religious fractionalization	−1.474	−1.639	−2.666^	−1.488	−1.472	−1.467
	(1.251)	(1.422)	(1.499)	(1.248)	(1.319)	(1.252)
Logged PAD revenues	0.074					
	(0.186)					
Logged area	1.170***	1.210***	1.085***	1.170***	1.279***	1.162***
	(0.151)	(0.186)	(0.182)	(0.152)	(0.191)	(0.153)
Logged population	−0.151	−0.324	2.271***	−0.009	−0.210	−0.072
	(0.277)	(0.267)	(0.577)	(0.481)	(0.329)	(0.257)
Poverty rate (% of population)		0.016				
		(0.022)				
Logged DAU transfer per capita			3.798***			
			(0.817)			
Logged staff expenditure per capita				0.237		
				(0.767)		
Logged natural resource revenues per capita					−0.083	
					(0.065)	
Observations	1,209	1,003	1,208	1,205	1,168	1,270
AIC	339.582	270.414	308.352	338.423	319.809	349.602
Log likelihood	−162.791	−128.207	−147.176	−162.211	−152.904	−168.801

Notes: Dependent variable is a binary variable for whether or not a split occurred within a district-year. Aceh and Papua observations were excluded from the model. Observations included in these estimations are from units in 1999 through 2005. Coefficients are based on logit models with standard errors corrected for panel datasets. ^$p < 0.10$, *$p < 0.05$, **$p < 0.01$, ***$p < 0.001$.

Table B.12. *Robustness: alternative Golkar dominance and fractionalization measures (post-2005 sample)*

	(1)	(2)	(3)	(4)	(5)
Golkar_share_all	-0.182	1.545	1.602	-2.106	3.938*
	(1.793)	(1.703)	(1.795)	(1.743)	(1.607)
L.count of ethnic riots	-0.113	-0.257	-0.175	-0.077	-0.458°
	(0.123)	(0.255)	(0.168)	(0.092)	(0.275)
Logged PAD revenues	-0.502				
	(0.330)				
Religious fractionalization	2.391°	2.393	1.581	2.242	3.437**
	(1.362)	(1.491)	(1.534)	(1.583)	(1.137)
Logged area	0.753***	0.731***	0.642***	0.683***	
	(0.169)	(0.161)	(0.154)	(0.150)	
Logged population	0.749	0.600	1.578***	0.618	0.400
	(0.455)	(0.373)	(0.436)	(0.437)	(0.265)
Poverty rate (% of population)		0.060*			
		(0.026)			
Logged DAU transfer per capita			1.834**		
			(0.675)		
Logged staff expenditure per capita				0.277	
				(0.357)	
Logged natural resource revenues per capita					-0.084
					(0.085)
Observations	955	975	967	827	1566
AIC	173.051	190.493	189.756	152.174	223.658
Log likelihood	-79.525	-88.246	-87.878	-69.087	-105.829

Notes: Dependent variable is a binary variable for whether or not a split occurred within a district-year. Aceh and Papua observations were excluded from the model. Observations included in these estimations are from units in 2006 through 2012. Coefficients are based on logit models with standard errors corrected for panel datasets. $°p < 0.10$, $*p < 0.05$, $**p < 0.01$, $***p < 0.001$.

267

Table B.13. *Turnover and change in levels of violence*

	Full sample			No-split districts in conflict areas			Parent districts in conflict areas			Child districts in conflict areas		
	(1)	(2)	(3)	(4)	(5)	(6)	(7)	(8)	(9)	(10)	(11)	(12)
0/1 turnover to opposition in 1999 election?	-0.264**			-0.717**			-1.130*			-0.619^		
	(0.086)			(0.267)			(0.635)			(0.315)		
L.count of idenviol	-0.584***	-0.584***	-0.584***	-0.604***	-0.606***	-0.608***	-0.582***	-0.605***	-0.590***	-0.267	-0.269	-0.256
	(0.063)	(0.063)	(0.063)	(0.075)	(0.076)	(0.076)	(0.107)	(0.117)	(0.114)	(0.212)	(0.209)	(0.222)
Religious fractionalization	0.693***	0.567**	0.560**	0.429	0.179	0.473	2.334	3.531^	2.630^	-0.642	-0.469	-0.900
	(0.198)	(0.184)	(0.183)	(0.690)	(0.692)	(0.728)	(1.432)	(2.054)	(1.494)	(0.491)	(0.430)	(0.673)
0/1 turnover to opposition in 2004 election?		0.181			-0.243			1.866			0.640*	
		(0.120)			(0.228)			(1.266)			(0.306)	
Change in vote margins from the 1999 to 2004 election			0.002			0.008			0.016			-0.005
			(0.002)			(0.007)			(0.019)			(0.010)
Logged GDP per capita (with oil)	✓	✓	✓	✓	✓	✓	✓	✓	✓	✓	✓	✓
Logged population	✓	✓	✓	✓	✓	✓	✓	✓	✓	✓	✓	✓
Logged area	✓	✓	✓	✓	✓	✓	✓	✓	✓	✓	✓	✓
Poverty rate	✓	✓	✓	✓	✓	✓	✓	✓	✓	✓	✓	✓
Observations	2,057	2,057	2,057	289	289	289	187	187	187	94	94	94
AIC	6446.775	6458.579	6462.560	1246.903	1252.322	1251.594	914.364	914.434	919.389	275.083	273.758	278.329
Log likelihood	-3215.387	-3221.289	-3223.280	-615.451	-618.161	-617.797	-449.182	-449.217	-451.695	-129.541	-128.879	-131.165

Note: The dependent variable in these models is the change in the count of ethnocommunal violence in a district from one year to the next. Conflict districts refer to units that had ethnocommunal violence from 1997 through 2012. Coefficients are based on OLS regressions with robust standard errors. ^$p < 0.10$, *$p < 0.05$, **$p < 0.01$, ***$p < 0.001$.

Table B.14. *Turnover and count of ethnic riots*

	Full sample			Conflict districts			Parent districts in conflict areas			Child districts in conflict areas		
	(1)	(2)	(3)	(4)	(5)	(6)	(7)	(8)	(9)	(10)	(11)	(12)
0/1 turnover to opposition in 1999 election?	-1.207***			-0.819***			-0.603^			0.214		
	(0.259)			(0.198)			(0.360)			(0.738)		
L.count of ethnic riots	0.456***	0.526***	0.526***	0.128**	0.139**	0.133**	0.089**	0.070**	0.095**	0.528**	0.511**	0.528***
	(0.086)	(0.088)	(0.088)	(0.037)	(0.044)	(0.042)	(0.029)	(0.027)	(0.032)	(0.164)	(0.161)	(0.157)
Religious fractionalization	5.501***	4.370***	4.371***	2.217***	1.540**	1.556**	3.922***	4.353***	3.935***	-0.963	-0.714	-2.518*
	(0.677)	(0.608)	(0.606)	(0.563)	(0.587)	(0.537)	(1.145)	(1.081)	(1.110)	(1.061)	(0.990)	(1.137)
0/1 turnover to opposition in 2004 election?		-0.027			0.134			1.300*			0.231	
		(0.277)			(0.281)			(0.607)			(0.537)	
Change in vote margins from the 1999 to 2004 election			-0.001			0.001			0.001			-0.037^
			(0.010)			(0.006)			(0.012)			(0.020)
Logged GDP per capita (with oil)		✓	✓		✓	✓		✓	✓		✓	✓
Logged population		✓	✓		✓	✓		✓	✓		✓	✓
Logged area		✓	✓		✓	✓		✓	✓		✓	✓
Poverty rate		✓	✓		✓	✓		✓	✓		✓	✓
Observations	2,057	2,057	2,057	476	476	476	187	187	187	94	94	94
AIC	1453.208	1476.242	1476.242	1142.103	1157.727	1156.263	396.441	394.731	399.356	139.968	139.927	137.918
Log likelihood	-717.604	-729.121	-729.121	-562.052	-569.863	-569.131	-189.220	-188.365	-190.678	-60.984	-60.963	-59.959

Notes: The dependent variable in these models is the count of ethnocommunal violence in a district-year. Conflict districts refer to units that had ethnocommunal violence from 1997 through 2012. Coefficients are based on negative binomial regressions with robust standard errors.
^$p < 0.10$, *$p < 0.05$, **$p < 0.01$, ***$p < 0.001$.

Glossary

ABRI	Angkatan Bersenjata Republik Indonesia
BKR	Badan Keamanan Rakyat
CSIS	Centre for Strategic and International Studies
DOM	Daerah Operasi Militer
DPD	Dewan Perwakilan Daerah
DPR	Dewan Perwakilan Rakyat
DPRD	Dewan Perwakilan Rakyat Daerah
ECK	Electoral Commission of Kenya
GAM	Gerakan Aceh Merdeka
Gerindra	Partai Gerakan Indonesia Raya
GKST	Gereja Kristen Sulawesi Tengah
Golkar	Golongan Karya
GPM	Gereja Protestan Maluku
HMI	Himpunan Muslim Indonesia
ICMI	Ikatan Cendekiawan Muslim se-Indonesia
IPKI	Partai Ikatan Pendukung Kemerdekaan Indonesia
KANU	Kenya African National Union
MPR	Majelis Permusyawaratan Rakyat
MUI	Majelis Ulama Indonesia
NaRC	National Rainbow Coalition
NU	Nahdlatul Ulama
NVMS	National Violence Monitoring System
ODM	Orange Democratic Movement
OPM	Operasi Papua Merdeka
OSVIA	Opleiding School Voor Inlandsche Ambtenaren
PAN	Partai Amanat Nasional
Parkindo	Partai Kristen Indonesia
PDI	Partai Demokrasi Indonesia
PDIP	Partai Demokrasi Indonesia-Perjuangan
PERTI	Pergerakan Tarbiyah Islamiyah
PETA	Pembela Tanah Air
PKB	Partai Kebangkitan Bangsa

PKI	Partai Komunis Indonesia
PKS	Partai Kesejahteraan Sosial
PNI	Partai Nasional Indonesia
PNU	Party of National Unity
PODES	Potensi Desa
PPP	Partai Persatuan Pembangunan
PRRI	Revolutionary Government of the Republic of Indonesia
PSII	Partai Sarekat Islam Indonesia
PUSA	Persatuan Ulama Seluruh Aceh
PUTERA	Pusat Tenaga Rakyat
RMS	Republik Maluku Selatan
SARA	Suku Agama Ras Antar-golongan
SBKRI	Surat Bukti Kewarganegaraan Republik Indonesia
TMII	Taman Mini Indonesia Indah
TNI	Tentara Nasional Indonesia
UNSFIR	United Nations Support for Indonesian Recovery
USDP	Union Solidarity and Development Party
VOC	Vereenigde Oost-Indische Compagnie

References

Abdullah, Taufik (2010). "Nationalist Activities during the Japanese Period." In: *The Encyclopedia of Indonesia in the Pacific War*, ed. by Peter Post, William H. Frederick, Iris Heidebrink, and Shigeru Sato. Leiden and Boston: Brill, pp. 113–127.

Abulai, Abdul-Gafaru and Gordon Crawford (Feb. 2010). "Consolidating Democracy in Ghana: Progress and Prospects?" *Democratization* 17 (1): 26–67.

Acemoglu, Daron and James Robinson (2006). *Economic Origins of Dictatorship and Democracy*. New York: Cambridge University Press.

Acemoglu, Daron, James Robinson, and Thierry Verdier (2004). "Kleptocracy and Divide-and-Rule: A Model of Personal Rule." *Journal of the European Economic Association* 2 (2/3): 162–192.

Adhuri, Dedi S. (2013). *Selling the Sea, Fishing for Power: A Study of Conflict over Marine Tenure in Kei Islands, Eastern Indonesia*. Asia-Pacific Environment Monograph 8. Canberra: Australian National University Press.

Aditjondro, George (2001). "Guns, Pamphlets, and Handie-Talkies: How the Military Exploited Local Ethno-Religious Tensions in Maluku to Preserve Their Political and Economic Privileges." In: *Violence in Indonesia* ed. by Ingrid Wessel and Georgia Wimhofer. Hamburg: Abera-Verl, pp. 10–128.

— (2004). "Kerusuhan Poso dan Morowali: Akar Permasalahan dan Jalan Keluarnya." Paper presented at Propatria, Jakarta, January 7. Jakarta, Indonesia.

Aditya, Arys. and Karlis. Salna (2019). *Indonesia Says There Was No Fraud in Presidential Vote*. Bloomberg. URL: www.bloomberg.com/news/articles/20190424/indonesia-says-no-fraud-in-presidential-vote-as-count-disputed.

Adnanes, Marian. (2004). "Exit and/or Voice? Youth and Post-Communist Citizenship in Bulgaria." *Political Psychology* 25 (5): 795–815.

Adri, N. (Mar. 2018). *Military and Police Chiefs Vow to Maintain Neutrality during Elections*. The Jakarta Post. URL: www.thejakartapost.com/news/218/3/28/military-and-police-chiefs-vow-to-maintain-neutrality-during-elections.html.

Afriyadi, Achmad Dwi (Apr. 2017). *Bolehkan PNS Jadi Anggota Parpol?* Liputan6. URL: www.liputan6.com/bisnis/read/293566/bolehkah-pns-jadi-anggota-parpol.

Akaev, Askar (1993). *Chelovek Bez Serediny*. Асаба, Bishkek: Asaba.

Al Qurtuby, Sumanto (2016). *Religious Violence and Conciliation in Indonesia: Christians and Muslims in the Moluccas*. New York: Routledge Press.

Albertus, Michael and Victor Menaldo (2013). "Gaming Democracy: Elite Dominance during Transition to Democracy." *British Journal of Political Science* 44 (3): 575–603.

Allers, Maarten and J. Bieuwe Geertsma (2016). "The Effects of Local Government Amalgamation on Public Spending, Taxation, and Service Levels: Evidence from 15 Years of Municipal Consolidation." *Journal of Regional Science* 56 (4): 659–682.

Amal, Ichlasul (1992). *Regional and Central Government in Indonesian Politics: West Sumatra and South Sulawesi 1949–1979*. Yogyakarta: Gadjah Mada University Press.

Amelia, Mei (Nov. 2016). *Kronologi Demo 4 November: Dari Damai hingga Berakhir Ricuh*. DetikNews. URL: https://news.detik.com/berita/d-3339694/kronologi-demo-4-november-dari-damai-hingga-berakhir-ricuh

Amelin, V. V. (1993). *Mezhnatsional'nye Konflikty v Respublikakh Srednei Azii Na Rybezhe 8–90 Godov*. Moscow: Izdatel'skii Tsentr "ROSS."

Amindoni, Ayomi (Oct. 2019). *Kabinet Jokowi: "Koalisi gemuk" setelah Prabowo Subianto merapat ke pemerintah, sinyal negatif demokrasi Indonesia?* BBC. URL: www.bbc.com/indonesia/indonesia-512592.

Amnesty International (1993). *Indonesia Shock Therapy: Restoring Order in Aceh, 1989–1993*. Technical Report London: Amnesty International.

Ananta, Aris, Evi Nurvidya Arifin, Sairi Hasbullah, N. B. Handayani, and A. Pramono (2015). *Demography of Indonesia's Ethnicity*. Singapore: Institute of Southeast Asian Studies.

Ananta, Aris, Evi Nurvidya Arifin, and Leo Suryadinata (2005). *Emerging Democracy in Indonesia*. Singapore: Institute of Southeast Asian Studies.

Andaya, Barbara Watson and Leonard Y. Andaya (2015). *A History of Early Modern Southeast Asia, 140–1830*. New York: Cambridge University Press.

Anderson, Benedict (1982). *Imagined Communities: Reflections on the Origin and Spread of Nationalism*. London: Verso.

Ansell, Ben and David Samuels (2014). *Inequality and Democratization: An Elite-Competition Approach*. Cambridge Studies in Comparative Politics. New York: Cambridge University Press.

Antara News (2008). *Mantan Aktivis Mahasiswa: Tidak Ada Rekayasa Dalam Pendudukan Gedung DPR/MPR 1998*. Antara News. URL: www.antaranews.com/berita/100488/mantan-aktivis-mahasiswa-tidak-ada-rekayasa-dalam-pendudukan-gedung-dpr-mpr-1998.

(2015). *Tujuh Gelombang Pilkada Serentak 2015 hingga 2027*. ANTARA. URL: www.antaranews.com/berita/48618/tujuh-gelombang-pilkada-serentak-215-hingga-227.

Antara News (2007). *Kota Banggai Sulteng Semakin Mencekam*. Bahasa Indonesia. Antara News. URL: www.antaranews.com/berita/54483/kota-banggai-sulteng-semakin-mencekam.

Antlov, Hans (1994). "Village Leaders and the New Order." In: *Leadership on Java: Gentle Hints, Authoritarian Rule*, ed. by Hans Antlov and Sven Cederroth. London and New York: Nordic Institute of Asian Studies, pp. 73–96.

(2003). "Civic Engagement in Local Government Renewal in Indonesia." Quezon City: Institute for Popular Democracy.

Aragon, Lorraine (2000). *Fields of the Lord; Animism, Christian Minorities, and State Development in Indonesia*. Honolulu: University of Hawaii Press.

(2001). "Communal Violence in Poso, Central Sulawesi: Where People Eat Fish and Fish Eat People." *Indonesia* 72: 45–79.

(2007). "Elite Competition in Central Sulawesi." In: *Renegotiating Boundaries: Local Politics in Post-Suharto Indonesia*, ed. by Henk Schulte and Gerry van Klinken. Leiden: KITLV Press, pp. 39–66.

(2013). "Development Strategies, Religious Relations, and Communal Violence in Central Sulawesi, Indonesia: A Cautionary Tale." In: *Development Strategies, Identities, and Conflict in Asia. Politics, Economics and Inclusive Development*, ed. by William Ascher and Natalia Mirovitskaya. New York: Palgrave and Macmillan, pp. 153–182.

Arifin, Evi N., M. Sairi Hasbullah, and Agus Pramono (2017). "Chinese Indonesians: How Many, Who and Where?" *Asian Ethnicity* 18 (3): 31–329.

Aristotle (1944). *Aristotle's Politics*. Ed. and translated by H. Rackham. Cambridge, MA: Harvard University Press.

Aritonang, Jan and Karel Steenbrink (2008). *A History of Christianity in Indonesia*. Ed. by Jan Aritonang and Karel Steenbrink. Leiden and Boston: Brill.

Arivia, Gadis (2007). "Politik Representasi Suara Ibu Peduli." In: Paper presented at Peringatan 9 Tahun Reformasi. Jakarta, Indonesia, pp. 1–6.

Arriola, Leonardo and Martha Johnson (2014). "Ethnic Politics and Women's Empowerment in Africa: Ministerial Appointments to Executive Cabinets." *American Journal of Political Science* 58 (2): 495–510.

Asal, Victor, Michael Findley, James Piazza, and James Igoe Walsh (2016). "Political Exclusion, Oil, and Ethnic Armed Conflict." *Journal of Conflict Resolution* 60 (8): 1343–1367.

Asher, Sam and Paul Novosad (2017). "Politics and Local Economic Growth: Evidence from India." *American Economic Journal: Applied Economics* 9 (1): 229–273.

Aspinall, Edward (1997). "What Price Victory? The 1997 Elections." *Inside Indonesia* 51. URL: www.insideindonesia.org/what-price-victory-the-1997-elections.

(2005). *Opposing Suharto: Compromise, Resistance, and Regime Change in Indonesia*. Stanford, CA: Stanford University Press.

(2006). "Violence and Identity Formation in Aceh under Indonesian Rule." In: *Verandah of Violence: The Background to the Aceh Problem*, ed. by Anthony Reid. Singapore: National University of Singapore Press, pp. 149–176.

(2014). "Parliament and Patronage." *Journal of Democracy* 25 (4): 96–110.

Babatunde, Abosede Omowumi. (2015). "Youth Uprising and the Quest for Political Reform in Africa." *African Security Review* 24 (2): 107–121.

Baldwin, Kate (2016). *The Paradox of Traditional Chiefs in Democratic Africa*. New York: Cambridge University Press.

Banggai, BPS Kabupaten (2015). *Jumlah Penduduk dan Laju Pertumbuhan Penduduk Menurut Kecamatan di Kabupaten Banggai 2010, 2014, dan 2015*. BPS Kabupaten Banggai. URL: https://banggaikab.bps.go.id/statictable/217/

2/2/134/jumlah-penduduk-dan-laju-pertumbuhan-penduduk-menurut-kecamatan-di-kabupaten-banggai-21-2014-dan-2015.html.

Barber, Richard, ed. (2000). *Aceh: The Untold Story*. Bangkok: Asian Forum for Human Rights and Development.

Bardhan, Pranab (2002). "Decentralization of Governance and Development." *Journal of Economic Perspectives* 16 (4):185–205.

Barron, Patrick. 2008. "Managing the Resources for Peace: Reconstruction and Peacebuilding in Aceh." In: *Reconfiguring Politics: The Indonesia-Aceh Peace Process*, ed. Aguswandi and Judith Large. London: Conciliation Resources, pp. 58–61.

Barron, Patrick, Anders Engvall, and Adrian Morel (2016). *Understanding Violence in Southeast Asia: The Contribution of Violent Incidents Monitoring Systems*. Technical Report. The Asia Foundation. URL: https://asiafoundation.org/wp-content/uploads/2016/10/UnderstandingViolenceinSEAsia.pdf.

Barron, Patrick, Sana Jaffrey, and Ashutosh Varshney (2016). "When Large Conflicts Subside: The Ebbs and Flows of Violence in Post-Suharto Indonesia." *Journal of East Asian Studies* 16 (2):191–217.

Bartels, Dieter (1978). *Guarding the Invisible Mountain: Invisible Alliances, Religious Syncretism, and Ethnic Identity among AmbAmbon Christians and Moslems in the Moluccas*. Ithaca, NY: Cornell University Press.

Barth, Frederik (1969). *Ethnic Groups and Boundaries*. Prospect Heights, IL: Waveland Press.

Bartolini, Stefano (2000). *The Political Mobilization of the European Left, 1860–1980: The Class Cleavage*. New York: Cambridge University Press.

Bates, Robert (1973). *Ethnicity in Contemporary Africa*. Program in East African Studies. Syracuse, NY.

(1983). "Modernization, Ethnic Competition, and the Rationality of Politics in Contemporary Africa." In: *State versus Ethnic Claims: African Policy Dilemmas*, ed. by Donald Rothchild and Victor Olorunsola. Westview Special Studies on Africa. Boulder, CO: Westview Press, pp. 152–171.

Bates, Robert and Da-Hsiang Lien (1985). "A Note on Taxation, Development, and Representative Government." *Politics and Society* 14 (1): 53–70.

Bazzi, Samuel and Matthew Gudgeon (2021). "The Political Boundaries of Ethnic Divisions." *American Economic Journal: Applied Economics* 13 (1): 235–266.

BBC (Oct. 2010). *Serbia Quietly Marks 10 Years since Milosevic Was Ousted*. URL: www.bbc.com/news/world-europe-11478533.

(2015). *Tujuh hal yang perlu Anda ketahui tentang Pilkada 2015*. BBC. URL: www.bbc.com/indonesia/berita_indonesia/215/12/15128_indonesia_pilkada_explainer.

Becker, Gary. (1968). "Crime and Punishment: An Economic Approach." *Journal of Political Economy* 76 (2): 169–217. DOI: http://dx.doi.org/10.1086/259394.

Beetham, David (June 1994). "Conditions for Democratic Consolidation." *Review of African Political Economy* 21 (60): 157–172.

Beissinger, Mark (2002). *Nationalist Mobilization and the Collapse of the Soviet State*. New York: Cambridge University Press.

Beittinger-Lee, Verena (2010). *(Un)Civil Society and Political Change in Indonesia: A Contested Arena*. New York: Routledge.

Bekoe, Dorina and Stephanie Burchard (2017). "The Contradictions of Pre-election Violence: The Effects of Violence on Voter Turnout in Sub-Saharan Africa." *African Studies Review* 60 (2): 73–92.

Bertrand, Jacques (2002). "Legacies of the Authoritarian Past: Religious Violence in Indonesia's Moluccan Islands." *Pacific Affairs* 75 (1): 57–85.

(2004). *Nationalism and Ethnic Conflict in Indonesia*. New York: Cambridge University Press.

Besley, Timothy and Torsten Persson (2009). "Repression or Civil War?" *American Economic Review: Papers and Proceedings* 99 (2): 292–297.

Biberaj, Elez (1999). *Albania in Transition: The Rocky Road to Democracy*. Boulder, CO: Westview Press.

Billing, Trey (2019). "Government Fragmentation, Administrative Capacity, and Public Goods: The Negative Consequences of Reform in Burkina Faso." *Political Research Quarterly.* 72 (3): 669–685.

Birnir, Johanna K. (2007). *Ethnicity and Electoral Politics*. New York: Cambridge University Press.

Blesse, Sebastian and Thushyanthan Baskaran (2016). "Do Municipal Mergers Result in Scale Economies? Evidence from a German Federal State." *Regional Science and Urban Economics* 59 (59): 54–74.

Blom-Hansen, Jens, Kurt Houlberg, Søren Serritzlew, and Daniel Treisman (2016). "Jurisdiction Size and Local Government Policy Expenditure: Assessing the Effect of Municipal Amalgamation." *American Political Science Review* 110 (4): 812–831.

Blussé, Leonard (1986). *Strange Company: Chinese Settlers, Mestizo Women and the Dutch in VOC Batavia*. Dordrecht and Riverton: Foris Publications.

Blussé, Leonard (2003). "One Hundred Weddings and Many More Funerals a Year: Chinese Civil Society in Batavia at the end of the Eighteenth Century." In: *The Archives of the Kong Koan of Batavia*, ed. by Leonard Blussé and Menghong Chen. Leiden: Brill, pp. 8–28.

Boileau, Julian (1983). *Golkar: Functional Group Politics in Indonesia*. Jakarta: Yayasan Proklamasi, Centre for Strategic and International Studies Jakarta.

Boix, Carles (2003). *Democracy and Redistribution*. Cambridge Studies in Comparative Politics. New York: Cambridge University Press.

Boland, B. (1982). *The Struggle of Islam in Modern Indonesia*. The Hague: Nijhoff.

Bond, Andrew and Natalie Koch (2010). "Interethnic Tensions in Kyrgyzstan: A Political Geographic Perspective." *Eurasian Geography and Economics* 51 (4): 531–562.

Boone, Catherine (2003). "Decentralization as a Political Strategy in West Africa." *Comparative Political Studies* 36 (4): 355–380.

Booth, Anne (2011). "Splitting, Splitting, and Splitting Again: A Brief History of the Development of Regional Government in Indonesia since Independence." *Bijdragen tot de Taal-, Land- en Volenkunde* 167 (1): 31–59.

(2016). *Economic Change in Modern Indonesia: Colonial and Post-Colonial Comparisons*. New York: Cambridge University Press.

Boyle, Michael (2014). *Violence after War: Explaining Instability in Post-Conflict States*. Baltimore: Johns.

BPS (2000). *Sensus Penduduk Propinsi Maluku*. Jakarta: Badan Pusat Statistik.

(2003). *Kota Ambon Dalam Angka 2003*. Jakarta: Badan Pusat Statistik.

(2012). *Kota Ambon Dalam Angka 2012*. Ambon: Badan Pusat Statistik.

(2016a). *Maluku Tenggara Dalam Angka 2016*. Maluku Tenggara: Badan Pusat Statistik.

(2016b). *Provinsi Maluku Dalam Angka 2016*. Jakarta: Badan Pusat Statistik.

Brass, Paul (1997). *Theft of an Idol: Text and Context in the Representation of Collecti Violence*. Princeton, NJ: Princeton University Press.

Bratakusumah, Deddy Supriadi and Dadang Solihin (2001). *Otonomi Penyelenggaraan Pemerintahan Daerah*. Jakarta: Gramedia Pustaka Utama.

Bresnan, John (1993). *Managing Indonesia: The Modern Political Economy*. New York: Columbia University Press.

Brownlee, Jason (2009). "Portents of Pluralism: How Hybrid Regimes Affect Democratic Transitions." *American Journal of Political Science* 53 (3): 515–532.

Brownlee, Jason, Tarek Masoud, and Andrew Reynolds (Oct. 2013). "Tracking the 'Arab Spring': Why the Modest Harvest?" *Journal of Democracy* 24 (4): 29–44.

(2015). *The Arab Spring: Pathways of Repression and Reform*. New York: Oxford University Press.

Budi S. P., Johan, Iwan Setiawan, and Dailis Muhamad (June 2000). "Tragedi Poso, Duka Kita Bersama." *Tempo*.

Budianta, Melani (2006). "Decentralizing Engagement: Women and the Democratization Process in Indonesia." *Signs* 31 (4): 915–923.

Buehler, Michael (2014). "Elite Competition and Changing State-Society Relations: Shari'a Policymaking in Indonesia." In: *Beyond Oligarchy: Wealth, Power, and Contemporary Indonesian Politics*, ed. by Michele Ford and Thomas Pepinsky. Cornell Modern Indonesia Project No. 77. Ithaca, NY: Southeast Asia Program, pp. 157–175.

(2016). *The Politics of Shari'a Law: Islamist Activists and the State in Democratizing Indonesia*. New York: Cambridge University Press.

Cao, Xun, Haiyan Duan, Chuyu Liu, James Piazza, and Yingjie Wei (May 2018). "Digging the 'Ethnic Violence in China' Database: The Effects of Inter-Ethnic Inequality and Natural Resources Exploitation in Xinjiang." *China Review* 18 (2): 121–154.

Carey, Sabine (Mar. 2006). "The Dynamic Relationship between Protest and Repression." *Political Research Quarterly* 59 (1): 1–11.

Carnes, Nicholas (2016). "Why Are There So Few Working-Class People in Political Office? Evidence from State Legislatures." *Politics, Groups, and Identities* 4 (1): 84–109.

Caruthers, Thomas (2002). "The End of the Transition Paradigm." *Journal of Democracy* 13 (1): 5–21.

CAVR (2006). *Chega! Final Report for the Commission for Reception, Truth, and Reconciliation in East Timor (CAVR)*. Dili, Timor Leste: The Commission for Reception, Truth, and Reconciliation Timor Leste (CAVR).

Cederman, Lars-Erik, Kristian Skrede Gleditsch, and Julian Wucherpfennig (2017). "Predicting the Decline of Ethnic Civil War: Was Gurr Right and for the Right Reasons?" *Journal of Peace Research* 54 (2): 262–274.

Cederman, Lars-Erik, Simon Hug, and Lutz Krebs (2010). "Democratization and Civil War: Empirical Evidence." *Journal of Peace Research* 47 (4): 377–394.

Cederman, Lars-Erik, Andreas Wimmer, and Brian Min (2010). "Why Do Ethnic Groups Rebel? New Data and Analysis." *World Politics* 62 (1): 87–119.

Chandra, Elizabeth (Oct. 2012a). "'We the (Chinese) People': Revisiting the 1945 Constitutional Debate on Citizenship." *Indonesia* 94: 85–110.

Chandra, Kanchan (2004). *Why Ethnic Parties Succeed: Patronage and Ethnic Head Counts in India.* Cambridge: Cambridge University Press.

(2006). "What Is Ethnic Identity and Does It Matter?" *Annual Review of Political Science* 9 (1): 397–424.

(2012b). "What Is Ethnic Identity? A Minimalist Definition." In: *Constructivist Theories of Ethnic Politics,* ed. by Kanchan Chandra. New York: Oxford University Press, pp. 51–96.

Chapman, Thomas and Philip Roeder (2007). "Partition as a Solution to Wars of Nationalism: The Importance of Nationalism." *American Political Science Review* 101 (4): 677–691.

Chatty, Dawn, Nisrine Mansour, and Nasser Yassin (2013). "Bedouin in Lebanon: Social Discrimination, Political Exclusion, and Compromised Health Care." *Social Science and Medicine* 82: 43–50.

Chauvel, Richard (1990). *Nationalist, Soldiers, and Separatists.* Leiden: KITLV Press.

Cheeseman, Nic (July 2008). "The Kenyan Elections of 2007: An Introduction." *Journal of Eastern African Studies* 2 (2): 166–184.

Cheeseman, Nic and Blessing-Miles Tendi (June 2010). "Power-Sharing in Comparative Perspective: The Dynamics of 'Unity Government' in Kenya and Zimbabwe." *Journal of Modern African Studies* 48 (2): 203–229.

Chernov-Hwang, Julie and Kamal Sadiq (2010). "Legislating Separation and Solidarity in Plural Societies: The Chinese in Indonesia and Malaysia." *Nationalism and Ethnic Politics* 16 (2): 192–215.

Chua, Amy (2003). *World on Fire: How Exporting Free Market Democracy Breeds Ethnic Hatred and Global Instability.* New York: Doubleday.

Claver, Alexander (2011). "Crisis Management and Creative Adjustment: Margo-Redjo in the 1930s." In: *Chinese Indonesians and Regime Change,* ed. by Marlene Dieleman, Juliette Koning, and Peter Post. Brill. pp. 139–167.

CNN (1998). *Indonesian Opposition Leader Tries to Call Off Protest: Fear of Bloodshed at Rallies Planned for Wednesday.* CNN International. URL: http://edition.cnn.com/WORLD/asiapcf/9805/19/indonesia.pm/index.html.

(Jan. 2019). *Ahok sang pemicu rentetan aksi bela Islam dan nama besar 212.* CNN. URL: www.cnnindonesia.com/nasional/20190115135955-32-360979/ahok-sang-pemicu-rentetan-aksi-bela-islam-dan-nama-besar-212.

CNN Indonesia (2019a). *BPN Prabowo Tak Merasa Tanggung Jawab atas Kerusuhan Bawaslu.* CNN Indonesia. URL: www.cnnindonesia.com/nasional/2019 0522132302-32-397379/bpn-prabowo-tak-merasa-tanggung-jawab-atas-kerusuhan-bawaslu?

(June 2019b). *Misteri Tim Mawar, Kerusuhan 22 Mei dan Prabowo*. URL: www.cnnindonesia.com/nasional/20190611180827204025O5/misteri-tim-mawar-kerusuhan-22-mei-dan-prabowo.

Coedes, George (1968). *The Indianized States of Southeast Asia*. Ed. by Walter F. Vella. Translated by Sue Brown Cowing. Honolulu: University of Hawaii Press.

Colenbrander, H.T. (1920). *Jan Pietersz. Coen: Bescheiden omtrent zijn Bedriff in Indie*. Vol. I–IV. Martinus Nijhoff.

Collier, Paul, Anke Hoeffler, and M. Soderbom (2008). "Post-Conflict Risks." *Journal of Peace Research* 45 (4): 461–478.

Collier, Paul and Pedro C. Vicente (2014). "Votes and Violence: Evidence from a Field Experiment in Nigeria." *The Economic Journal* 124 (574): F327–F355. ISSN: 1468–0297. DOI: http://dx.doi.org/10.1111/ecoj.12109.

Colombo, Andrea, Olivia D'Aoust, and Olivier Sterck (2015). "From Rebellion to Electoral Violence: Evidence from Burundi." Working Paper.

Commercio, Michael (2018). "Structural Violence and Horizontal Inequalities: Conflict in Southern Kyrgyzstan." *Politics, Groups, and Identities* 6 (4): 764–784.

Condra, Luke, James Long, Andrew Shaver, and Austin Wright (2018). "The Logic of Insurgent Electoral Violence." *American Economic Review* 108 (11): 3199–3231.

Coppel, Charles (1983). *Indonesian Chinese in Crisis*. Kuala Lumpur: Oxford University Press.

Cribb, Robert (2001a). "Genocide in Indonesia, 1965 (M." *Journal of Genocide Research* 3 (2): 219–239.

— (2001b) "How Many Deaths? Problems in the Statistics of Massacre in Indonesia (1965–1966) and East Timor (1975–1980)." In: *Violence in Indonesia*, ed. by Ingrid Wessel and Georgia Wimhofer. Hamburg: Abera-Verl, pp. 82–98.

— (2010). "Institutions." In: *The Encyclopedia of Indonesia in the Pacific War*, ed. by Peter Post, William H. Frederick, Iris Heidebrink, and Shigeru Sato. Vol. 19. Handbook of Oriental Studies. Section 3 Southeast Asia. Leiden and Boston: Brill, pp. 102–113.

Cribb, Robert and Charles Coppel (2009). "A Genocide that Never Was: Explaining the Myth of Anti-Chinese Massacre in Indonesia, 1965–66." *Journal of Genocide Research* 11 (4): 447–465.

Crouch, Harold (1978). *The Army and Politics in Indonesia*. Ithaca, NY: Cornell University Press.

— (1979). "Patrimonialism and Military Rule in Indonesia." *World Politics* 31 (4): 571–587.

Damanik, Rynaldi (2003). *Tragedi Kemanusiaan Poso: Menggapai Surya Pagi Melalui Kegelapan Malam [Humanitarian Tragedy in Poso: Reaching for the Light of Dawn after the Darkness of Night]*. Jakarta: Yakoma PGI.

Davidson, Jamie (2008). *From Rebellion to Riots: Collective Violence on Indonesian Borneo*. Madison: University of Wisconsin Press.

— (2009). "Dilemmas of Democratic Consolidation in Indonesia." *The Pacific Review* 22 (3): 293–310.

Departemen Penerangan Indonesia (1945). *Political manifesto of the Government of the Republic of Indonesia*. Jakarta, November 1, 1945. Ministry of Information of the Republic of Indonesia. Jakarta: Ministry of Information of the Republic of Indonesia.

Diamond, Larry (2008). "The Democratic Rollback: The Resurgence of the Predatory State." *Foreign Affairs* 87 (2): 36–48.

Doera, Mgr. R. Isak (2003). *Memori pelaksanaan tugas sebagai pastor militer*. Ed. by Fabian Thomas. Jakarta: Yasol Mentari.

Dowding, Keith and Peter John (2012). *Exits, Voices and Social Investment: Citizens' Reaction to Public Services*. New York: Cambridge University Press.

DPP Golkar (1988a). *Anak Lampiran LXXVIII s/d CV dari Lampiran Pertanggung-Pertang DPP Golkar Masa Bhakti 1983–1988*. Jakarta: DPP Golkar.

— (1988b). *Lampiran Pertanggungjawaban DPP-Golkar Masa Bakti 1983–1988*. DPP Golkar.

Duncan, Christopher (2013). *Violence and Vengeance: Religious Conflict and Its Aftermath in Eastern Indonesia*. Ithaca, NY: Cornell University Press.

Dunning, Thad (2011). "Fighting and Voting: Violent Conflict and Electoral Politics." *Journal of Conflict Resolution* 55 (3): 327–339.

Ecip, S. Sinansari (1999). *Menyulut Ambon: Kronologi Merambatnya berbagai Kerusuhan Lintas Wilayah di Indonesia*. Kronik Indonesia Baru. Bandung: Mizan Pustaka.

Eifert, Benn, Edward Miguel, and Daniel N. Posner (2010). "Political Competition and Ethnic Identification in Africa." *American Journal of Political Science* 54 (2): 494–510. ISSN: 1540-5907. DOI: http://dx.doi.org/1.1111/j.154-597.210.00443.x.

EISA (July 2010a). *Kenya: 2002 Presidential Election Results*. Electoral Institute for Sustainable Democracy in Africa. URL: www.eisa.org.za/wep/ken2002results.htm.

— (July 2010b). *Kenya: Election Archive*. Electoral Institute for Sustainable Democracy in Africa. URL: www.eisa.org.za/wep/kenelectarchive.htm.

Elfversson, Emma and Anders Sjögren (2020). "Do Local Power-Sharing Deals Reduce Ethnopolitical Hostility? The Effects of 'Negotiated Democracy' in a Devolved Kenya." *Ethnopolitics* 19 (1): 45–63.

Ellis-Petersen, Hannah (2018). *From Peace Icon to Pariah: Aung San Suu Kyi's Fall from Grace*. The Guardian. URL: www.theguardian.com/world/2018/nov/23/aung-san-suu-kyi-fall-from-grace-myanmar.

Elson, Robert (2001). *Suharto: A Political Biography*. New York: Cambridge University Press.

— (2008). *The Idea of Indonesia*. New York: Cambridge University Press.

Emmerson, Donald (2000). "Will Indonesia Survive?" *Foreign Affairs* 79 (3): 95–106.

Endi, Severianus (2017). *Tjhai Chui Mie, Singkawang's First Female Mayor*. The Jakarta Post. URL: www.thejakartapost.com/news/2017/02/18/tjhai-chui-mie-singkawangs-first-female-mayor.html

Englebert, Pierre and N. Sangare (2010). *Comparative Assessment of Decentralization in Africa: Burkina Faso Desk Study*. Technical Report Washington, DC: United States Agency for International Development.

Epstein, David, Robert Bates, Jack Goldstone, Ida Kristensen, and Sharyn O'Halloran (2006). "Democratic Transitions." *American Journal of Political Science* 50 (3): 551–569.

Fadillah, Ramadhian (2014). "Kisah Soeharto dielu-elukan Muslim sedunia saat naik haji." *Merdeka.* URL: www.merdeka.com/peristiwa/kisah-soeharto-dielu-elukan-muslim-sedunia-saat-naik-haji.html.

Fasseur, C. (2007). "Colonial Dilemma: Van Vollenhoven and the Struggle between Adat Law and Western Law in Indonesia." In: *The Revival of Tradition in Indonesian Politics: The Deployment of Adat from Colonialism to Indigenism*, ed. by Jamie Davidson and David Henley. Contemporary Southeast Asia Series. New York: Routledge Press, pp. 5–67.

Fealy, Greg (Dec. 2016). *Bigger than Ahok: Explaining the 2 December Mass Rally.* Indonesia at Melbourne. URL: https://indonesiaatmelbourne.unimelb.edu .au/bigger-than-ahok-explaining-jakartas-2-december-mass-rally/.

Fearon, James (1995). "Rationalist Explanations for War." *International Organization* 49 (3): 379–414.

(2004). "Why Do Some Civil Wars Last So Much Longer than Others?" *Journal of Peace Research* 41 (3): 275–301.

Fearon, James and David Laitin (1996). "Explaining Interethnic Cooperation." *American Political Science Review* 90 (4): 715–735.

Federspiel, H. M. (2001). *Islam and Ideology in the Emerging Indonesian State: The Persatuan Islam (Persis), 1923 to 1957.* Leiden: Brill.

Feith, Herbert (1962). *The Decline of Constitutional Democracy in Indonesia.* Ithaca: Cornell University Press.

Fitrani, Fitria, Bert Hoffman, and Kai Kaiser (2005). "Unity in diversity? The creation of new local governments in a decentralising Indonesia." *Bulletin of Indonesian Economic Studies* 41 (1): 57–79. DOI: http://dx.doi.org/1.18/ 0074915007269Q.

Fjelde, Hanne and Gudrun Ostby (2014). "Socioeconomic Inequality and Communal Conflict: A Disaggregated Analysis of Sub-Saharan Africa, 199– 2008." *International Interactions* 40 (5): 737–762.

Fogg, Kevin (2019). *Indonesia's Islamic Revolution.* New York: Cambridge University Press. DOI: https://doi-org.libproxy1.nus.edu.sg/1.1017/ 9781108768214.

Formichi, Chiara (2010). "Pan-Islam and Religious Nationalism: The Case of Kartosuwiryo and Negara Islam Indonesia." *Indonesia* 90:125–146.

Fortna, Virgina Page (2008). *Does Peacekeeping Work? Shaping Belligerents' Choices after Civil War.* Princeton, NJ: Princeton University Press.

Fox, James J. (2011). "Re-Considering Eastern Indonesia." *Asian Journal of Social Sciences* 39 (2): 131–149.

Frederick, William (1978). "Indonesian Society in Transition: Surabaya, 1926– 1946." PhD thesis. University of Hawaii.

Freedom House (1999). *Freedom in the World: East Timor 1999.* Technical Report Freedom House, URL: www.refworld.org/docid/5278c8b914.html.

Furnivall, J. S. (2010). *Netherlands India: A Study of Plural Economy.* Cambridge Library Collection – East and South-East Asian History. Cambridge, UK· Cambridge University Press.

(1948). *Colonial Policy and Practice: A Comparative Study of Burma and the Netherlands India*. New York: Cambridge University Press.

Gagnon, Victor (1994/1995). "Ethnic Nationalism and International Conflict: The Case of Serbia." *International Security* 19 (3):130–166.

Galdini, Franco (July 2014). *Kyrgyzstan Violence: Four Years On*. Al Jazeera. URL: www.aljazeera.com/indepth/opinion/2014/06/kyrgyzstan-violence-2010-201463016460195835.html.

Garthoff, Raymond (2000). *The Great Transition: American-Soviet Relations and the End of the Cold War*. Washington, DC: Brookings Institution Press.

Gasiorowski, Mark and Timothy Power (1998). "The Structural Determinants of Democratic Consolidation: Evidence from the Third World." *Comparative Political Studies* 31 (6): 740–771.

Geertz, Clifford (1973). *The Interpretation of Cultures*. New York: Basic Books.

(1976). *The Religion of Java*. Chicago: Univeristy of Chicago Press.

Geser, Hans (1999). "The Local Party as an Object of Interdisciplinary Comparative Study: Some Steps toward Theoretical Integration." In: *Local Parties in Political and Organizational Perspective*, ed. by Martin Saiz and Hans Geser. Boulder, CO: Westview Press, pp. 3–43.

Glaeser, Edward (2005). "The Political Economy of Hatred." *Quarterly Journal of Economics* 120 (1): 45–86.

Goksoy, Ismail (2002). "The Policy of the Dutch Government towards Islam in Indonesia." *The American Journal of Islamic Social Sciences* 19 (1): 73–94.

Gorbiano, Marchio (Oct. 2019). *Jokowi Announces His New Cabinet. Here's the Line Up*. The Jakarta Post. URL: www.thejakartapost.com/news/2019/10/23/breaking-jokowis-new-cabinet-announced-here-is-the-lineup.html.

Green, Elliott (2010). "Patronage, District Creation, and Reform in Uganda." *Studies in Comparative International Development* 45 (1): 83–103.

Groffman, Bernard (1985). "Excerpts from the First Declaration of Bernard Grofman in Badham v. Eu." *PS: Political Science & Politics* 18 (Summer): 544–550.

Grossman, Guy and Janet Lewis (Feb. 2014). "Administrative Unit Proliferation." *American Political Science Review* 108 (1): 196–217.

Grossman, Guy, Jan Pierskalla, and Emma B. Dean (2017). "Government Fragmentation and Public Goods Provision." *Journal of Politics* 79 (3): 823–840.

Grzymala-Busse, Anna (2002). *Redeeming the Communist Past: The Regeneration of Communist Parties in East Central Europe*. New York: Cambridge University Press.

Guillemin, Marylis and Lynn Gillam (2004). "Ethics, Reflexivity, and 'Ethically Important Moments' in Research." *Qualitative Inquiry* 10 (2): 261–280.

Gupta, Dipak, Harinder Singh, and Tom Sprague (1993). "Government Coercion of Dissidents: Deterrence or Provocation." *Journal of Conflict Resolution* 37 (2): 301–339.

Gurr, Ted (1993). *Minorities at Risk: A Global View of Ethnopolitical Conflict*. Washington, DC: United States Institute of Peace.

(2000). *People versus States: Ethnopolitical Conflict and Accommodation at the End of the Twentieth Century*. Washington, DC: United States Institute of Peace Press.

Guterres, António (June 2018). *Religious Conflicts Normally Product of Political or Geostrategic Manipulation, Proxies for Other Antagonisms, Secretary-General Tells Security Council*. www.un.org/press/en/20198/sgsm19104.doc.htm Remarks to the Security Council.

Habyarimana, James, Macartan Humphreys, Daniel Posner, and Jeremy Weinstein (2007). "Why Does Ethnic Diversity Undermine Public Goods Provision." *American Political Science Review* 101 (4): 709–725.

Hack, Karl and Tobias Rettig (2006). "Demography and Domination in Southeast Asia." In: *Colonial Armies in Southeast Asia*, ed. by Karl Hack and Tobias Rettig. London and New York: Routledge. pp. 36–67.

Hadiz, Vedi (2010). *Localising Power in Post-Authoritarian Indonesia: A Southeast Asia Perspective*. Stanford, CA: Stanford University Press.

Hadler, Jeffrey (2009). *Muslims and Matriarchs: Cultural Resilience in Minangkabau through Jihad and Colonialism*. Singapore: National University of Singapore Press.

Haggard, Stephan and Robert Kaufman (1995). *The Political Economy of Democratic Transitions*. Princeton, NJ: Princeton University Press.

— (1999). "The Political Economy of Democratic Transitions." In: *Transitions to Democracy*, ed. by Lisa Anderson. New York: Columbia University Press, pp. 72–96.

— (2012). "Inequality and Regime Change: Democratic Transitions and the Stability of Democratic Rule." *American Political Science Review* 106 (3): 495–516.

Haggard, Stephan, Robert Kaufman, and Terence Teo (2016). "Distributive Conflict and Regime Change: A Qualitative Dataset." *Harvard Dataverse*, doi: 10.7910/DVN/O0GRQK.

Hahadi (2004). *DPRD Poso, 1952–1999: Studi Sejarah Parlemen Lokal*. Indonesia: Pustaka Timur.

Hamka (1973). "Hamka: The Shocking Draft Bill on Marriage." In: *Indonesian Politics and Society: A Reader*, ed. by David Bourchier and Vedi Hadiz. Asia Research Center, Murdoch University, Western Australia. London and New York: Routledge, pp. 85–88.

Hardin, Russell (1995). *One for All: The Logic of Group Conflict*. Princeton, NJ: Princeton University Press.

Haring, Melinda and Michael Cecire (Mar. 2013). *Why the Color Revolutions Failed. Foreign Policy* URL: https://foreignpolicy.com/2013/03/18/why-the-color-revolutions-failed/

Harjanto, Nicolaus (2010). "Political Party Survival: The Golongan Karya Party and Electoral Politics in Indonesia 1999–2009." PhD thesis. Northern Illinois University.

Harvey, Barbara (1974). "Tradition, Islam, and Rebellion: South Sulawesi 1950–1965." PhD thesis. Ithaca, NY: Cornell University.

Hassan, Mai (2016). "A State of Change: District Creation in Kenya after the Beginning of Multiparty Elections." *Political Research Quarterly* 69 (3): 510–521.

Hassan, Mai and Ryan Sheely (2016). "Executive–Legislative Relations, Party Defections, and Lower Level Administrative Unit Proliferation: Evidence From Kenya." *Comparative Political Studies* 50 (12): 1595–1631.

Hasurullah (2009). *Dendam Konflik Poso (Periode 1998–2001): Konflik Poso dari Perspektif Komunikasi Politik.* Jakarta: Gramedia Pustaka Utama.

Hechter, Michael (2000). *Containing Nationalism.* New York: Oxford University Press.

Henley, David (1996). *Nationalism and Regionalism in a Colonial Context: Minahasa in the Dutch East Indies.* Leiden: KITLV Press.

Hering, B. B. and G. A. Willis (1973). *The Indonesia General Election of 1971.* Centre D'Etude Du Sud-Est Asiatique et de L'Extreme Orient.

Hernawan, Budi (2016). "Torture as Theatre in Papua." *International Journal of Conflict and Violence* 10 (1): 78–92.

Heryanto, Ariel (1999). "Rape, Race and Reporting." In: *Reformasi: Crisis and Change in Indonesia,* ed. by Arief Budiman, B. Hatley, and Damien Kingsbury. Australia: Monash Asia Institute, pp. 299–334.

Heuken SJ, Adolf (2008). "Catholic Converts in the Moluccas, Minahasa and Sangihe-Talaud, 1512–1680." In: *A History of Christianity in Indonesia,* ed. by Jan Aritonang and Karel Steenbrink. Leiden: Brill, pp. 23–72.

Hierman, Brent (2015). "Central Asian Ethnicity Compared: Evaluating the Contemporary Social Salience of Uzbek Identity in Kyrgyzstan and Tajikistan." *Europe-Asia Studies* 67 (4): 519–539.

Hill, Hal (2000). *The Indonesian Economy.* New York: Cambridge University Press.

Hillman, Ben (2012). "Ethnic Politics and Local Political Parties in Indonesia." *Asian Ethnicity* 13 (4): 419–440.

(2017). "Increasing Women's Parliament Representation in Asia and the Pacific: The Indonesian Experience." *Asia and the Pacific Policy Studies* 4 (1): 38–49.

Hinnerich, B.T. (2009). "Do Merging Local Governments Free Ride on Their Counterparts When Facing Boundary Reform?" *Journal of Public Economics* 93 (5–6): 721–728.

Hirschman, Albert (1970). *Exit, Voice, and Loyalty: Responses to Decline in Firms, Organizations, and States.* Cambridge, MA: Harvard University Press.

(1978). "Exit, Voice, and the State." *World Politics* 31 (1): 9–107.

Hobsbawm, Eric (1996). "Are All Tongues Equal?" In: *Living as Equals,* ed. by Paul Barker. New York: Oxford University Press, pp. 85–98.

Hoffman, Bert, Kadjatmiko, Kai Kaiser, and Sjahrir (May 2006). "Evaluating Fiscal Equalization in Indonesia." World Bank Policy Research Working Paper 3911.

Hooe, Todd Ryan. (2012). "'Little Kingdoms': Adat and Inequality in the Kei Islands, Eastern Indonesia." PhD thesis. University of Pittsburgh.

Hoon, Chang Yau (2006). "Assimilation, Multiculturalism, Hybridity: The Dilemmas of the Ethnic Chinese in Post-Suharto Indonesia." *Asian Ethnicity* 7 (2): 149–166.

Horowitz, Donald (1985). *Ethnic Groups in Conflict.* Los Angeles: University of California Press.

(2001). *The Deadly Ethnic Riots.* Berkeley: University of California Press.

(2013). *Constitutional Change and Democracy in Indonesia.* New York: Cambridge University Press.

HRW (2007). *Protest and Punishment: Political Prisoners in Papua.* Vol. 19 4c. Washington, DC: Human Rights Watch.

Htun, Mala (2016). *Inclusion without Representation in Latin America: Gender Quotas and Ethnic Reservations.* New York: Cambridge University Press.

Human Rights Watch (1999). *The Violence in Ambon.* Technical Report 1. New York: Human Rights Watch.

— (2002). *Four Years of Communal Violence in Central Sulawesi.* Technical Report Washington, DC: Human Rights Watch.

— (Mar. 2008). *Ballots to Bullets: Organized Political Violence and Kenya's Crisis of Governance.* Technical Report Vol. 20 No. 1(A). Washington, DC: Human Rights Watch. URL: www.hrw.org/sites/default/files/reports/kenya38web.pdf.

— (Aug. 2010). *"Where Is the Justice?" Interethnic Violence in Southern Kyrgyzstan and Its Aftermath.* Technical Report. Washington, DC: Human Rights Watch.

— (Aug. 2017). *Kenya: Post-Election Killings, Abuse.* Technical Report. Washington, DC: Human Rights Watch. URL: www.hrw.org/news/2017/08/27/kenya-post-election-killings-abuse.

— (2019). *Indonesia: Set Independent Inquiry into Jakarta Riots: 8 Protesters Fatally Shot.* Washington, DC: Human Rights Watch. URL: www.hrw.org/news/2019/05/31/indonesia-set-independent-inquiry-jakarta-riots.

Huntington, Samuel (1991). *The Third Wave: Democratization in the Late Twentieth Century.* Norman: University of Oklahoma Press.

Huskey, Eugene (1995). "The Rise of Contested Politics in Central Asia: Elections in Kyrgyzstan, 1989–90." *Europe-Asia Studies* 47 (5): 813–833.

ICG (2000). *Indonesia: Overcoming Murder and Chaos in Maluku.* ICG Asia Report 10. Jakarta and Brussels: International Crisis Group.

— (2002). *Indonesia: The Search for Peace in Maluku.* ICG Asia Report 31. Jakarta and Brussels: International Crisis Group.

— (2007). *Indonesia: Decentralisation and Local Power Struggles in Maluku.* Asia Briefing 64. Jakarta and Brussels: International Crisis Group.

— (2017). *Buddhism and State Power in Myanmar.* Asia Report no. 290. International Crisis Group.

ICMI (2018). *Sejarah ICMI.* URL: https://icmi.or.id/profil/sejarah.

IDN Times (2017). *Henk Ngantung, Pria Kristen dan Keturunan Tionghoa Pertama yang Jadi Gubernur Jakarta.* IDN Times. URL: www.idntimes.com/news/indonesia/rosa-folia/henk-ngantung-pria-non-muslim-pertama-yang-jadi-gubernur-jakarta/full.

IFES (Apr. 2014). "Elections in Indonesia: 2014 National Legislative Elections." *International Foundation for Electoral Systems*, 1–12. URL: www.ifes.org/sites/default/files/indonesia_214_national_legislative_election_faq.pdf.

IMF (1998). *Indonesia Memorandum of Economic and Financial Policies.* Technical Report International Monetary Fund.

The Jakarta Post (Mar. 2018). *EDITORIAL. What 'Pilkada' Can Offer.* The Jakarta Post. URL: www.thejakartapost.com/academia/2018/03/05/editorial-what-pilkada-can-offer.html.

Jenkins, David (1984). *Suharto and His Generals: Indonesian Military Politics 1975–1983.* Cornell Modern Indonesia Project Monograph Series. Ithaca, NY: Cornell University Press.

Jung, Dietrich (2010). "'Islam as a Problem': Dutch Religious Politics in the East Indies." *Review of Religious Research* 51 (3): 288–301.

Jusuf, Ester Indahyani, Hotma Timbul, Olisias Gultom, and Sondang Frishka (2007). *Kerusuhan Mei 1998 Fakta, Data, dan Analisa: Mengungkap Kerusuhan Mei 1998 sebagai Kejahatan terhadap Kemanusiaan*. Ed. by Raymond Simanjorang. Jakarta: Solidaritas Nusa Bangsa (SNB) and Assosiasi Penasehat Hukum dan Hak Asasi Manusia (APHI).

Kahin, Audrey (1999). *Rebellion to Integration: West Sumatra and the Indonesian Polity*. Amsterdam: Amsterdam University Press.

Kahin, George McTurnan (1970). *Nationalism and Revolution in Indonesia*. Ithaca, NY: Cornell University Press.

Kapoor, Kanupriya, and Tommy. Ardiansyah (2019). *Protesters, Police Crash, in Second Night of Post-election Protests in Indonesia*. Reuters. URL: www.reuters.com/article/us-indonesia-election-casualties/protesters-police-clash-in-second-night-of-post-election-protests-in-indonesia-idUSKCN1SSAS.

Kapstein, Ethan and Nathan Converse (2008). *The Fate of Young Demcoracies*. New York: Cambridge University Press.

Kaptein, Nico (2014). *Islam, Colonialism, and the Modern Age in the Netherlands East Indies: A Biography of Sayyid Uthman (1822–1914)*. Leiden: Brill.

Karatnycky, Adrian and Peter Ackerman (2005). *How Freedom Is Won: From Civic Resistance to Durable Democracy*. Technical Report Freedom House.

Kartasasmita, Ginandjar and Joseph Stern (2016). *Reinventing Indonesia*. Singapore: World Scientific.

Kasfir, Nelson (1979). "Explaining Ethnic Political Participation." *World Politics* 31: 365–388.

Kastor, Rustam (2000). *Badai Pembalasan Laskar Mujahidin: Ambno-Maluku (cetakan 2)*. Jakarta: Wihdah Press.

Kaufman, Chaim (1996). "Possible and Impossible Solution to Ethnic Civil Wars." *International Security* 20 (4): 136–175.

Keefer, Philip (2007). "Clientelism, Credibility, and the Policy Choices of Young Democracies." *American Journal of Political Science* 51 (4): 804–821.

Khamidov, Alisher (May 2010). *Provisional Government Grappling with Simmering Ethnic Tension in Kyrgyzstan*. EurasiaNet. URL: www.refworld.org/docid/4c15f7d926.html.

Kiernan, Ben (2007). *Genocide and Resistance in Southeast Asia: Documentation, Denial, and Justice in Cambodia and East Timor*. New Brunswick: Transaction Publishers.

Kimura, Ehito (2013). *Political Change and Territoriality in Indonesia: Provincial Proliferation*. Contemporary Southeast Asia Series. New York: Routledge Press.

King, Dwight (1982). "Indonesia's New Order Regime as a Bureaucratic Polity, a Neopatrimonial Regime, or a Bureaucratic-Authoritarian Regime: What Differences Does It Make?" In: *Interpreting Indonesian Politics: Thirteen Contributions to the Debate*, ed. by Benedict Anderson and Audrey Kahin. Coernll Modern Indonesian Project, Southeast Asia Program. Ithaca, NY: Cornell University (Interim Report Series), pp. 104–116.

(2003). *Half-Hearted Reform: Electoral Institutions and the Struggle for Democracy in Indonesia*. Westport, CT: Praeger.

(2010). *The White Book on the 1992 General Election in Indonesia*. Jakarta: Equinox Publishing.

King, Gary (1998). *Unifying Political Methodology: The Likelihood Theory of Statistica Inference.* Ann Arbor The University of Michigan Press.

King, Gary and Langche Zeng (2001). "Logistic Regression in Rare Events Data." *Political Analysis* 9 (2): 137–163.

Kompas (1998). *Masyarakat Berkabung.* Harian KOMPAS. URL: www.seasite.niu .edu/indonesian/reformasi/Chronicle/Kompas/May14/masy01.htm.

(2008). *Situasi Banggai Masih Mencekam.* Bahasa Indonesia. Kompas. URL: https://nasional.kompas.com/read/2008/06/19/22202744/Situasi .Banggai.Masih.Mencekam.

(2009). *Gong Perdamaian Dunia Siap Dikirab ke Ambon.* URL: https://nasional .kompas.com/read/2009/11/24/03323479/gong.perdamaian.dunia.siap .dikirab.ke.ambon.

(Aug. 2014). *MK Tolak Seluruh Gugatan Prabowo-Hatta.* KOMPAS. URL: https://nasional.kompas.com/read/2014/08/21/20472051/MK.Tolak. Seluruh.Gugatan.Prabowo-Hatta.

(Sept. 2016). *Gara-Gara Ahok, Pilkada DKI Berasa Pilpres.* KOMPAS. URL: https:// megapolitan.kompas.com/read/2016/09/24/14010271/gara-gara.ahok .pilkada.dki.berasa.pilpres.?page=all.

Kompas (July 2015). *Kemendagri Perketat Pemekaran Daerah Baru.* Kompas. https://nasional.kompas.com/read/2015/07/11/16491141/Kemendagri. Perketat.Pemekaran.Daerah.Baru?page=all

Kompasiana (Sept. 2012). *Peluang Prabowo Subianto.* URL: www.kompasiana .com/djohans/5517b5a1813311a3689de467/peluang-prabowo-subianto.

KONTRAS (2004). *Laporan Penelitian Bisnis Militer di Poso, Sulawesi Tengah.* Technical Report Poso, Sulawesi Tengah: Komisi untuk Orang Hilang dan Korban Tindak Kekerasan (KONTRAS).

Kraxberger, Brennan (2004). "The Geography of Regime Survival: Abacha's Nigeria." *African Affairs* 103 (412): 413–430.

Kuhn, Philip (2009). *Chinese among Others: Emigration in Modern Times.* Lanham, MD: Rowman and Littlefield.

Kwok, Yenni (July 2014). *With the Election of Joko Widodo, Indonesia Writes a New Chapter.* TIME. URL: https://time.com/3020999/indonesia-joko-widodo-jokowi-declared-president/

Kymlicka, Will (1995). *Multicultural Citizenship: A Liberal Theory of Minority Rights.* Oxford: Clarendon Press.

La Ode, M. D. (2012). *Etnis Cina Indonesia dalam Politik : Politik Etnis Cina Pontianak dan Singkawang di Era Reformasi, 1998–2008.* Jakarta: Yayasan Pustaka Obor Indonesia.

Laitin, David (1986). *Hegemony and Culture: Politics and Religious Change among the Yoruba.* Chicago: University of Chicago Press.

Lake, David and Donald Rothchild (2005). "Territorial Decentralization and Civil War Settlements." In: *Sustainable Peace: Power and Democracy after Civil Wars,* ed. by Philip Roeder and Donald Rothchild. Ithaca, NY: Cornell University Press.

Laksono, Paschalis Maria (2002). *The Common Ground in the Kei Islands: Eggs from One Fish and One Bird.* Yogyakarta: Galang Press.

Lamb, Kate (Dec. 2016). *Trial of Jakarta Governor Ahok Begins as Hundreds of Islamic Hardliners Protest*. The Guardian. URL: www.theguardian.com/world/2016/dec/13/trial-of-jakarta-governor-ahok-begins-as-hundreds-of-islamic-hardliners-protest.

Lasahido, Tahmidy, Christian Tindjabate, Meyni Walalangi, M. Tasrief Siara, Darwis Waru, and Iwan Lapasere (2003). *Suara dari Poso: Kerusuhan, Konflik, dan Resolusi*. Jakarta: YAPPIKA.

Lee, Jung Ok (2018). *Korea: From Teargas to Candlelight*. Democracy International. URL: www.democracy-international.org/korea-teargas-candlelight

Levitsky, Steven and Lucan Way (2002). "The Rise of Competitive Authoritarianism." *Journal of Democracy* 13 (2): 51–65.

(2015). "The Myth of Democratic Recession." *Journal of Democracy* 26 (1): 45–58.

Lewis, David G. and Saniya Sagnayeva (2020). "Corruption, Patronage and Illiberal Peace: Forging Political Settlement in Post-conflict Kyrgyzstan." *Third World Quarterly* 41 (1): 77–95.

Lichbach, Mark (1987). "Deterrence or Escalation? The Puzzle of Aggregate Studies of Repression and Dissent." *Journal of Conflict Resolution* 31 (2): 266–297.

Liddle, Richard W. (1999). "Regime: The New Order." In: *Indonesia beyond Soeharto: Polity, Economy, Society, and Transition*, ed. by Don Emmerson. Armonk, NY: M.E. Sharpe, pp. 39–70.

Liddle, William R. (1978). "The 1977 Indonesian Election and New Order Legitimacy." *Southeast Asian Affairs* 5: 122–38.

(1996). "The Islamic Turn in Indonesia: A Political Explanation." *Journal of Asian Studies* 55 (3): 613–634.

(Feb. 1973). "Evolution from Above: National Leadership and Local Development in Indonesia." *Journal of Asian Studies* 32 (2): 287–309.

Lidstrom, Anders. (2010). "The Swedish Model under Stress: The Waning of the Egalitarian, Unitary State?" In: *Territorial Choice: The Politics of Boundaries and Borders*, ed., by Harald Baldersheim and Lawrence E. Rose. New York: Palgrave, pp. 61–79.

Lieberman, Victor (2003). *Strange Parallels: Southeast Asia in Global Context, c. 800–1830*. Volume 2: Mainland Mirrors: Europe, Japan, China, South Asia, and the Islands. New York: Cambridge University Press.

Lijphart, Arendt (1977). *Demoracy in Plural Societies: A Comparative Exploration*. New Haven, CT: Yale University Press.

Lima, Ricardo Carvalho de Andrade and Raul da Mota Silveira Neto (2018). "Secession of Municipalities and Economies of Scale: Evidence from Brazil." *Journal of Regional Science* 58 (1): 159–180.

Linz, Juan and Alfred Stepan (1996). *Problems of Democratic Transition and Consolidation: Southern Europe, South America, and Post-Communist Europe*. Baltimore, MD: Johns Hopkins University Press.

Liputan 6 (2007). *Tujuh Otak Kerusuhan Banggai Diburuju*. Liputan 6. URL: www.liputan6.com/news/read/138118/tujuh-otak-kerusuhan-banggai-diburu.

Liputan 6 (2013). *15 Tahun Silam, 4 Mahasiswa Trisakti Tewas Ditembak.* Liputan6.com. URL: www.liputan6.com/news/read/584057/15-tahun-silam-4-mahasiswa-trisakti-tewas-ditembak.

Liu, Morgan (2012). *Under Solomon's Throne: Uzbek Visions of Renewal in Osh. Central Eurasia in Context.* Pittsburgh, PA: University of Pittsburgh Press.

Lohanda, Mona (1996). *The Kapitan Cina of Batavia: 1837–1942.* Jakarta: Penerbit Djambatan.

(2002). *Growing Pains: The Chinese and the Dutch in Colonial Java, 1890–1942.* Jakarta: Yayasan Cipta Loka Caraka.

Lutz, Nancy (Nov. 1991). "Colonization, Decolonization and Integration: Language Policies in East Timor, Indonesia." In: Paper presented at the annual meetings of the American Anthropological Association. Chicago. URL: www.ci.uc.pt/timor/language.htm.

Machado, Fabiana, Carlos Scartascini, and Mariano Tommasi (2011). "Political Institutions and Street Protests in Latin America." *Journal of Conflict Resolution* 55 (3): 34–365.

Machiavelli, Niccolo (1531). *Discourses on Livy.* Ed. and Translated by Harvey Mansfield and Nathan Tarcov. Chicago and London: University of Chicago Press.

Madubun, Jusuf (1997). "Jaringan Elite dan Mekanisme Perwakilan Politik di tingkat Lokal: Kasus DPRD Kabupaten Daerah Tk.II Maluku Tenggara." MA thesis. Yogyakarta: Universitas Gadjah Mada.

Magenda, Burhan (1989). "The Surviving Aristocracy in Indonesia: Politics in Three Provinces of the Outer Islands." PhD thesis. Ithaca, NY: Cornell University, 1036 pp.

Mahid, Syakir, Haliadi Saliadi, and Wilman Darsono (2012). *Sejarah Kerajaan Bungku.* Palu: Universitas Tadulako Palu.

Malesky, Edmund (2009). "Gerrymandering–Vietnamese Style: Escaping the Partial Reform Equilibrium in a Nondemocratic Regime." *Journal of Politics* 71 (1): 132–159.

Mancini, Luca (2008). "Horizontal Inequality and Communal Violence: Evidence from Indonesian Districts." In: *Horizontal Inequalities and Conflict: Understanding Group Violence in Multiethnic Societies,* ed. by Frances Stewart. New York: Palgrave Macmillan, pp. 106–135.

Mansbridge, Jane (1999). "Should Blacks Represent Blacks and Women Represent Women? A Contingent 'Yes'" *Journal of Politics* 61 (3): 628–657.

Marat, Erica (2008). "March and After: What Has Changed? What Has Stayed the Same?" *Central Asian Survey* 27 (3): 229–240.

Marelius, John (2005). "Governor, Democrats, Spar over Redistricting." *San Diego Union Tribune,* February 25, A1.

Mark, Ethan (2018). *Japan's Occupation of Java in the Second World War: A Transnational History.* London: Bloomsbury Publishing.

Martinez-Bravo, Monica, Priya Mukherjee, and Andreas Stegman (2017). "The Non-Democratic Roots of Elite Capture: Evidence from Soeharto Mayors in Indonesia." *Econometrica* 85 (6): 1991–2010.

Masoed, Mochtar (1983). "The Indonesian Economy and Political Structure during the Early New Order, 1966–1971." PhD thesis. Ohio State University.

Masuhara, Ayako (2015). *The End of Personal Rule in Indonesia: Golkar and the Transformation of the Suharto Regime.* Kyoto Area Studies on Asia: Center for Southeast Asian Studies, Kyoto University.

Matveeva, Anna (Feb. 2007). "Zagadka Iuga." *Nezavisimaia Gazeta.*

Maxon, Robert M. (2016). "The Demise and Rise of Majimbo in Independent Kenya" In: *Kenya after 50: Reconfiguring Historical, Political, and Policy Milestones,* ed. by Michael M. Kithinji, Mickie M. Koster, and Jerono P. Rotich. African Histories and Modernities. New York, NY: Palgrave Macmilllan, pp. 19–48.

McCargo, Duncan (1999). "Killing the Messenger: The 1994 Press Bannings and the Demise of Indonesia's New Order." *Press/Politics* 1 (4): 29–45.

McCauley, John F. (2017). *The Logic of Ethnic and Religious Conflict in Africa.* New York: Cambridge University Press.

McDonald, Hamish and Richard Tanter (2006). "Introduction." In: *Masters of Terror: Indonesia's Military Violence in East Timor* ed. by Richard Tanter, Desmond Ball, and Gerry van Klinken. Lanham, MD: Rowman & Littlefield Publishers, pp. 1–12.

McGlinchey, Eric (2011). "Exploring Regime Instability and Ethnic Violence in Kyrgyzstan." *Asia Policy* 12: 79–98.

(2014). "Fast Forwarding the Brezhnev Years: Osh in Flames." *Russian History* 41 (3): 373–391.

McRae, Dave (2013). *A Few Poorly Organized Men: Interreligious Violence in Poso, Indonesia.* Leiden: KITLV Press.

Megoran, Nick (2013). "Shared Space, Divided Space: Narrating Ethnic Histories of Osh." *Environment and Planning* 45 (4): 892–907.

Melvin, Jess (2017). "Mechanics of Mass Murder: A Case for Understanding the Indonesian Killings as Genocide." *Journal of Genocide Research* 19 (4): 487–511.

Mietzner, Marcus (1999). "From Soeharto to Habibie: The Indonesian Armed Forces and Political Islam during the Transition." In: *Post-Soeharto Indonesia: Renewal or Chaos? Indonesia Assessment 1998,* ed. by Geoff Forrester. Barthus, New South Wales: Crawford House, pp. 65–102.

(2010). "Indonesia's Direct Elections: Empowering the Electorate or Entrenching the New Order Oligarchy?" In: *Soeharto's New Order and Its Legacy,* ed. by Edward Aspinall and Greg Feally. Canberra: ANU Press, pp. 173–190.

(2013). *Money, Power, and Ideology: Political Parties in Post-Authoritarian Indonesia.* Singapore: National University of Singapore Press.

(2018). "Authoritarian Elections, State Capacity, and Performance Legitimacy: Phases of Regime Consolidation and Decline in Suharto's Indonesia." *International Political Science Review* 39 (1): 83–96.

Mietzner, Marcus and Burhanuddin Muhtadi (2018). "*The Mobilisation of Intolerance and Its Trajectories: Indonesian Muslims' Views of Religious Minorities and Ethnic Chinese.*" In: *Contentious Belonging: The Place of Minorities in Indonesia,* Indonesia Update Series. Singapore: ISEAS, pp. 155–174.

Migdal, Joel (1988). *Strong Societies and Weak States: State-Society Relations and State Capabilities in the Third World.* Princeton, NJ: Princeton University Press.

Miguel, Edward and Mary K. Gugerty (2005). "Ethnic Diversity, Social Sanctions, and Public Goods in Kenya." *Journal of Public Economics* 89 (11–12): 2325–2368.

Minorities at Risk Project (2004). *Chronology for Uzbeks in Kyrgyzstan, 2004.* Minorities at Risk Project. URL: www.refworld.org/docid/469f38b1c.html.

Mobini-Kesheh, Natalie (1999). *The Hadrami Awakening: Community and Identity in the Netherlands East Indies, 1900–1942*. Ithaca, NY: Cornell Southeast Asia Program Publications.

Montalvo, Jose and Martha Reynal-Querol (2010). "Ethnic Polarization and the Duration of Civil Wars." *Economics of Governance* 11: 123–43.

Monteiro, Nuno P. and Alexandre Debs (2019). "An Economic Theory of War." *Journal of Politics* 82 (1): 255–268.

Moore, Barrington (1966). *Social Origins of Dictatorship and Democracy: Lord and Peasant in the Making of the Modern World*. Boston, MA: Beacon Press.

Moore, Will (1998). "Repression and Dissent: Substitution, Context, and Timing." *American Journal of Political Science* 42 (3): 851–873.

(2000). "The Repression of Dissent: A Substitution Model of Government Coercion." *Journal of Conflict Resolution* 44 (1): 107–127.

Moser, Robert and Ethan Scheiner (2012). *Electoral Systems and Political Context: How the Effects of Rules Vary Across New and Established Democracies*. New York: Cambridge University Press.

Mubyarto, Loekman Soetrisno, Hudiyanto, Edhie Djatmiko, Ita Setiawati, and Agnes Mawarni (1991). *East Timor: The Impact of Integration, an Indonesian Socio-Anthropological Study*. Northcote. Indonesia Resources and Information Program (IRIP).

Mujiburrahman (2006). *Feeling Threatened: Muslim-Christian Relations in Indonesia's New Order*. Leiden: Amsterdam University Press.

Murunga, Godwin and Shadrack Nasong'o (2006). "Bent on Self-Destruction: The Kibaki Regime in Kenya." *Journal of Contemporary African Studies* 24 (1): 1–28.

Mutua, Makau (2008). *Kenya's Quest for Democracy: Taming Leviathan*. London: Lynne Rienner Publishers.

Mylonas, Harris (2012). *The Politics of Nation-Building: Making Co-Nationals, Refugees, and Minorities*. New York: Cambridge University Press.

Nakazawa, K. (2013). "Amalgamation, Free-Rider Behavior, and Regulation." Joint Discussion Paper Series in Economics no. 39, Tokyo University.

Nathalia, Telly (May 2019). *Prabowo and Allies Reported to Police for Causing Post-Election Riots*. Jakarta Globe. URL: https://jakartaglobe.id/news/prabowo-and-allies-reported-to-police-for-causing-postelection-riots/

Nathalia, Telly and Yustinus Paat (Apr. 2019). *Prabowo Feeds Voters Nativist Themes, Promises; Jokowi Keeps Highlighting Own Achievements*. Jakarta Globe. URL: https://jakartaglobe.id/news/prabowo-feeds-voters-nativist-themes-promises-jokowi-keeps-highlighting-own-achievements/

Nathaniel, Felix (May 2019). *TKN: Prabowo Harus Tanggung Jawab Terhadap Kericuhan Aksi 22 Mei*. URL: https://tirto.id/tkn-prabowo-harus-tanggung-jawab-terhadap-kericuhan-aksi-22-mei-dU9z.

Ndegwa, Stephen (1998). "The Incomplete Transition: The Constitutional and Electoral Context in Kenya." *Africa Today* 45 (2): 193–211.

Nellis, John R. (1974). *The Ethnic Composition of Leading Kenyan Government Positions*. Research Report No. 24. The Scandinavian Institute of African Studies.

Nessen, William (2006). "Sentiments Made Visible: The Rise and Reason for Aceh's National Liberation Movement." In: *Verandah of Violence: The Background of the Aceh Problem*, ed. by Anthony Reid. Singapore: National University of Singapore Press, pp. 177–198.

The News Minute (2018). *Telangana to Get Two More Districts, KCR Fulfills Election Promise*. The News Minute. URL: www.thenewsminute.com/article/telangana-get-two-more-districts-kcr-fulfils-election-promise-93493.

Ng, Su Fang (2012). "Dutch Wars, Global Trade, and the Heroic Poem: Dryden's Annus mirabilis (1666) and Amin's Sya'ir perang Mengkasar (1670)." *Modern Philology* 109 (3): 352–384.

Noer, Deliar (1973). *The Modernist Muslim Movement in Indonesia 1900–1942*. Oxford, New York, and Jakarta: Oxford University Press.

Oates, Wallace (1972). *Fiscal Federalism*. Cheltenham, UK: Edward Elgar.

Obama, Barack (July 2015). *Remarks by President Obama to the Kenyan People*. The White House Archives. URL: https://obamawhitehouse.archives.gov/the-press-office/2015/07/26/remarks-president-obama-kenyan-people.

OHCHR (2008). *Report from OHCHR Fact-finding Mission to Kenya, 6–28 February 2008*. Technical Report Geneva, Switzerland: United Nations High Commissioner for Human Rights.

Okamoto, Dina and Rima Wilkes (2008). "The Opportunities and Costs of Voice and Exit: Modelling Ethnic Group Rebellion and Integration." *Journal of Ethnic and Migration Studies* 34 (3): 347–369.

Olzak, Susan (1992). *The Dynamics of Ethnic Competition and Conflict*. Stanford, CA: Stanford University Press.

Olzak, Susan and Suzanne Shanahan (1996). "Deprivation and Race Riots: An Extension of Spillerman's Analysis." *Social Forces* 74 (3): 931–961.

Ordeshook, Peter (1997). "Constitutions for New Democracies: Reflections of Turmoil or Agents of Stability?" *Public Choice* 90: 55–72.

Pamanawa News (2018). *Mabuk Picu Bentrokan di Sirimau, Satu Luka*. URL: https://pamanawanews.com/news/hukrim/mabuk-picu-bentrokan-di-sirimau-satu-luka-87686206/

Paulus Jozlas, D. G. Stibbe, and Simon de Graaff (1917–1939). *Encyclopaedie van Nederlandsch Oost Indie* (6 vols.). 's-Gravenhage: Nijhoff; Leiden: Brill.

PemiluAsia (2018). PemiluAsia. URL: www.pemilu.asia/?lang=ind&c=54&opt=5&s=13.

Pepinsky, Thomas (2009). *Economic Crisis and The Breakdown of Authoritarian Regimes: Indonesia and Malaysia in Comparative Perspective*. New York: Cambridge University Press.

(2016). "Colonial Migration and the Origins of Governance: Theory and Evidence from Java." *Comparative Political Studies* 49 (9): 1201–1237.

Pfaff, Steven and Hyojoung Kim (2003). "Exit-Voice Dynamics of Collective Action: An Analysis of Emigration and Protest in the East German Revolution." *American Journal of Sociology* 109 (2): 401–444.

Pieris, John (2004). *Tragedi Maluku: Sebuah Krisis Peradaban*. Jakarta: Yayasan Obor Indonesia.

Pierskalla, Jan (2016). "Splitting the Difference? The Politics of District Creation in Indonesia." *Comparative Political Studies* 48 (2): 249–268.

Pierskalla, Jan and Audrey Sacks (Feb. 2017). "Unpacking the Effects of Decentralization on Local Conflict: Lessons from Indonesia." *World Development* 90: 213–228.

Pires, Tome (1515). *Suma Oriental of Tome Pires: An Account of the East, from the Red Sea to China, Written in Malacca and India in 1512–1515.* Ed. by Armando Cortesao. Translated from the Portuguese MS in the Bibliotheque de la Chambre des Deputes, Paris. New Delhi: J. Jetley for Asian Educational Services.

Pitkin, Hannah (1967). *The Concept of Representation.* Berkeley: University of California Press.

Posen, Barry (1993). "The Security Dilemma and Ethnic Conflict." *Survival* 35 (1): 27–47.

Posner, Daniel (2004). "Measuring Ethnic Fractionalization in Africa." *American Journal of Political Science* 48 (4): 849–863.

(2005). *Institutions and Ethnic Politics in Africa.* New York: Cambridge University Press.

(2017). "When and Why Do Some Social Cleavages become Politically Salient Rather than Others?" *Ethnic and Racial Studies* 40 (12): 2001–2019.

Post, Peter (2011). "The Oei Tiong Ham Concern and the Change of Regimes in Indonesia, 1931–1950." In: *Chinese Indonesians and Regime Change,* ed. by Marleen Dieleman, Juliette Koning, and Peter Post. Leiden and Boston: Brill, pp. 169–199.

Powell, Robert (1996). "Uncertainty, Shifting Power, and Appeasement." *American Political Science Review* 90 (4): 749–764.

Prempeh, H. Kwasi (2008). "Presidents Untamed." *Journal of Democracy* 19 (2): 109–123.

Przeworski, Adam, Michael Alvarez, Jose Antonio Cheibub, and Fernando Limongi (2000). *Democracy and Development: Political Institutions and Well-Being in the World, 195–1990.* New York: Cambridge University Press.

Purdey, Jemma (2006). *Anti-Chinese Violence in Indonesia, 1996–1999.* Honolulu: University of Hawaii Press.

Putra, Lutfy Mairizal (1998). *Pendudukan Gedung DPR Mei 1998 dalam Ingatan Taufik Basari.* KOMPAS. URL: https://nasional.kompas.com/read/2016/05/21/18110421/pendudukan.gedung.dpr.mei.1998.dalam.ingatan.taufik .basari?page=1.

Putri, Budiarti Utami (May 2019). *Prabowo Buka Suara soal Kerusuhan 22 Mei.* Tempo. URL: https://pilpres.tempo.co/read/1208220/prabowo-buka-suara-soal-kerusuhan-22-mei.

Raben, Remco (1996). "Batavia and Colombo: The Ethnic and Spatial Order of Two Colonial Cities, 1600–1800." PhD thesis. University of Leiden.

Rabushka, Alvin and Kenneth Shepsle (1972). *Politics in Plural Societies: A Theory of Democratic Instability.* Columbus, OH: Charles Merill.

Radelet, Steven and Jeffrey Sachs (1998). "The Onset of the East Asian Financial Crisis." Working Paper 6680.

Ramadhani, Nurul Fitri (May 2019). *Prabowo to Challenge Election Results at Constitutional Court*. The Jakarta Post. URL: www.thejakartapost.com/news/2019/05/21/prabowo-to-challenge-election-results-at-constitutional-court.html.

Rasyid, Ryaas (2003). "Regional Autonomy and Local Politics in Indonesia." In: *Local Power and Politics in Indonesia: Decentralisation and Democratisation*, ed. by Edward Aspinall and Greg Fealy. Singapore: ISEAS, pp. 63–71.

Ravallion, Martin (2016). *The Economics of Poverty: History, Measurement, Policy*. New York: Oxford University Press.

Razakov, Talant (2011). *Oshskie Sobbitiia*. Bishkek.

Rei, Claudia (2014). "Careers and Wages in the Dutch East India Company." *Cliometrica* 8 (1): 27–48.

Reid, Anthony (1988). *Southeast Asia in the Age of Commerce: 1450–1680*. Volume One: The Lands below the Winds. New Haven, CT: Yale University Press.

— (1993). *Southeast Asia in the Early Modern Era: Trade, Power, and Belief*. Ithaca, NY: Cornell University Press.

— (1996). "Flows and Seepages in the Long-term Chinese Interaction with Southeast Asia." In: *Sojourners and Settlers: Histories of Southeast Asia and the Chinese*, ed. by Anthony Reid. Sydney: Allen & Unwin, pp. 15–49.

— (2005). *An Indonesian Frontier: Acehnese and Other Histories of Sumatra*. Singapore: National University of Singapore Press.

— (2010). *Imperial Alchemy: Nationalism and Political Identity in Southeast Asia*. New York: Cambridge University Press.

— (2013). *The Blood of the People: Revolution and the End of Traditional Rule in Northern Sumatra*. Singapore: National University of Singapore Press.

Reilly, Benjamin (2001). *Democracy in Divided Societies: Electoral Engineering for Conflict Management*. New York: Cambridge University Press.

Resnick, Danielle (2017). "Democracy, Decentralization, and District Proliferation: The Case of Ghana." *Political Geography* 59: 47–60.

Ressa, Maria (1998a). *Indonesia Orders Crackdown on Riots oover Prices*. CNN. URL: http://edition.cnn.com/WORLD/9802/12/indonesia/

— (1998b). *Indonesian Assembly Set to Re-Elect Sharto: His Choice of VP is Controversial*. CNN. URL: http://edition.cnn.com/WORLD/9802/27/indonesia/

Ricklefs, Merle (1983). "The Crisis of 1740-1 in Java: The Javanese, Chinese, Madurese and Dutch, and the Fall of the Court of Kartasura." *Bijdragen tot de Taal-, Land- en Volkenkunde* 139 (2/3): 268–290.

— (2008). *A History of Modern Indonesia since c. 1200*. New York: Palgrave Macmillan.

— (2012). *Islamisation and its Opponents in Java: A Political, Social, Cultural, and Religious History, c. 1930 to the Present*. Singapore: National University of Singapore Press.

Robinson, Geoffrey (1995). *The Dark Side of Paradise: Political Violence in Bali*. Ithaca, NY: Cornell University Press.

— (2010). *"If You Leave Us Here, We Will Die": How Genocide Was Stopped in East Timor*. Princeton, NJ: Princeton University Press.

— (2018). *The Killing Season: A History of the Indonesian Massacre, 1965–66*. Human Rights and Crimes against Humanity. Princeton, NJ: Princeton University Press.

Robison, Richard and Vedi Hadiz (2004). *Reorganising Power in Indonesia: The Politics of Oligarchy in an Age of Markets.* New York: Routledge Press.

Robison, Richard and Andrew Rosser (1998). "Contesting Reform: Indonesia's New Order and the IMF." *World Development* 26 (8): 1593–1609.

Roeder, Philip (1991). "Soviet Federalism and Ethnic Mobilization." *World Politics* 43 (2): 196–232.

Rohde, David (2001). "Indonesia Unravelling?" *Foreign Affairs.* URL: https://www.foreignaffairs.com/articles/asia/2001-07-01/indonesia-unraveling.

Roosa, John (2006). *Pretext for Mass Murder: The September 30th Movement and Suharto's Coup d'Etat in Indonesia.* Madison: University of Wisconsin Press.

(2016). "The State of Knowledge about an Open Secret: Indonesia's Mass Disappearances of 1965–66." *Journal of Asian Studies* 75 (2): 281–297.

Rosengard, Jay (2004). "Will Bank Bailouts Bust Budgets? Fiscalisation of the East Asian Financial Crisis." Harvard University John F. Kennedy School of Government Faculty Research Working Papers Series.

Rosenthal, Andrew (1992). *CONFLICT IN THE BALKANS; Bush Urges U.N. to Back Force to Get Aid to Bosnia* (Aug. 1992).

Rotar, Igor (June 2007). *Property Disputes Fuel Uzbek-Kyrgyz Tension in Southern Kyrgyzstan.* EurasiaNet. URL: www.refworld.org/docid/46cc321914.html.

Rothchild, Donald. (1997). *Managing Ethnic Conflict in Africa: Pressures and Incentives.* Washington, DC: Brookings Institution Press.

Rotheroe, Dominic (Sept 1998). *The Green Guerrillas.* The Independent. URL: www.independent.co.uk/arts-entertainment/the-green-guerrillas-1197901.html.

Rudbeck, Jens, Erica Mukherjee, and Kelly Nelson (2016). "When Autocratic Regimes Are Cheap and Play Dirty: The Transaction Costs of Repression in South Africa, Kenya, and Egypt." *Comparative Politics* 48 (2): 147–166.

Rude, George (1981). *The Crowd in History: A Study of Popular Disturbances in France and England, 1730–1848.* London: Serif.

Rusyana, Yus (1999). "Penyelenggaraan Pengajaran Bahasa Daerah." In: *Bahasa Nusantara Suatu Pemetaan Awal: Gambaran tentang Bahasa-Bahasa Daerah di Indonesia,* ed. by Ajip Rosid. Jakarta: Dunia Pustaka Jaya, pp. 71–78.

Ryter, Loren (2001). "Pemuda Pancasila: The Last Loyalist Free Men of Suharto's Order?" In: *Violence and the State in Suharto's Indonesia,* ed. by Benedict Anderson. Ithaca, NY: Cornell University Press, pp. 124–155.

Saldanha, Joao Mariano de Sousa (1994). *The Political Economy of East Timor Development.* Jakarta: Pustaka Sinar Harapan.

Salehyan, Idean and Christopher Linebarger (2015). "Elections and Social Conflict in Africa, 1990–2009." *Studies in Comparative International Development* 50: 23–49.

Sambanis, Nicholas (2000). "Partition as a Solution to Ethnic War: An Empirical Critique of the Theoretical Literature." *World Politics* 52 (4): 437–483.

Sangaji, Arianto (2007). "The Security Forces and Regional Violence in Poso." In: *Renegotiating Boundaries: Local Politics in Post-Suharto Indonesia,* ed. by Henk Schulte Nordholt and Gerry van Klinken. Leiden: KITLV Press, pp. 255–280.

Sangaji, Ruslan (2006). "Kekerasan Poso dan Ekspansi Modal." *Kompas.*

Sanger, David (1998). "International Business; Risking I.M.F. Aid, Suharto Dismises Central Banker." *New York Times*. URL: www.nytimes.com/1998/02/18/business/international-business-risking-imf-aid-suharto-dismisses-central-banker.html.

Sato, Shigeru (2006). "Indonesia 1939–1942: Prelude to the Japanese Occupation." *Journal of Southeast Asian Studies* 37 (2): 225–248.

(2010a). "Gatot Mangkupraja, PETA, and the Origins of the Indonesian National Army." *Bijdragen tot de Taal-, Land- en Volkenkunde* 166 (2/3): 189–217.

(2010b). "The PETA." In: *The Encyclopedia of Indonesia in the Pacific War*, ed. by Peter Post, William H. Frederick, Iris Heidebrink, and Shigeru Sato. Leiden and Boston: Brill, pp. 132–147.

Saunders, Joseph (1998). *Academic Freedom in Indonesia: Dismantling Soeharto-Era Barriers*. Human Rights Watch. URL: www.refworld.org/docid/3ae6a83a4.html.

Scacco, Alexandra (2010). "Who Riots? Explaining Individual Participation in Ethnic Violence." PhD thesis. Columbia University.

Scartascini, Carlos and Mariano Tommasi (2012). "The Making of Policy: Institutionalized or Not?" *American Journal of Political Science* 56 (4): 787–801.

Schedler, Andreas (2001). "Measuring Democratic Consolidation." *Studies in Comparative International Development* 36 (1): 66–92.

Schneider, Carsten and Philippe Schmitter (Dec. 2004). "Liberalization, Transition and Consolidation: Measuring the Components of Democratization." *Democratization* 11 (5): 59–90.

Schulze, Kirsten (2004). *The Free Aceh Movement (GAM): Anatomy of a Separatist Organization*. Technical Report Policy Studies 2. Washington, DC: East West Center.

(2006). "Insurgency and Counter-Insurgency: Strategy and the Aceh Conflic, October 1976–May 2004." In: *Verandah of Violence: The Background to the Aceh Problem*, ed. by Anthony Reid. Singapore: National University of Singapore Press, pp. 225–271.

(2017). "The 'Ethnic' in Indonesia's Communal Conflicts: Violence in Ambon, Poso, and Sambas." *Ethnic and Racial Studies* 40 (12): 2096–2114.

(Apr. 2019). "From Ambon to Poso: Comparative and Evolutionary Aspects of Local Jihad in Indonesia." *Contemporary Southeast Asia* 41 (1): 35–62.

Schwarz, Adam (1999). *A Nation in Waiting: Indonesia's Search for Stability*. Boulder, CO: Westview Press.

Scott, James (2010). *The Art of Not Being Governed: An Anarchist History of Upland Southeast Asia*. Singapore: National University of Singapore Press.

Selway, Joel and Kharis Templeman (2012). "The Myth of Consociationalism? Conflict Reduction in Divided Societies." *Comparative Political Studies* 45 (12):1542–71.

Setijadi, Charlotte (June 2017). *Ahok's Downfall and the Rise of Islamist Populism in Indonesia*. Research rep. 38. Perspectives. Singapore: ISEAS Yusof Ishak Institute. URL: www.iseas.edu.sg/images/pdf/ISEAS_Perspective_217_38.pdf.

Shair-Rosenfield, Sarah (2012). "The Alternative Incumbency Effect: Electing Women Legislators in Indonesia." *Electoral Studies* 31 (3): 576–587.

Sharma, Shalendra (2003). *The Asian Financial Crisis: Crisis, Reform, and Recovery.* New York: Manchester University Press.

Sherlock, Stephen (July 2005). *Indonesia's Regional Representative Assembly: Democracy, Representation and the Regions.* Technical Report Canberra: Centre for Democratic Institutions.

Shin, Jae-Hyeok (2012). "Electoral System Choice and Parties in New Democracies: Lessons from the Philippines and Indonesia." In: *Party Politics in Southeast Asia: Clientelism and Electoral Competition in Indonesia, Thailand, and the Philippines*, ed. by Dirk Tomsa and Andreas Ufen. London and New York: Routledge Press, pp. 101–119.

(2015). "The Choice of Candidate-Centered Electoral Systems in New Democracies." *Party Politics* 23 (2): 160–171 1–19. DOI: 10.1177/1354068815581539

Shiraishi, Takeshi (1997). "Anti-Sinicism in Java's New Order." In: *Essential Outsiders: Chinese and Jews in the Modern Transformation of Southeast Asia and Central Europe*, ed. by Daniel Chirot and Anthony Reid. Seattle: University of Washington Press, pp. 187–207.

Siddik, Abdullah F. (May 2010). "Toward Integration: Ethnic Chinese Movements in Post-Suharto Indonesia." PhD thesis. Ithaca, NY: Cornell University.

Siddique, Sharon and Leo Suryadinata (1981–1982). "Bumiputra and Pribumi: Economic Nationalism (Indigenism) in Malaysia and Indonesia." *Pacific Affairs* 54 (4): 662–687.

Sidel, John T. (2006). *Riots, Pogroms, Jihad: Religious Violence in Indonesia.* Ithaca, NY: Cornell University Press.

Silva, Romesh and Patrick Ball. 2006. "The Profile of Human Rights Violations in Timor-Leste, 1974–1999: A Report by the Benetech Human Rights Data Analysis Group to the Commission on Reception, Truth, and Reconciliation of Timor Leste." URL: https://hrdag.org/timorleste/.

Simandjuntak, Deasy (2009). "Milk-Coffee at 10 AM: Encountering the State through Pilkada in North Sumatra." In: *State of Authority: The State in Society in Indonesia*, ed. by Gerry van Klinken and Joshua Barker. Ithaca, NY: Cornell Southeast Asia Program Publication, pp. 73–94.

Simanjuntak, P. N. H. (2003). *Kabinet-Kabinet Republik Indonesia: Dari Awal Kemerdekaan sampai Reformasi.* Jakarta: Penerbit Djambatan.

Simons, Marlise and Hannah Beech (2019). *Aung San Suu Kyi Defends Myanmar Against Rohingya Genocide Accusations* The New York Times. URL: www.nytimes.com/2019/12/11/world/asia/aung-san-suu-kyi-rohingya-myanmar-genocide-hague.html.

Simpson, Bradley (2008). *Economists with Guns: Authoritarian Development and U.S.-Indonesian Relations, 1960–1968.* Stanford, CA: Stanford University Press.

Sjahrir, Bambang Suharnoko, Krisztina Kis-Katos, and Gunther Schulze (2013). "Political Budget Cycle in Indonesia at the District Level." *Economics Letters* 120: 342–345.

Slater, Daniel (2010). *Ordering Power: Contentious Politics and Authoritarian Leviathans in Southeast Asia*. Cambridge Studies in Comparative Politics. New York: Cambridge University Press.

Slater, Daniel and Lucan Ahmad Way (2017). *Was the 2016 U.S. Election Democratic? Here Are 7 Serious Shortfalls* URL: www.washingtonpost .com/news/monkey-cage/wp/2017/01/12/was-the-2016-u-s-election-democratic-we-see-7-serious-shortfalls/?utm_term=.f47acff8dd28.

Snyder, Jack (2000). *From Voting to Violence: Democratization and Nationalist Violence*. New York and London: Norton.

Soeharto (1968). *Pidato di depan Dewan Perwakilan Rakyat-Gotong Royong*. Jakarta: Departemen Penerangan R.I.

Somers Heidhues, Mary (2003). *Golddiggers, Farmers, and Traders in the "Chinese Districts" of West Kalimantan, Indonesia*. Ithaca, NY: Southeast Asia Program, Cornell University.

(2009). "1740 and the Chinese Massacre in Batavia: Some German Eyewitness Accounts." *Archipel* 77:117–147.

(2012). "Anti-Chinese Violence in Java during the Indonesian Revolution, 1945–49." *Journal of Genocide Research* 14 (3–4): 381–401.

Spilerman, S. (1976). "Structural Characteristics of Cities and the Severity of Racial Disorders." *American Sociological Review* 41 (5): 771–793.

Spolaore, Enrico and Romain Wacziarg (2009). "The Diffusion of Development." *Quarterly Journal of Economics* 124 (2): 469–529.

Steele, Janet (2003). "Representations of 'The Nation' in Tempo Magazine." *Indonesia* 76:127–145.

Steenbrink, Karel (1993). *Dutch Colonialism and Indonesian Islam: Contacts and Conflicts 1596–1950*. Amsterdam and Atlanta: Editions Rodopi B.V.

(2008). "The Arrival of Protestantism and the Consolidation of Christianity in the Moluccas 1605–1800." In: *A History of Christianity in Indonesia* ed. by Jan Aritonang and Karel Steenbrink. Leiden: Brill, pp. 99–136.

Stephan, Alfred (1986). "Paths toward Redemocratization: Theoretical and Comparative Considerations." In: *Transitions from Authoritarian Rule: Comparative Perspectives*, ed. by Guillermo O'Donnell, Philippe Schmitter, and Laurence Whitehead. Vol. 4. Baltimore, MD: Johns Hopkins University Press, pp. 64–84.

Suberu, Rotimi (2001). *Federalism and Ethnic Conflict in Nigeria*. Washington, DC: United States Institute of Peace Press.

Subhan, S. D. and Rudy F. X. Gunawan, eds. (2004). *Mereka Bilang di sini Tidak Ada Tuhan: Suara Korban Tragedi Priok*. Jakarta: Kontras dan Gagas Media.

Subianto, Benny (2009). "Ethnic Politics and the Rise of the Dayak Bureaucrats in Local Elections: Pilkada in Six Kabupaten in West Kalimantan." In: *Deepening Democracy in Indonesia? Direct Elections for Local Leaders (Pilkada)*, ed. by Maribeth Erb and Priya Sulistiyanto. Singapore: ISEAS, pp. 1–37.

Sudharmono (1997). *Sudharmono, S.H.: Pengalaman dalam Masa Pengabdian: Sebuah Otobiografi*. Jakarta: Grasindo.

Sulaiman, M. Isa (2006). "From Autonomy to Periphery: A Critical Evaluation of the Acehnese Nationalist Movement." In: *Verandah of Violence: The*

Background of the Aceh Problem, ed. by Anthony Reid. Singapore: National University of Singapore Press, pp. 121–148.

Suleiman, Ezra (1999). "Bureaucracy and Democratic Consolidation: Lessons from Eastern Europe" In: *Transitions to Democracy*, ed. by Lisa Anderson. New York: Columbia University Press, pp. 141–167.

Sumaktoyo, Nathanael (June 2019). "Double Minority Candidates and Muslim Voting Behavior: Evidence from Indonesia." Paper presented at SEAREG 2019.

Sunstein, Cass (2001). *Designing Democracy: What Constitutions Do*. New York: Oxford University Press.

Suryadinata, Leo (1982). *Political Parties and the 1982 General Election in Indonesia*. Singapore: Institute of Southeast Asian Studies.

(1989). *The Ethnic Chinese in the ASEAN States: Bibliographical Essays*. Singapore: ISEAS.

(1986). *Pribumi Indonesians, the Chinese Minority, and China: A Study of Perceptions and Policies*. Asian Studies Series. Singapore: Heinemann Asia.

ed. (1999). *Political Thinking of the Indonesian Chinese, 1900–1955: A Sourcebook*. Singapore: Singapore University Press.

(2015). *Prominent Indonesian Chinese: Biographical Sketches*. 4th edition. Singapore: Institute of Southeast Asian Studies.

Suryadinata, Leo, Evi N. Arifin, and Aris Ananta (2003). *Indonesia's Population: Ethnicity and Religion in a Changing Political Landscape*. Singapore: Institute of Southeast Asian Studies.

Sutherland, Heather (Oct. 2001). "The Makassar Malays: Adaptation and Identity, c. 1660–1790." *Journal of Southeast Asian Studies* 32 (3): 397–421.

Sutrimo (2013). "Kiprah Pak Harto dalam Kenangan." In: *34 Wartawan Istana Bicara Tentang Pak Harto*, ed. by Tarman Azzam. Jakarta: UMB Press, pp. 281–295.

Suyono, Seno and Verrianto Madjowa (Apr. 2000). "Mereka Berebut Kuasa, Poso Terbakar." *Tempo*.

Svolik, Milan (2014). "Which Democracies Will Last?Coups, Incumbent, Takeovers, and the Dynamic of Democratic Consolidation." *British Journal of Political Science* 45 (4): 715–738.

Swianiewicz, Pawel. (2010). "If Territorial Fragmentation is a Problem, Is Amalgamation a Solution? An East European Perspective." *Local Government Studies* 36 (2):183–203.

Swidler, Ann (2013). "Cultural Sources of Institutional Resilience: Lessons from Chieftancy in Rural Malawi." In: *Social Resilience in the Neoliberal Era*, ed. by Peter Hall and Michele Lamont. New York: Cambridge University Press, pp. 319–345.

Tadjoeddin, Muhammad Zulfan (2011). "The Economic Origins of Indonesia's Seccesionist Conflicts." *Civil Wars* 13 (3): 312–332.

Tadjoeddin, Muhammad Zulfan and Syed Mansoob Murshed (2007). "Socio-Economic Determinants of Everyday Violence in Indonesia: An Empirical Investigation of Javanese Districts, 1994–2003." *Journal of Peace Research* 44 (6): 689–709.

Tadjoeddin, Zulfan (2013). "Educated but Poor: Explaining Localized Ethnic Violence During Indonesia's Democratic Transition." *International Area Studies Review* 16 (1): 24–49.

Tajima, Yuhki (Jan. 2013). "The Institutional Basis of Intercommunal Order: Evidence from Indonesia's Democratic Transition." *American Journal of Political Science* 57 (1): 104–119.

(2014). *The Institutional Origins of Communal Violence: Indonesia's Transition from Authoritarian Rule*. New York: Cambridge University Press.

Tajima, Yuhki, Krislert Samphantharak, and Kai Ostwald (2018). "Ethnic Segregation and Public Goods: Evidence from Indonesia." *American Political Science Review* 112 (3): 637–653.

Tambiah, Stanley (1997). *Leveling Crowds: Ethnonationalist Conflicts and Collective Violence in South Asia*. Berkeley: University of California Press.

Tan, Mely (2004). "Unity in Diversity: Ethnic Chinese and Nation-Building in Indonesia." In: *Ethnic Relations and Nation-Building in Southeast Asia: The Case of the Ethnic Chinese*, ed. by Leo Suryadinata. Singapore: Institute of Southeast Asian Studies, pp. 20–44.

Tan, Paige Johnson (2015). "Explaining Party System Institutionalization in Indonesia." In: *Party System Institutionalization in Asia: Democracies, Autocracies, and the Shadows of the Past*, ed. by Allen Hicken and Erik Martinez Kuhonta. New York: Cambridge University Press, pp. 236–259.

Tanasaldy, Taufiq (2012). *Regime Change and Ethnic Politics in Indonesia: Dayak Politics of West Kalimantan*. Leiden, the Netherlands: KITLV Press.

Tavits, Margit (2012). "Organizing for Success: Party Organizational Strength and Electoral Performance in Postcommunist Europe." *Journal of Politics* 74 (1): 83–97.

Taylor, Jean Gelman (1983). *The Social World of Batavia: European and Eurasian in Dutch Asia*. Madison: University of Wisconsin Press.

Taylor, John (1991). *Indonesia's Forgotten War: The Hidden History of East Timor*. Highland, NJ: Zed Books.

Tempo (2003). *Vonis Sisa Perang: Tokoh Kristen dalam Konflik Poso Divonis 3 Tahun* URL: https://majalah.tempo.co/read/hukum/88508/vonis-sisa-perang.

Tempo (2004a). *495 PNS Menjadi Anggota Partai Politik* (May 2004). URL: https://nasional.tempo.co/read/42948/495-pns-menjadi-anggota-partai-politik.

Tempo (2004b). *Pendeta Damanik Bebas* (Nov. 2004). URL: https://nasional.tempo.co/read/50818/pendeta-damanik-bebas.

Tempo (2010). *Pemerintah Dinilai Anaktirikan Alkhairaat* (2010). URL: https://nasional.tempo.co/read/279437/pemerintah-dinilai-anaktirikan-alkhairaat/full&view=ok.

Tempo (2011). *Presiden Resmikan Gong Perdamaian Kupang* (2011). URL: https://nasional.tempo.co/read/311980/presiden-resmikan-gong-perdamaian-di-kupang/full&view=ok.

Tempo (2016). *Wapres Kalla Bicara Soal Moratorium Pemekaran Wilayah*.

Teorell, Jan (2010). *Determinants of Democratization: Explaining Regime Change in the World, 1972–2006*. London: Cambridge University Press.

Thorburn, Craig (2002). "Musibah: Entitlements, Violence, and Reinventing Tradition in the Kei Islands, Southeast Maluku." In: Paper submitted for the International Association for the Study of Common Property, 9th Biennial Confernece, Victoria Falls, Zimbabwe, pp. 1–31.

(2008). "Adat Law, Conflict, and Reconciliation: The Kei Islands, Southeast Maluku." In: *Indonesia: Law and Society*, ed. by Tim Lindsey. New South Wales, Australia Federation Press, pp. 115–143.

Thornley, Andrew (2015). *Indonesia's Local Elections: High Drama and Humdrum*. The Asia Foundation.

Tianlean, Bakri A. G. (2005). *Fitnah: Seputar Kerusuhan Ambon-Maluku (Dari Theo Syafei sampai RMS)*. Jakarta: Komite Penyelamat Maluku.

Tiebout, C. M. (1956). "A Pure Theory of Local Expenditures." *Journal of Political Economy*. 64: 416–424.

Tilly, Charles (1978). *From Mobilization to Revoluion*. New York: McGraw-Hill.

(2007). *Democracy*. New York: Cambridge University Press.

The Times of India (2016). *KCR Announces Schedule for Creation of New Districts*. The Times of India. URL: https://timesofindia.indiatimes.com/city/hyderabad/KCR-announces-schedule-for-creation-of-new-districts/articleshow/52664910.cms.

Tirtosudarmo, Riwanto (2008). "State Formation, Decentralisation, and East Sulawesi Province: Conflict and the Politics of Transcending Boundaries in Eastern Indonesia." CRISE Working Paper 56. Oxford: CRISE, Oxford University.

Tishkov, Valery (1995). "'Don't Kill Me, I'm a Kyrgyz!': An Anthropological Analysis of Violence in the Osh Ethnic Conflict." *Journal of Peace Research* 32 (2): 133–149.

Tocqueville, Alexis de (1988). *Democracy in America*. New York: Harper Collins.

Toha, Risa J. (2017). "Political Competition and Ethnic Riots in Democratic Transition: A Lesson from Indonesia." *British Journal of Political Science* 47 (3): 631–651. ISSN: 1469-2112. DOI: 10.1017/S0007123415000423. URL: http://journals.cambridge.org/article_S0007123415000423.

Toha, Risa J. and S. P. Harish (2017). "A New Typology of Electoral Violence: Insights from Indonesia." *Terrorism and Political Violence* 31 (4): 687–711.

(2020). "Electoral Violence in Indonesia 20 Years after Reformasi." In: *Democracy in Indonesia: From Stagnation to Regression*, ed. by Thomas Power and Eve Warburton. Singapore: ISEAS, pp. 346–370.

Tomsa, Dirk (2014). "Party System Fragmentation in Indonesia: The Subnational Dimension." *Journal of East Asian Studies* 14 (2): 249–278.

Treisman, Daniel (2007). *The Architecture of Government: Rethinking Political Decentralization*. New York: Cambridge University Press.

Tribune, ed. (2016). *Pemekaran, Pemerintah Lihat Banyak Daerah Belum Siap*. URL: www.tribunnews.com/nasional/2016/10/08/pemekaran-pemerintah-lihat-banyak-daerah-belum-siap.

Uar, Eka Dahlan (2005). "Larvul Ngabal sebagai Sistem Adat dalam Penyelesaian Masalah Konflik Sosial di Maluku Tenggara." MA Thesis. Yogyakarta: Gadjah Mada University.

Ueda, Kaoru, Sonny Wibisono, Naniek Harkatiningsih, and Chen Sian Lim (2016). "Paths to Power in the Early Stage of Colonialism: An Archaeological

Study of the Sultanate of Banten, Java, Indonesia, the Seventeenth to Early Nineteenth Century." *Asian Perspectives* 55 (1): 89–119.

Ufen, Andreas (2010). "Electoral Campaigning in Indonesia: The Professionalization and Commercialization after 1998." *Journal of Contemporary Southeast Asian Affairs* 29 (4): 11–37.

UNHCR (2017). *"This Is Our Home": Stateless Minorities and Their Search for Citizenship*. UNHCR Statelessness Report. UNHCR.

van Dijk, Kees (1992). "The Indonesian General Elections 1971–92." *Indonesia Circle* 58: 48–66.

van de Berghe, Pierre (1981). *The Ethnic Phenomenon*. Westport, CT: Praeger.

van Klinken, Gerry (2005). "New Actors, New Identities: Post-Suharto Ethnic Violence in Indonesia." In: *Violent internal Conflicts in Asia Pacific: Histories, Political Economies, and Policies*, ed. by Dewi Fortuna Anwar, Helene Bouvier, Glenn Smith, and Roger Tol. Jakarta: Yayasan Obor Indonesia, pp. 79–100.

(2006). "The Maluku Wars: Communal Contenders in a Failing State." In: *Violent Conflicts in Indonesia: Analysis, Representation, Resolution*, ed. by Charles Coppel. London: Routledge, pp. 129–43.

(2007). *Communal Violence and Democratization in Indonesia: Small Town Wars*. New York: Routledge.

van Klinken, Helene (2012). "The New Order in East Timor." In: *Making Them Indonesian: Child Transfers Out of East Timor*, Melbourne, Australia: Monash University Publishing, pp. 1–19.

van Randwijck, S. C. Graaf (1981). *Handelen en Denken in Dienst der Zending: Oegstgeest 1897–1942*. The Hague: Boekencentrum.

Vanhanen, Tatu (1999). "Domestic Ethnic Conflict and Ethnic Nepotism: A Comparative Analysis." *Journal of Peace Research* 36 (1): 55–73.

Varshney, Ashutosh (2002). *Ethnic Conflict and Civic Life: Hindus and Muslims in India*. Vol. 8. 361–394. New Haven, CT: Yale University Press.

(2009). "Ethnicity and Ethnic Conflict." In: *The Oxford Handbook of Comparative Politics*, ed. by Carles Boix and Susan Stokes. New York: Oxford University Press, pp. 1–24.

Varshney, Ashutosh, Mohammad Zulfan Tadjoeddin, and Rizal Panggabean (2008). "Creating Datasets in Information-Poor Environments: Patterns of Collective Violence in Indonesia, 1990–2003." *Journal of East Asian Studies* 8 (3): 361–394.

Wacana (2015). *Kerajaan Banggai; Menelusuri Jejak Kerajaan Banggai*. Bahasa Indonesia. Wacana. URL: www.wacana.co/2015/01/kerajaan-banggai/

Wachtel, Andrew (2013). "Kyrgyzstan between Democratization and Ethnic Intolerance." *Nationalities Papers* 41 (6): 971–986.

Waileruny, Semmy, Noija Fileo Pistos, Elda Loupatty, Anthoni Hatane, Richard Rahakbauw, Helen De Lima, Blandina Molle, Edwin Huwae, Lenarki Latupeirissa, Firel Sahetapy, and Willy Renyaan (1999). *Kepada Yth.: Sebagian Umat Islam di LUar Maluku (Yang Tidak Memahami Kerusuhan dan Kondisi Maluku)*. Bahasa Indonesia. Tim Pengacara Gereja (GPM dan Keuskupan Amboina). URL: http://media.isnet.org/kmi/ambon/Kristen06.html.

Walter, Barbara (2004). "Does Conflict Beget Conflict? Explaining Recurring Civil War." *Journal of Peace Research* 41 (3): 371–388.

Wan, Ming (2008). *The Political Economy of East Asia: Striving for Wealth and Power.* Washington, DC: Congressional Quarterly Press.

Wargadiredja, Arzia (Nov. 2018). *The Story Behind These Infamous Photographs of a Murder on the Streets of Jakarta.* VICE. URL: www.vice.com/en_asia/article/ mb3ykx/the-story-behind-these-infamous-photographs-of-a-murder-on-the-streets-of-jakarta.

Warsito, Kahar (2007). "Pendidikan dan Etnis: Sejarah Birokrasi kabupaten Banggai Kepulauan (1999–2005)." MA thesis. Palu: Universitas Tadulako.

Wertheim, W. F. (1959). *Indonesian Society in Transition: A Study of Social Change.* The Hague and Bandung: W. van Hoeve Ltd.

Wheatley, Paul (1983). "Nagara and Commander, Origins of the Southeast Asian Urban Tradition." The University of Chicago, Department of Geography Research Papers nos. 207–8.

Widjojo, Muridan. (2008). *The Revolt of Prince Nuku Cross-cultural Alliance-Making in Maluku* Leiden: Brill TANAP Monographs on the History of Asian-European Interaction.

Wieringa, Saskia (2011). "Sexual Slander and the 1965/66 Mass Killings in Indonesia: Political and Methodological Considerations." *Journal of Contemporary Asia* 41 (4): 544–565.

Wijaya, Lani Diana (Sept. 2019). *Pengakuan Relawan Prabowo Usai Divonis Bersalah Kerusuhan 22 Mei.* Tempo. URL: https://metro.tempo.co/read/1245802/ pengakuan-relawan-prabowo-usai-divonis-bersalah-kerusuhan 22-mei/ full&view=ok.

Wilkinson, Steven (2004). *Votes and Violence: Electoral Competition and Ethnic Riots in India.* New York: Cambridge University Press.

—— (2009). "Riots." *Annual Review of Political Science* 12: 329–343.

Wilkinson, Steven and Christopher Haid (2009). "Ethnic Violence as Campaign Expenditure: Riots, Competition, and Vote Swings in India." Working Paper.

Williams, Melissa (1998). *Voice, Trust, and Memory: Marginalized Groups and the Failings of Liberal Representation.* Princeton, NJ: Princeton University Press.

Williams, Richard (2016). "Analyzing Rare Events with Logistic Regression." University of Notre Dame. Unpublished manuscript. Last revised 2019. URL: www3.nd.edu/$\sim$rwilliam/stats3/RareEvents.pdf.

Wilson, Chris and Shahzad Akhtar (2019). "Repression, co-optation and insurgency: Pakistan's FATA, Southern Thailand and Papua, Indonesia." *Third World Quarterly* 40 (4): 71–726.

Wilson, Ian (Apr. 2017). *Jakarta: Inequality and the Poverty of Elite Pluralism.* New Mandala. URL: www.newmandala.org/jakarta-inequality-poverty-elite-pluralism/

Wimmer, Andreas (2002). *Nationalist Exclusion and Ethnic Conflict: Shadows of Modernity.* Cambridge: Cambridge University Press.

Wolters, O. W. (1970). *The Fall of Srivijaya in Malay History.* Ithaca, NY: Cornell University Press.

Wolters, Oliver (1982). *History, Culture, and Region in Southeast Asian Perspectives.* Singapore: Institute of Southeast Asian Studies.

World Bank (2005). *Aceh Public Expenditure Analysis Spending for Reconstruction and Poverty Reduction*. Technical Report. Washington, DC: World Bank.

Wright, Joseph (2008). "Political Competition and Democratic Stability in New Democracies." *British Journal of Political Science* 38 (2): 221–45.

Wucherpfennig, Julian, Nils Metternich, Lars-Erik Cederman, and Kristian Skrede (2012). "Ethnicity, the State, and the Duration of Civil War." *World Politics* 64 (1): 79–115.

Yang, Tsung-Rong Edwin (2001). "A Short History of Anti-Chinese Riots." In: *Perspectives on the Chinese Indonesians*, ed. by Michael R Godley and Grayson Lloyd. Adelaide: Crawford House Publishing, pp. 41–54.

Young, Crawford (1976). *The Politics of Cultural Pluralism*. Madison: University of Wisconsin Press.

Young, Iris (2000). *Inclusion and Democracy*. Oxford: Oxford University Press.

Yuliawati and Priska Sari Pratiwi (2016). *Deretan Kisah Mengerikan Pemerkosaan Massal Mei 1998*. CNN Indonesia. URL: www.cnnindonesia.com/nasional/20160519124757-20-131898/deretan-kisah-mengerikan-pemerkosaan-massal-mei-1998.

Ziblatt, Daniel (2006). "How Did Europe Democratize?" *World Politics* 58 (2): 11–38.

(2017). *Conservative Parties and the Birth of Democracy*. New York: Cambridge University Press.

Index

Printed in the USA
CPSIA information can be obtained
at www.ICGtesting.com
LVHW080540221123
764620LV00005B/149

9 781316 518977